MASASHI KISHIMOTO

In the process of creating this manga, I got into the habit of eating dried shredded squid, which is called *surume*. Overeating other foods makes me sleepy, but not this one, so it's just right for me. I hope that this becomes a surume manga for you— the more you chew on it, the more flavor you taste. If you're thinking, "Hey, that's just chewing gum!" then might I suggest you pick up volume 2 right away, before the flavor disappears?

(Volumes 1 and 2 were released simultaneously in Japan.)

AKIRA OKUBO

Hello, all you readers! I'm very new to this, but I'm making progress every day. I hope you'll stick with us until the end of the story.

01

SHONEN JUMP Manga Edition

Story MASASHI KISHIMOTO
Art AKIRA OKUBO

Translation/STEPHEN PAUL
Touch-Up Art & Lettering/SNIR AHARON
Design/JULIAN [JR] ROBINSON
Editor/ALEXIS KIRSCH

SAMURAI8 HACHIMARUDEN © 2019 by Masashi Kishimoto, Akira Okubo
All rights reserved.
First published in Japan in 2019 by SHUEISHA Inc., Tokyo.
English translation rights arranged by SHUEISHA Inc.

The stories, characters and incidents mentioned in this publication are
entirely fictional.

Printed in the U.S.A.

Published by VIZ Media, LLC
P.O. Box 77010
San Francisco, CA 94107

10 9 8 7 6 5 4 3 2 1
First printing, March 2020

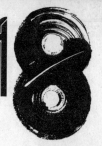

SAMURAI 8

THE TALE OF HACHIMARU

01

THE FIRST KEY

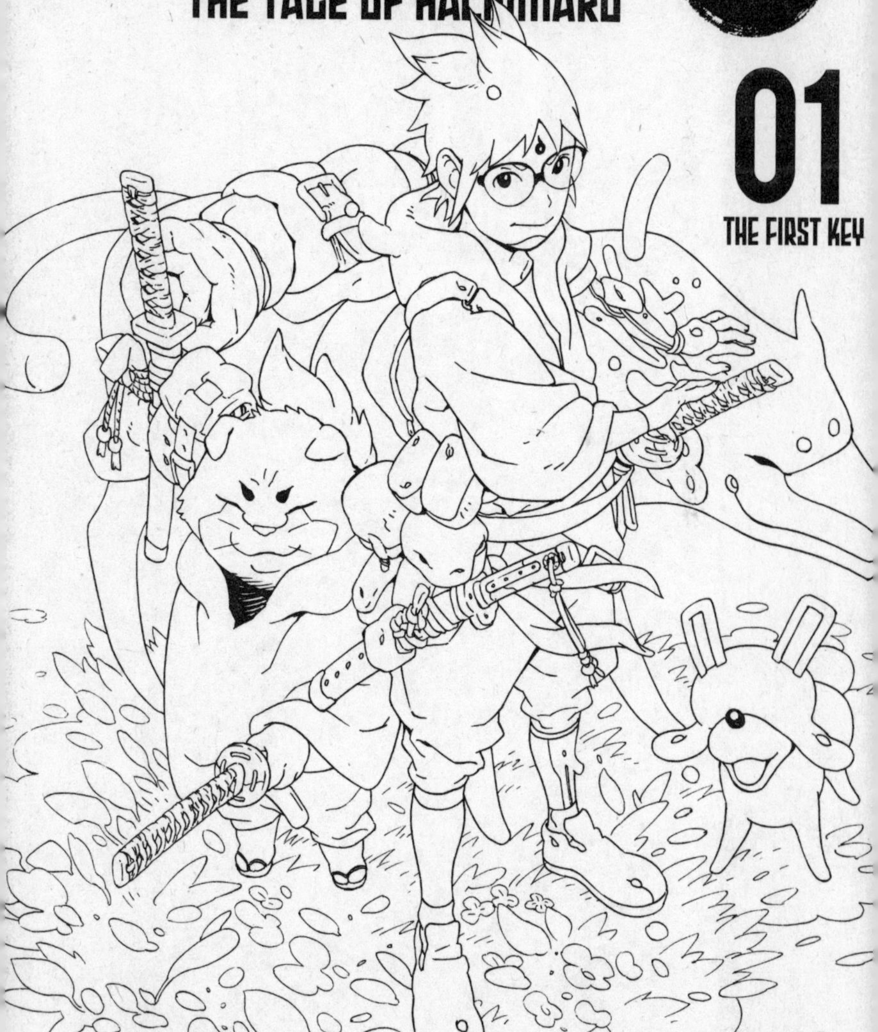

STORY BY
MASASHI KISHIMOTO

ART BY
AKIRA OKUBO

SAMURAI 8
THE TALE OF HACHIMARU

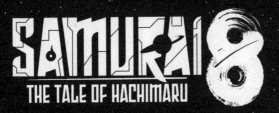

01
THE FIRST KEY

CONTENTS

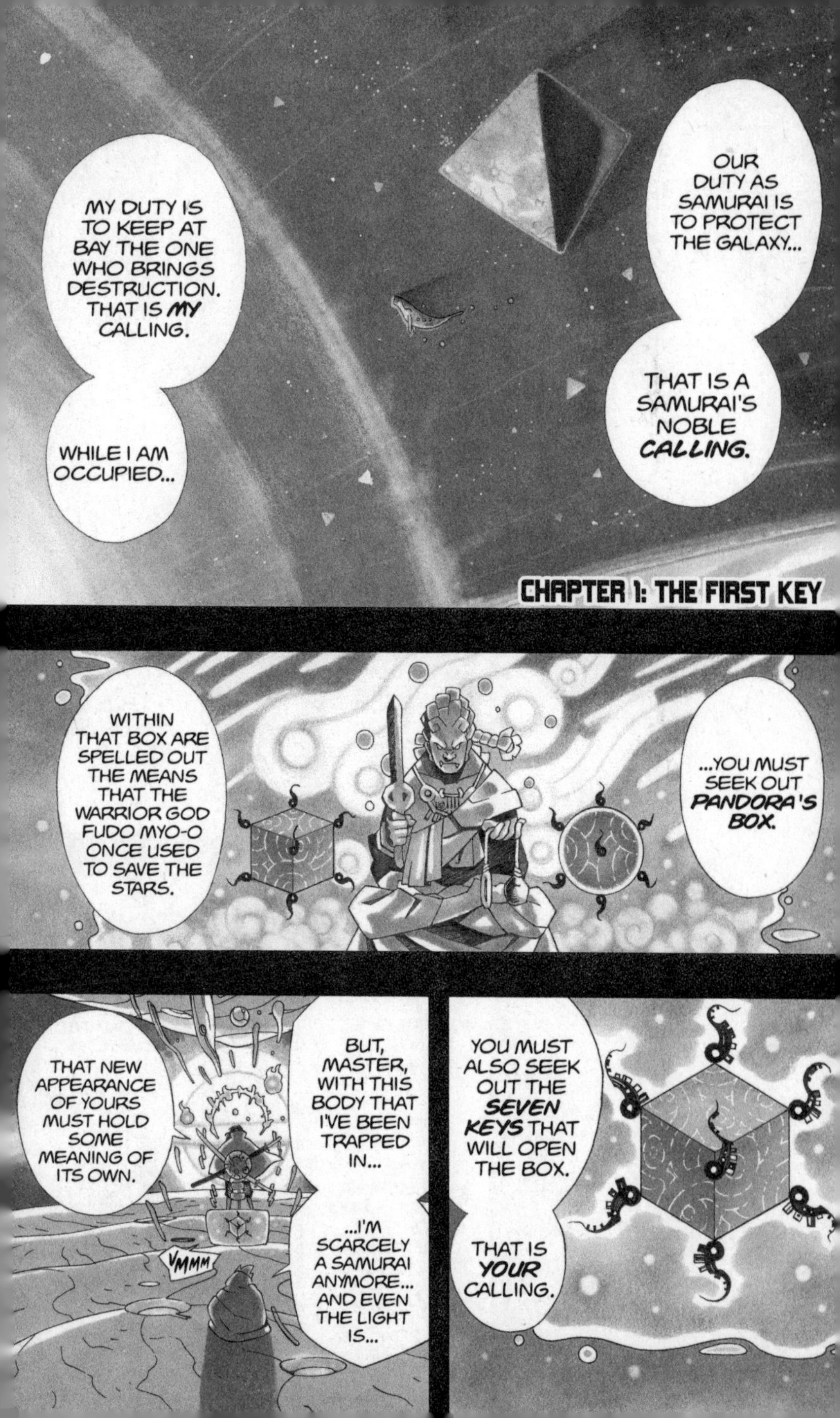
OUR DUTY AS SAMURAI IS TO PROTECT THE GALAXY...
THAT IS A SAMURAI'S NOBLE *CALLING.*
MY DUTY IS TO KEEP AT BAY THE ONE WHO BRINGS DESTRUCTION. THAT IS *MY* CALLING.
WHILE I AM OCCUPIED...
CHAPTER 1: THE FIRST KEY
...YOU MUST SEEK OUT *PANDORA'S BOX.*
WITHIN THAT BOX ARE SPELLED OUT THE MEANS THAT THE WARRIOR GOD FUDO MYO-O ONCE USED TO SAVE THE STARS.
YOU MUST ALSO SEEK OUT THE *SEVEN KEYS* THAT WILL OPEN THE BOX.
THAT IS *YOUR* CALLING.
BUT, MASTER, WITH THIS BODY THAT I'VE BEEN TRAPPED IN...
...I'M SCARCELY A SAMURAI ANYMORE... AND EVEN THE LIGHT IS...
THAT NEW APPEARANCE OF YOURS MUST HOLD SOME MEANING OF ITS OWN.
VMMM

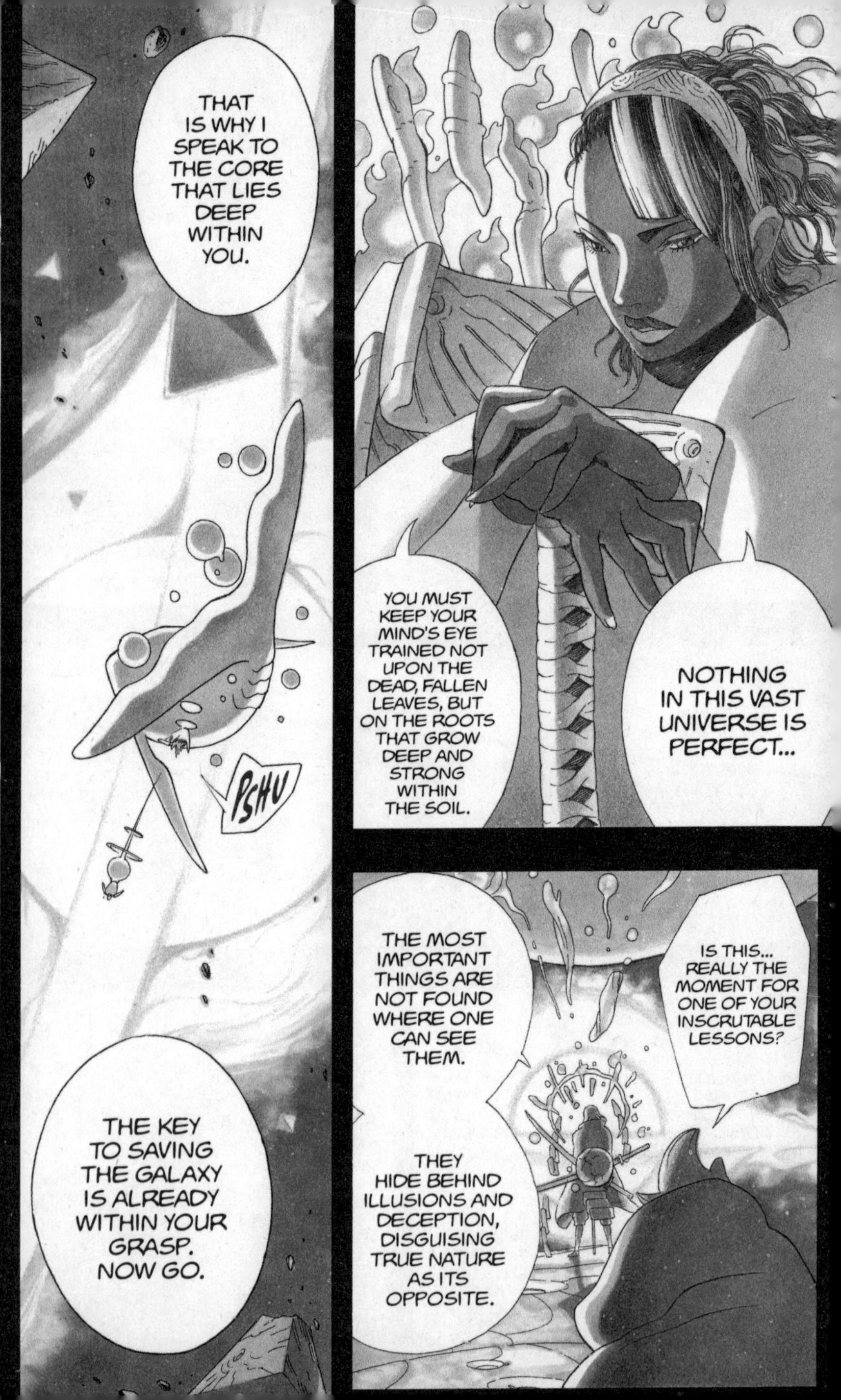
NOTHING IN THIS VAST UNIVERSE IS PERFECT...
YOU MUST KEEP YOUR MIND'S EYE TRAINED NOT UPON THE DEAD, FALLEN LEAVES, BUT ON THE ROOTS THAT GROW DEEP AND STRONG WITHIN THE SOIL.
IS THIS... REALLY THE MOMENT FOR ONE OF YOUR INSCRUTABLE LESSONS?
THE MOST IMPORTANT THINGS ARE NOT FOUND WHERE ONE CAN SEE THEM.
THEY HIDE BEHIND ILLUSIONS AND DECEPTION, DISGUISING TRUE NATURE AS ITS OPPOSITE.
THAT IS WHY I SPEAK TO THE CORE THAT LIES DEEP WITHIN YOU.
PSHU
THE KEY TO SAVING THE GALAXY IS ALREADY WITHIN YOUR GRASP. NOW GO.

CHAPTER 1: THE FIRST KEY

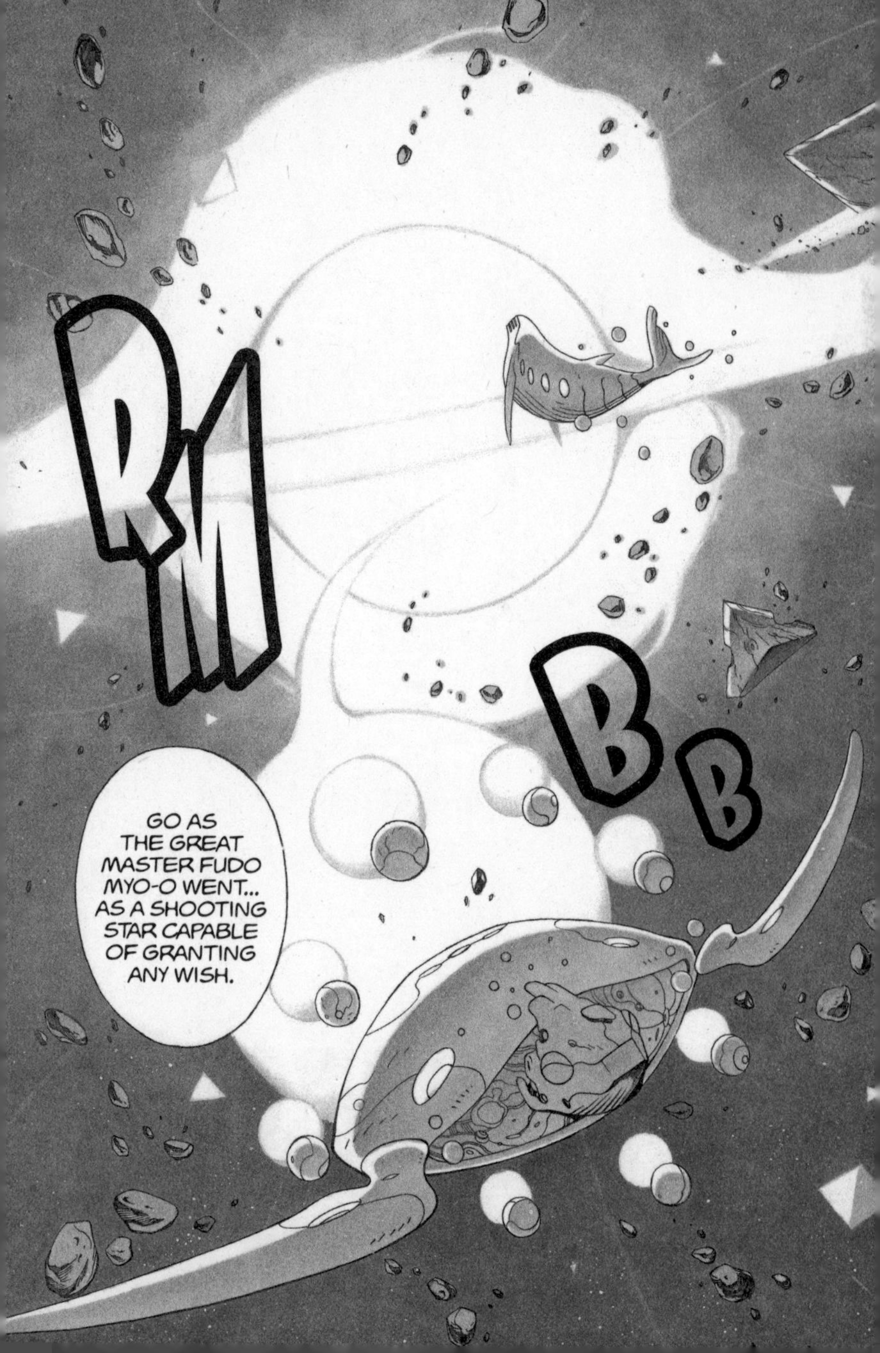
RM
BB
GO AS THE GREAT MASTER FUDO MYO-O WENT... AS A SHOOTING STAR CAPABLE OF GRANTING ANY WISH.

SAMURAI 8

THE TALE OF HACHIMARU

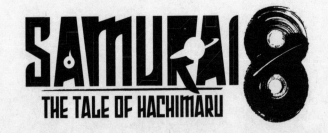

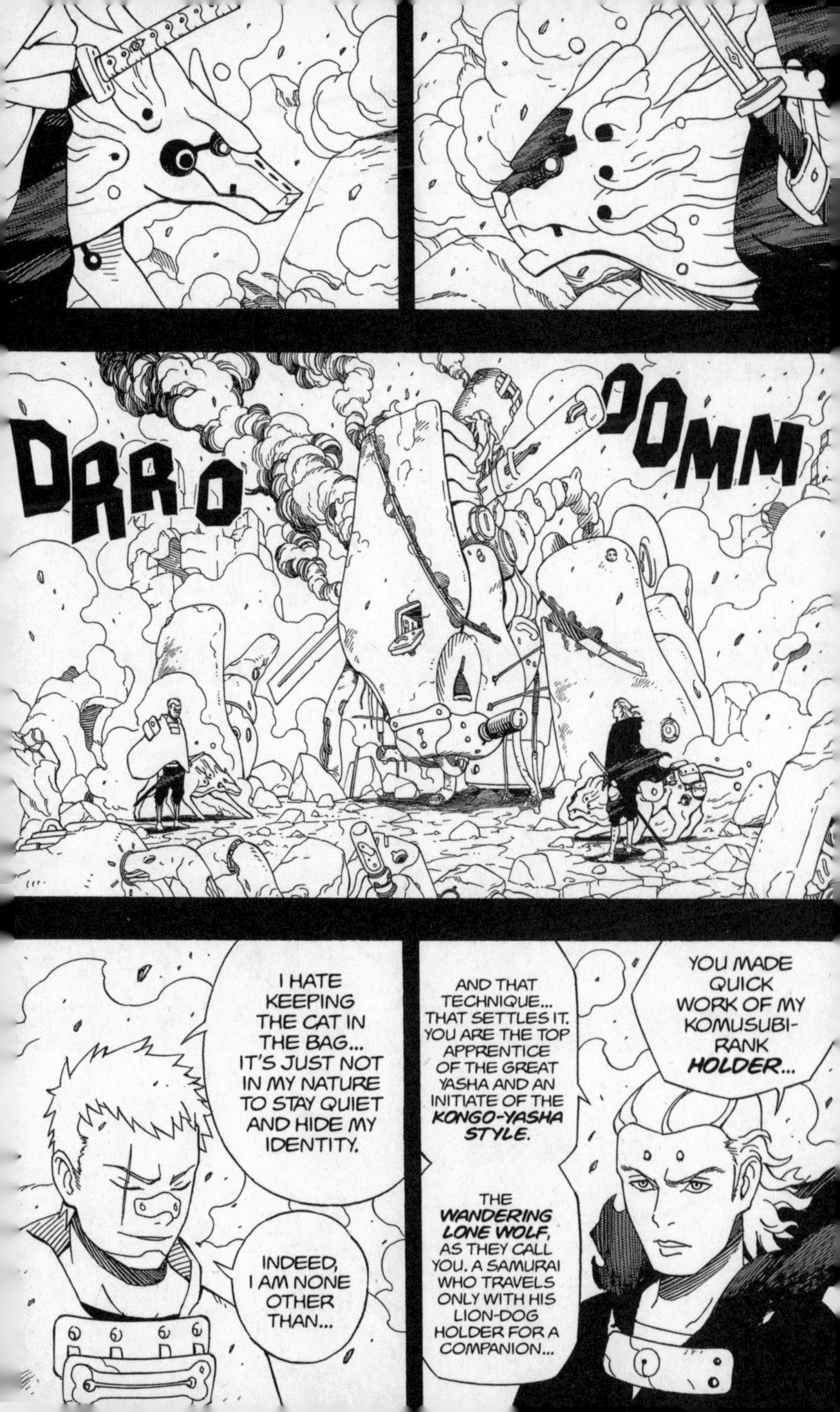

DRRO
OOMM
YOU MADE QUICK WORK OF MY KOMUSUBI-RANK ***HOLDER***...
AND THAT TECHNIQUE... THAT SETTLES IT. YOU ARE THE TOP APPRENTICE OF THE GREAT YASHA AND AN INITIATE OF THE ***KONGO-YASHA STYLE***.
THE ***WANDERING LONE WOLF***, AS THEY CALL YOU. A SAMURAI WHO TRAVELS ONLY WITH HIS LION-DOG HOLDER FOR A COMPANION...
I HATE KEEPING THE CAT IN THE BAG... IT'S JUST NOT IN MY NATURE TO STAY QUIET AND HIDE MY IDENTITY.
INDEED, I AM NONE OTHER THAN...

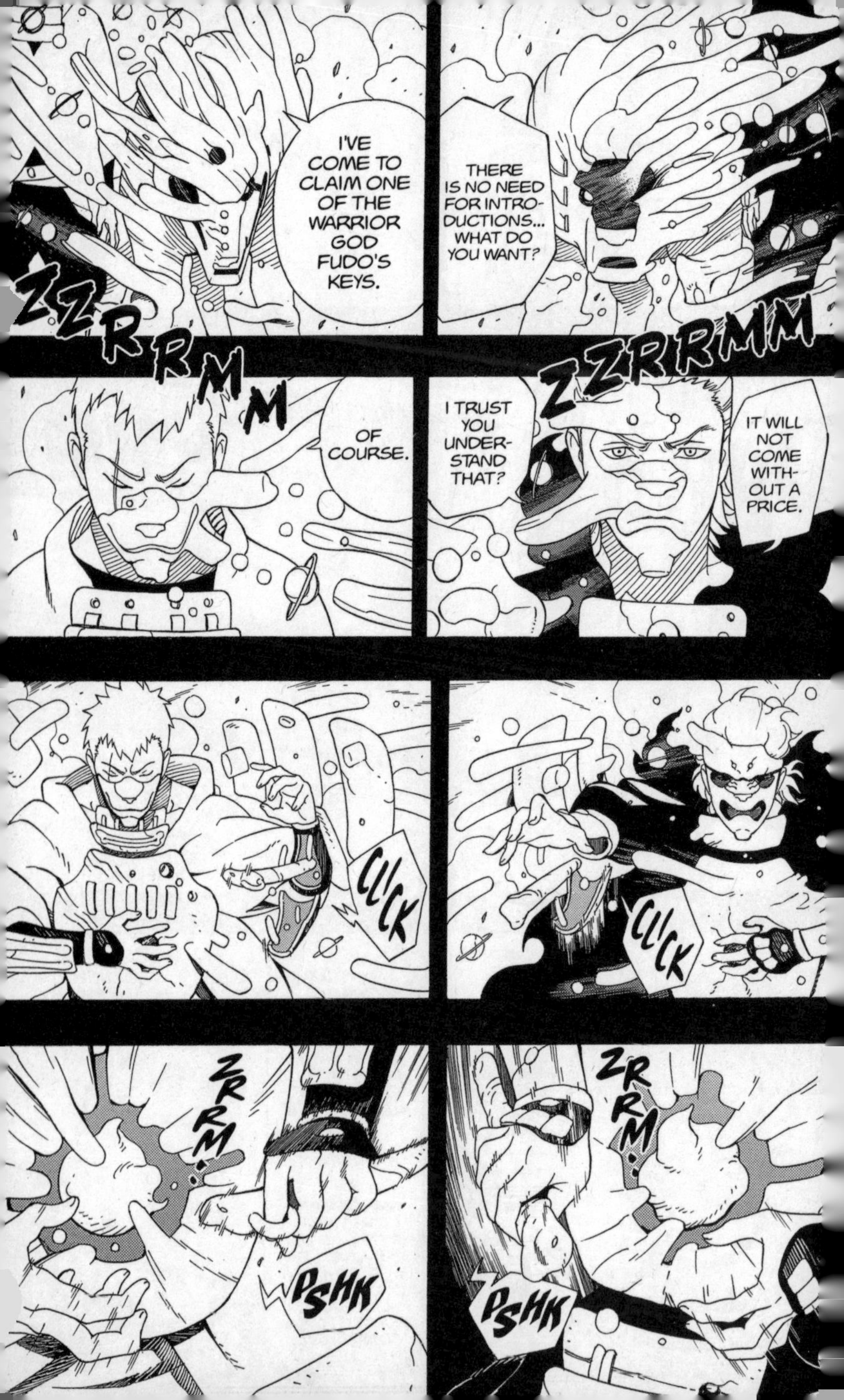
THERE IS NO NEED FOR INTRO-DUCTIONS... WHAT DO YOU WANT?
I'VE COME TO CLAIM ONE OF THE WARRIOR GOD FUDO'S KEYS.
ZZRRMM
ZZRRMM
IT WILL NOT COME WITH-OUT A PRICE.
I TRUST YOU UNDER-STAND THAT?
OF COURSE.
CLICK
CLICK
ZRRM
PSHK
ZRRM
PSHK

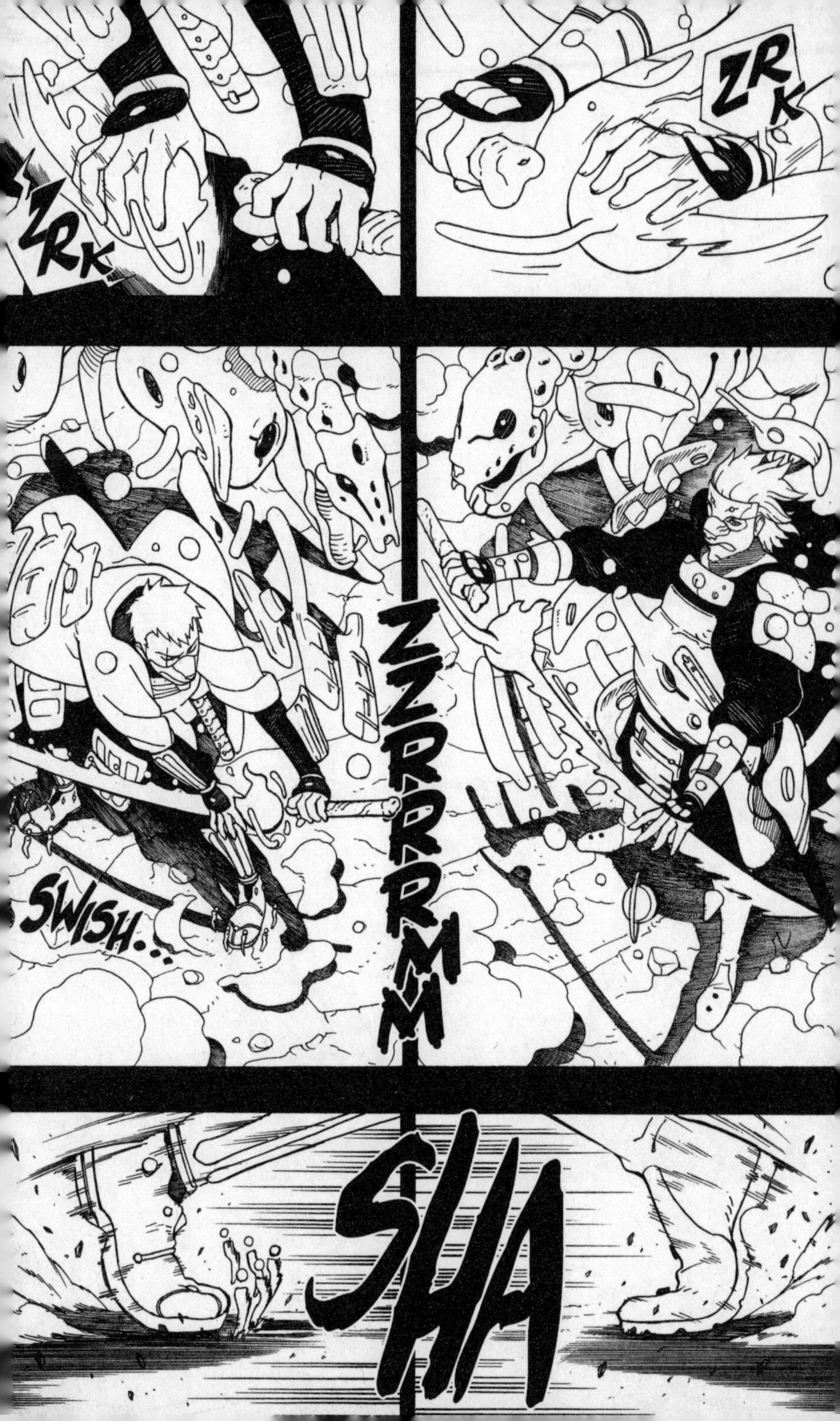
ZRK
ZRK
ZZRRRRRMM
SWISH...
SHA

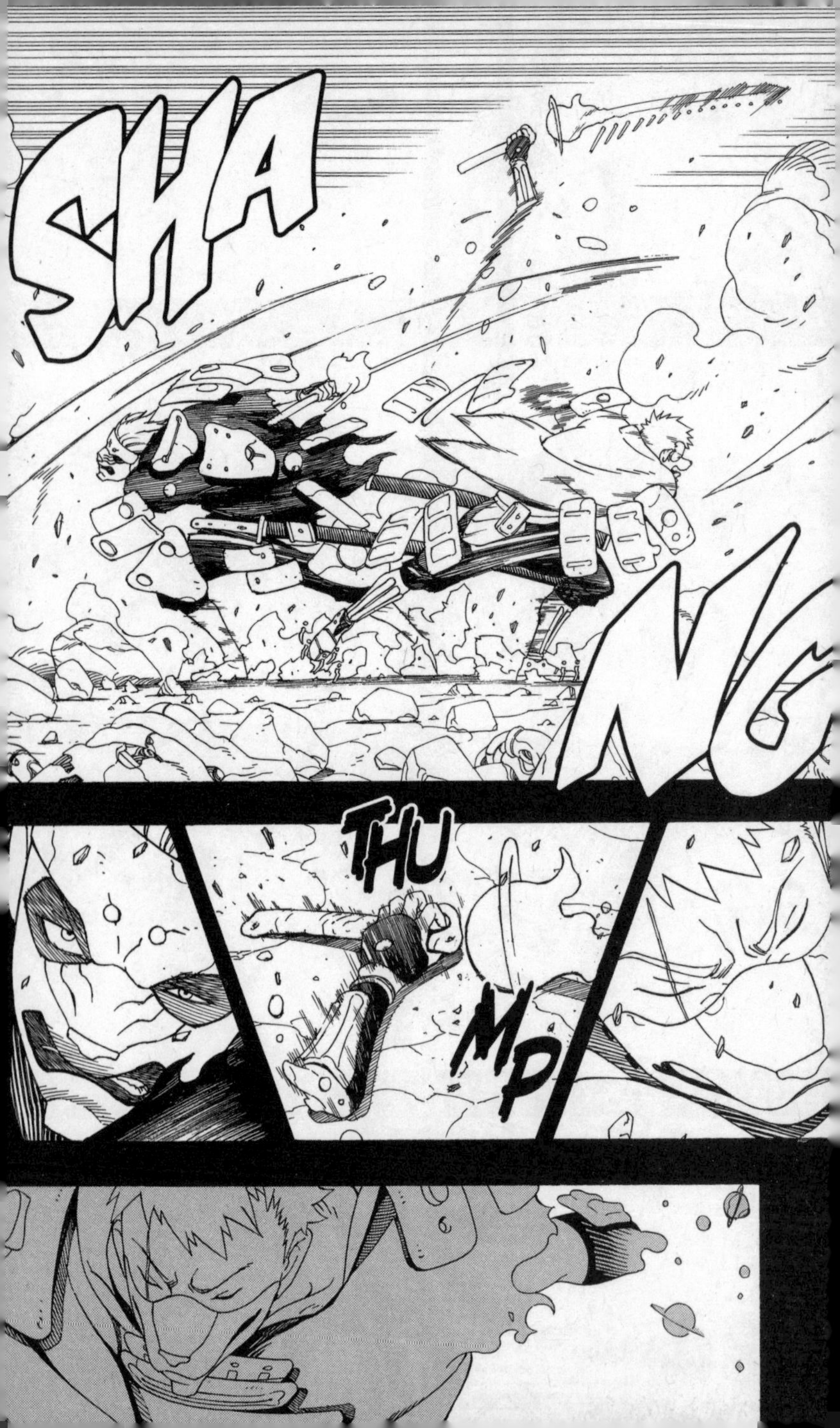
SHA
NG
THU
MP

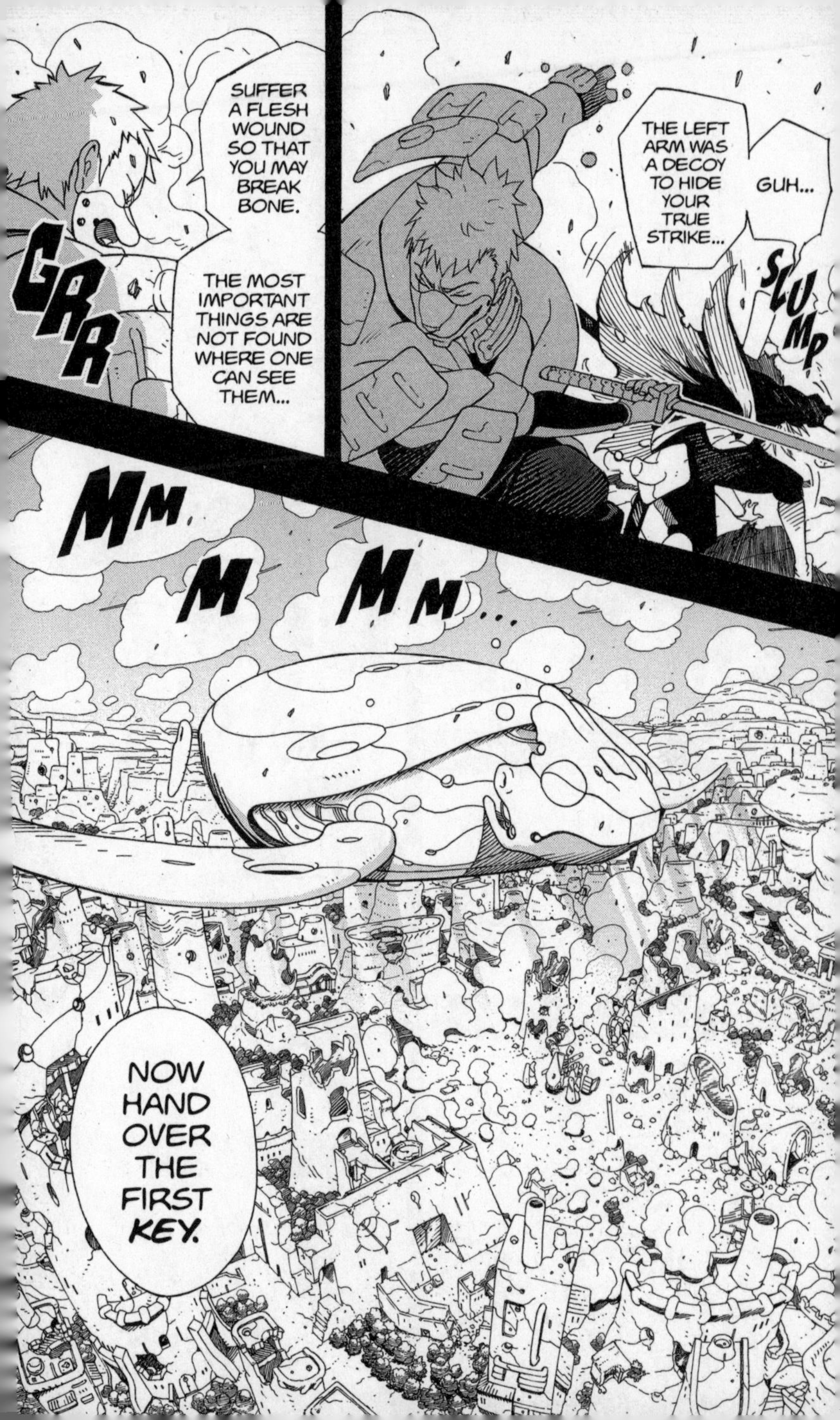
THE LEFT ARM WAS A DECOY TO HIDE YOUR TRUE STRIKE...
GUH...
SLUMP
SUFFER A FLESH WOUND SO THAT YOU MAY BREAK BONE.
THE MOST IMPORTANT THINGS ARE NOT FOUND WHERE ONE CAN SEE THEM...
GRR
MM M MM...
NOW HAND OVER THE FIRST *KEY*.

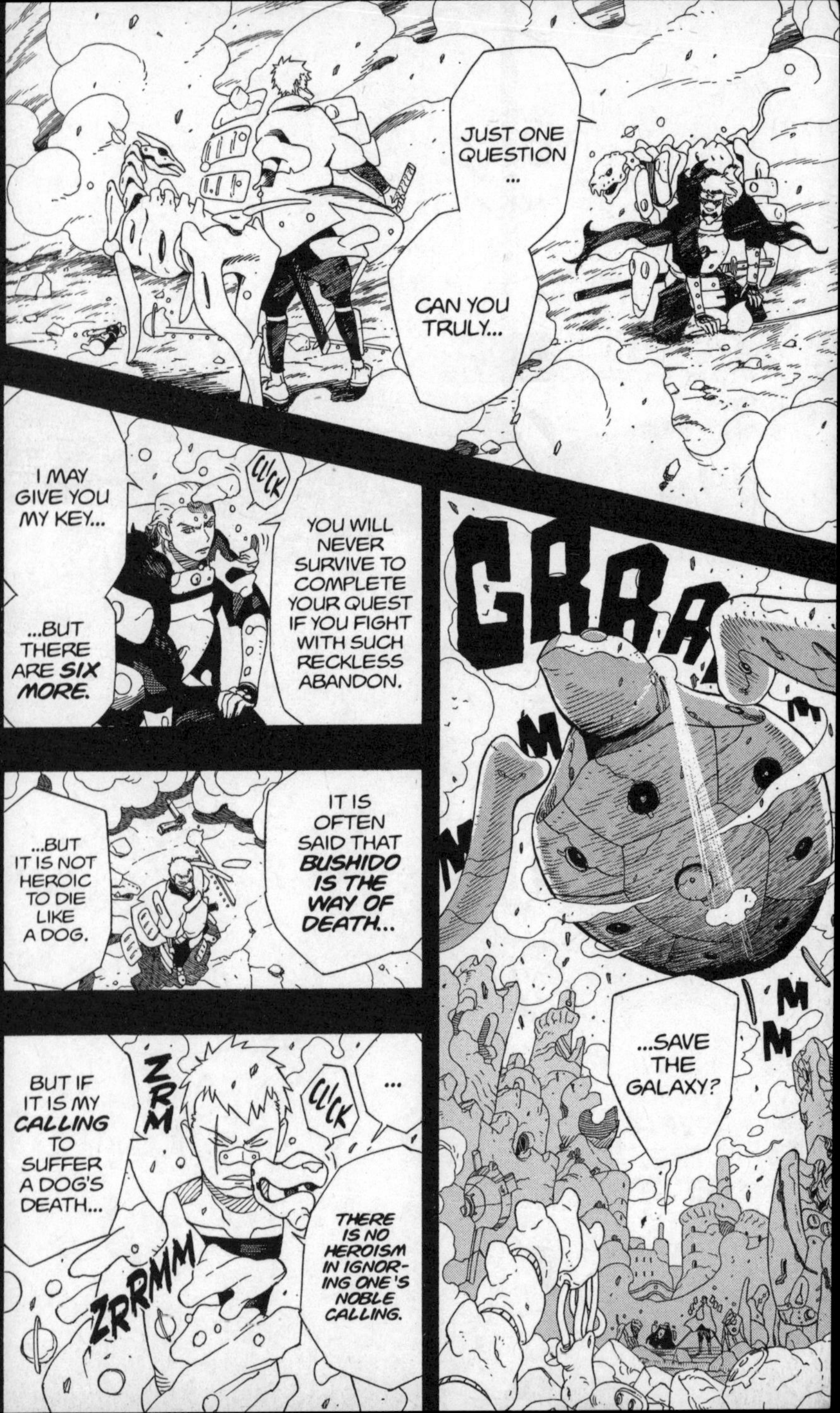
JUST ONE QUESTION ...
CAN YOU TRULY...
GRRRMMMM
...SAVE THE GALAXY?
CLICK
YOU WILL NEVER SURVIVE TO COMPLETE YOUR QUEST IF YOU FIGHT WITH SUCH RECKLESS ABANDON.
I MAY GIVE YOU MY KEY...
...BUT THERE ARE *SIX MORE.*
IT IS OFTEN SAID THAT ***BUSHIDO IS THE WAY OF DEATH...***
...BUT IT IS NOT HEROIC TO DIE LIKE A DOG.
...
CLICK
ZRM
BUT IF IT IS MY ***CALLING*** TO SUFFER A DOG'S DEATH...
THERE IS NO HEROISM IN IGNORING ONE'S NOBLE CALLING.
ZRRMM

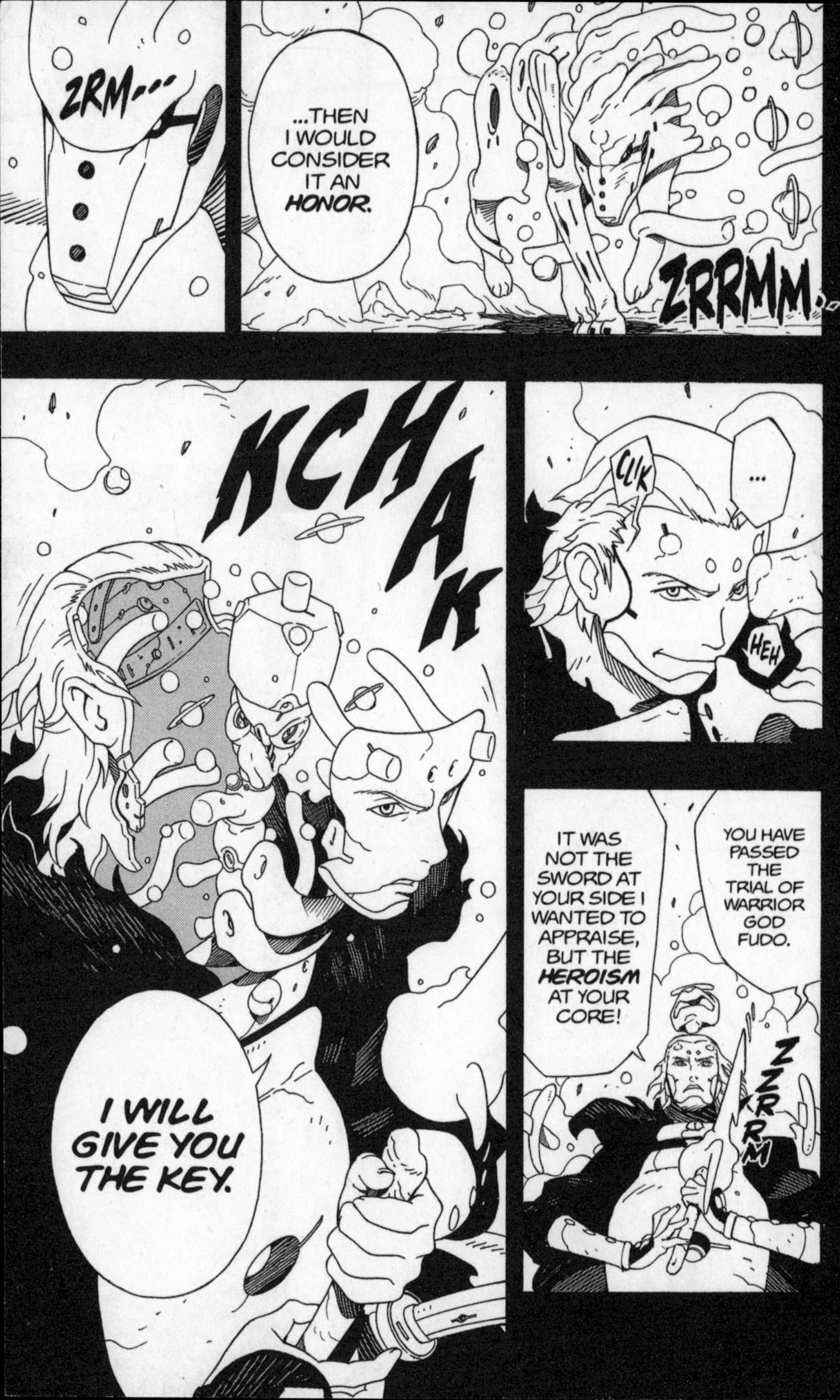
...THEN I WOULD CONSIDER IT AN HONOR.
ZRRMM
ZRM...
CLIK
...
HEH
YOU HAVE PASSED THE TRIAL OF WARRIOR GOD FUDO.
IT WAS NOT THE SWORD AT YOUR SIDE I WANTED TO APPRAISE, BUT THE HEROISM AT YOUR CORE!
ZZRRRM
KCHAK
I WILL GIVE YOU THE KEY.

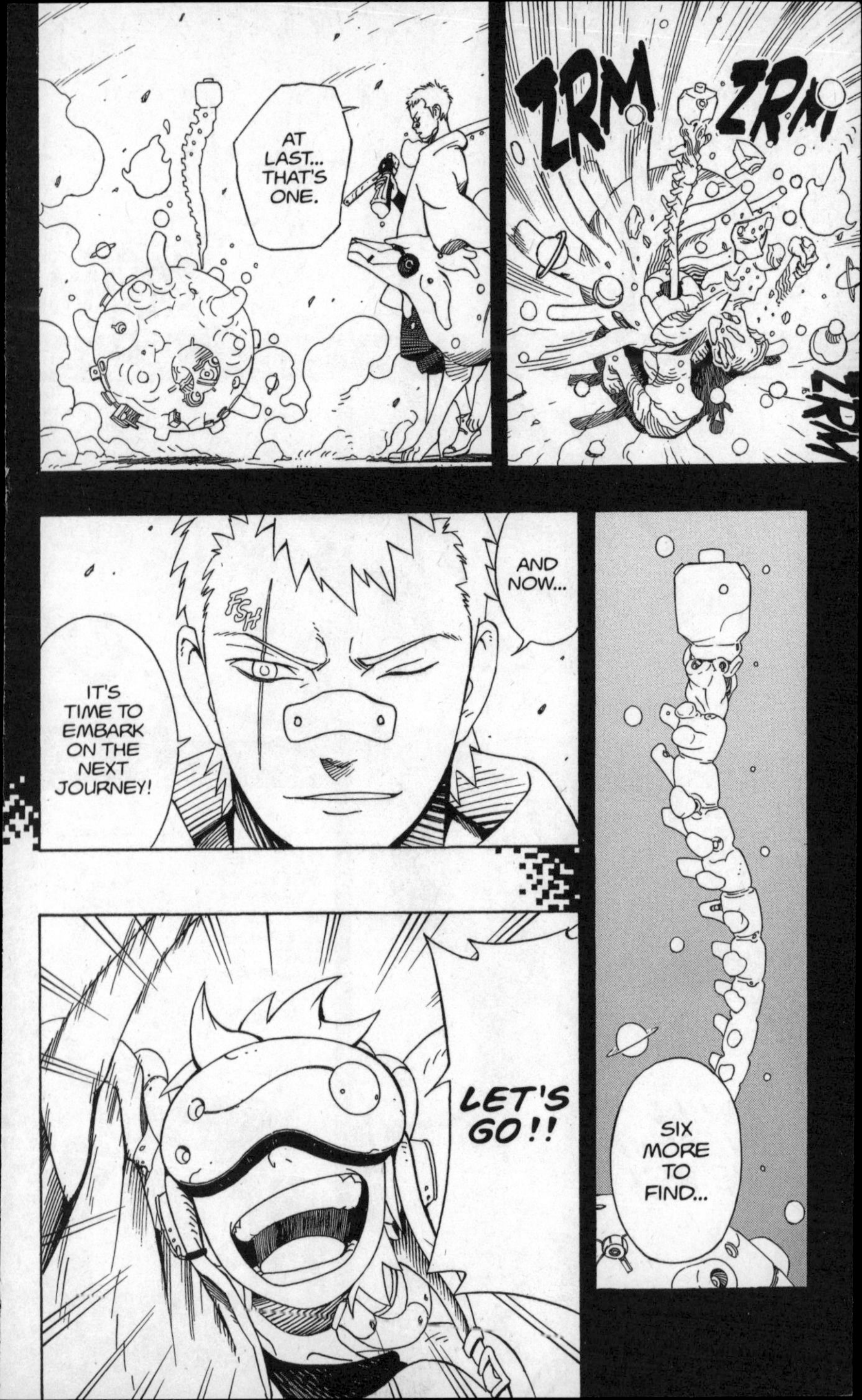
ZRM ZRM
ZRM
AT LAST... THAT'S ONE.
SIX MORE TO FIND...
AND NOW...
IT'S TIME TO EMBARK ON THE NEXT JOURNEY!
LET'S GO!!

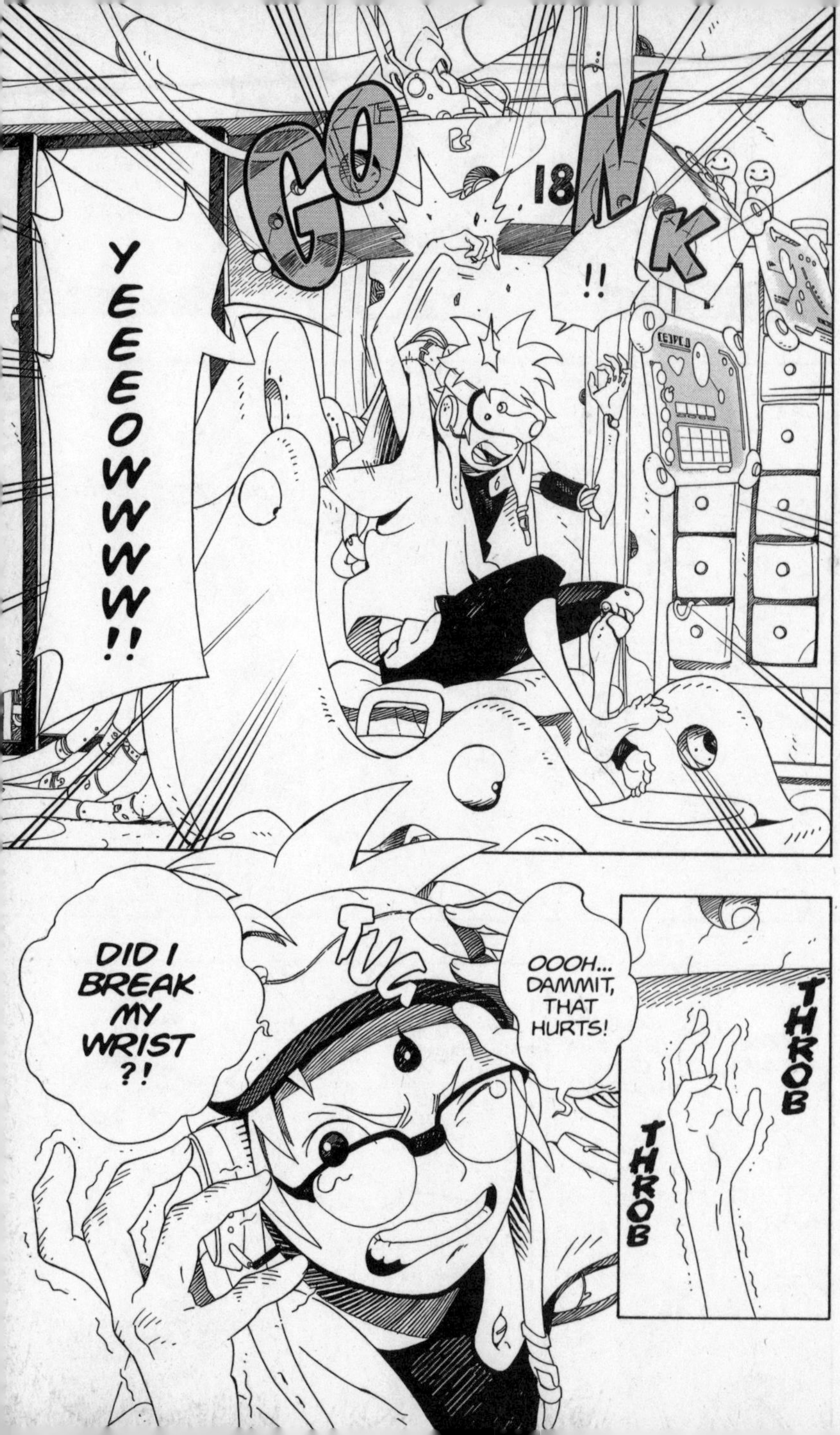
GONK
!!
YEEEOWWWWW!!
THROB
THROB
TUG
OOOH... DAMMIT, THAT HURTS!
DID I BREAK MY WRIST?!

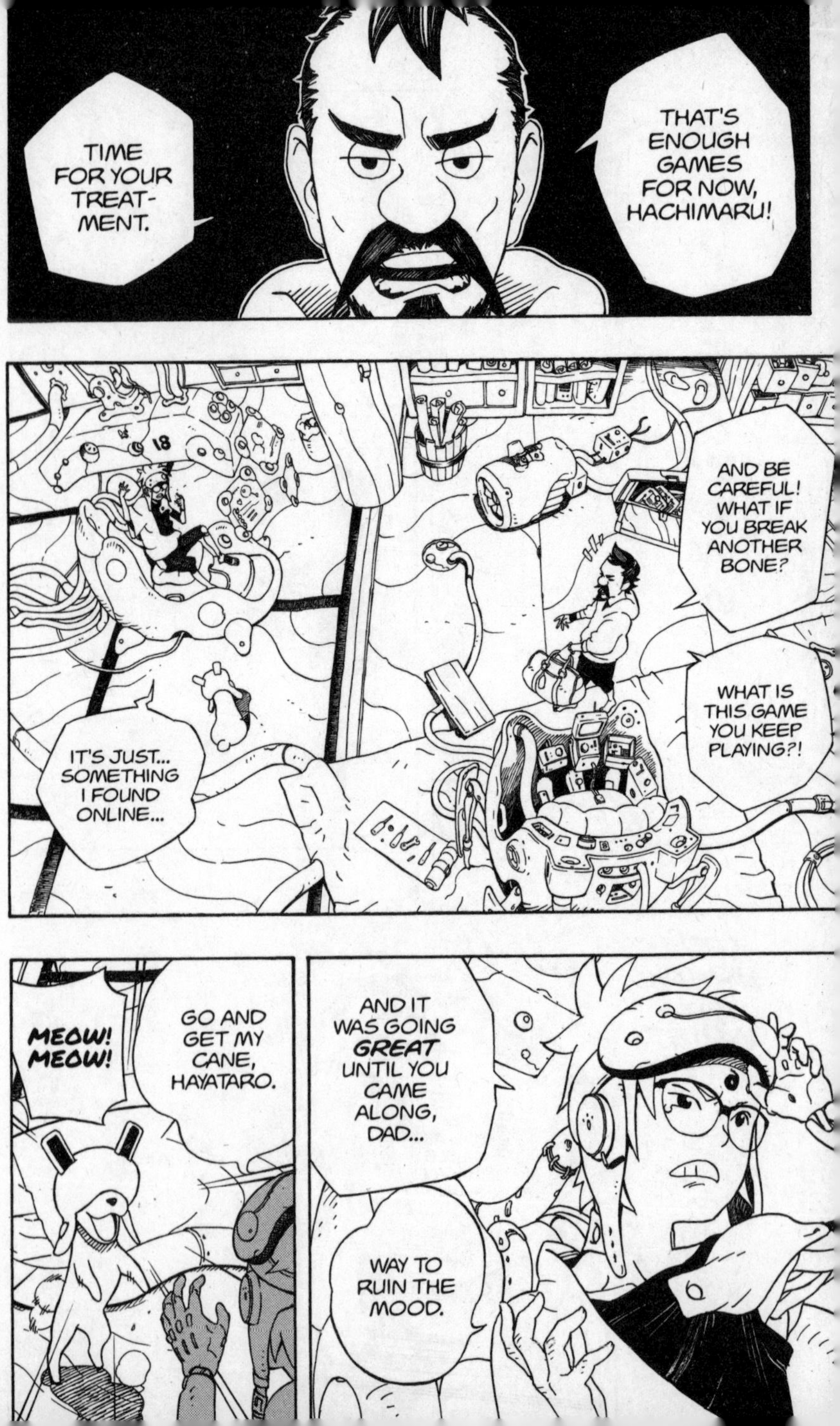

THAT'S ENOUGH GAMES FOR NOW, HACHIMARU!
TIME FOR YOUR TREAT-MENT.
AND BE CAREFUL! WHAT IF YOU BREAK ANOTHER BONE?
WHAT IS THIS GAME YOU KEEP PLAYING?!
IT'S JUST... SOMETHING I FOUND ONLINE...
AND IT WAS GOING **GREAT** UNTIL YOU CAME ALONG, DAD...
WAY TO RUIN THE MOOD.
GO AND GET MY CANE, HAYATARO.
MEOW! MEOW!

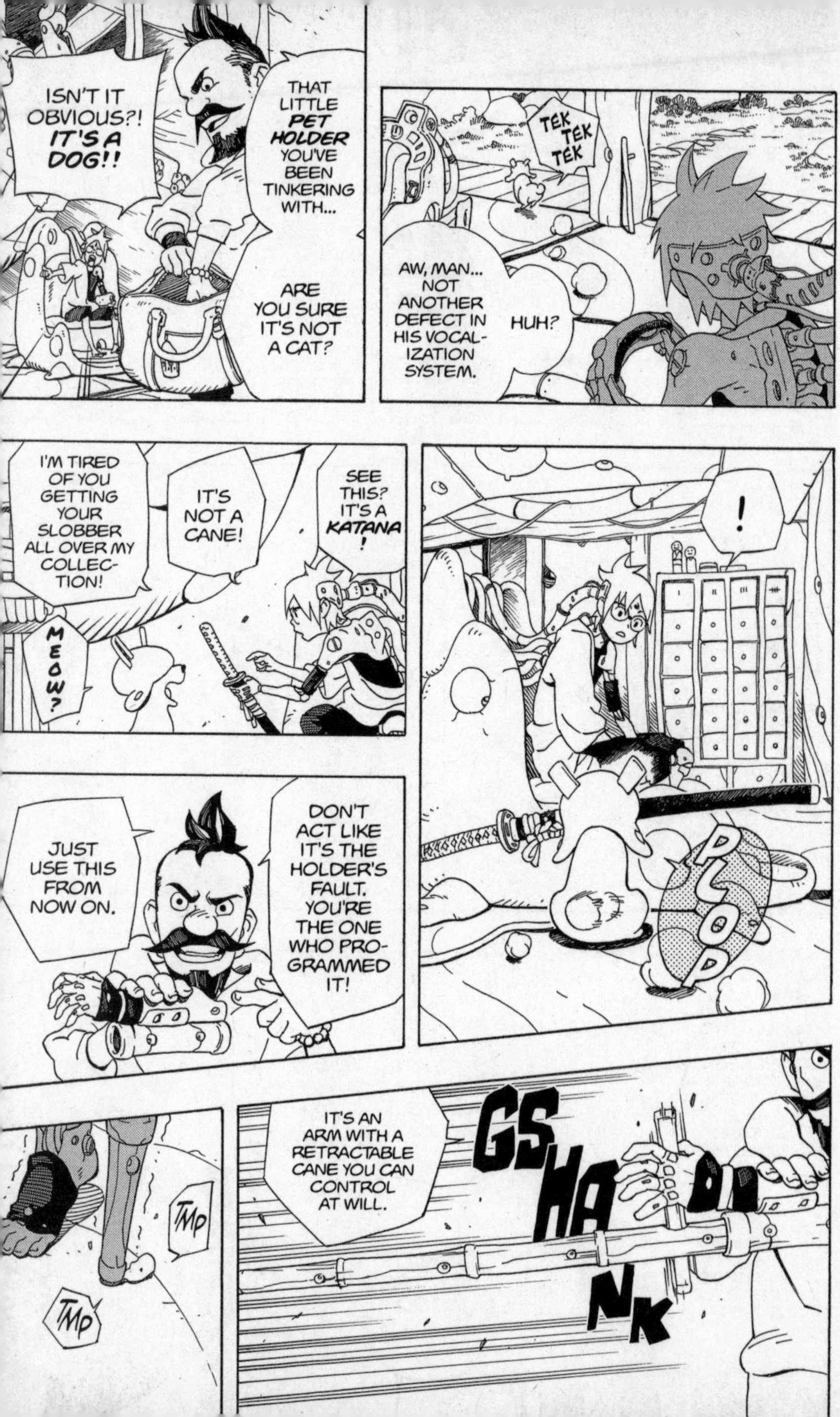

TEK TEK TEK
HUH?
AW, MAN... NOT ANOTHER DEFECT IN HIS VOCALIZATION SYSTEM.
THAT LITTLE *PET HOLDER* YOU'VE BEEN TINKERING WITH...
ARE YOU SURE IT'S NOT A CAT?
ISN'T IT OBVIOUS?! *IT'S A DOG!!*
!
PLOP
SEE THIS? IT'S A *KATANA*!
IT'S NOT A CANE!
I'M TIRED OF YOU GETTING YOUR SLOBBER ALL OVER MY COLLECTION!
MEOW?
DON'T ACT LIKE IT'S THE HOLDER'S FAULT. YOU'RE THE ONE WHO PROGRAMMED IT!
JUST USE THIS FROM NOW ON.
GSHANK
IT'S AN ARM WITH A RETRACTABLE CANE YOU CAN CONTROL AT WILL.
TMP
TMP

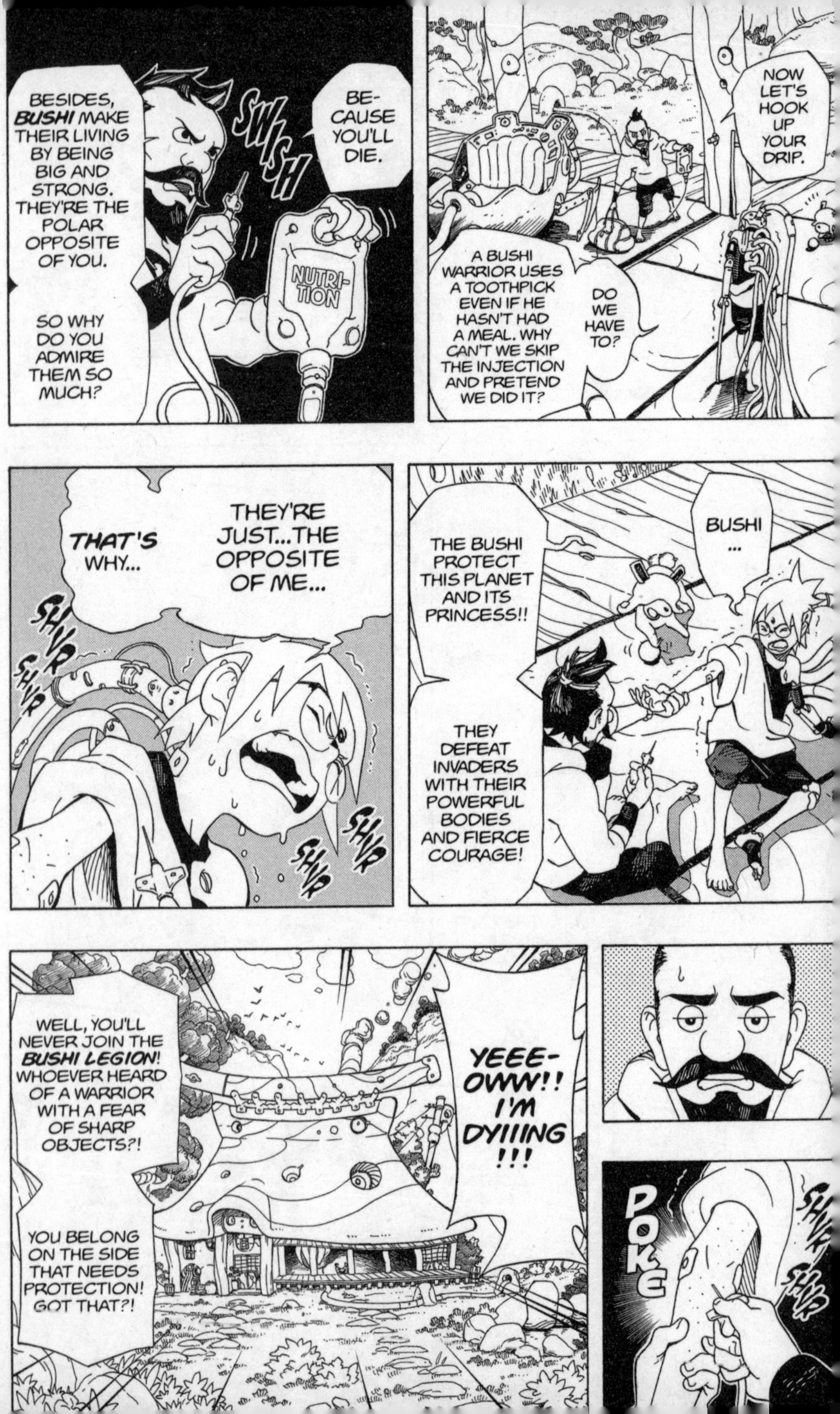

NOW LET'S HOOK UP YOUR DRIP.
DO WE HAVE TO?
A BUSHI WARRIOR USES A TOOTHPICK EVEN IF HE HASN'T HAD A MEAL. WHY CAN'T WE SKIP THE INJECTION AND PRETEND WE DID IT?
BE-CAUSE YOU'LL DIE.
SWISH
NUTRI-TION
BESIDES, **BUSHI** MAKE THEIR LIVING BY BEING BIG AND STRONG. THEY'RE THE POLAR OPPOSITE OF YOU.
SO WHY DO YOU ADMIRE THEM SO MUCH?
BUSHI ...
THE BUSHI PROTECT THIS PLANET AND ITS PRINCESS!!
THEY DEFEAT INVADERS WITH THEIR POWERFUL BODIES AND FIERCE COURAGE!
THEY'RE JUST...THE OPPOSITE OF ME...
THAT'S WHY...
SHVR SHVR
SHVR SHVR
POKE
SHVR SHVR
YEEE-OWW!! I'M DYIIING!!!
WELL, YOU'LL NEVER JOIN THE ***BUSHI LEGION***! WHOEVER HEARD OF A WARRIOR WITH A FEAR OF SHARP OBJECTS?!
YOU BELONG ON THE SIDE THAT NEEDS PROTECTION! GOT THAT?!

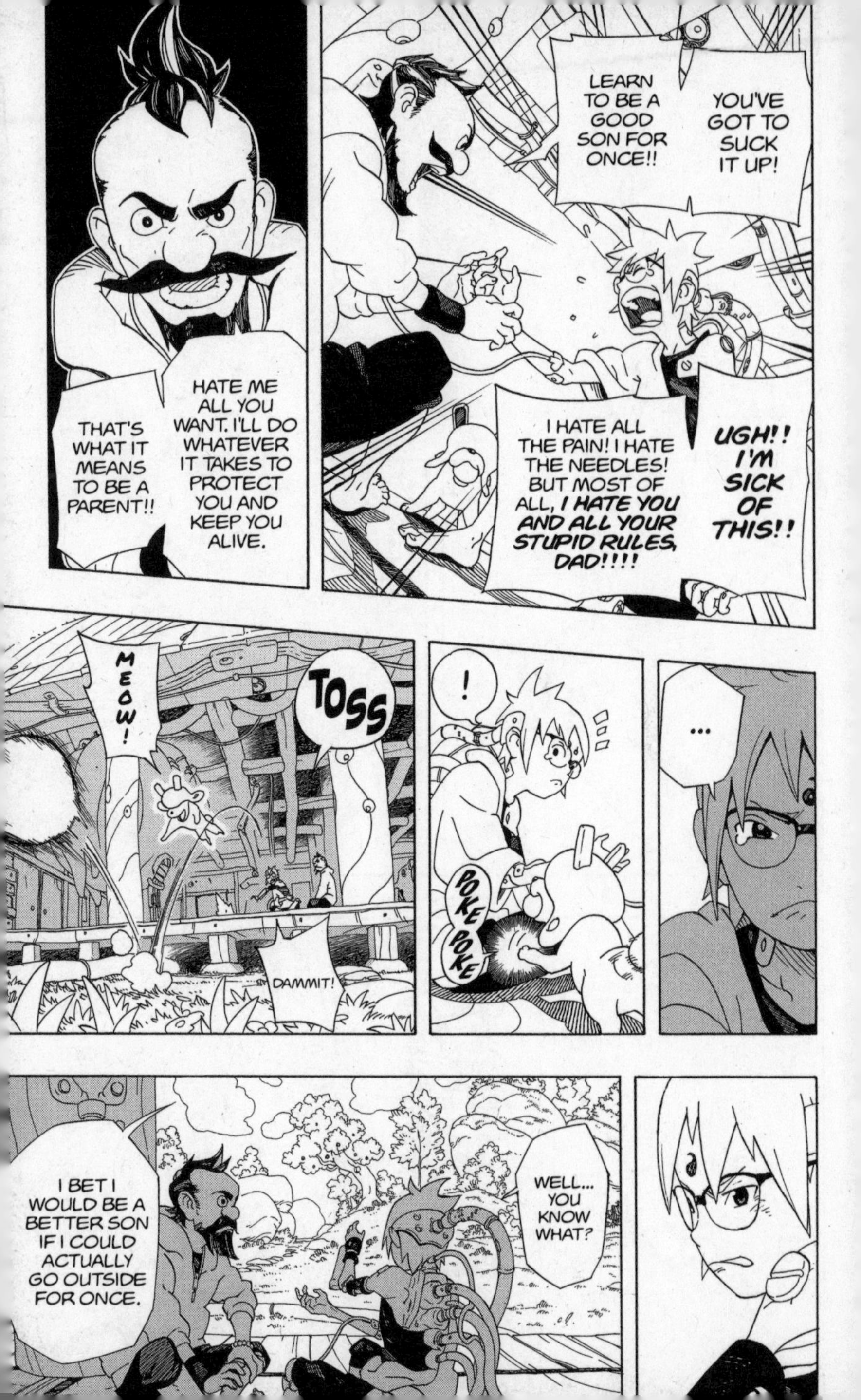
YOU'VE GOT TO SUCK IT UP!
LEARN TO BE A GOOD SON FOR ONCE!!
UGH!! I'M SICK OF THIS!!
I HATE ALL THE PAIN! I HATE THE NEEDLES! BUT MOST OF ALL, ***I HATE YOU AND ALL YOUR STUPID RULES, DAD!!!!***
HATE ME ALL YOU WANT. I'LL DO WHATEVER IT TAKES TO PROTECT YOU AND KEEP YOU ALIVE.
THAT'S WHAT IT MEANS TO BE A PARENT!!
...
!
POKE POKE
TOSS
MEOW!
DAMMIT!
WELL... YOU KNOW WHAT?
I BET I WOULD BE A BETTER SON IF I COULD ACTUALLY GO OUTSIDE FOR ONCE.

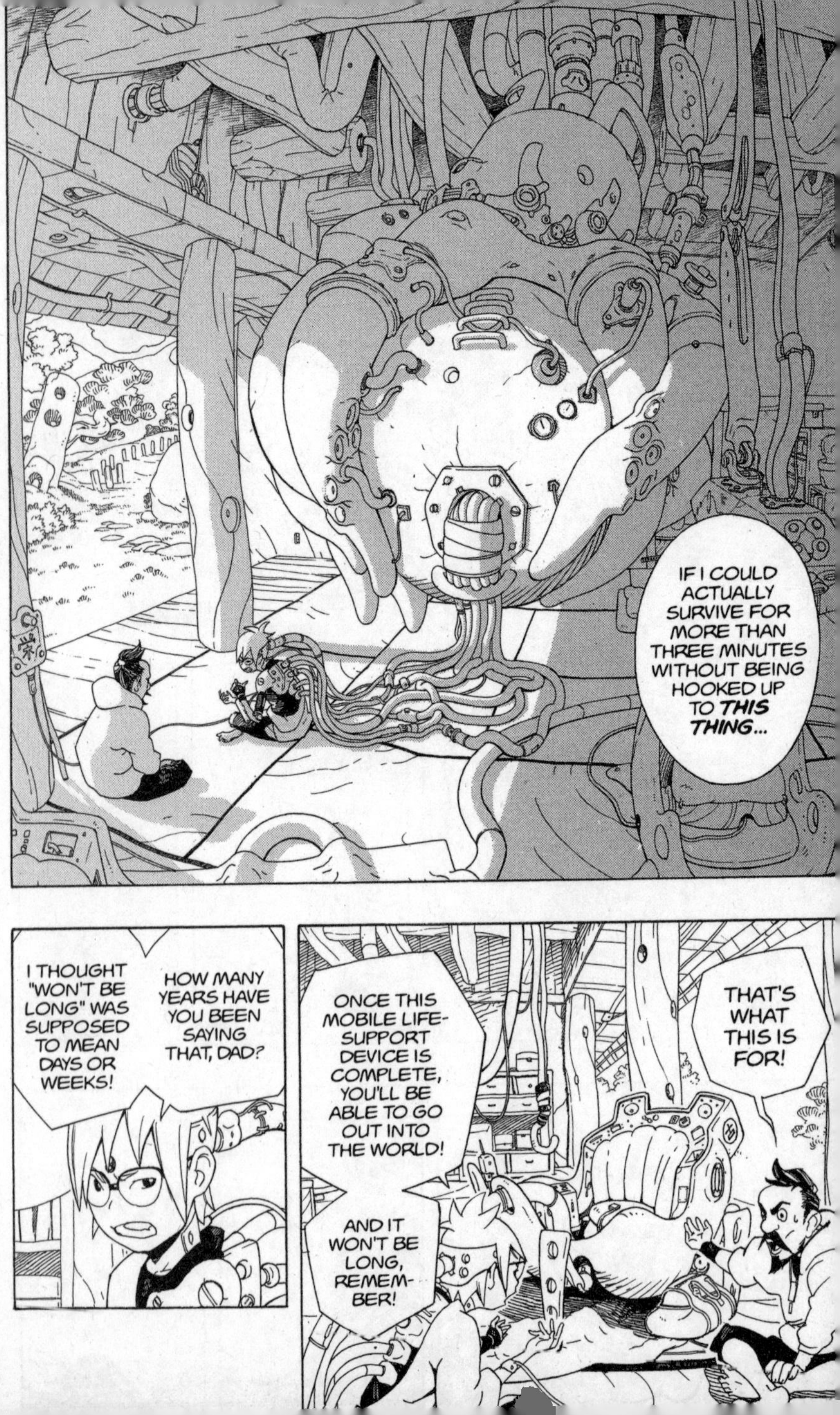
IF I COULD ACTUALLY SURVIVE FOR MORE THAN THREE MINUTES WITHOUT BEING HOOKED UP TO **THIS THING...**
THAT'S WHAT THIS IS FOR!
ONCE THIS MOBILE LIFE-SUPPORT DEVICE IS COMPLETE, YOU'LL BE ABLE TO GO OUT INTO THE WORLD!
AND IT WON'T BE LONG, REMEMBER!
HOW MANY YEARS HAVE YOU BEEN SAYING THAT, DAD?
I THOUGHT "WON'T BE LONG" WAS SUPPOSED TO MEAN DAYS OR WEEKS!

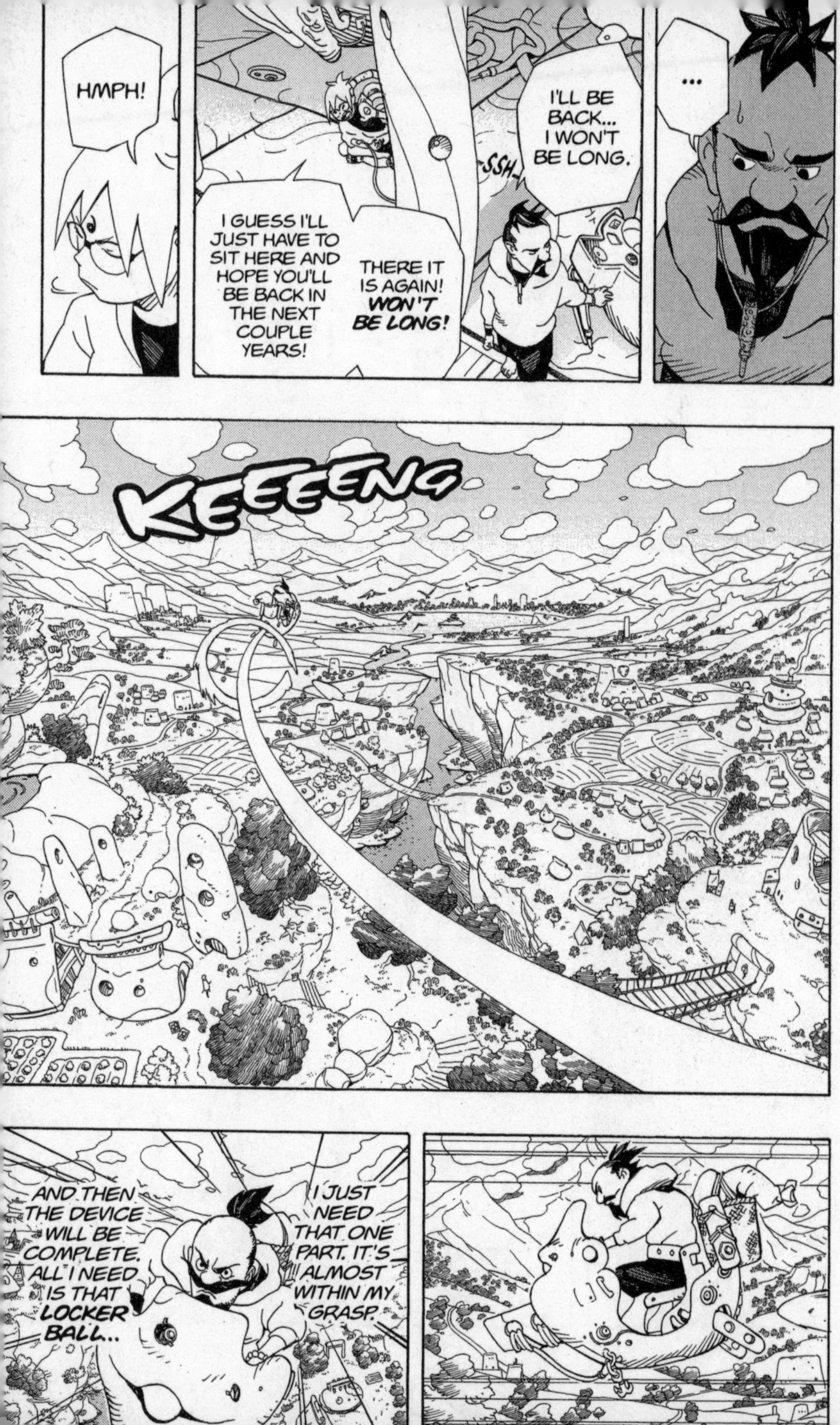
...
I'LL BE BACK... I WON'T BE LONG.
-SSH-
I GUESS I'LL JUST HAVE TO SIT HERE AND HOPE YOU'LL BE BACK IN THE NEXT COUPLE YEARS!
THERE IT IS AGAIN! WON'T BE LONG!
HMPH!
KEEEENG
I JUST NEED THAT ONE PART. IT'S ALMOST WITHIN MY GRASP.
AND THEN THE DEVICE WILL BE COMPLETE. ALL I NEED IS THAT LOCKER BALL...

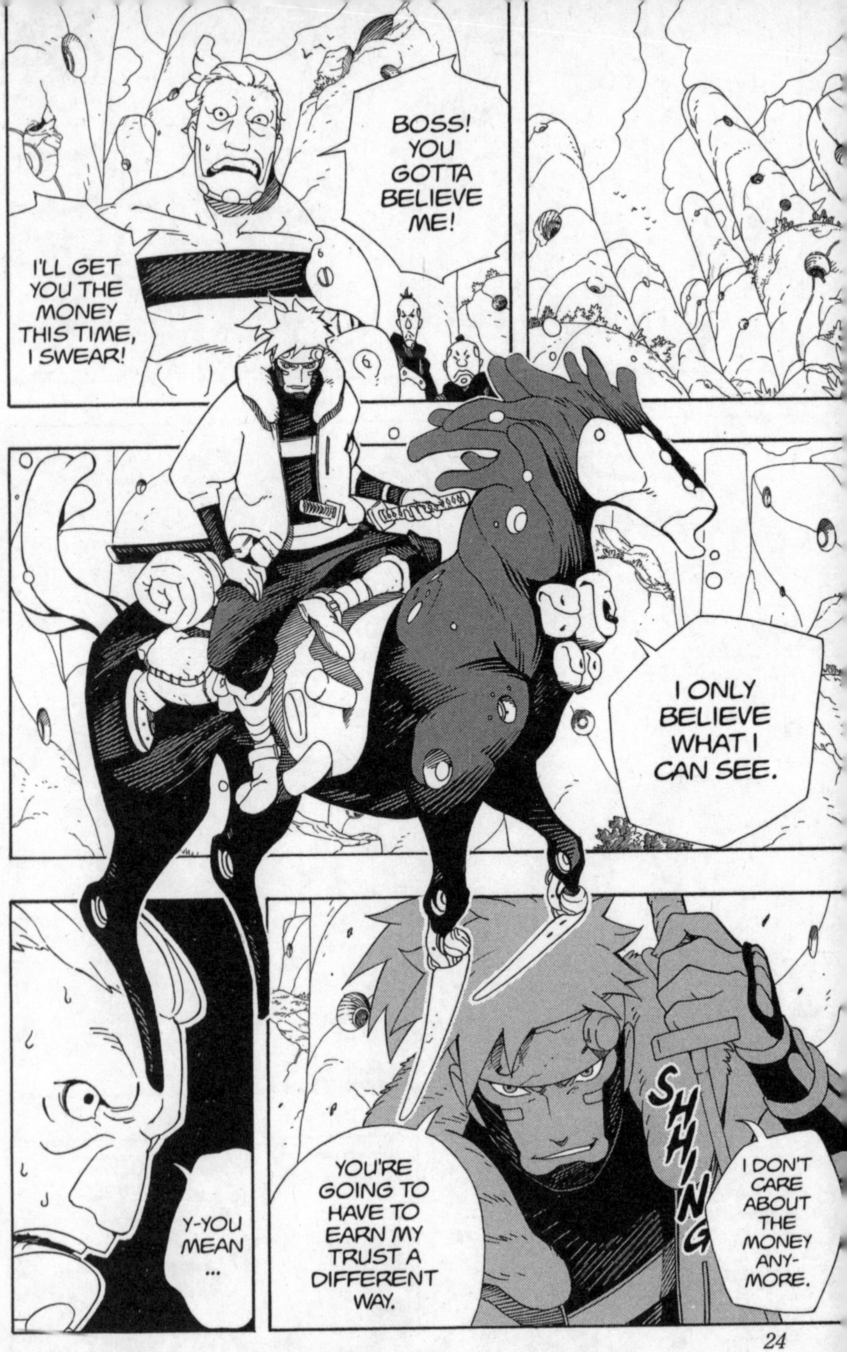
BOSS! YOU GOTTA BELIEVE ME!
I'LL GET YOU THE MONEY THIS TIME, I SWEAR!
I ONLY BELIEVE WHAT I CAN SEE.
I DON'T CARE ABOUT THE MONEY ANY-MORE.
SHHING
YOU'RE GOING TO HAVE TO EARN MY TRUST A DIFFERENT WAY.
Y-YOU MEAN ...

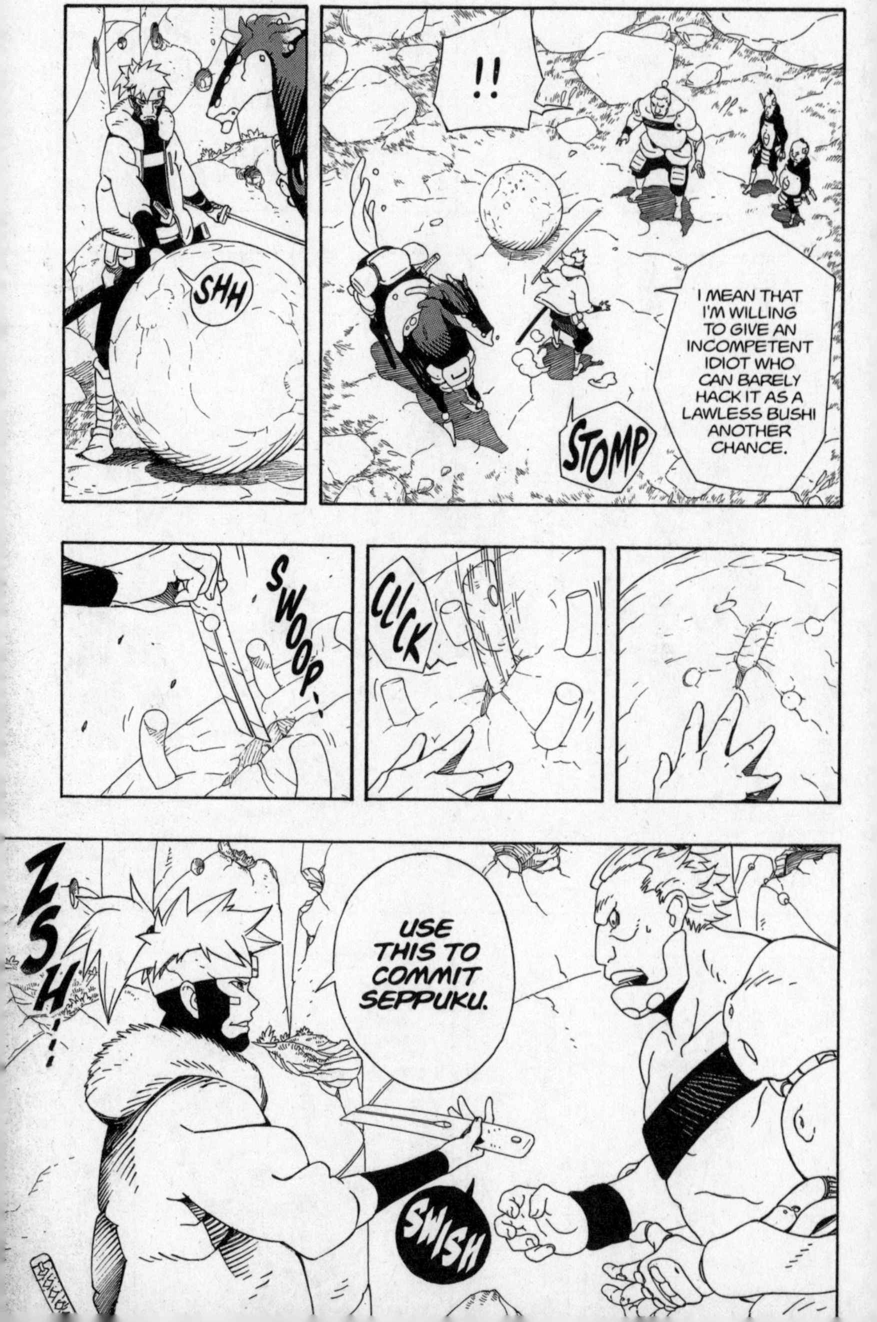

!!
I MEAN THAT I'M WILLING TO GIVE AN INCOMPETENT IDIOT WHO CAN BARELY HACK IT AS A LAWLESS BUSHI ANOTHER CHANCE.
STOMP
SHH
CLICK
SWOOOP
USE THIS TO COMMIT SEPPUKU.
ZSH
SWISH

HFF!! HFF!!

RATTLE

RATTLE RATTLE

I CAN'T... I CAN'T DO IT.

?!!

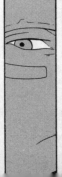

I THOUGHT YOU WANTED TO ADVANCE FROM A *BUSHI* TO A *SAMURAI*.

RATTLE

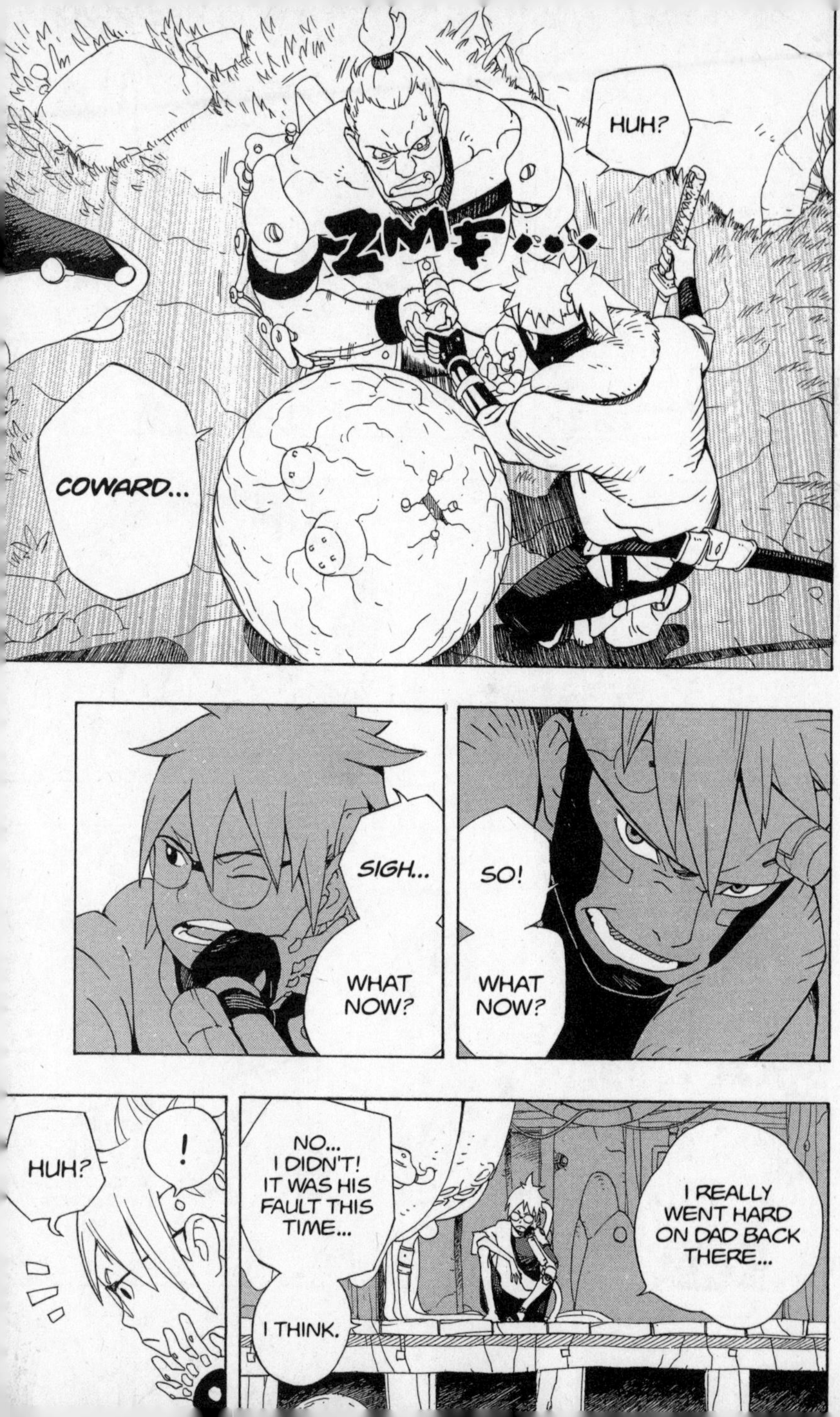
HUH?
ZMF...
COWARD...
SO!
WHAT NOW?
SIGH...
WHAT NOW?
I REALLY WENT HARD ON DAD BACK THERE...
NO... I DIDN'T! IT WAS HIS FAULT THIS TIME...
I THINK.
!
HUH?

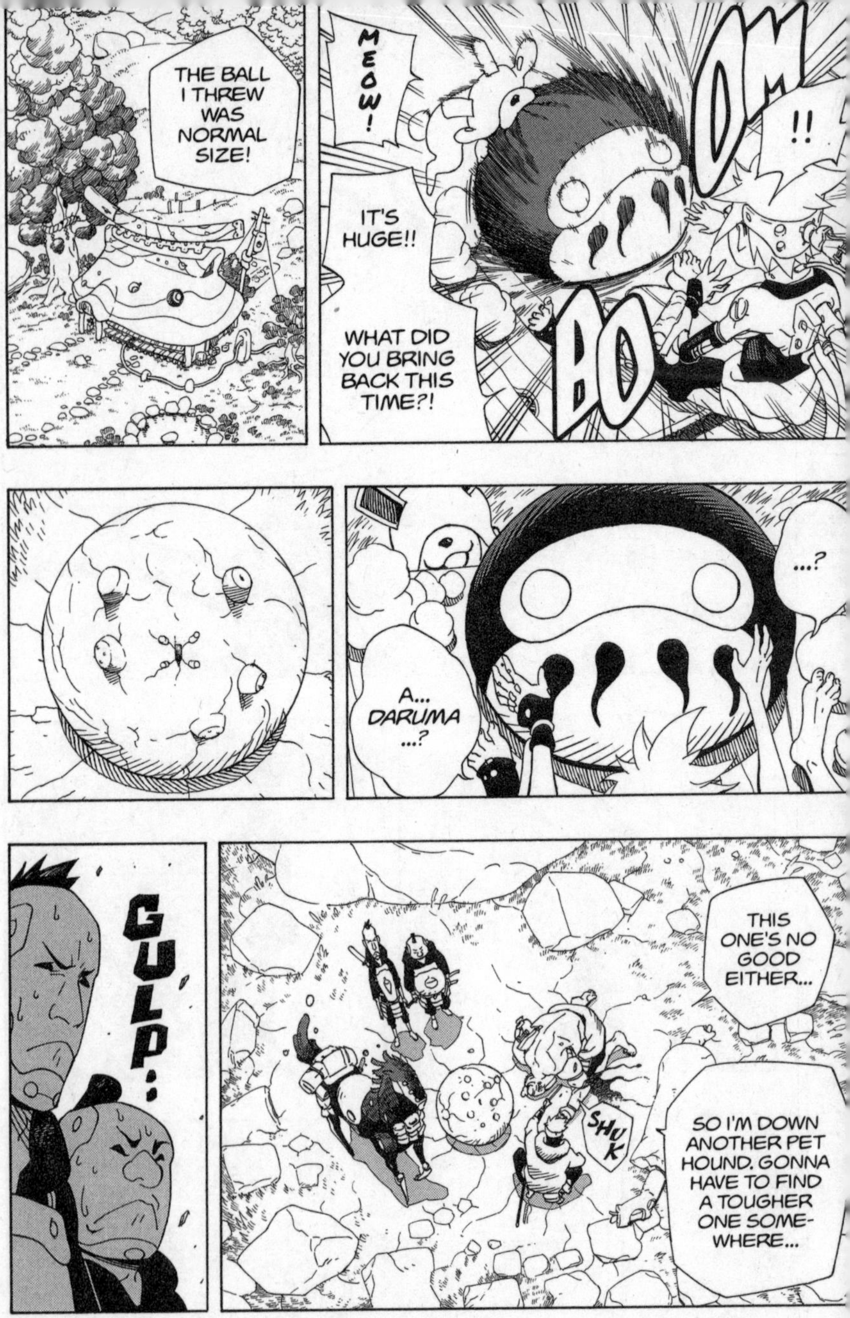
BOOM
!!
MEOW!
IT'S HUGE!!
WHAT DID YOU BRING BACK THIS TIME?!
THE BALL I THREW WAS NORMAL SIZE!
...?
A... DARUMA ...?
THIS ONE'S NO GOOD EITHER...
SO I'M DOWN ANOTHER PET HOUND. GONNA HAVE TO FIND A TOUGHER ONE SOME-WHERE...
SHUK
GULP

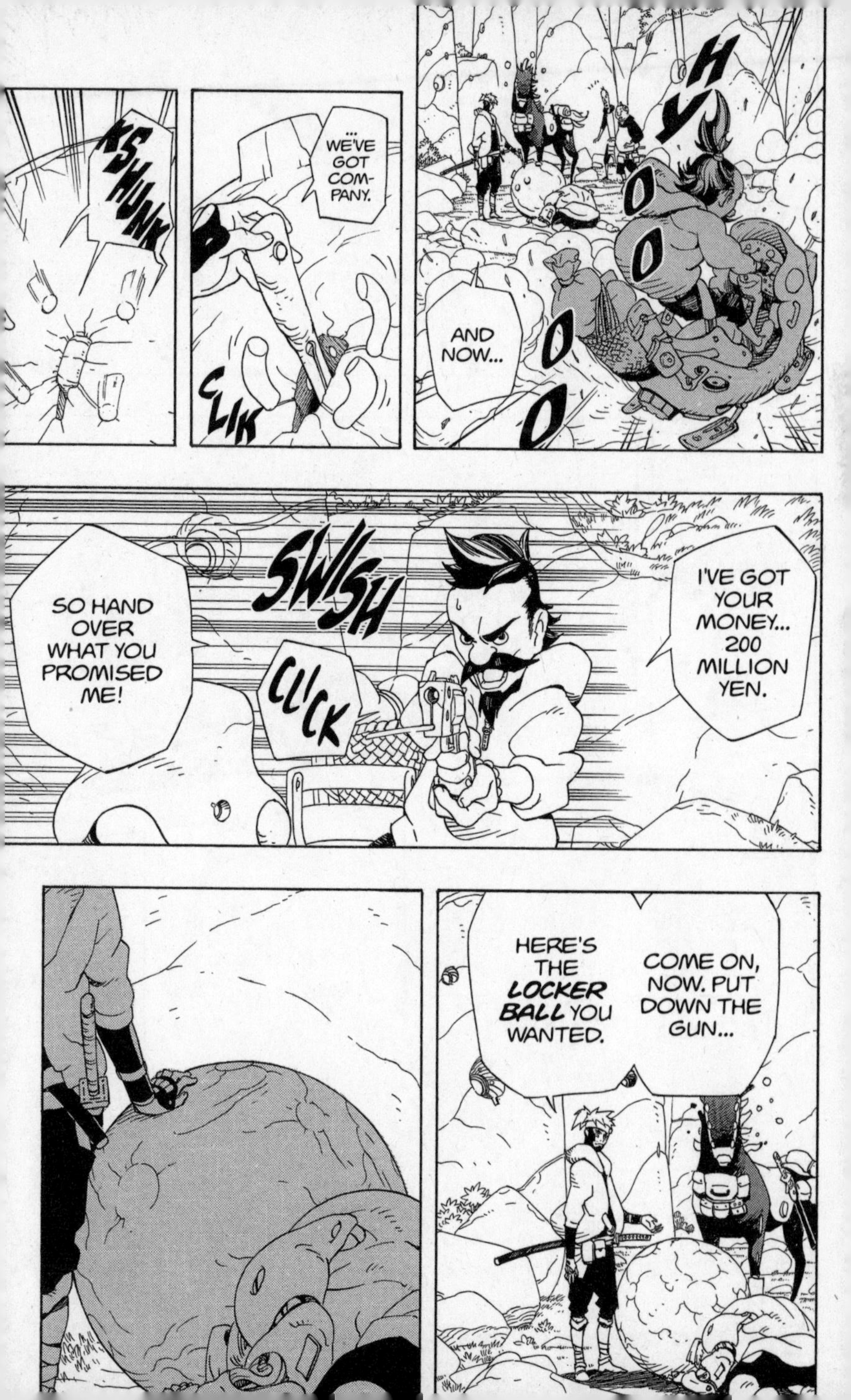
AND NOW...
... WE'VE GOT COMPANY.
CLIK
KSHUNK
I'VE GOT YOUR MONEY... 200 MILLION YEN.
SWISH
CLICK
SO HAND OVER WHAT YOU PROMISED ME!
COME ON, NOW. PUT DOWN THE GUN...
HERE'S THE **LOCKER BALL** YOU WANTED.

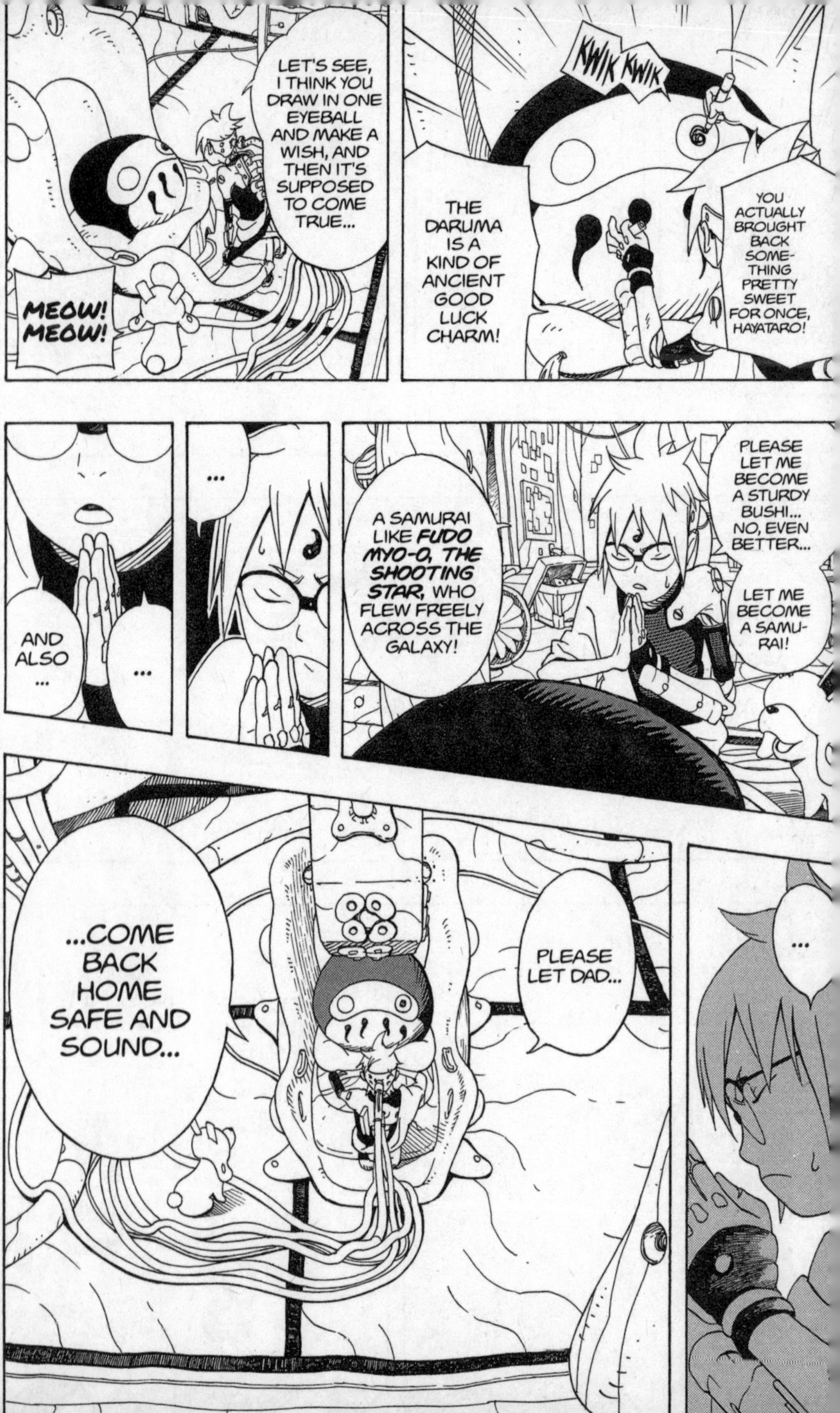
KWIK KWIK
YOU ACTUALLY BROUGHT BACK SOMETHING PRETTY SWEET FOR ONCE, HAYATARO!
THE DARUMA IS A KIND OF ANCIENT GOOD LUCK CHARM!
LET'S SEE, I THINK YOU DRAW IN ONE EYEBALL AND MAKE A WISH, AND THEN IT'S SUPPOSED TO COME TRUE...
MEOW! MEOW!
PLEASE LET ME BECOME A STURDY BUSHI... NO, EVEN BETTER...
LET ME BECOME A SAMURAI!
A SAMURAI LIKE FUDO MYO-O, THE SHOOTING STAR, WHO FLEW FREELY ACROSS THE GALAXY!
...
...
AND ALSO ...
...
PLEASE LET DAD...
...COME BACK HOME SAFE AND SOUND...

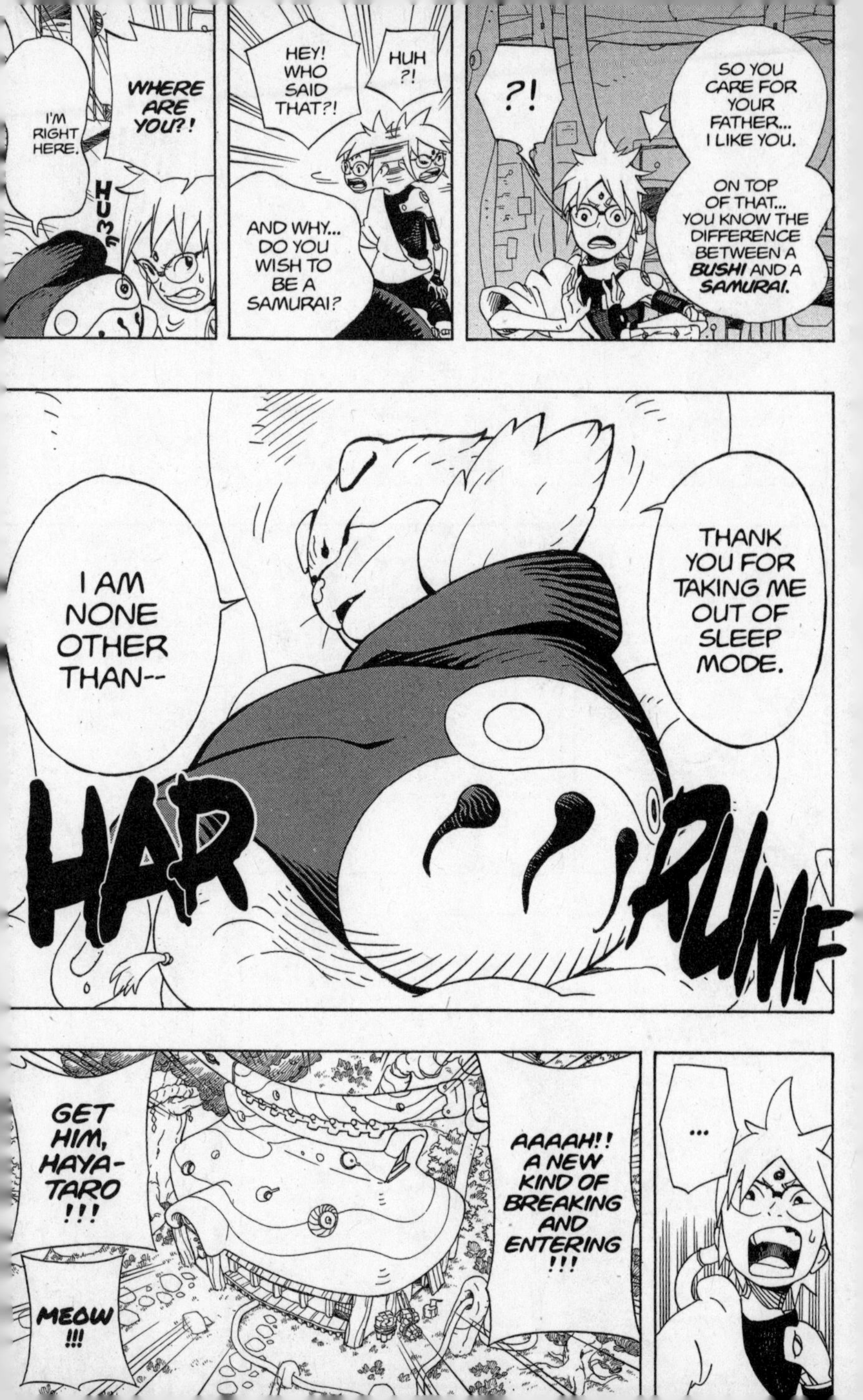
SO YOU CARE FOR YOUR FATHER... I LIKE YOU.
ON TOP OF THAT... YOU KNOW THE DIFFERENCE BETWEEN A BUSHI AND A SAMURAI.
?!
HUH ?!
HEY! WHO SAID THAT?!
AND WHY... DO YOU WISH TO BE A SAMURAI?
WHERE ARE YOU?!
I'M RIGHT HERE.
HUMF
THANK YOU FOR TAKING ME OUT OF SLEEP MODE.
I AM NONE OTHER THAN--
HARRUMF
...
AAAAH!! A NEW KIND OF BREAKING AND ENTERING !!!
GET HIM, HAYA-TARO !!!
MEOW !!!

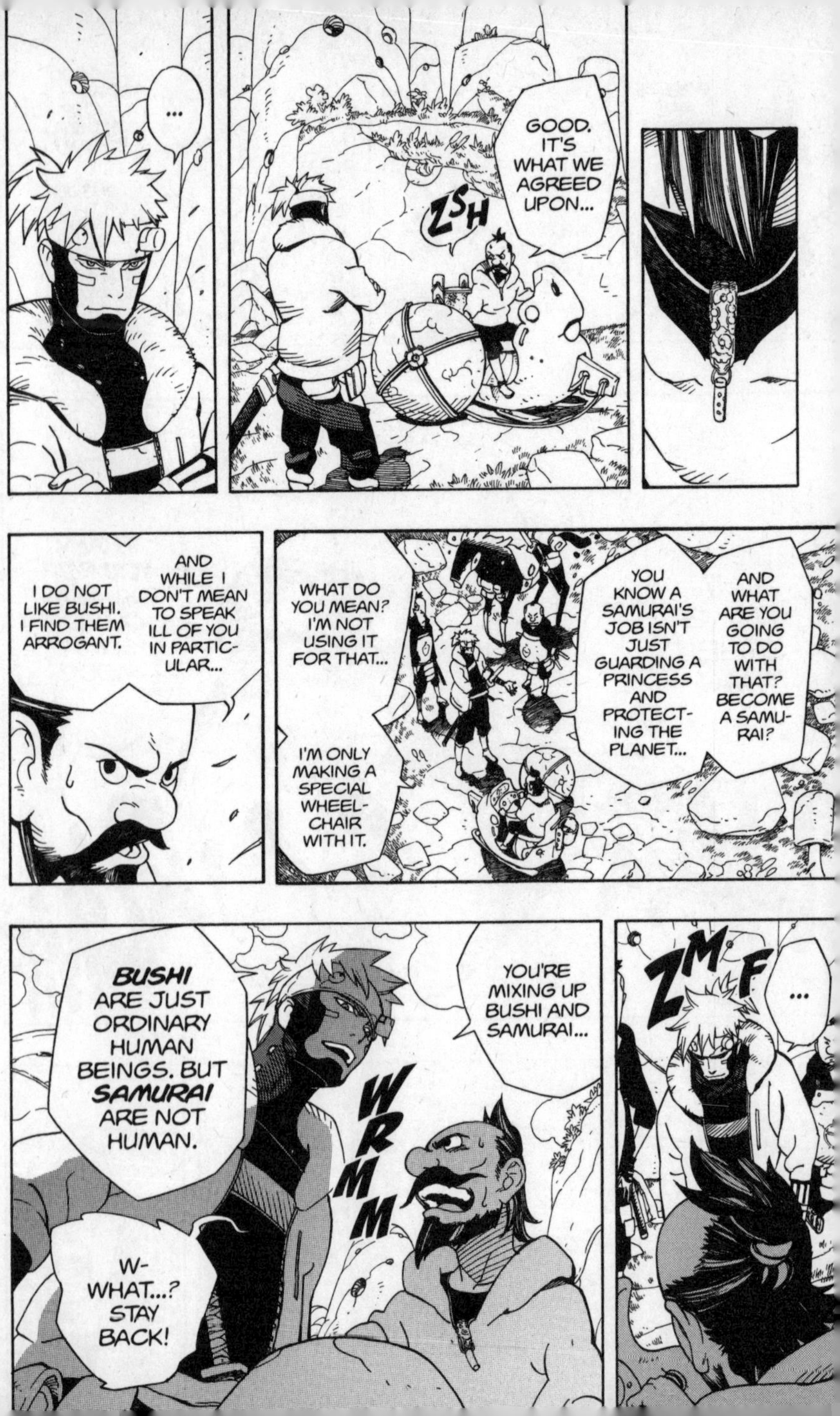
GOOD. IT'S WHAT WE AGREED UPON...
ZSH
...
AND WHAT ARE YOU GOING TO DO WITH THAT? BECOME A SAMURAI?
YOU KNOW A SAMURAI'S JOB ISN'T JUST GUARDING A PRINCESS AND PROTECTING THE PLANET...
WHAT DO YOU MEAN? I'M NOT USING IT FOR THAT...
I'M ONLY MAKING A SPECIAL WHEELCHAIR WITH IT.
AND WHILE I DON'T MEAN TO SPEAK ILL OF YOU IN PARTICULAR...
I DO NOT LIKE BUSHI. I FIND THEM ARROGANT.
ZMF
...
YOU'RE MIXING UP BUSHI AND SAMURAI...
BUSHI ARE JUST ORDINARY HUMAN BEINGS. BUT *SAMURAI* ARE NOT HUMAN.
WRMM
W-WHAT...? STAY BACK!

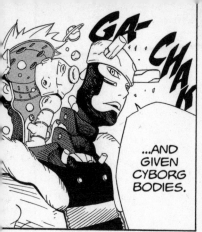

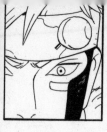

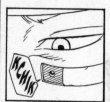

KCHIK
SAMURAI ARE CHOSEN BY THE WARRIOR GOD FOR BEING THE MOST ELITE OF BUSHI...
GA-CHAK
...AND GIVEN CYBORG BODIES.
VSHA
VMM
ZMF
A MEMORY UNIT CALLED A KEY, WHICH RESEMBLES A SPINE, BECOMES THE BASE OF THE SAMURAI.
KEY
BEEP
SAMURAI
KEY
BEEP BEEP
MACHINE
BEEP
EVERYTHING AROUND THE KEY IS CONSTRUCTED OF CYBORG PARTS.

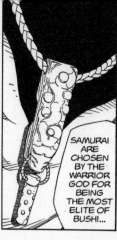

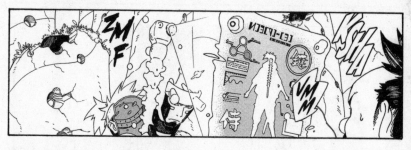

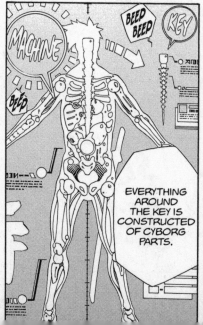

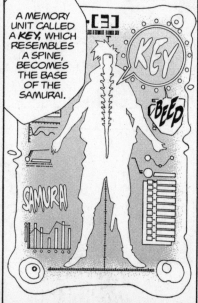

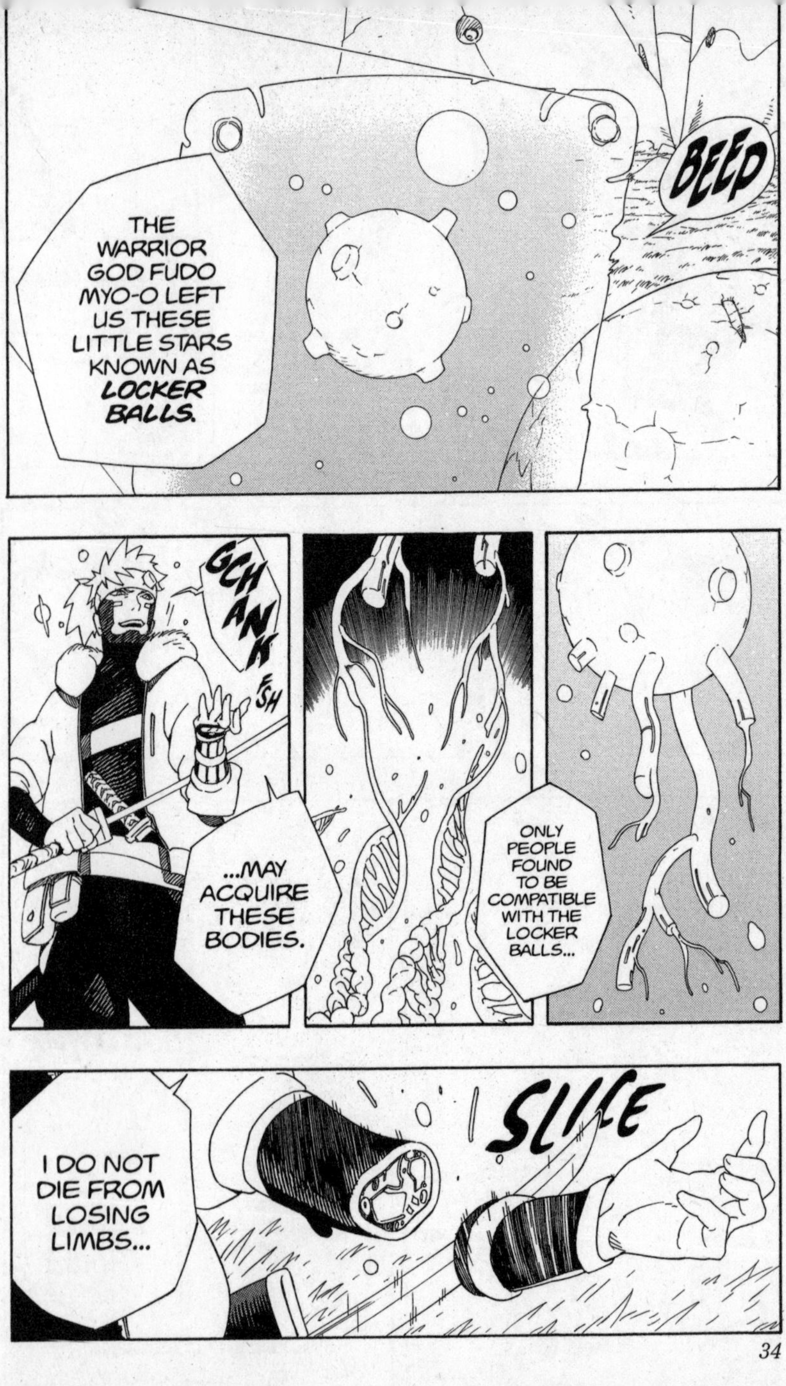
BEEP
THE WARRIOR GOD FUDO MYO-O LEFT US THESE LITTLE STARS KNOWN AS LOCKER BALLS.
ONLY PEOPLE FOUND TO BE COMPATIBLE WITH THE LOCKER BALLS...
GCHANK
FSH
...MAY ACQUIRE THESE BODIES.
SLICE
I DO NOT DIE FROM LOSING LIMBS...

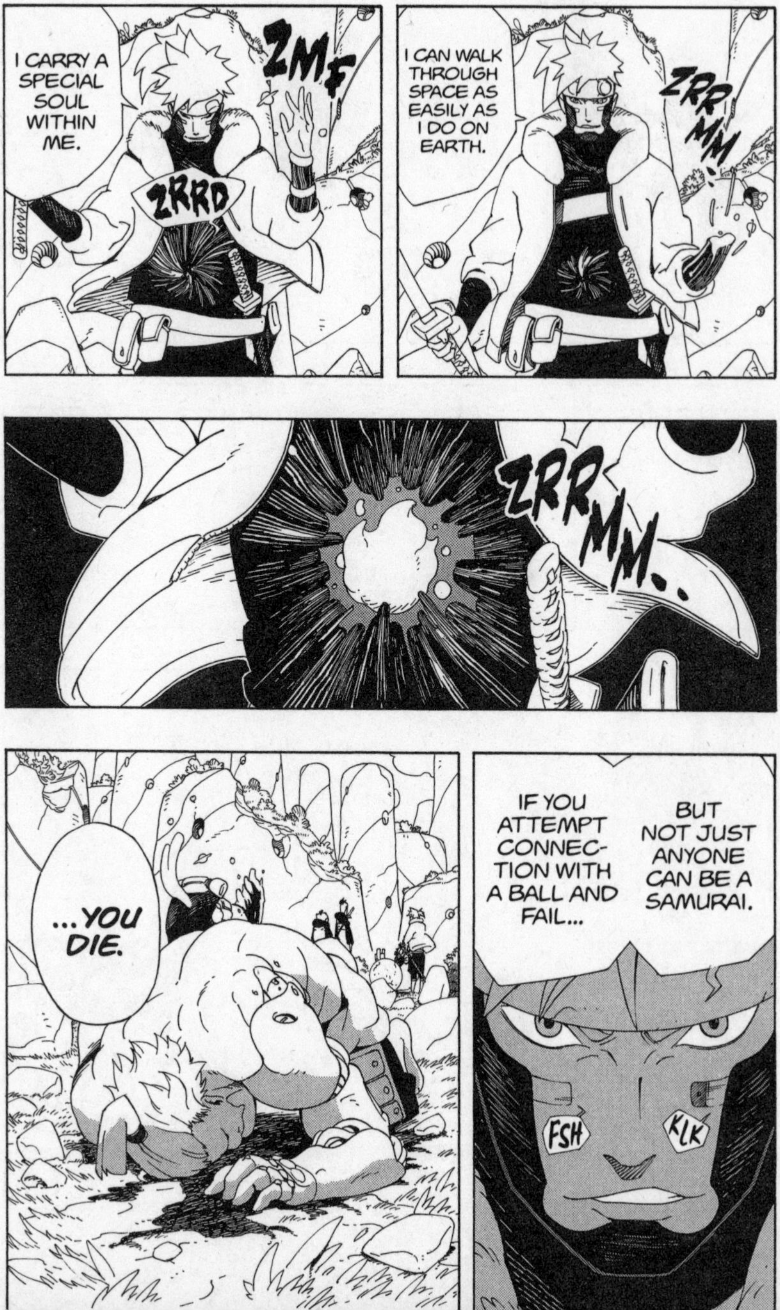
I CAN WALK THROUGH SPACE AS EASILY AS I DO ON EARTH.
ZRRMM!
I CARRY A SPECIAL SOUL WITHIN ME.
ZMF
ZRRD
ZRRMM...
BUT NOT JUST ANYONE CAN BE A SAMURAI.
IF YOU ATTEMPT CONNEC-TION WITH A BALL AND FAIL...
FSH
KLK
...YOU DIE.

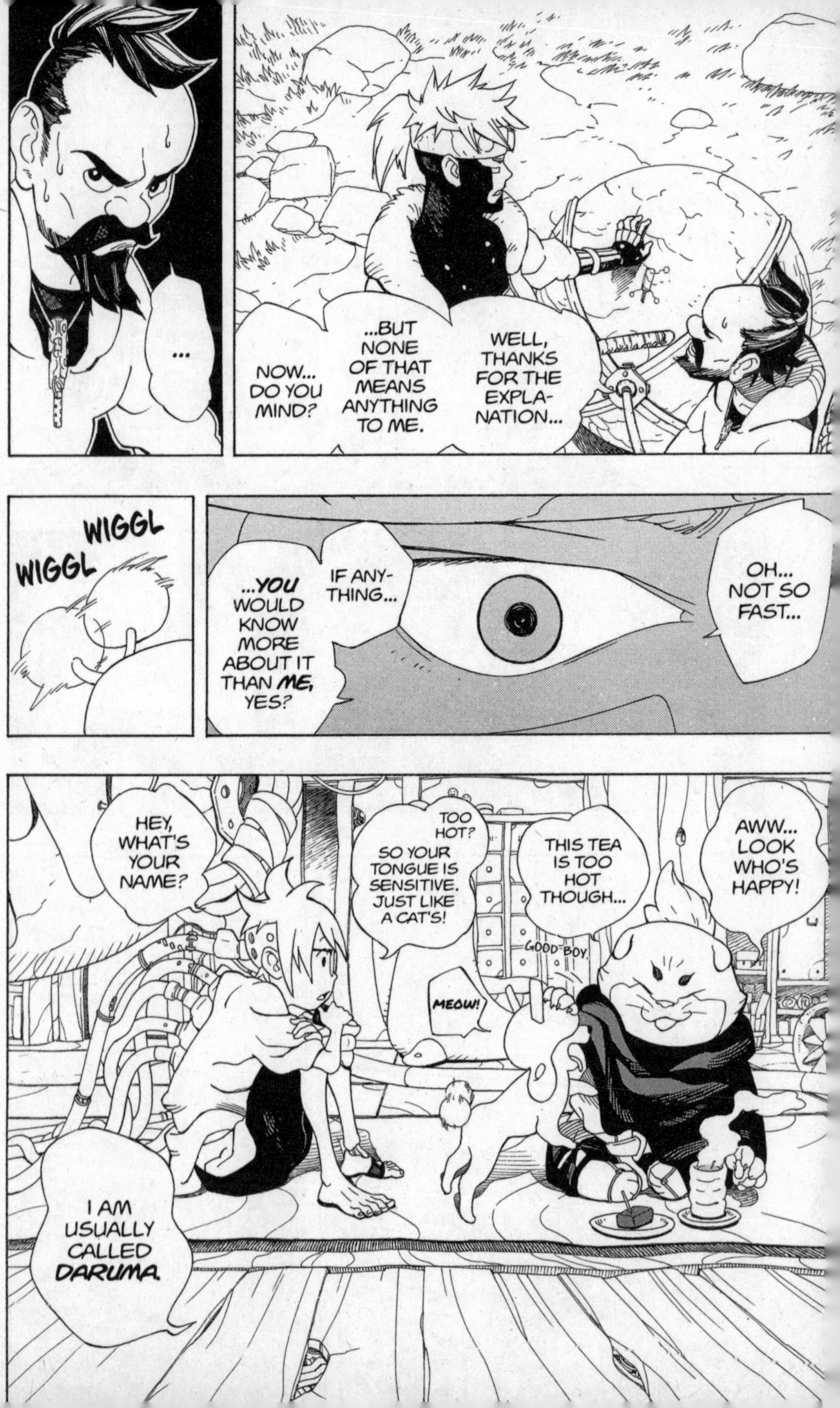
WELL, THANKS FOR THE EXPLA-NATION...
...BUT NONE OF THAT MEANS ANYTHING TO ME.
NOW... DO YOU MIND?
...
OH... NOT SO FAST...
IF ANY-THING...
...*YOU* WOULD KNOW MORE ABOUT IT THAN *ME*, YES?
WIGGL
WIGGL
AWW... LOOK WHO'S HAPPY!
GOOD BOY.
THIS TEA IS TOO HOT THOUGH...
TOO HOT?
SO YOUR TONGUE IS SENSITIVE. JUST LIKE A CAT'S!
MEOW!
HEY, WHAT'S YOUR NAME?
I AM USUALLY CALLED *DARUMA*.

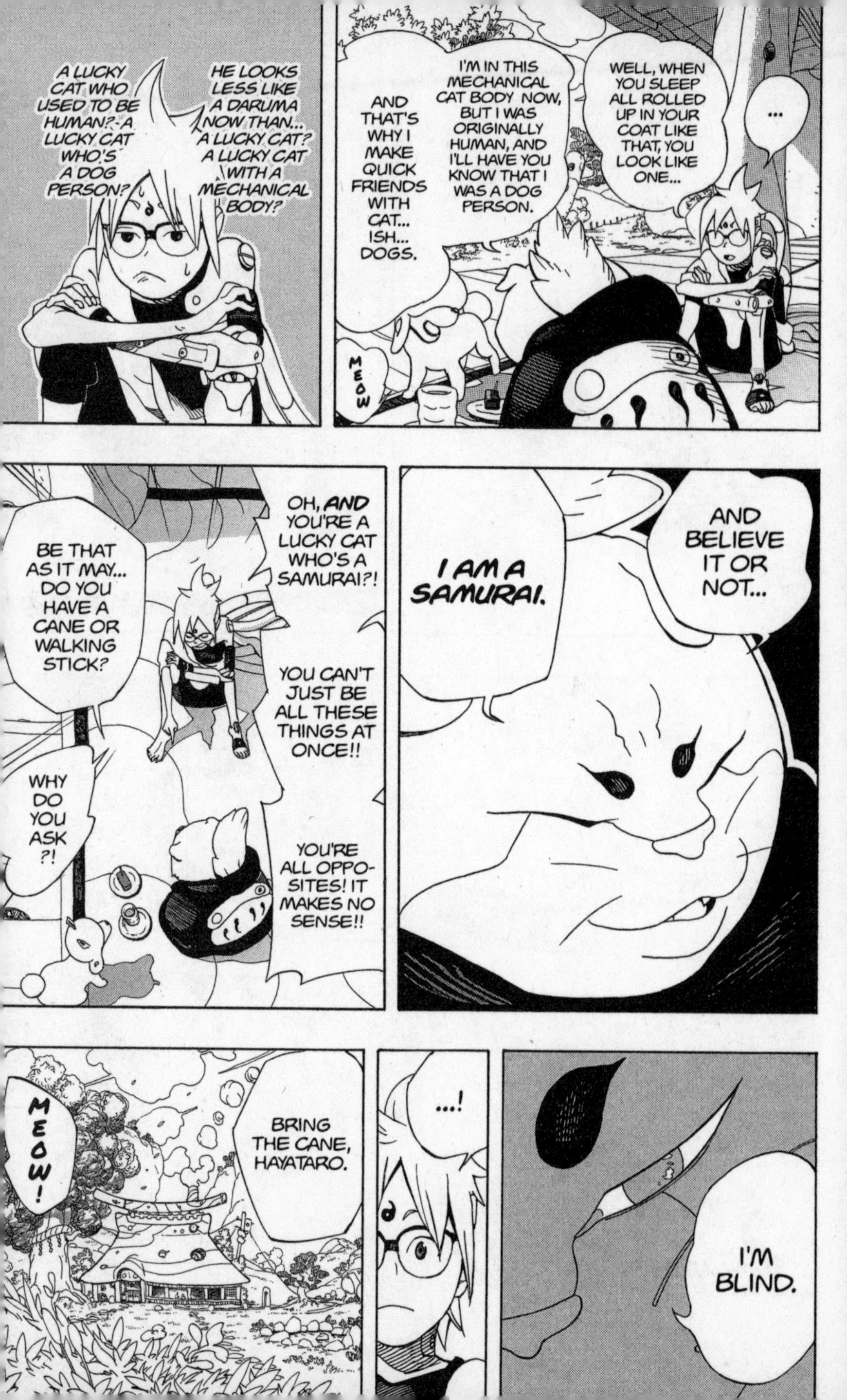
...
WELL, WHEN YOU SLEEP ALL ROLLED UP IN YOUR COAT LIKE THAT, YOU LOOK LIKE ONE...
I'M IN THIS MECHANICAL CAT BODY NOW, BUT I WAS ORIGINALLY HUMAN, AND I'LL HAVE YOU KNOW THAT I WAS A DOG PERSON.
AND THAT'S WHY I MAKE QUICK FRIENDS WITH CAT... ISH... DOGS.
MEOW
HE LOOKS LESS LIKE A DARUMA NOW THAN... A LUCKY CAT? A LUCKY CAT WITH A MECHANICAL BODY?
A LUCKY CAT WHO USED TO BE HUMAN?-A LUCKY CAT WHO'S A DOG PERSON?
AND BELIEVE IT OR NOT...
I AM A SAMURAI.
OH, AND YOU'RE A LUCKY CAT WHO'S A SAMURAI?!
YOU CAN'T JUST BE ALL THESE THINGS AT ONCE!!
YOU'RE ALL OPPOSITES! IT MAKES NO SENSE!!
BE THAT AS IT MAY... DO YOU HAVE A CANE OR WALKING STICK?
WHY DO YOU ASK?!
I'M BLIND.
...!
BRING THE CANE, HAYATARO.
MEOW!

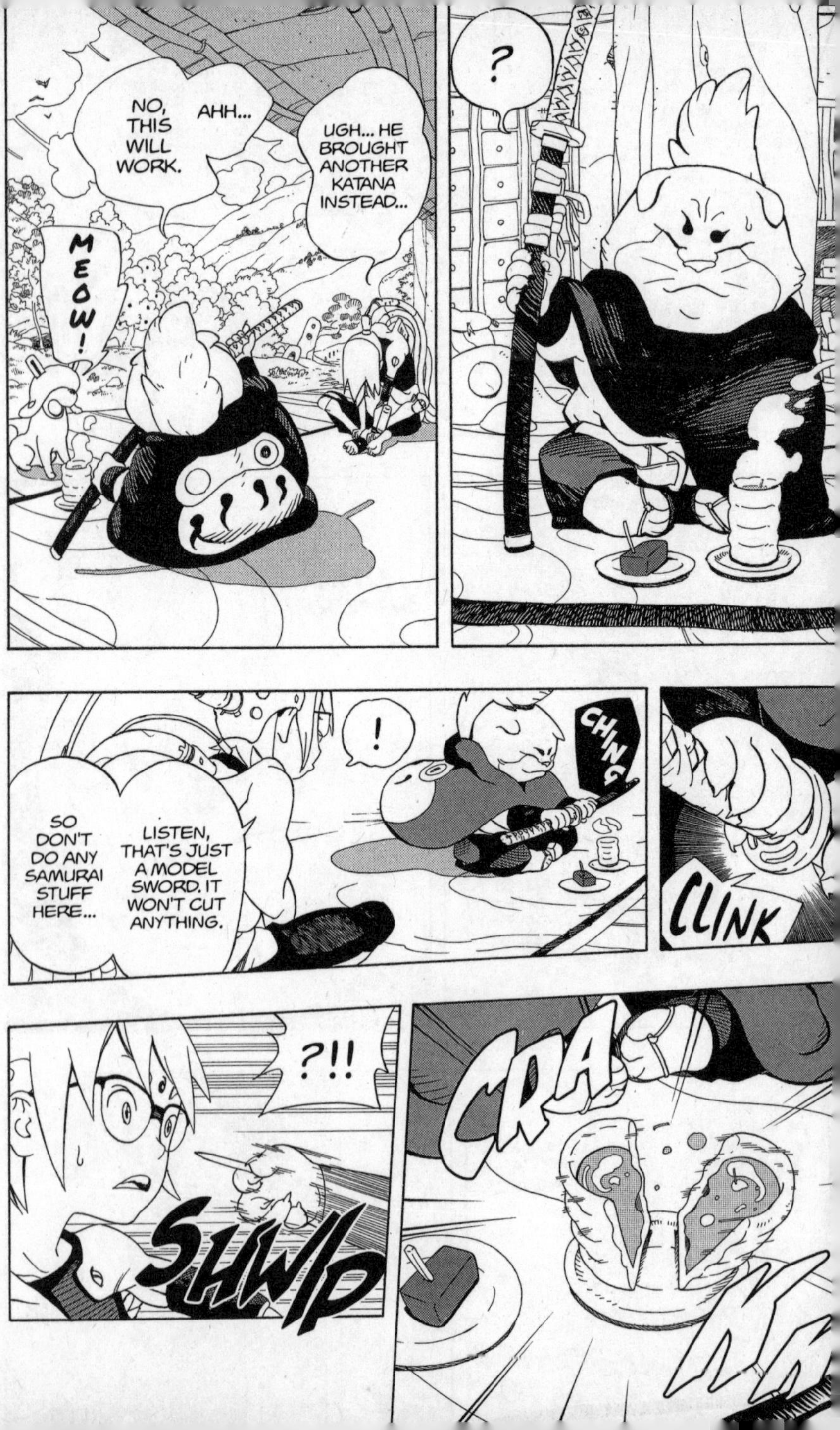
?
UGH... HE BROUGHT ANOTHER KATANA INSTEAD...
AHH...
NO, THIS WILL WORK.
MEOW!
CLINK
CHING
!
LISTEN, THAT'S JUST A MODEL SWORD. IT WON'T CUT ANYTHING.
SO DON'T DO ANY SAMURAI STUFF HERE...
CRA
?!!
SHWIP

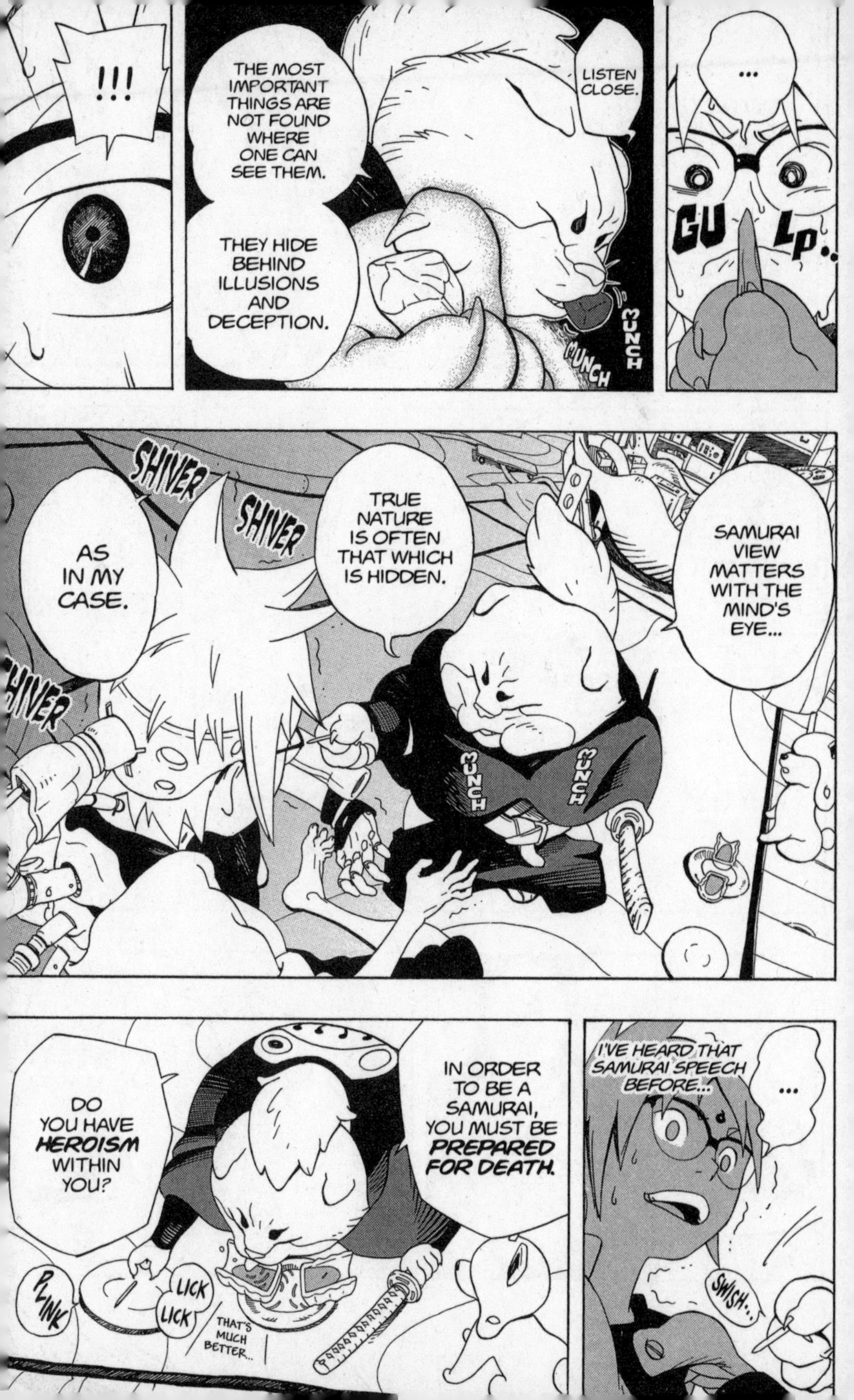
...
GULP..
LISTEN CLOSE.
THE MOST IMPORTANT THINGS ARE NOT FOUND WHERE ONE CAN SEE THEM.
THEY HIDE BEHIND ILLUSIONS AND DECEPTION.
MUNCH
MUNCH
!!!
SAMURAI VIEW MATTERS WITH THE MIND'S EYE...
TRUE NATURE IS OFTEN THAT WHICH IS HIDDEN.
MUNCH
MUNCH
SHIVER
SHIVER
AS IN MY CASE.
I'VE HEARD THAT SAMURAI SPEECH BEFORE...
...
SWISH...
IN ORDER TO BE A SAMURAI, YOU MUST BE ***PREPARED FOR DEATH.***
DO YOU HAVE ***HEROISM*** WITHIN YOU?
THAT'S MUCH BETTER...
LICK
LICK
PLINK

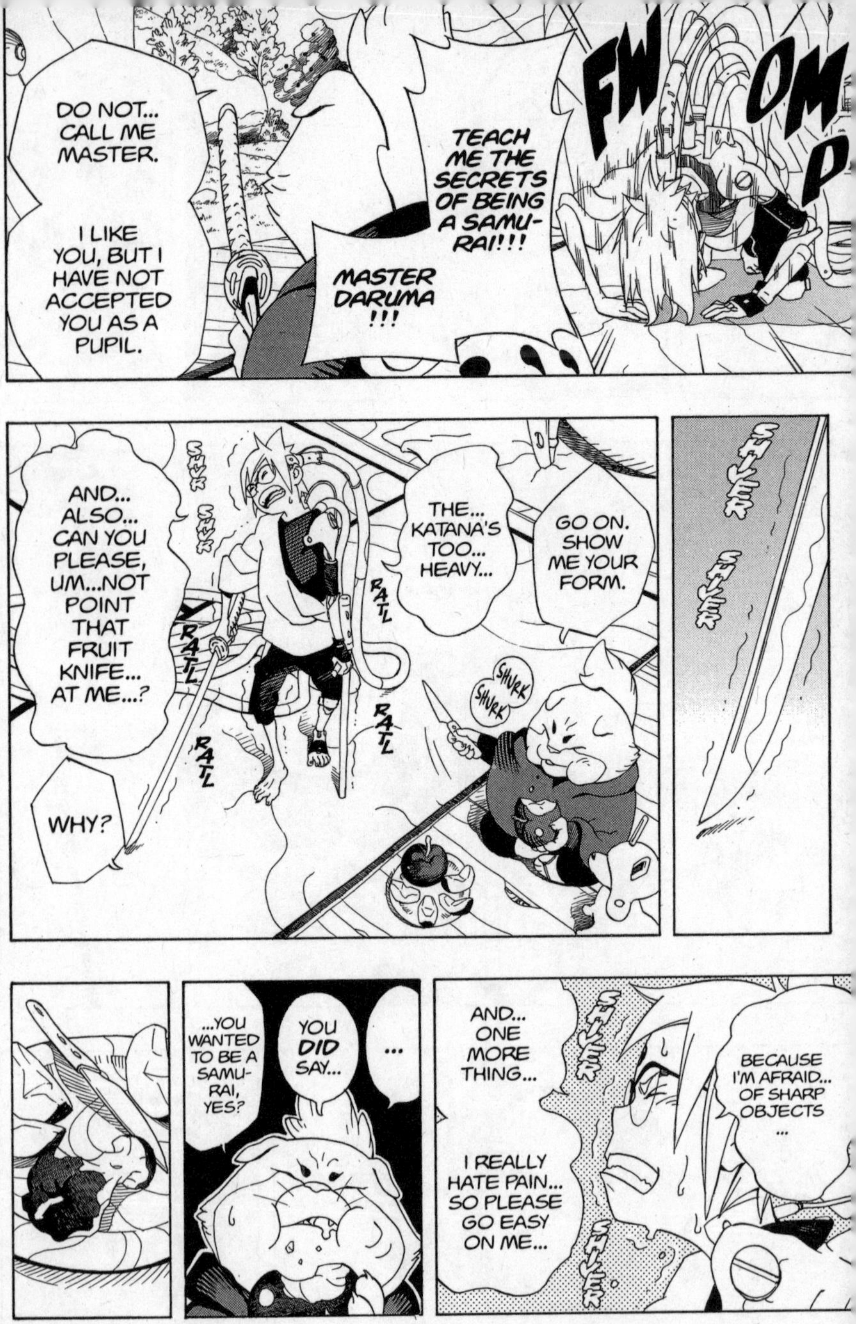
FWOMP
TEACH ME THE SECRETS OF BEING A SAMU-RAI!!!
MASTER DARUMA!!!
DO NOT... CALL ME MASTER.
I LIKE YOU, BUT I HAVE NOT ACCEPTED YOU AS A PUPIL.
SHIVER
SHIVER
GO ON. SHOW ME YOUR FORM.
THE... KATANA'S TOO... HEAVY...
SHURK
SHURK
RATL
RATL
RATL
RATL
SHVK
SHVK
AND... ALSO... CAN YOU PLEASE, UM...NOT POINT THAT FRUIT KNIFE... AT ME...?
WHY?
SHIVER
BECAUSE I'M AFRAID... OF SHARP OBJECTS...
AND... ONE MORE THING...
I REALLY HATE PAIN... SO PLEASE GO EASY ON ME...
SHIVER
...
YOU DID SAY...
...YOU WANTED TO BE A SAMU-RAI, YES?

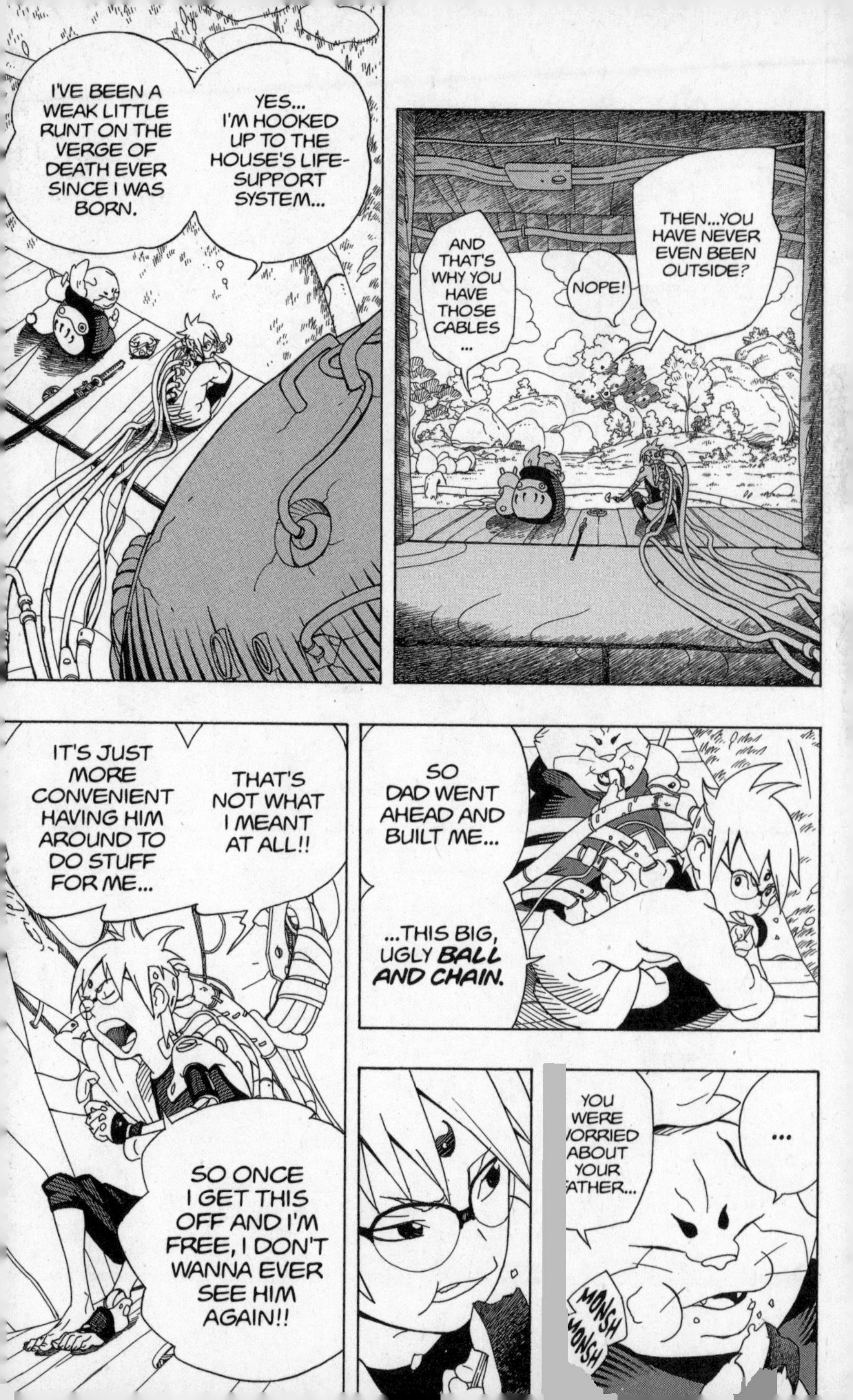
THEN...YOU HAVE NEVER EVEN BEEN OUTSIDE?
NOPE!
AND THAT'S WHY YOU HAVE THOSE CABLES ...
YES... I'M HOOKED UP TO THE HOUSE'S LIFE-SUPPORT SYSTEM...
I'VE BEEN A WEAK LITTLE RUNT ON THE VERGE OF DEATH EVER SINCE I WAS BORN.
SO DAD WENT AHEAD AND BUILT ME...
...THIS BIG, UGLY BALL AND CHAIN.
THAT'S NOT WHAT I MEANT AT ALL!!
IT'S JUST MORE CONVENIENT HAVING HIM AROUND TO DO STUFF FOR ME...
SO ONCE I GET THIS OFF AND I'M FREE, I DON'T WANNA EVER SEE HIM AGAIN!!
YOU WERE WORRIED ABOUT YOUR FATHER...
...
MONSH MONSH

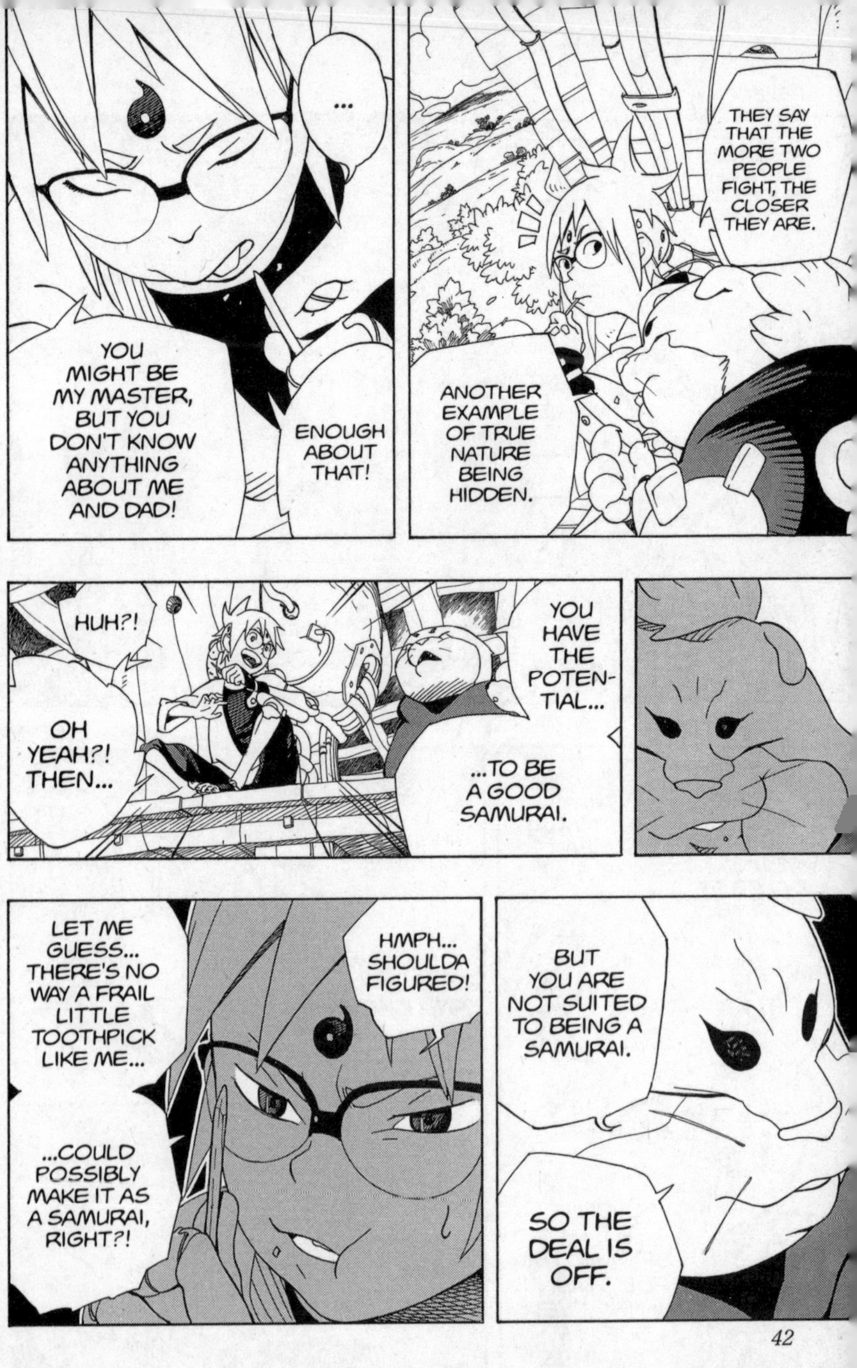
THEY SAY THAT THE MORE TWO PEOPLE FIGHT, THE CLOSER THEY ARE.
ANOTHER EXAMPLE OF TRUE NATURE BEING HIDDEN.
...
YOU MIGHT BE MY MASTER, BUT YOU DON'T KNOW ANYTHING ABOUT ME AND DAD!
ENOUGH ABOUT THAT!
YOU HAVE THE POTEN-TIAL...
...TO BE A GOOD SAMURAI.
HUH?!
OH YEAH?! THEN...
BUT YOU ARE NOT SUITED TO BEING A SAMURAI.
SO THE DEAL IS OFF.
HMPH... SHOULDA FIGURED!
LET ME GUESS... THERE'S NO WAY A FRAIL LITTLE TOOTHPICK LIKE ME...
...COULD POSSIBLY MAKE IT AS A SAMURAI, RIGHT?!

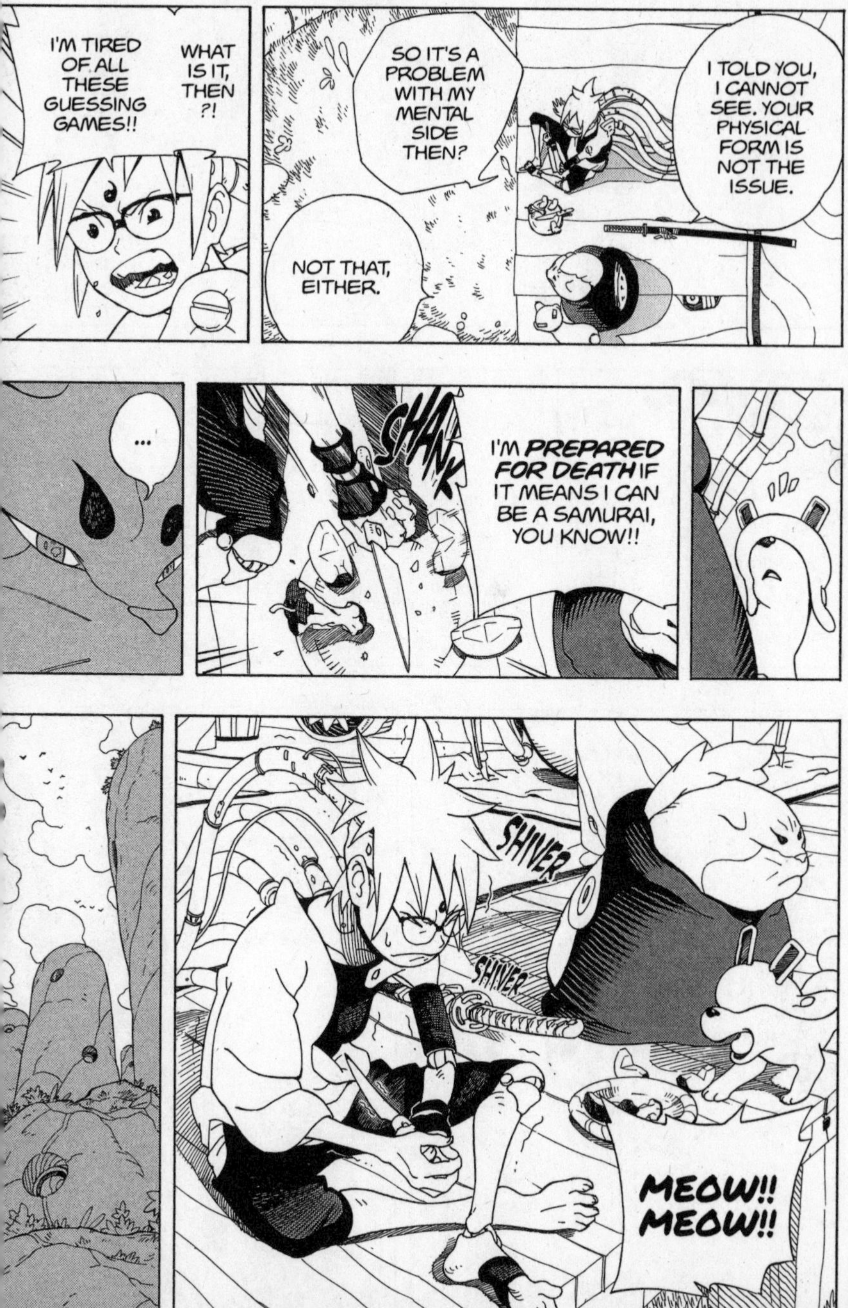
I TOLD YOU, I CANNOT SEE. YOUR PHYSICAL FORM IS NOT THE ISSUE.
SO IT'S A PROBLEM WITH MY MENTAL SIDE THEN?
NOT THAT, EITHER.
WHAT IS IT, THEN ?!
I'M TIRED OF ALL THESE GUESSING GAMES!!
SHANK
I'M **PREPARED FOR DEATH** IF IT MEANS I CAN BE A SAMURAI, YOU KNOW!!
...
SHIVER
SHIVER
MEOW!! MEOW!!

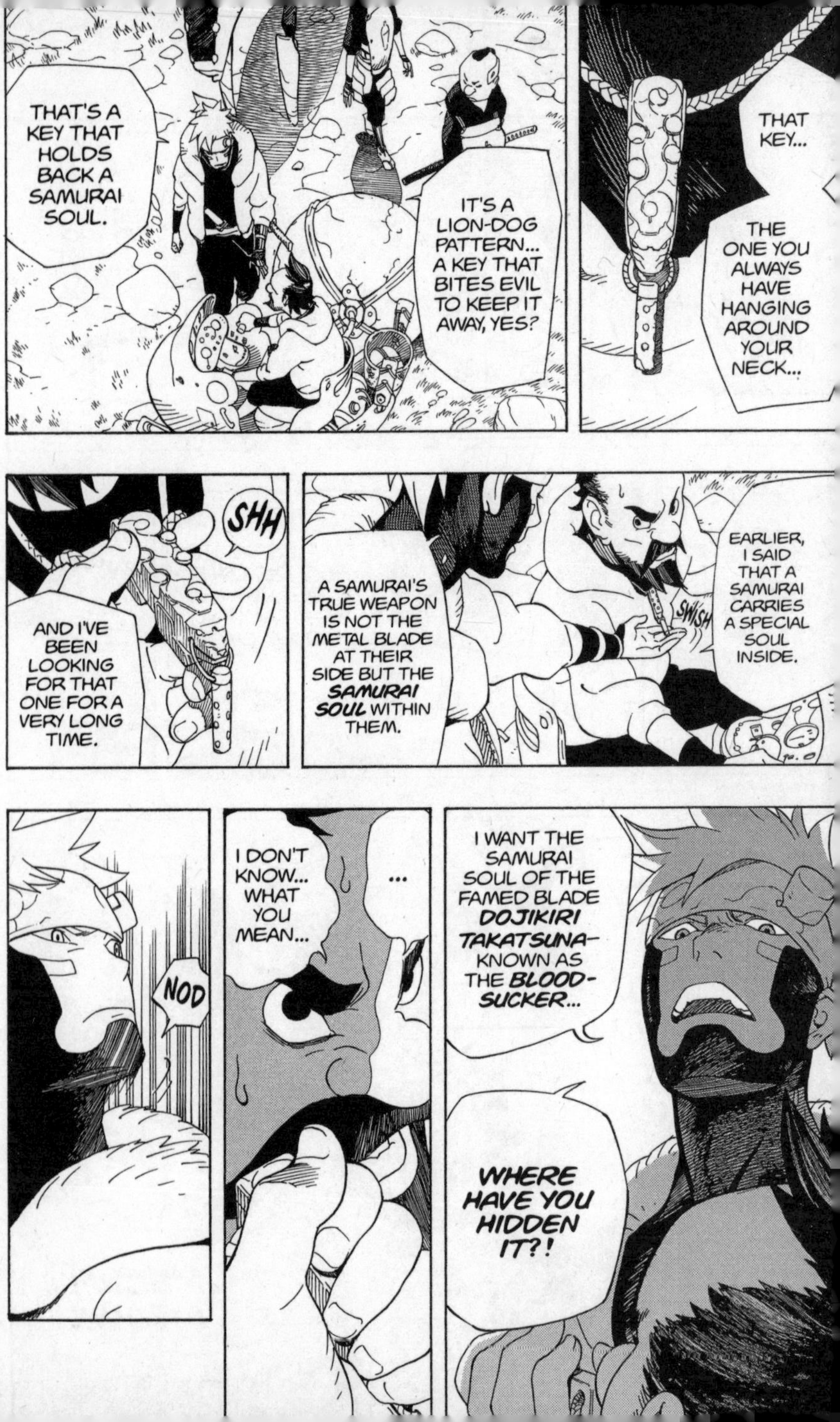
THAT KEY...
THE ONE YOU ALWAYS HAVE HANGING AROUND YOUR NECK...
IT'S A LION-DOG PATTERN... A KEY THAT BITES EVIL TO KEEP IT AWAY, YES?
THAT'S A KEY THAT HOLDS BACK A SAMURAI SOUL.
EARLIER, I SAID THAT A SAMURAI CARRIES A SPECIAL SOUL INSIDE.
SWISH
A SAMURAI'S TRUE WEAPON IS NOT THE METAL BLADE AT THEIR SIDE BUT THE SAMURAI SOUL WITHIN THEM.
SHH
AND I'VE BEEN LOOKING FOR THAT ONE FOR A VERY LONG TIME.
I WANT THE SAMURAI SOUL OF THE FAMED BLADE DOJIKIRI TAKATSUNA-KNOWN AS THE BLOOD-SUCKER...
WHERE HAVE YOU HIDDEN IT?!
...
I DON'T KNOW... WHAT YOU MEAN...
NOD

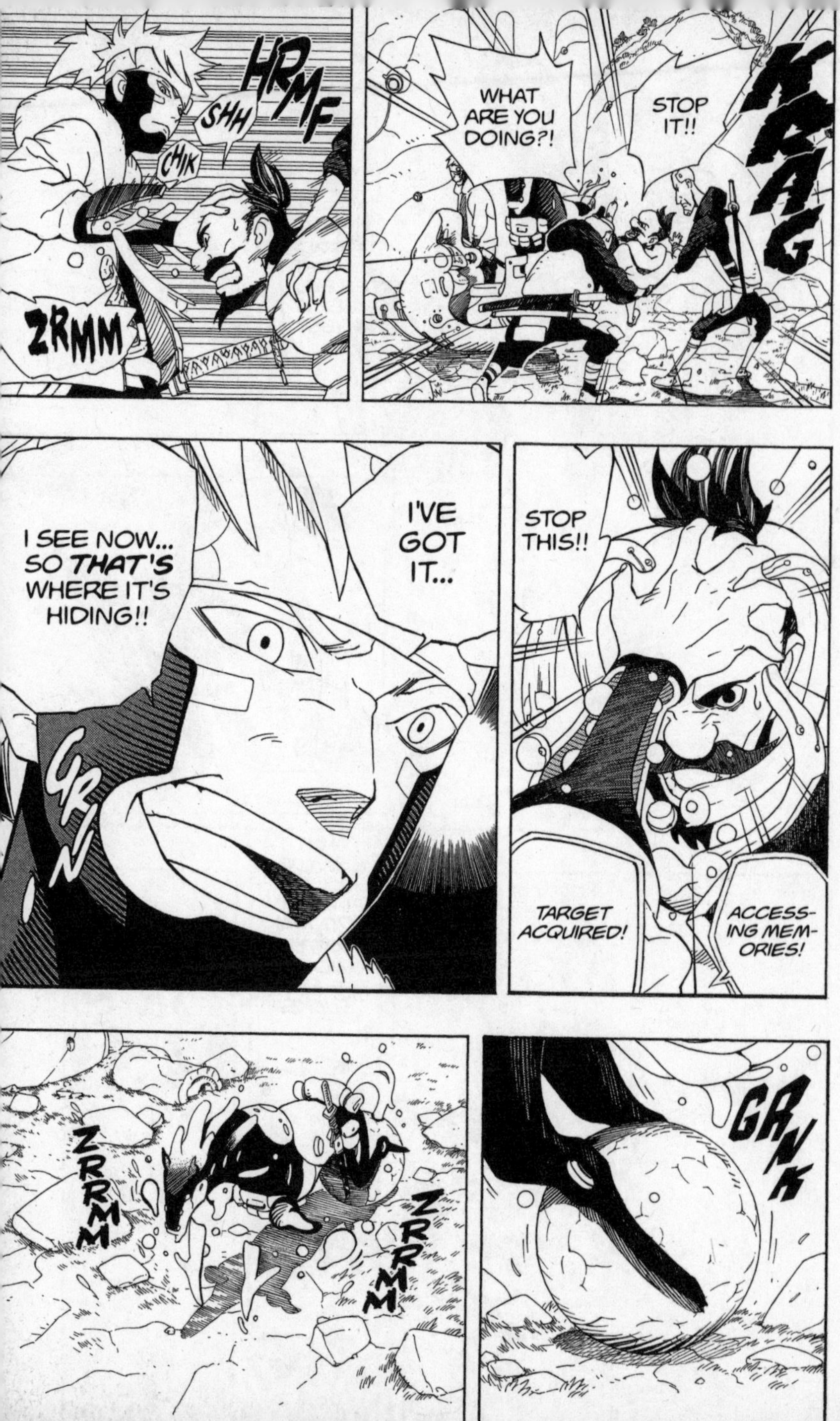
KRAG
STOP IT!!
WHAT ARE YOU DOING?!
HRMF
SHH
CHIK
ZRMM
STOP THIS!!
ACCESSING MEMORIES!
TARGET ACQUIRED!
I'VE GOT IT...
I SEE NOW... SO *THAT'S* WHERE IT'S HIDING!!
GRIN
GRNK
ZRRMM
ZRRMM

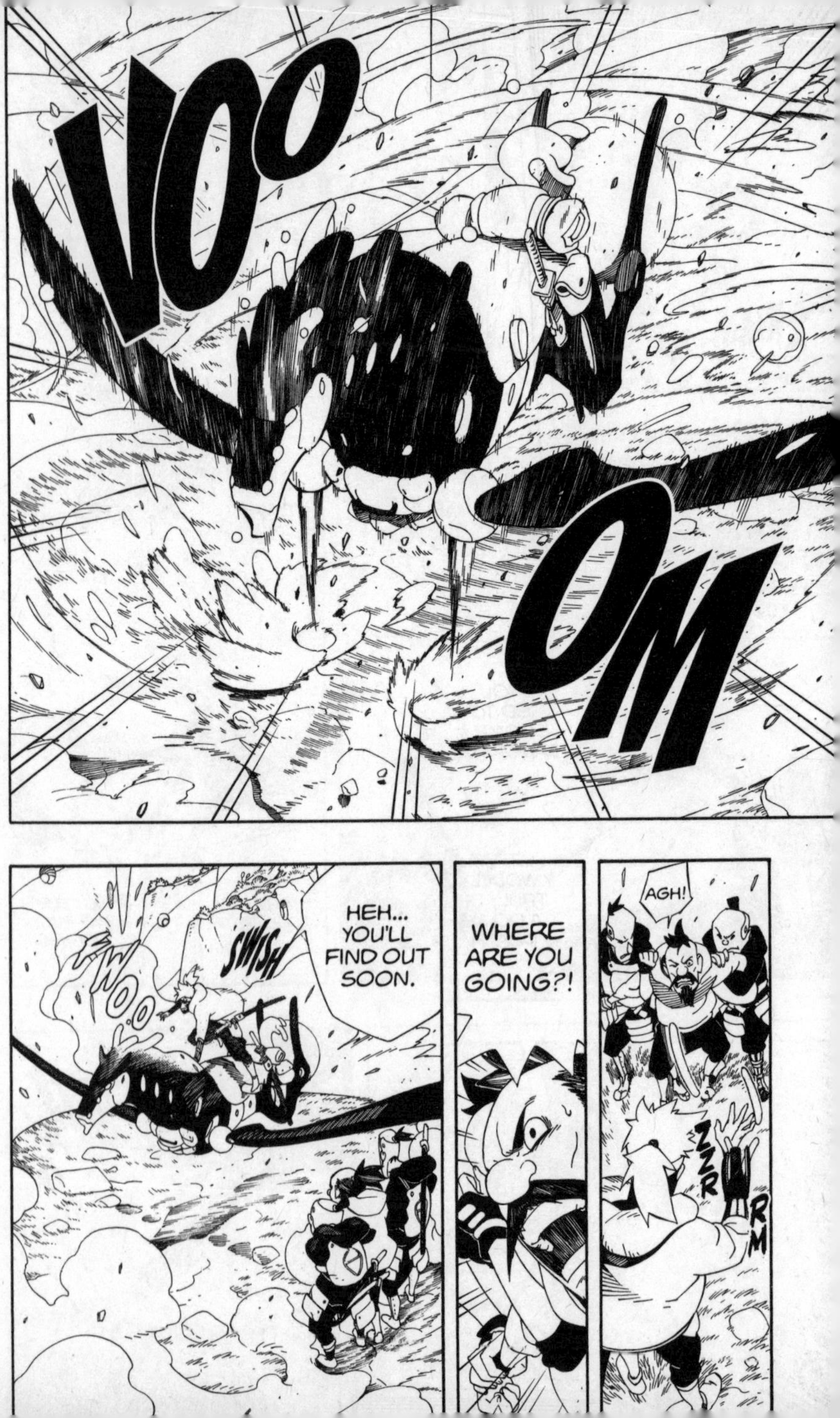
VOO
OM
AGH!
ZZR
RM
WHERE ARE YOU GOING?!
HEH... YOU'LL FIND OUT SOON.
SWISH
VWOO

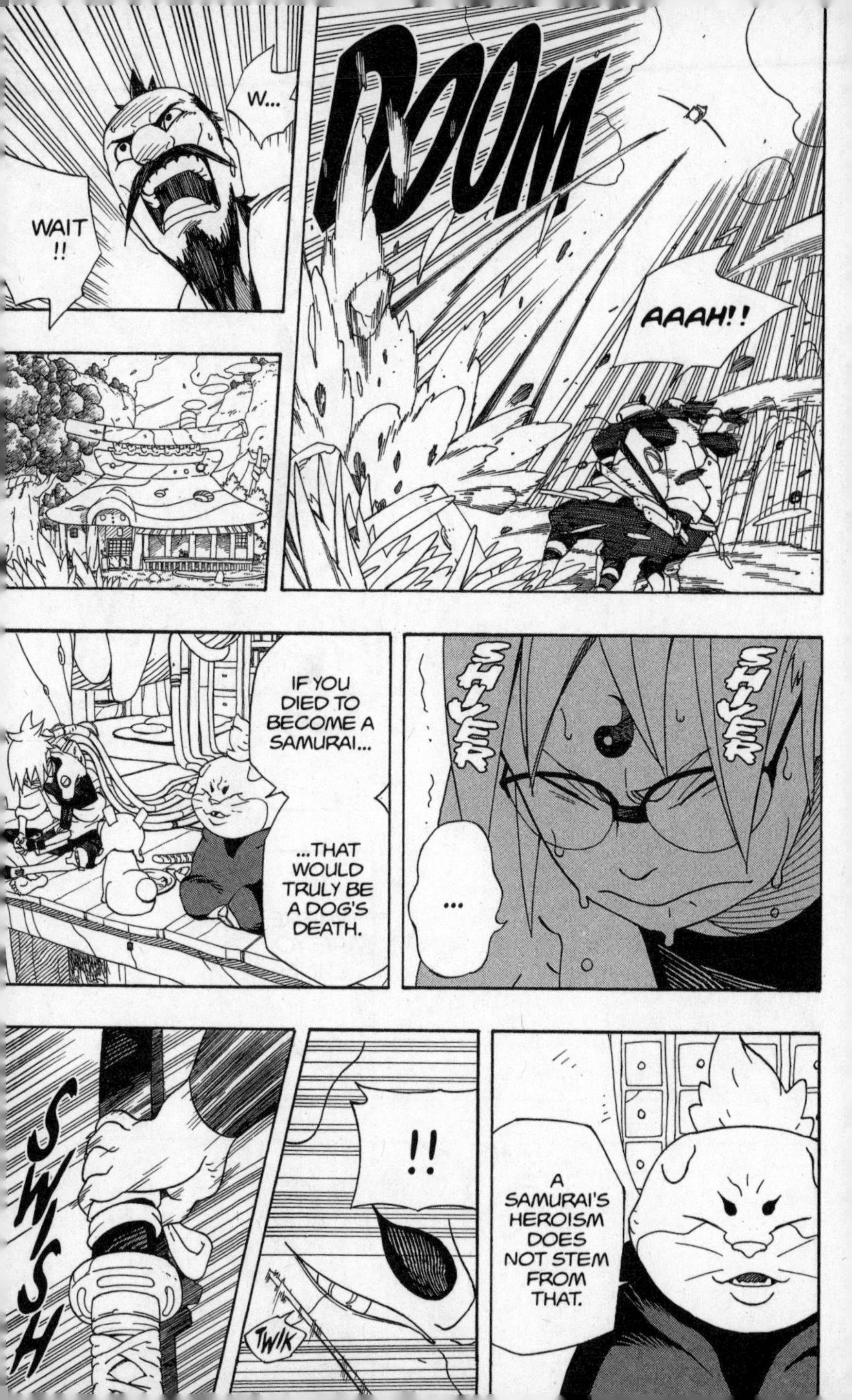
DOOM
AAAH!!
W...
WAIT !!
SHIVER
SHIVER
...
IF YOU DIED TO BECOME A SAMURAI...
...THAT WOULD TRULY BE A DOG'S DEATH.
A SAMURAI'S HEROISM DOES NOT STEM FROM THAT.
!!
TWIK
SWISH

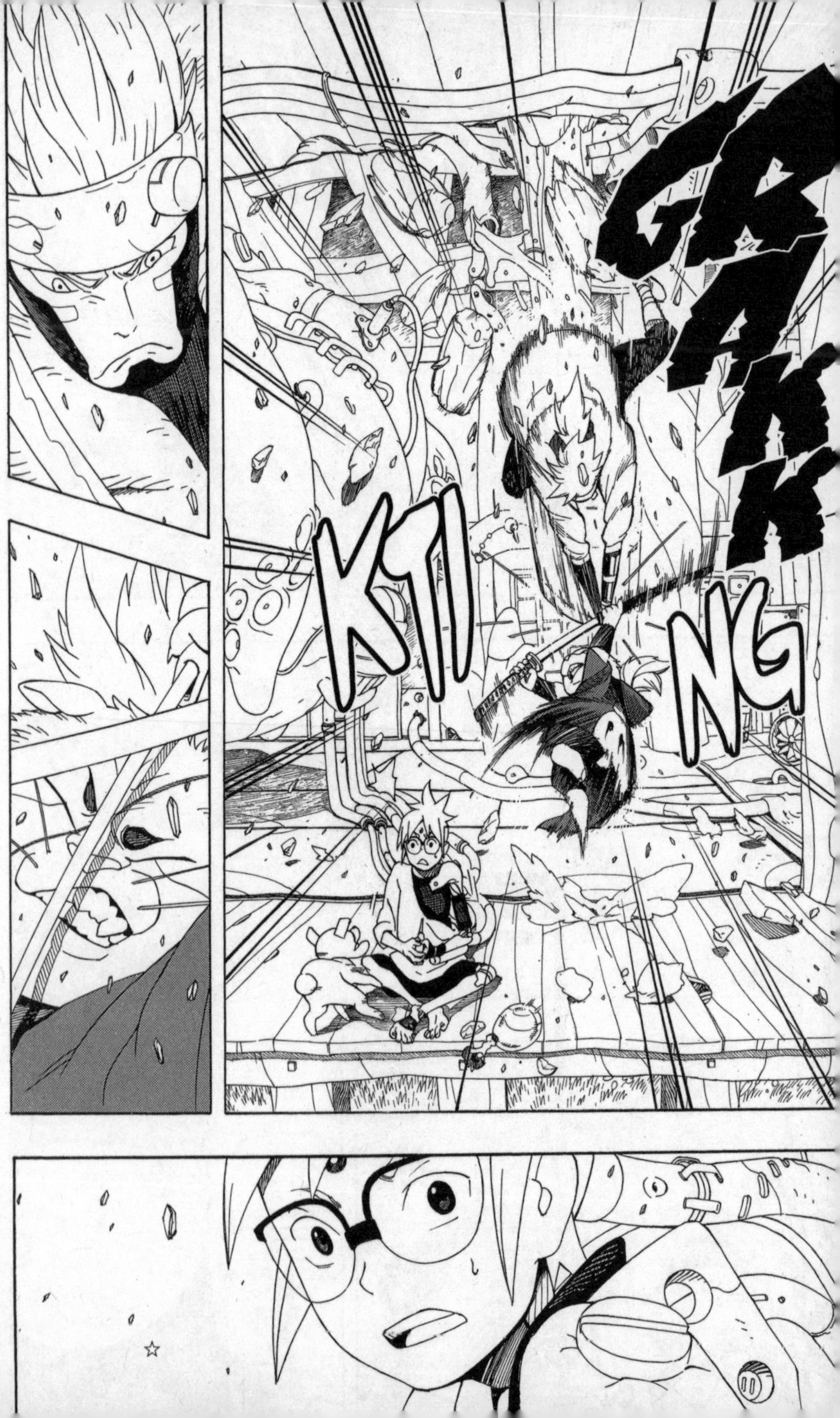
GRAKK
KTING

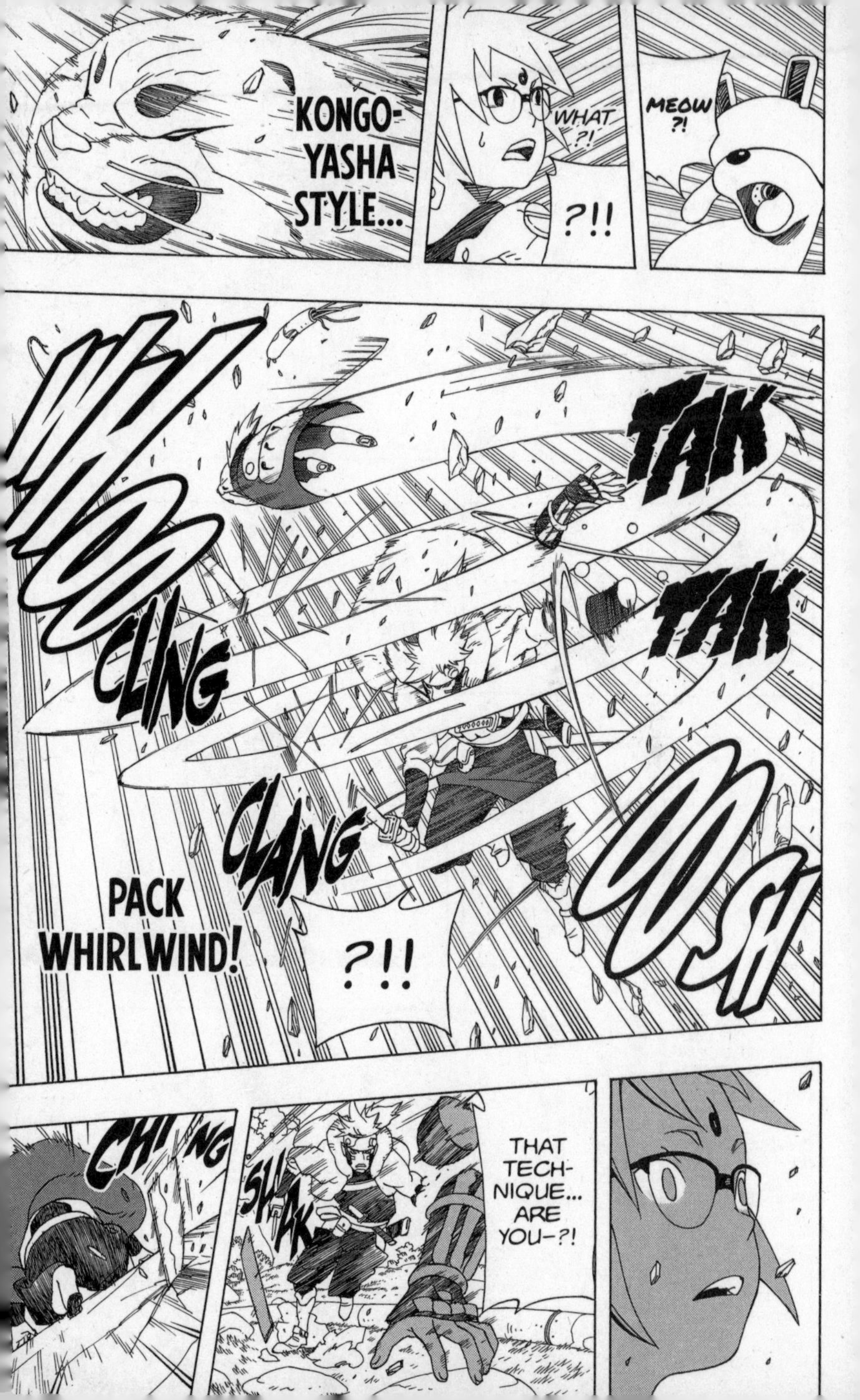
MEOW ?!
WHAT ?!
?!!
KONGO-YASHA STYLE...
TAK
TAK
WHOOO
CLING
WOOSH
CLANG
?!!
PACK WHIRLWIND!
THAT TECH-NIQUE... ARE YOU-?!
SHAK
CHING

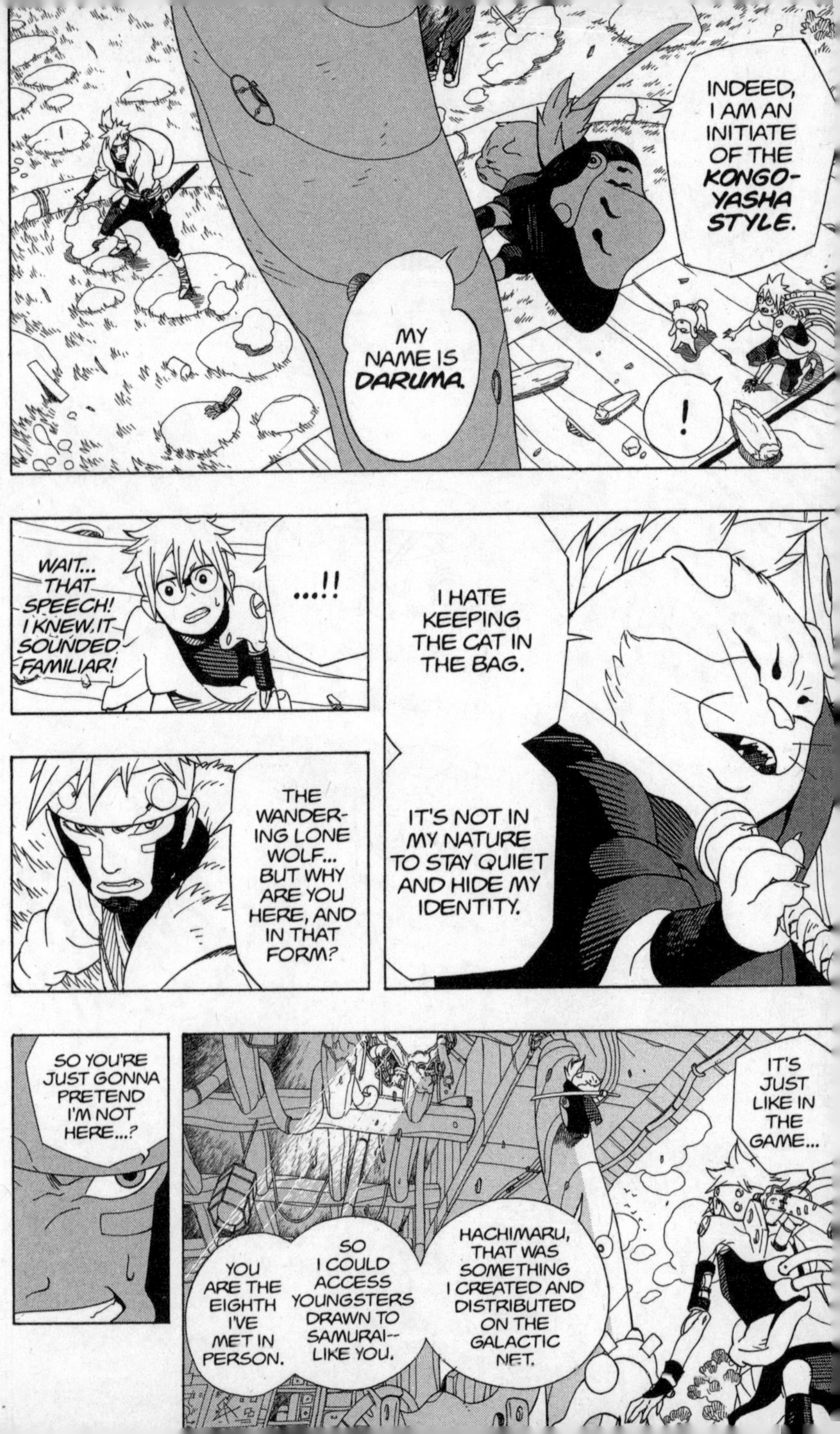
INDEED, I AM AN INITIATE OF THE KONGO-YASHA STYLE.
MY NAME IS DARUMA.
!
I HATE KEEPING THE CAT IN THE BAG.
IT'S NOT IN MY NATURE TO STAY QUIET AND HIDE MY IDENTITY.
...!!
WAIT... THAT SPEECH! I KNEW IT SOUNDED FAMILIAR!
THE WANDERING LONE WOLF... BUT WHY ARE YOU HERE, AND IN THAT FORM?
IT'S JUST LIKE IN THE GAME...
HACHIMARU, THAT WAS SOMETHING I CREATED AND DISTRIBUTED ON THE GALACTIC NET.
SO I COULD ACCESS YOUNGSTERS DRAWN TO SAMURAI--LIKE YOU.
YOU ARE THE EIGHTH I'VE MET IN PERSON.
SO YOU'RE JUST GONNA PRETEND I'M NOT HERE...?

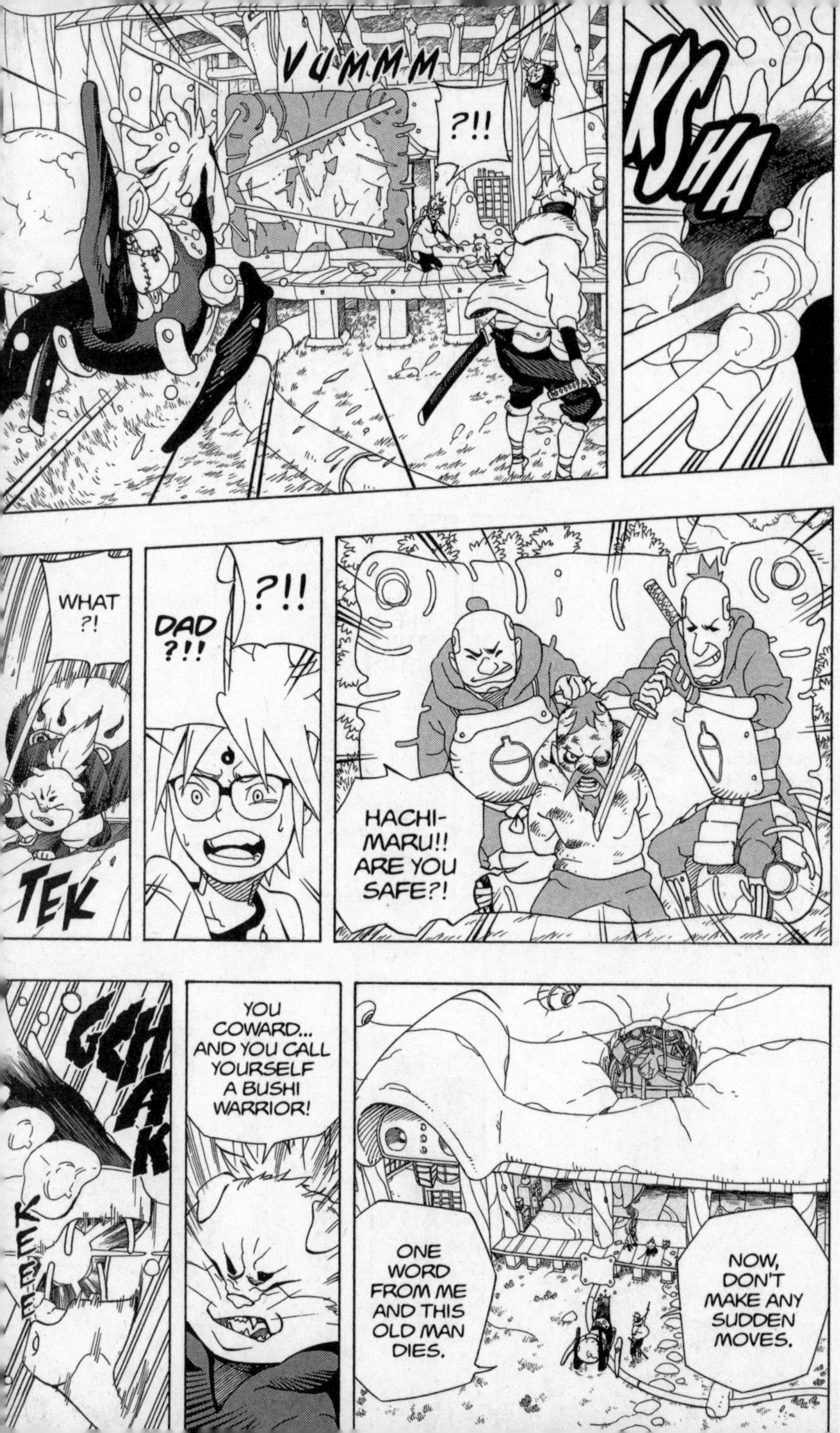
KSHA
VUMMM
?!!
HACHI-MARU!! ARE YOU SAFE?!
?!!
DAD?!!
WHAT?!
TEK
NOW, DON'T MAKE ANY SUDDEN MOVES.
ONE WORD FROM ME AND THIS OLD MAN DIES.
YOU COWARD... AND YOU CALL YOURSELF A BUSHI WARRIOR!
GCHAK

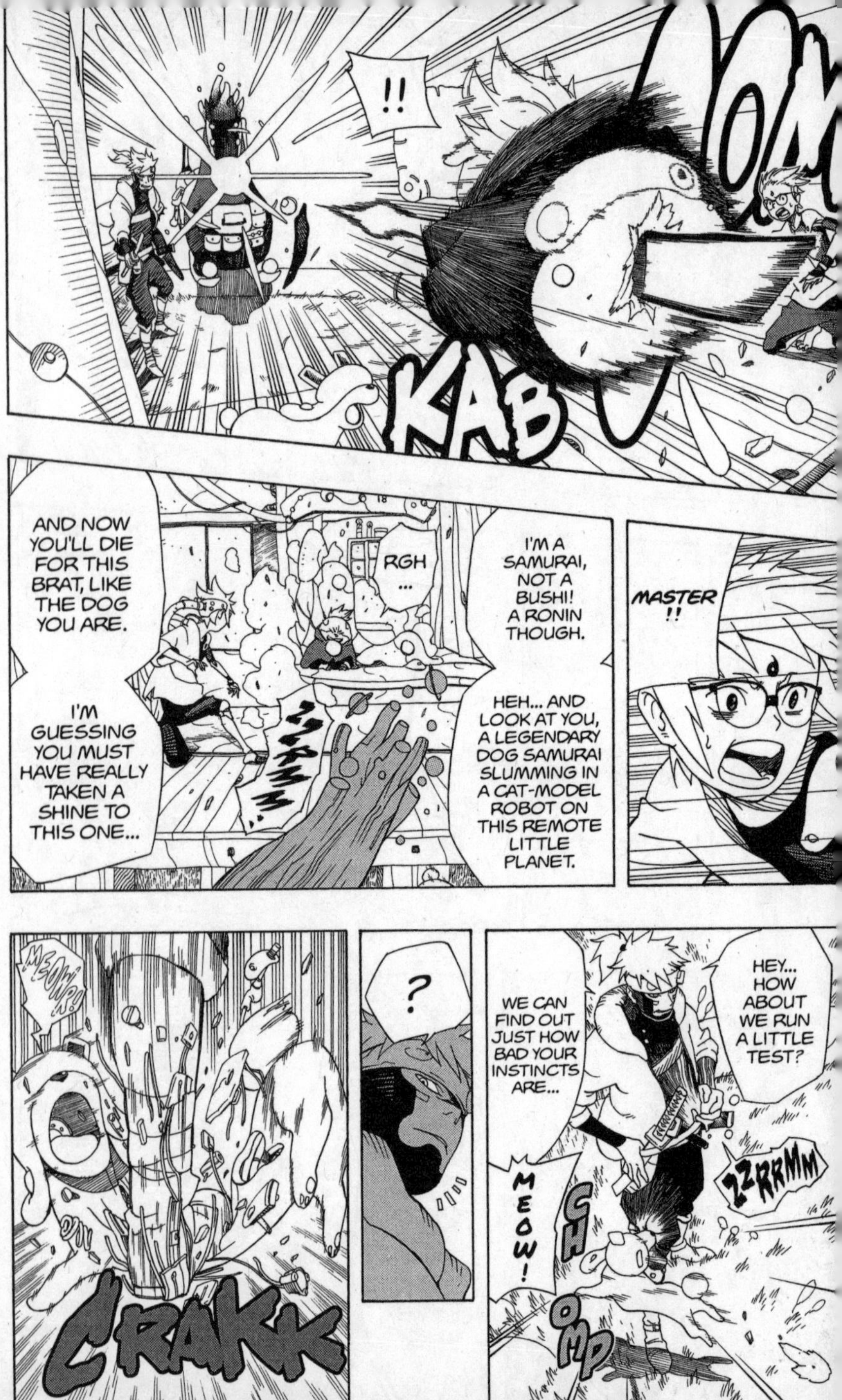

!!
KAB
MASTER !!
I'M A SAMURAI, NOT A BUSHI! A RONIN THOUGH.
RGH ...
HEH... AND LOOK AT YOU, A LEGENDARY DOG SAMURAI SLUMMING IN A CAT-MODEL ROBOT ON THIS REMOTE LITTLE PLANET.
ZZRRMM
AND NOW YOU'LL DIE FOR THIS BRAT, LIKE THE DOG YOU ARE.
I'M GUESSING YOU MUST HAVE REALLY TAKEN A SHINE TO THIS ONE...
HEY... HOW ABOUT WE RUN A LITTLE TEST?
WE CAN FIND OUT JUST HOW BAD YOUR INSTINCTS ARE...
ZZRRMM
MEOW!
CHOMP
?
MEOW!?
CRAKK

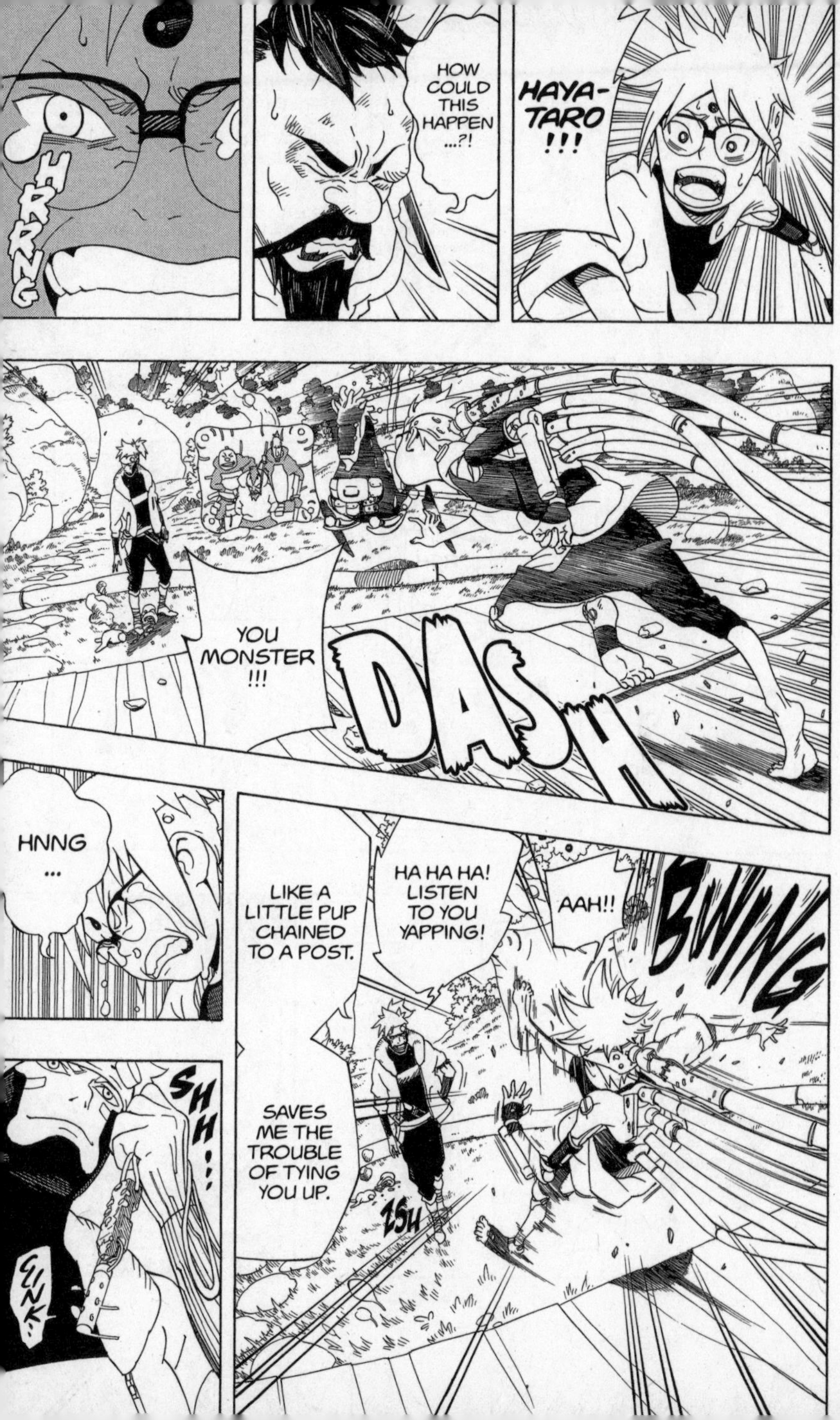
HAYA-TARO!!!
HOW COULD THIS HAPPEN...?!
HRRNG
YOU MONSTER!!!
DASH
AAH!!
BWING
HA HA HA! LISTEN TO YOU YAPPING!
LIKE A LITTLE PUP CHAINED TO A POST.
SAVES ME THE TROUBLE OF TYING YOU UP.
ZSH
HNNG...
SHH!!
CLINK

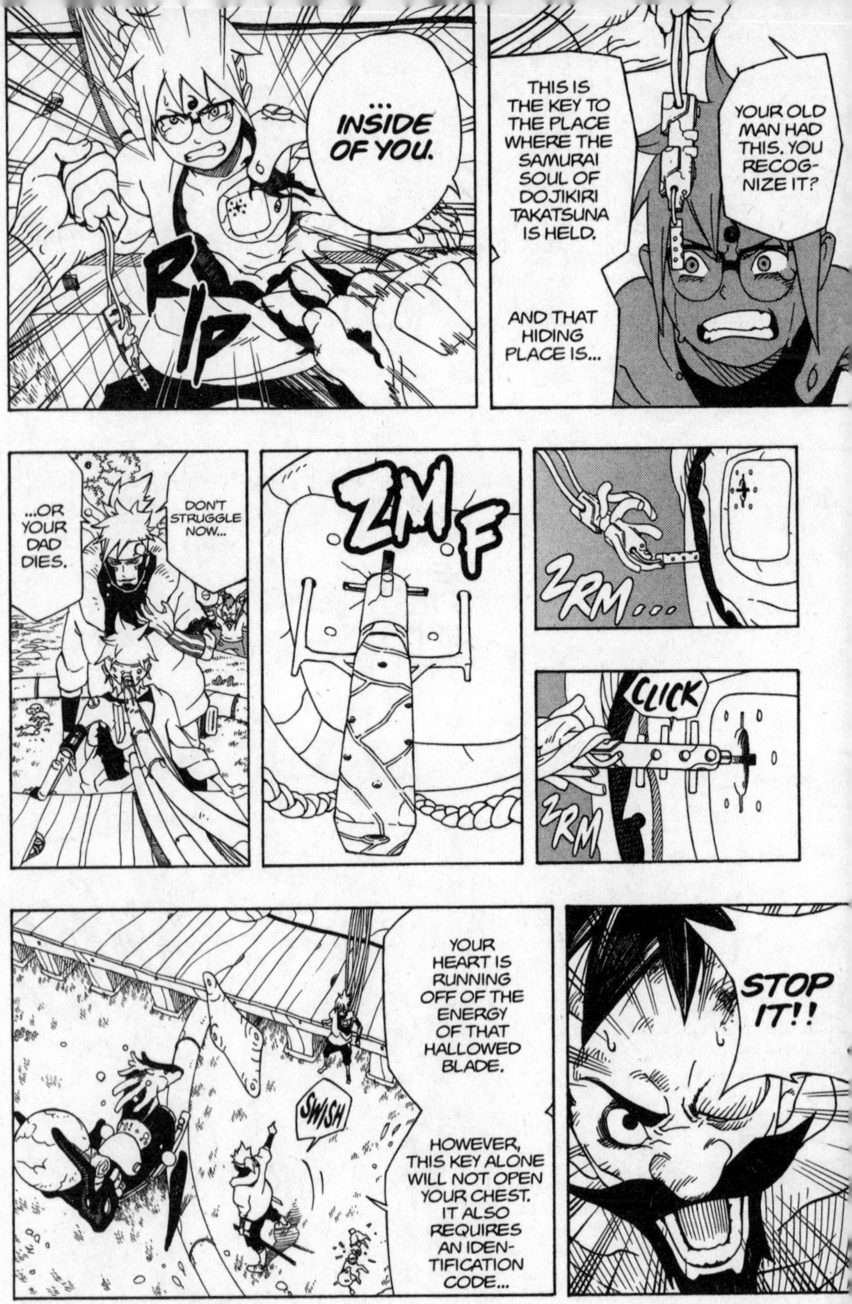

YOUR OLD MAN HAD THIS. YOU RECOGNIZE IT?
THIS IS THE KEY TO THE PLACE WHERE THE SAMURAI SOUL OF DOJIKIRI TAKATSUNA IS HELD.
AND THAT HIDING PLACE IS...
...INSIDE OF YOU.
RIP
ZRM...
CLICK
ZRM
ZMF
DON'T STRUGGLE NOW...
...OR YOUR DAD DIES.
STOP IT!!
YOUR HEART IS RUNNING OFF OF THE ENERGY OF THAT HALLOWED BLADE.
HOWEVER, THIS KEY ALONE WILL NOT OPEN YOUR CHEST. IT ALSO REQUIRES AN IDENTIFICATION CODE...
SWISH

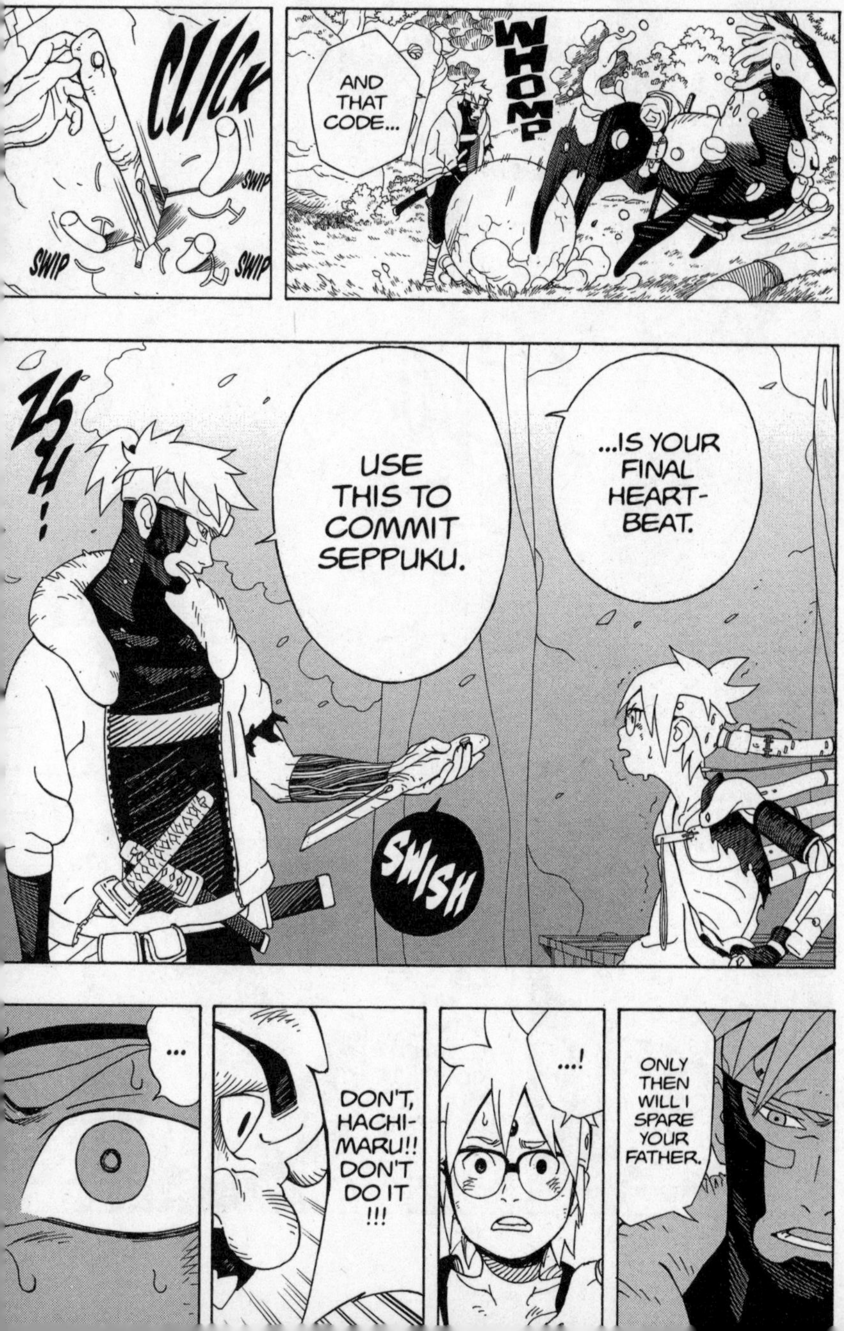
WHOMP
AND THAT CODE...
CLICK
SWIP
SWIP
SWIP
...IS YOUR FINAL HEART-BEAT.
USE THIS TO COMMIT SEPPUKU.
SWISH
ZSH!!
ONLY THEN WILL I SPARE YOUR FATHER.
...!
DON'T, HACHIMARU!!! DON'T DO IT!!!
...

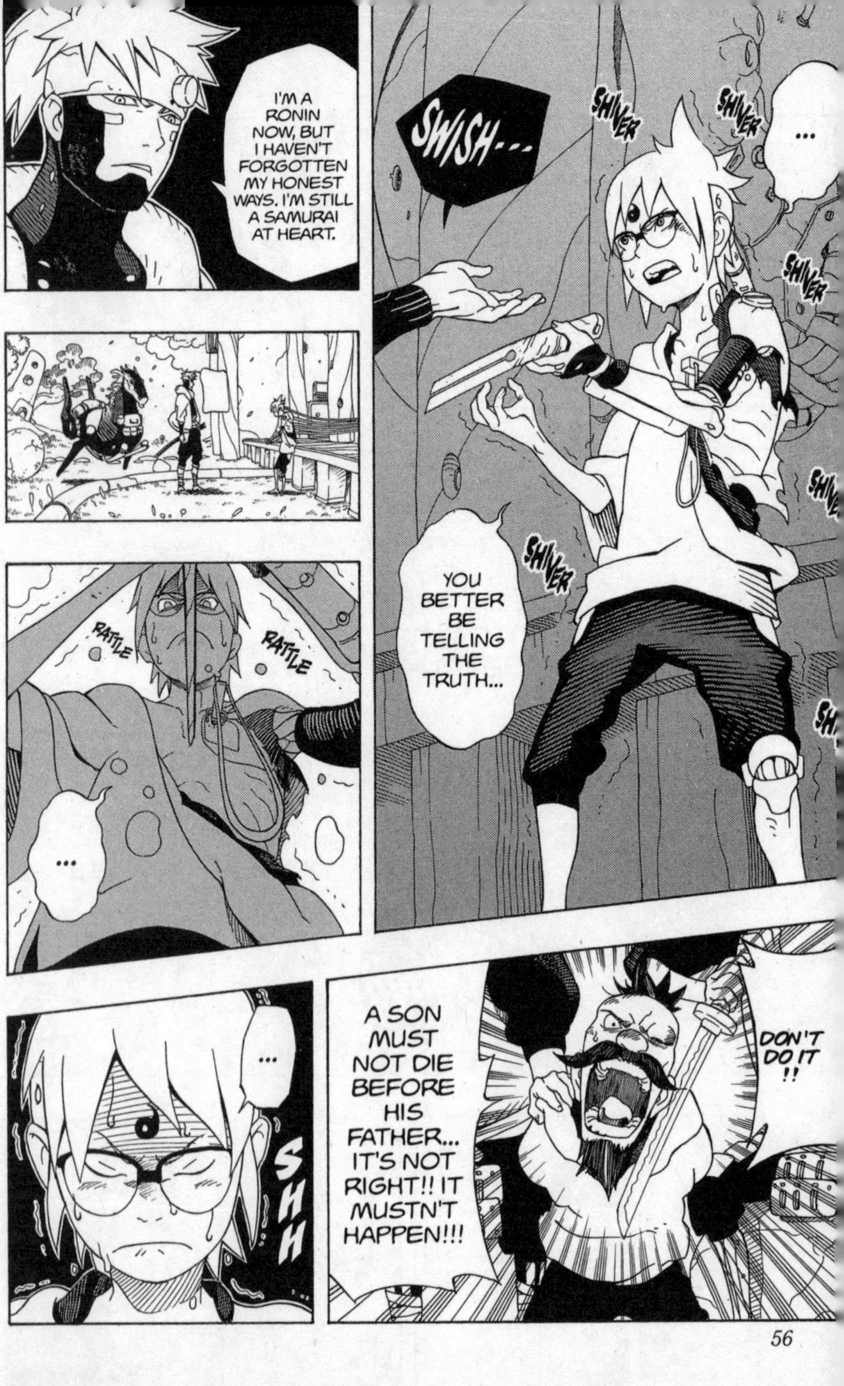
...
SHIVER
SHIVER
SHIVER
SWISH...
SHIVER
SHIVER
YOU BETTER BE TELLING THE TRUTH...
I'M A RONIN NOW, BUT I HAVEN'T FORGOTTEN MY HONEST WAYS. I'M STILL A SAMURAI AT HEART.
RATTLE
RATTLE
...
DON'T DO IT!!
A SON MUST NOT DIE BEFORE HIS FATHER... IT'S NOT RIGHT!! IT MUSTN'T HAPPEN!!!
...
SHH

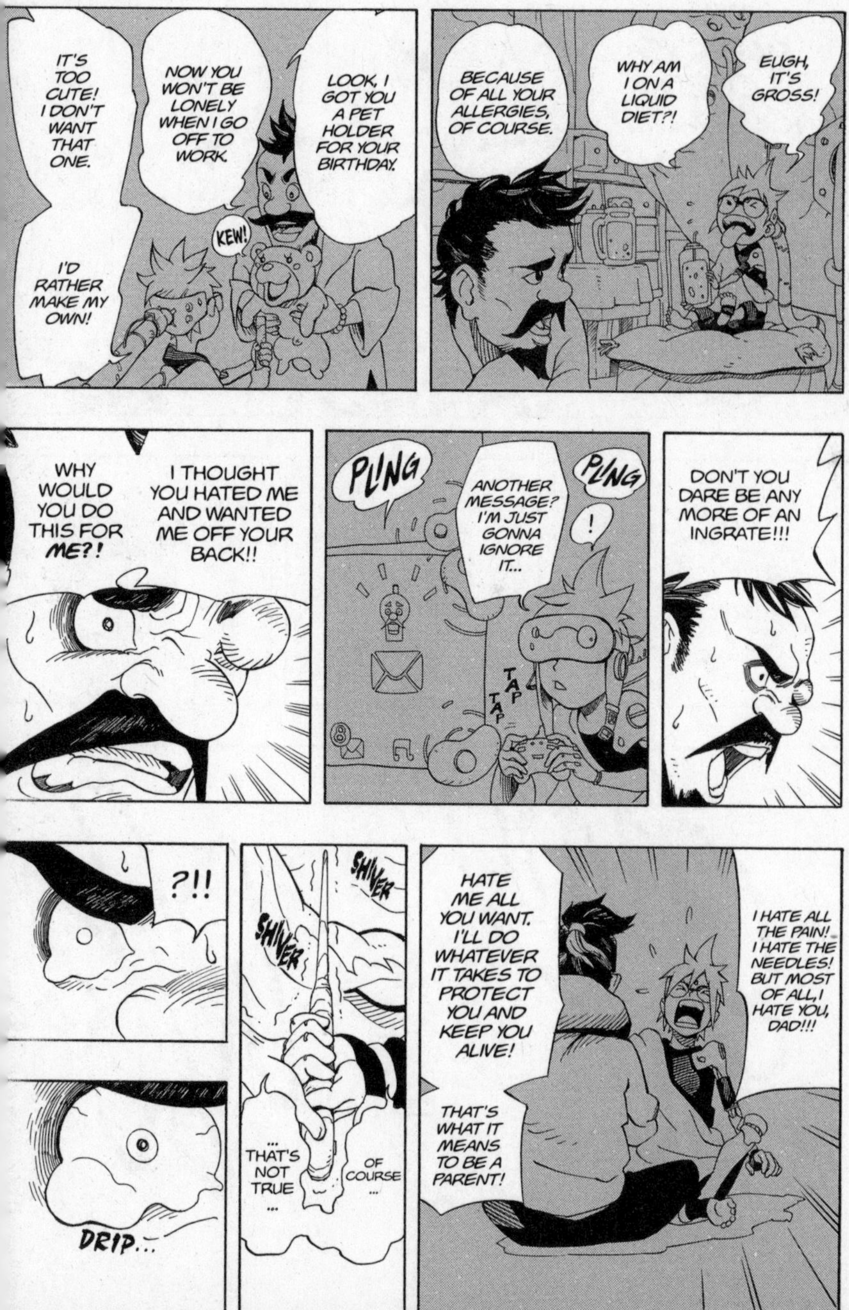
EUGH, IT'S GROSS!
WHY AM I ON A LIQUID DIET?!
BECAUSE OF ALL YOUR ALLERGIES, OF COURSE.
LOOK, I GOT YOU A PET HOLDER FOR YOUR BIRTHDAY.
NOW YOU WON'T BE LONELY WHEN I GO OFF TO WORK.
KEW!
IT'S TOO CUTE! I DON'T WANT THAT ONE.
I'D RATHER MAKE MY OWN!
DON'T YOU DARE BE ANY MORE OF AN INGRATE!!!
PLING
PLING
!
ANOTHER MESSAGE? I'M JUST GONNA IGNORE IT...
TAP TAP
I THOUGHT YOU HATED ME AND WANTED ME OFF YOUR BACK!!
WHY WOULD YOU DO THIS FOR ME?!
I HATE ALL THE PAIN! I HATE THE NEEDLES! BUT MOST OF ALL, I HATE YOU, DAD!!!
HATE ME ALL YOU WANT. I'LL DO WHATEVER IT TAKES TO PROTECT YOU AND KEEP YOU ALIVE!
THAT'S WHAT IT MEANS TO BE A PARENT!
SHIVER
SHIVER
OF COURSE...
...THAT'S NOT TRUE...
?!!
DRIP...

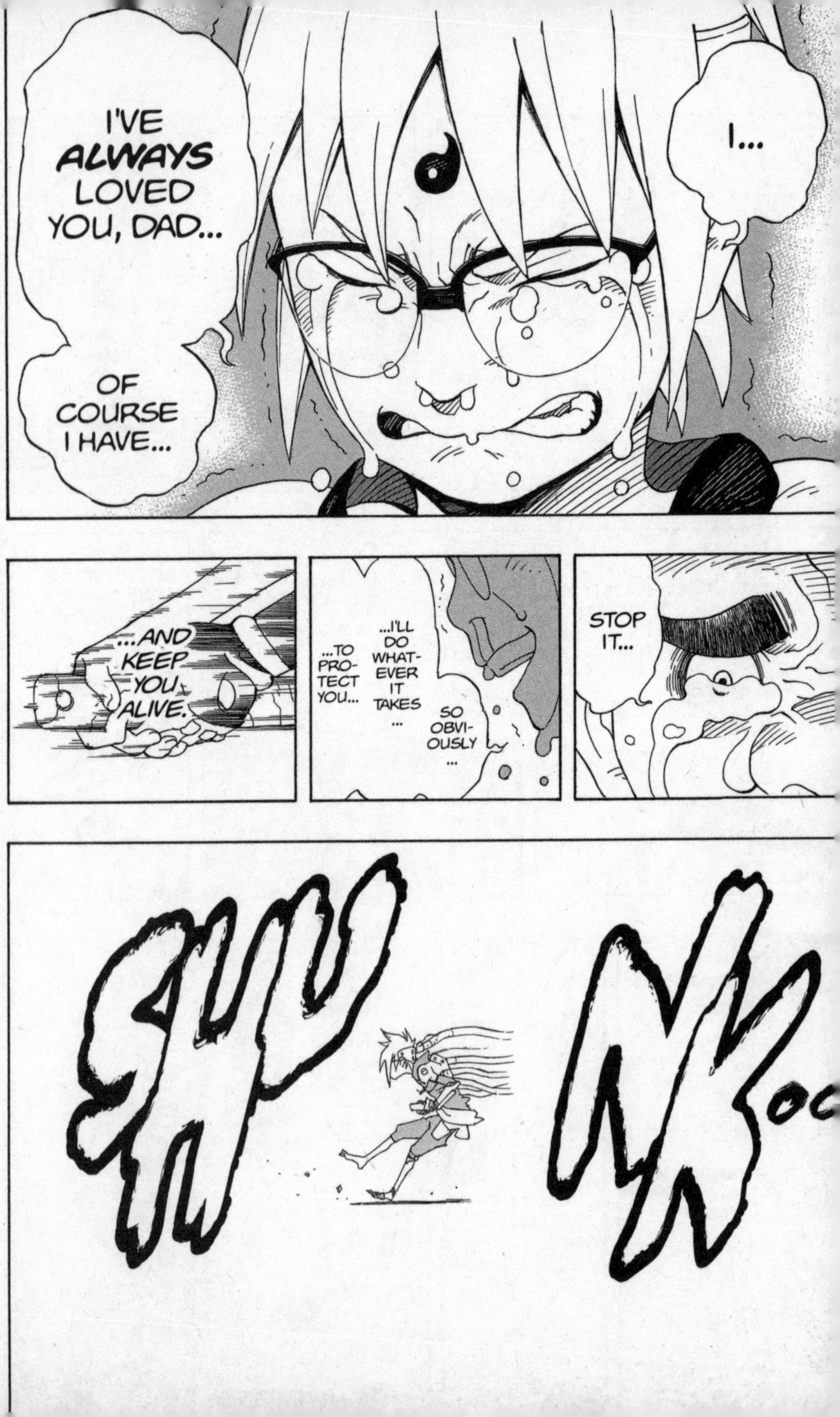
I...
I'VE ALWAYS LOVED YOU, DAD...
OF COURSE I HAVE...
STOP IT...
SO OBVIOUSLY...
...I'LL DO WHATEVER IT TAKES...
...TO PROTECT YOU...
...AND KEEP YOU ALIVE.

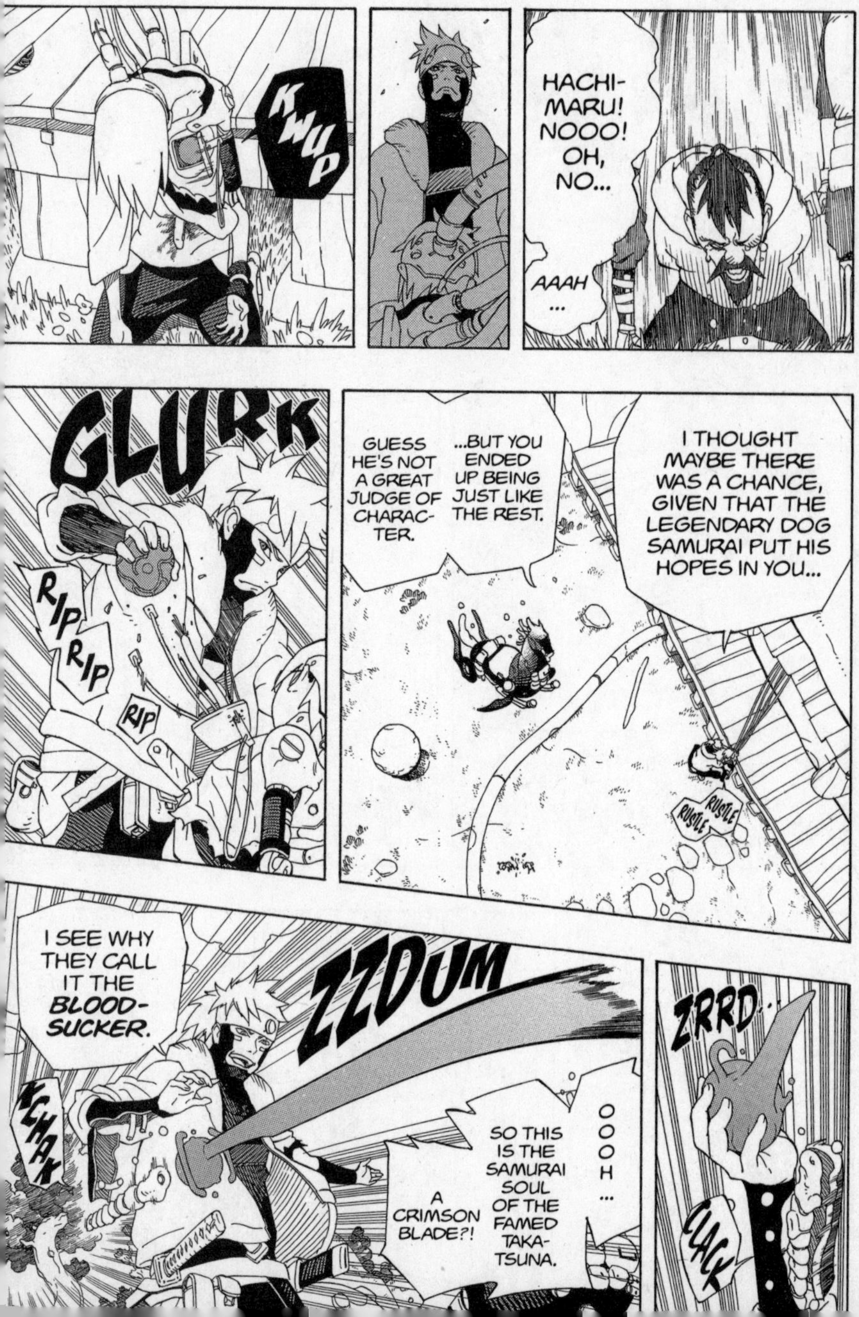
HACHI-MARU! NOOO! OH, NO...
AAAH ...
KWUP
I THOUGHT MAYBE THERE WAS A CHANCE, GIVEN THAT THE LEGENDARY DOG SAMURAI PUT HIS HOPES IN YOU...
...BUT YOU ENDED UP BEING JUST LIKE THE REST.
GUESS HE'S NOT A GREAT JUDGE OF CHARAC-TER.
RUSTLE
RUSTLE
GLURK
RIP
RIP
RIP
ZRRD...
CLACK
ZZDUM
I SEE WHY THEY CALL IT THE *BLOOD-SUCKER*.
OOOOH ...
SO THIS IS THE SAMURAI SOUL OF THE FAMED TAKA-TSUNA.
A CRIMSON BLADE?!
KCHAK

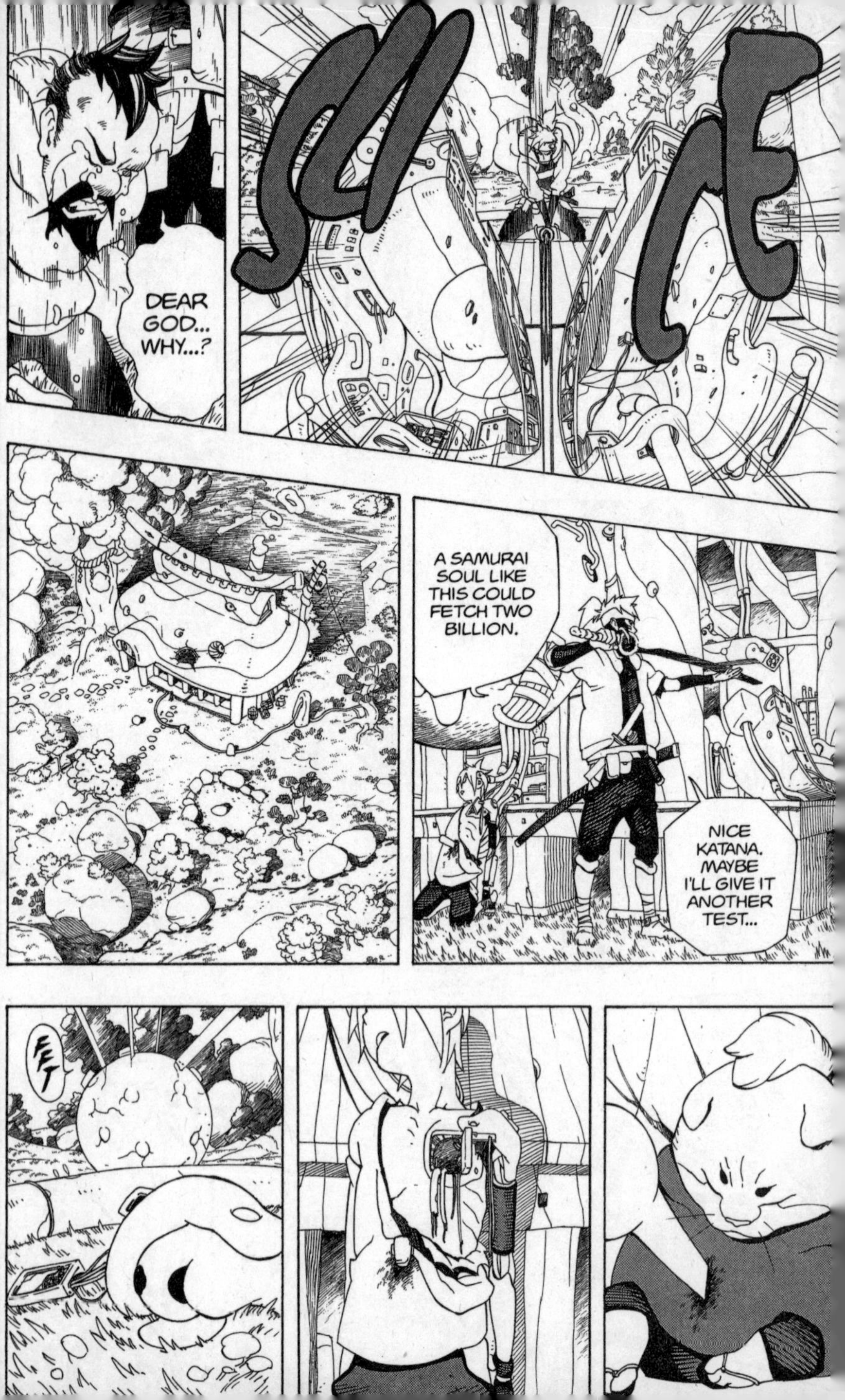
SLICE
DEAR GOD... WHY...?
A SAMURAI SOUL LIKE THIS COULD FETCH TWO BILLION.
NICE KATANA. MAYBE I'LL GIVE IT ANOTHER TEST...
FFT
...

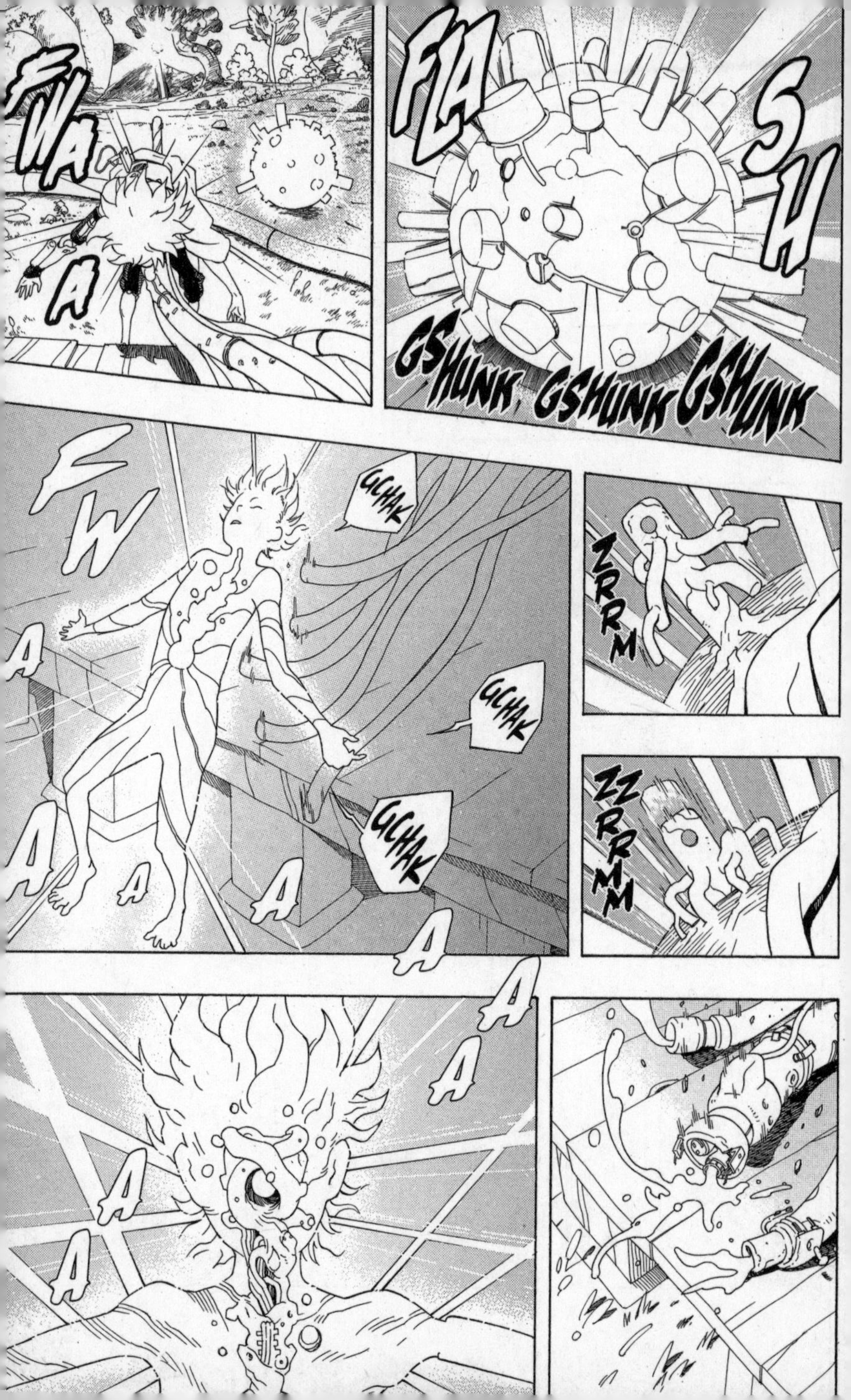
FLASH
GSHUNK GSHUNK GSHUNK
FWAA
ZRRRM
ZZRRRMM
FWAAAAAAA
GCHAK
GCHAK
GCHAK
AAAAAA

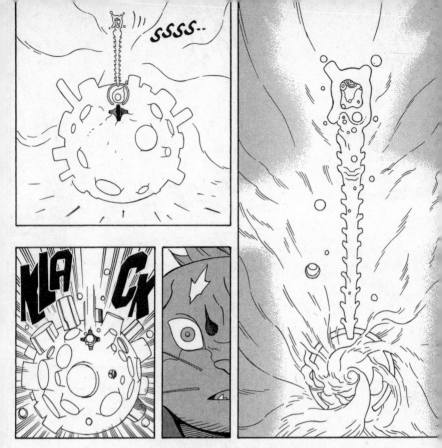

SSSS...

KLA CK

DID HE
JUST...?
...

!

ACK

ZZ
RR
MM

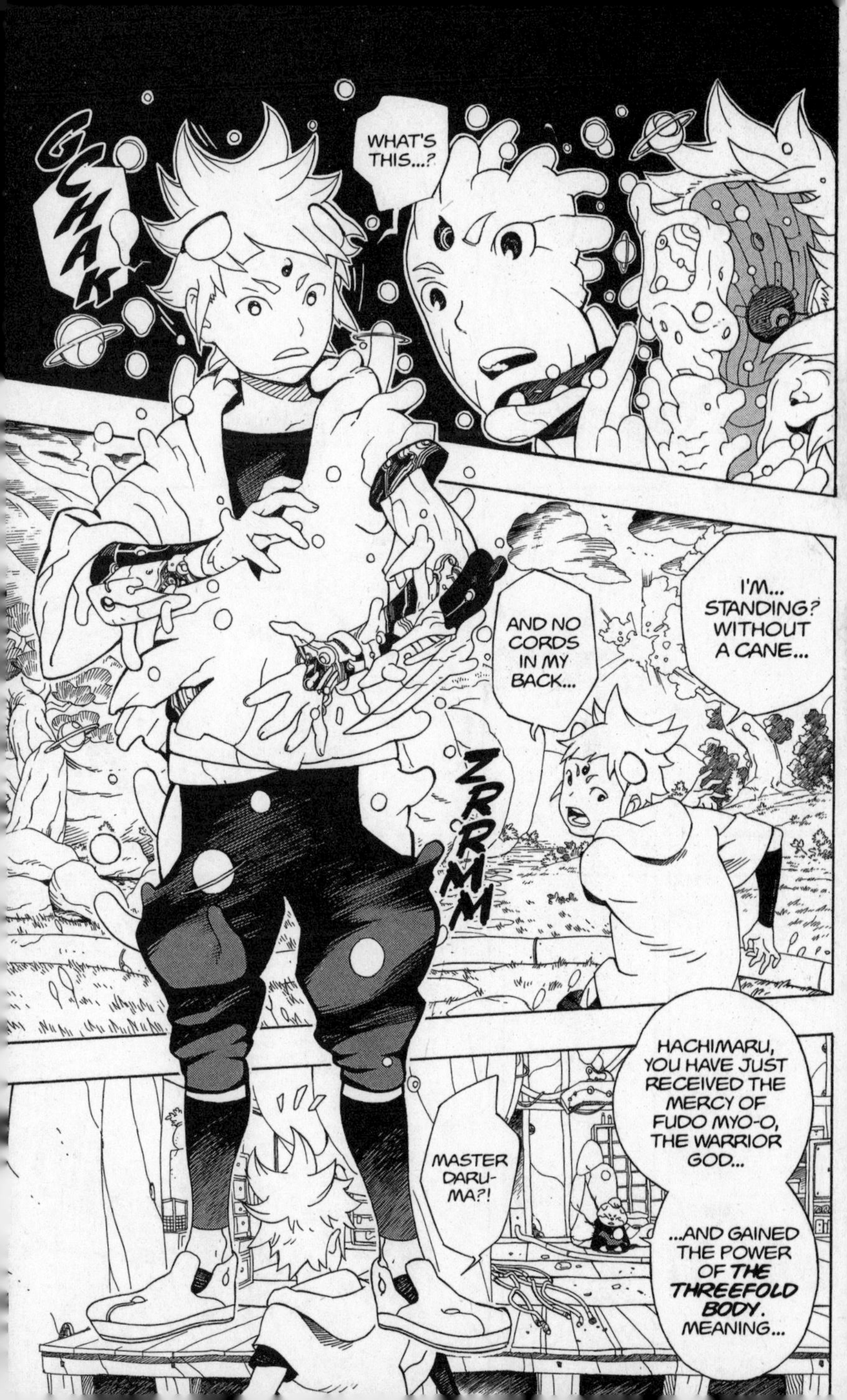
WHAT'S THIS...?
GCHAK
I'M... STANDING? WITHOUT A CANE...
AND NO CORDS IN MY BACK...
ZRRMM
HACHIMARU, YOU HAVE JUST RECEIVED THE MERCY OF FUDO MYO-O, THE WARRIOR GOD...
...AND GAINED THE POWER OF ***THE THREEFOLD BODY***. MEANING...
MASTER DARU-MA?!

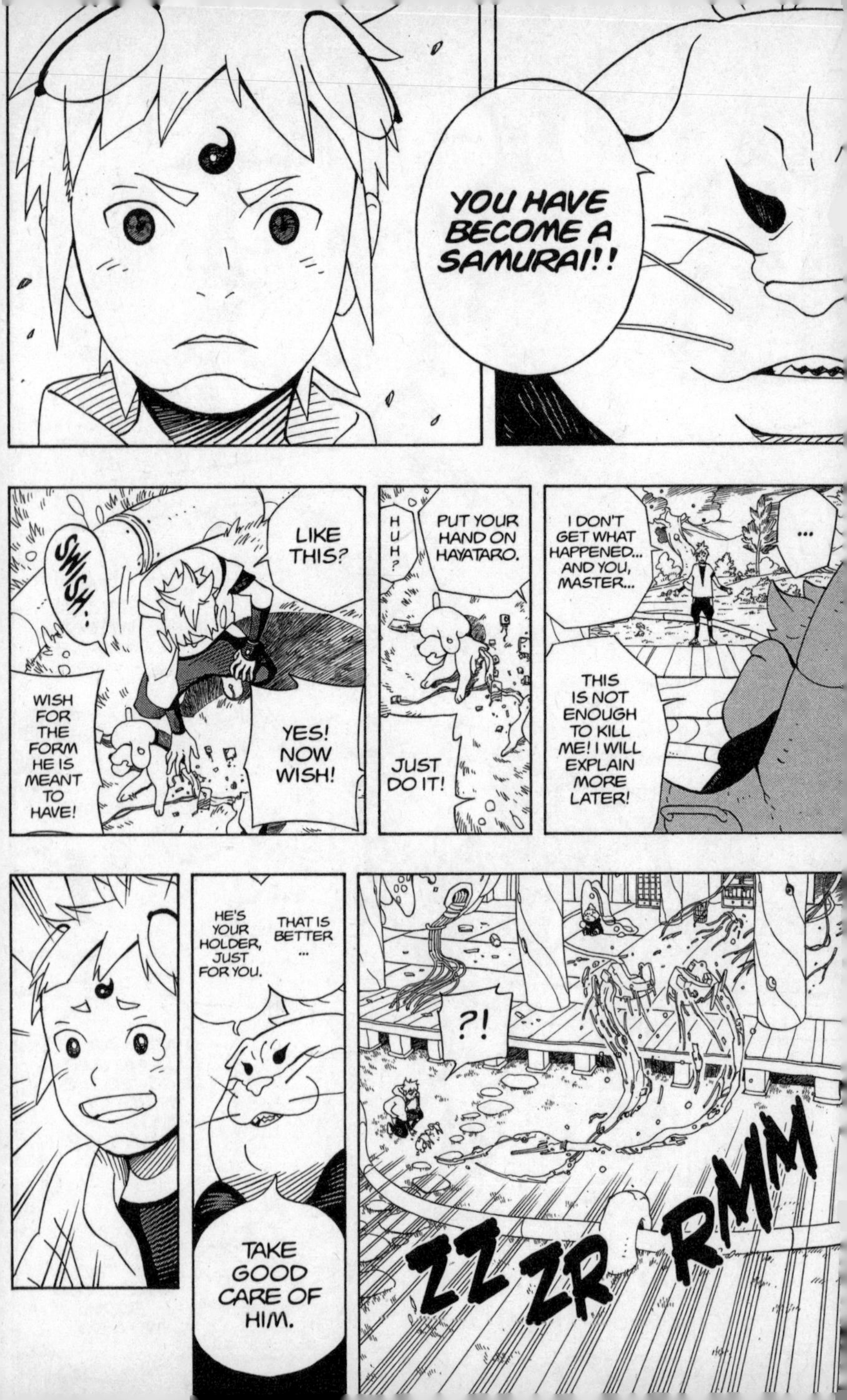
YOU HAVE BECOME A SAMURAI!!
...
I DON'T GET WHAT HAPPENED... AND YOU, MASTER...
THIS IS NOT ENOUGH TO KILL ME! I WILL EXPLAIN MORE LATER!
PUT YOUR HAND ON HAYATARO.
HUH?
JUST DO IT!
LIKE THIS?
YES! NOW WISH!
SWISH...
WISH FOR THE FORM HE IS MEANT TO HAVE!
?!
ZZZR RMM
THAT IS BETTER ...
HE'S YOUR HOLDER, JUST FOR YOU.
TAKE GOOD CARE OF HIM.

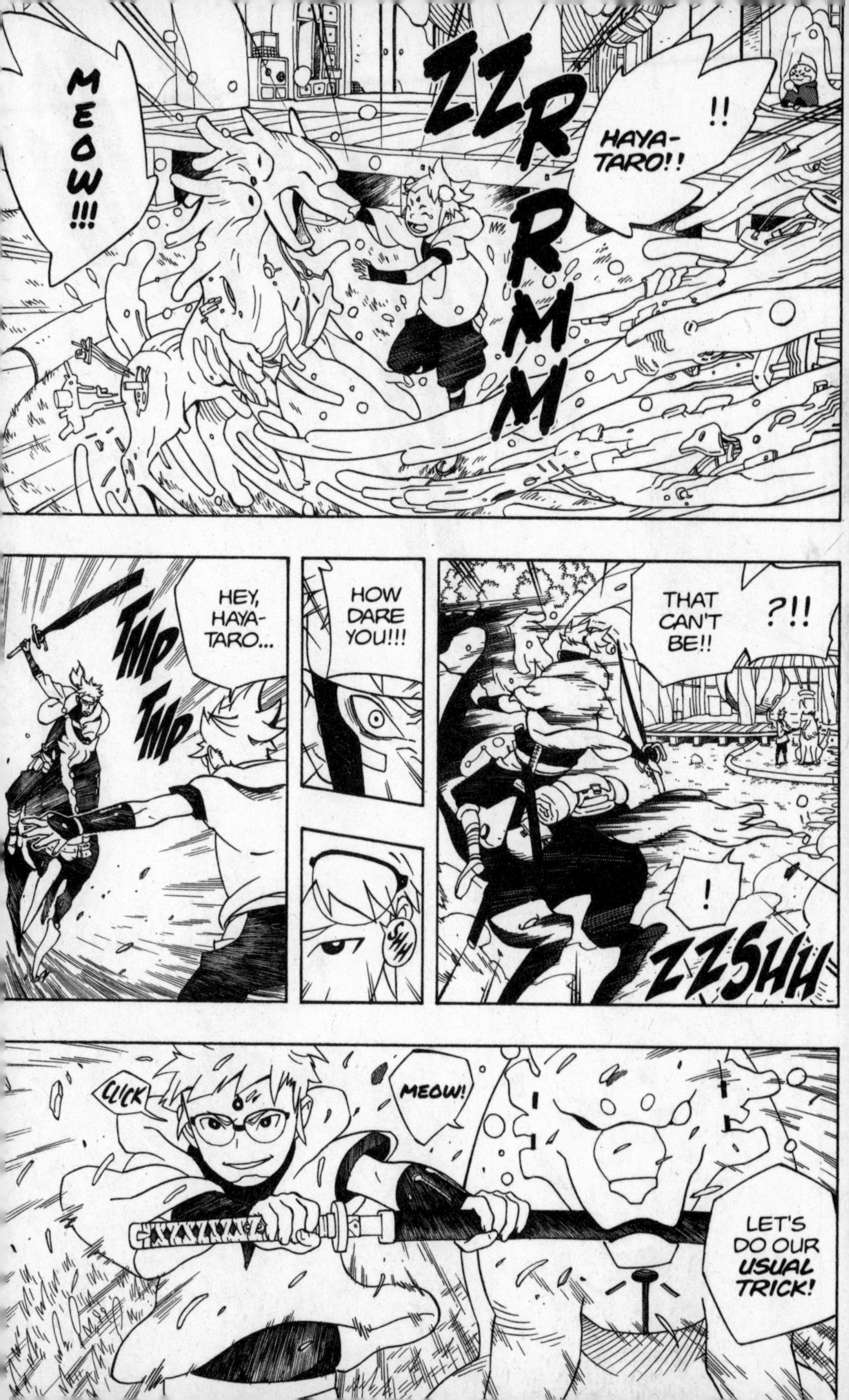
!!
HAYA-TARO!!
ZZRRMMM
MEOW!!!
?!!
THAT CAN'T BE!!
!
ZZSHU
HOW DARE YOU!!!
SHH
HEY, HAYA-TARO...
TMP TMP
LET'S DO OUR USUAL TRICK!
MEOW!
CLICK

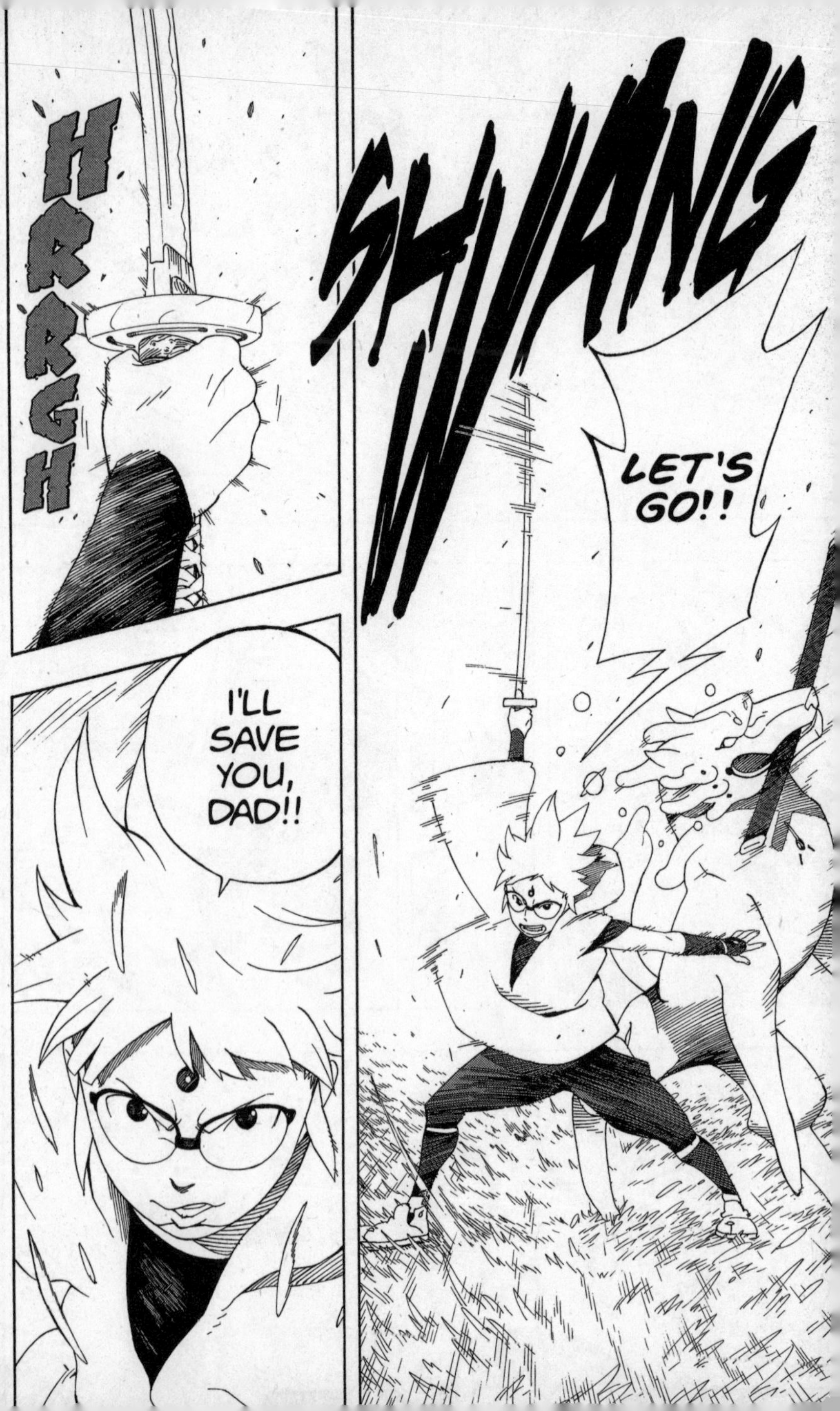
SHWANG
LET'S GO!!
HRRGH
I'LL SAVE YOU, DAD!!

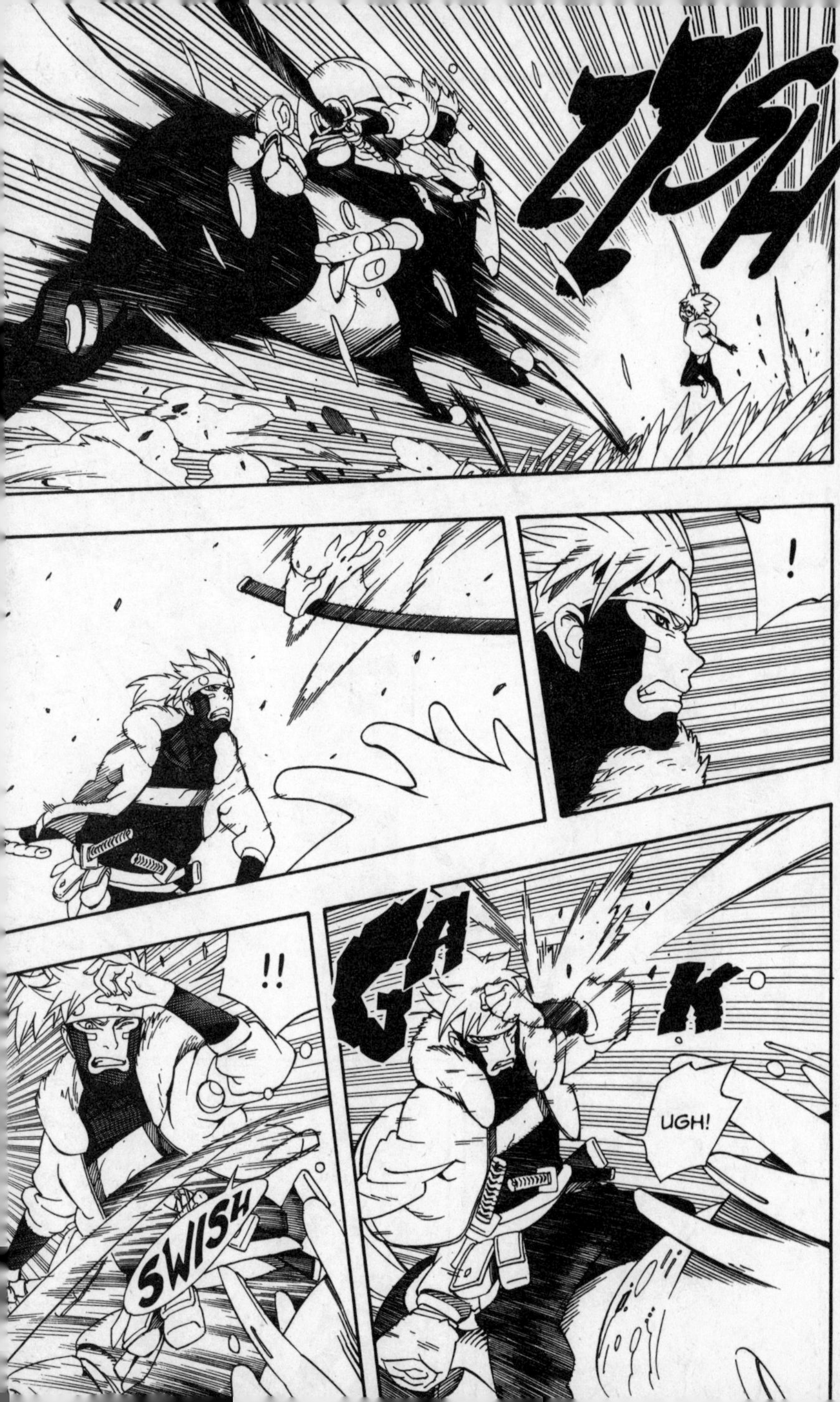
ZZSH
!
GA
K
UGH!
!!
SWISH

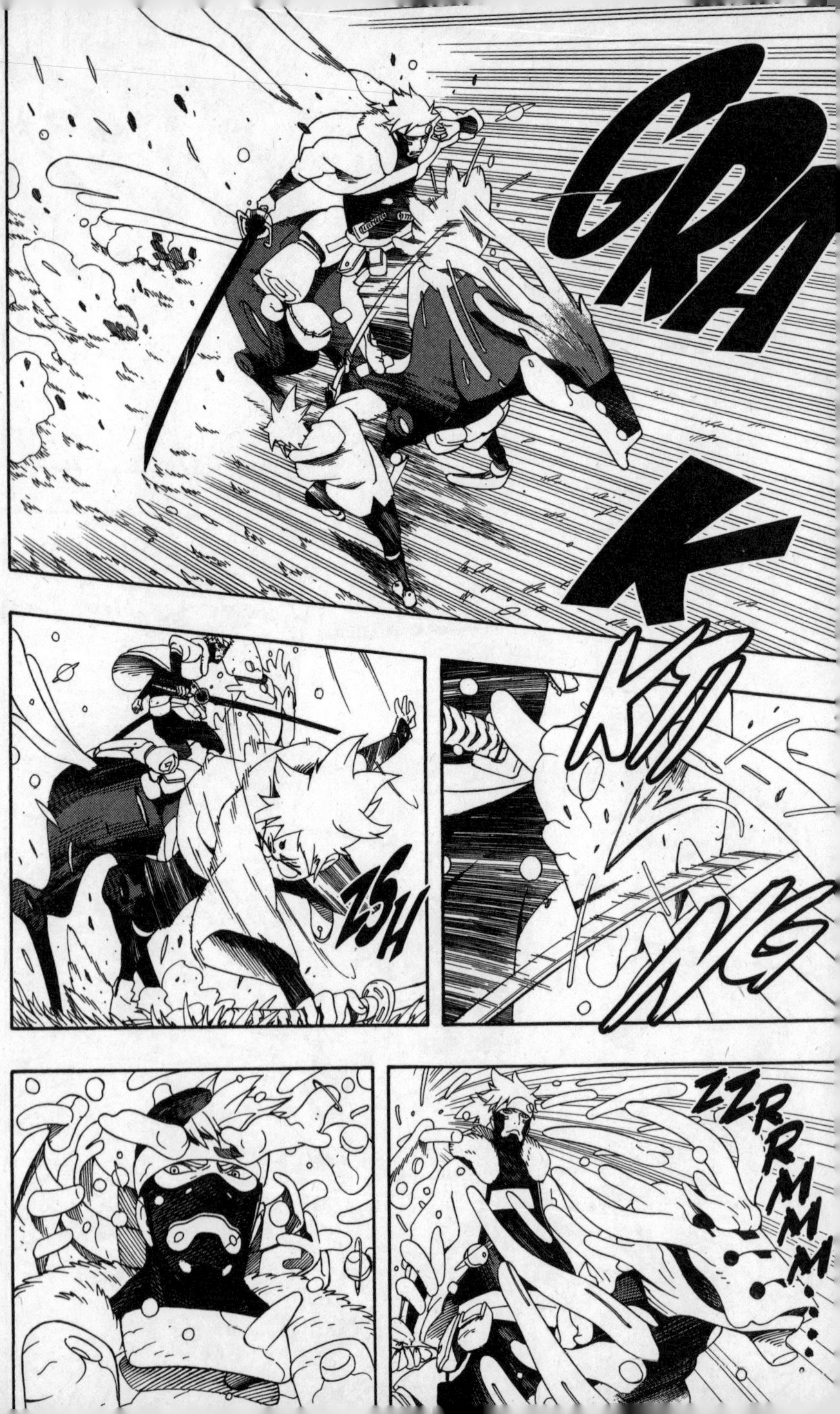
GRAKK
KTINNG
ZSH
ZZRRMMM

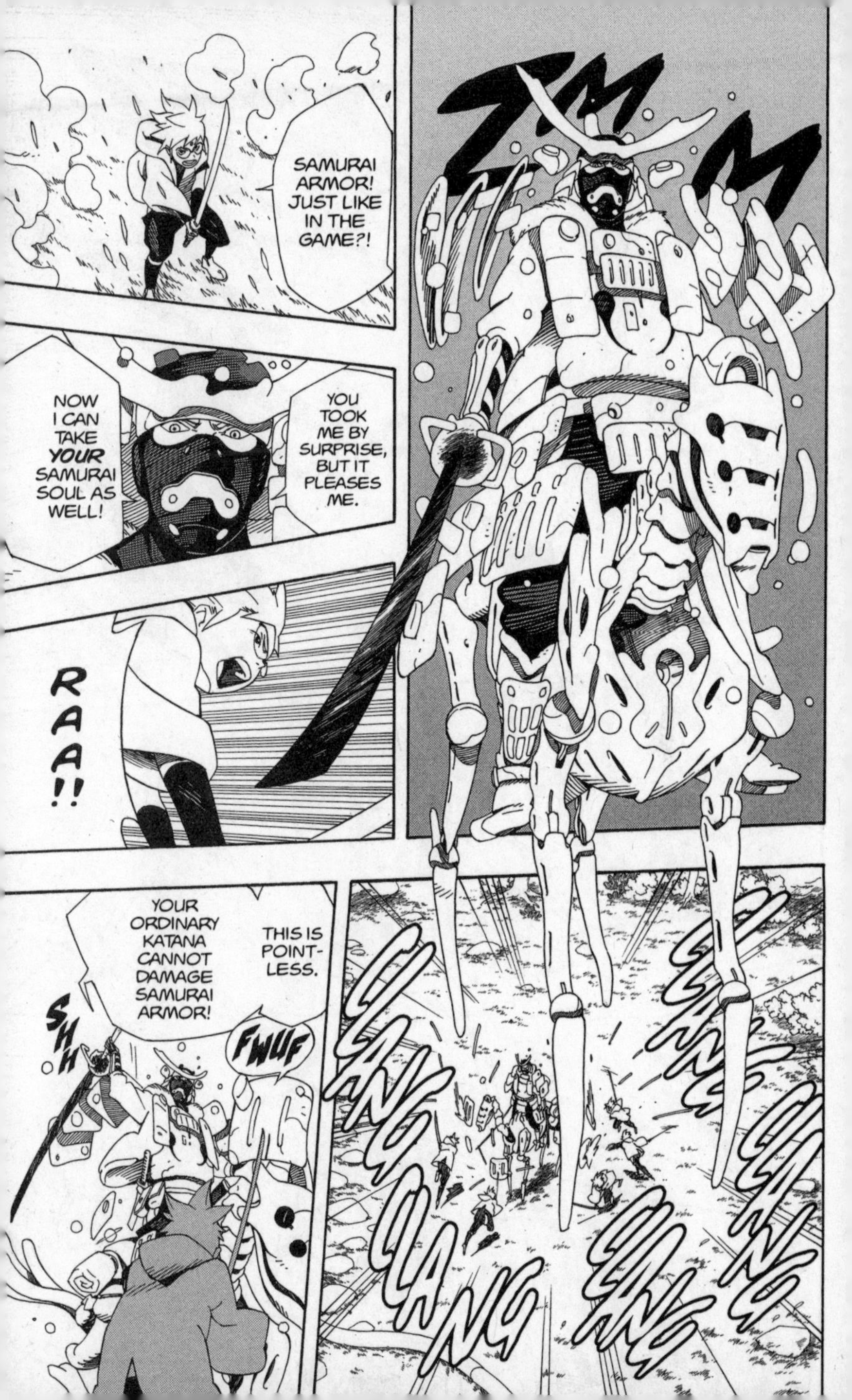
ZMM
SAMURAI ARMOR! JUST LIKE IN THE GAME?!
YOU TOOK ME BY SURPRISE, BUT IT PLEASES ME.
NOW I CAN TAKE YOUR SAMURAI SOUL AS WELL!
RAAA!!
CLANG CLANG
THIS IS POINTLESS.
YOUR ORDINARY KATANA CANNOT DAMAGE SAMURAI ARMOR!
SHH
FWUF

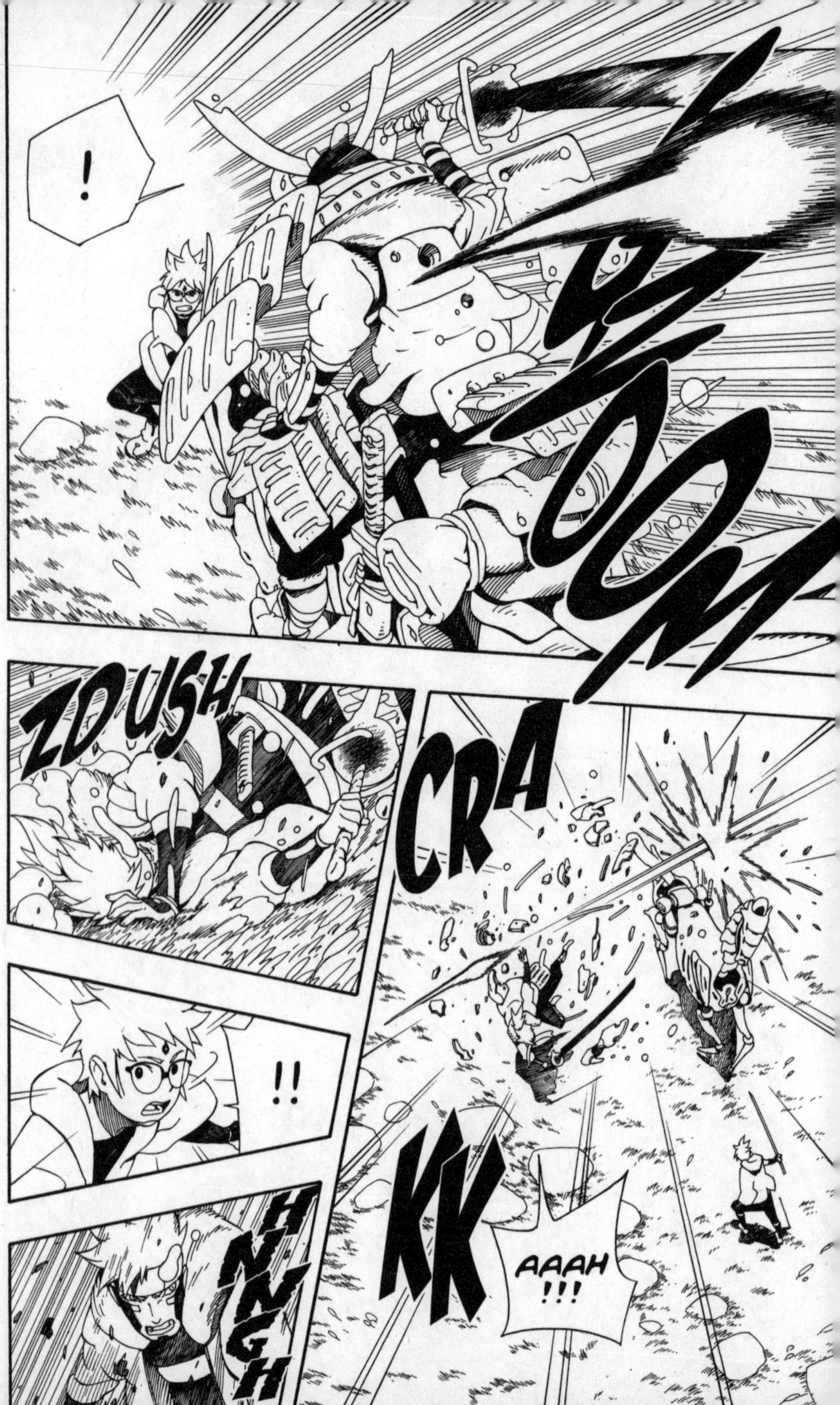
WHOOM
!
CRA
KK
AAAH!!!
ZDUSH
!!
HNGH

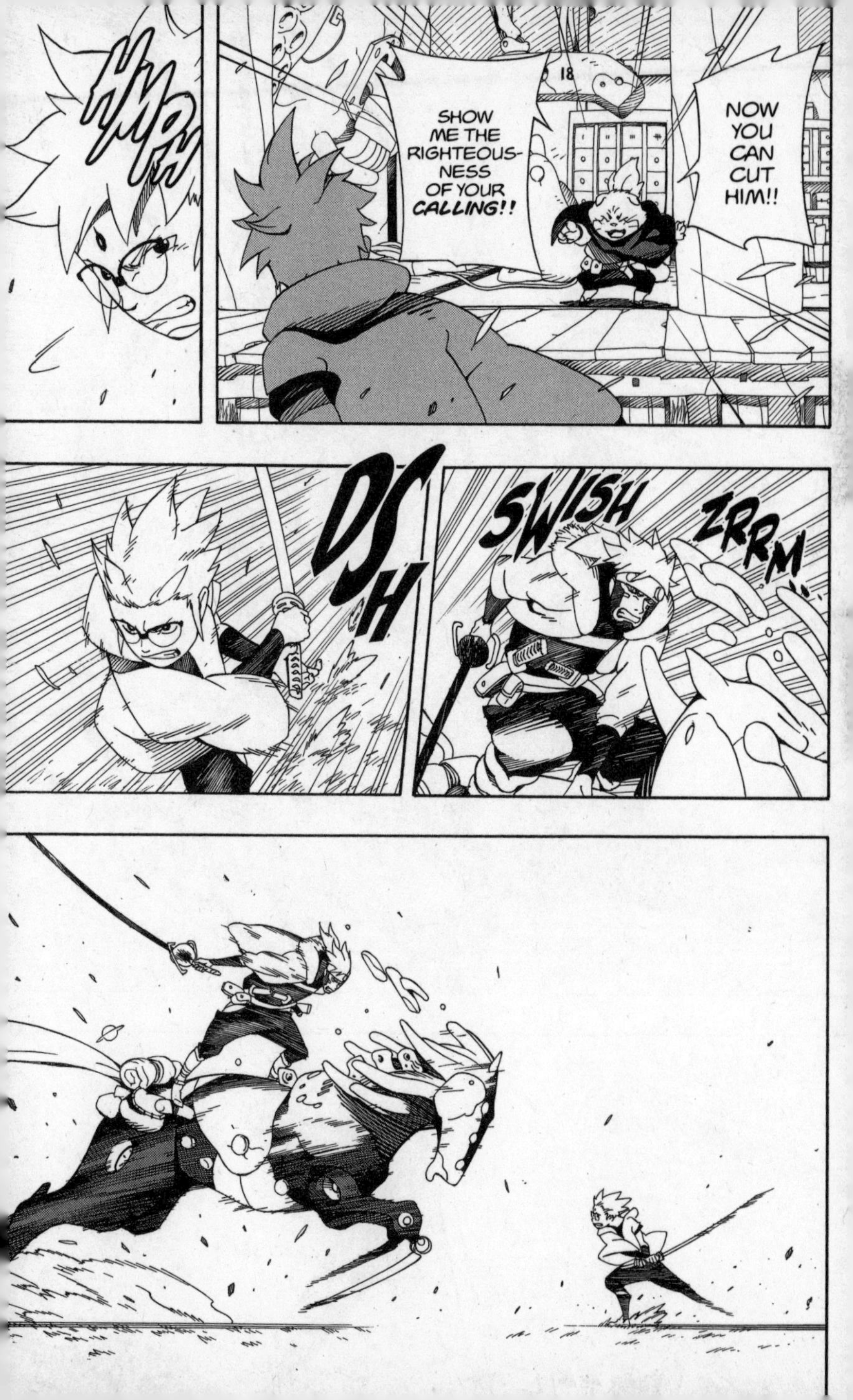
NOW YOU CAN CUT HIM!!
SHOW ME THE RIGHTEOUS-NESS OF YOUR CALLING!!
SWISH
ZRRM!!
DSH

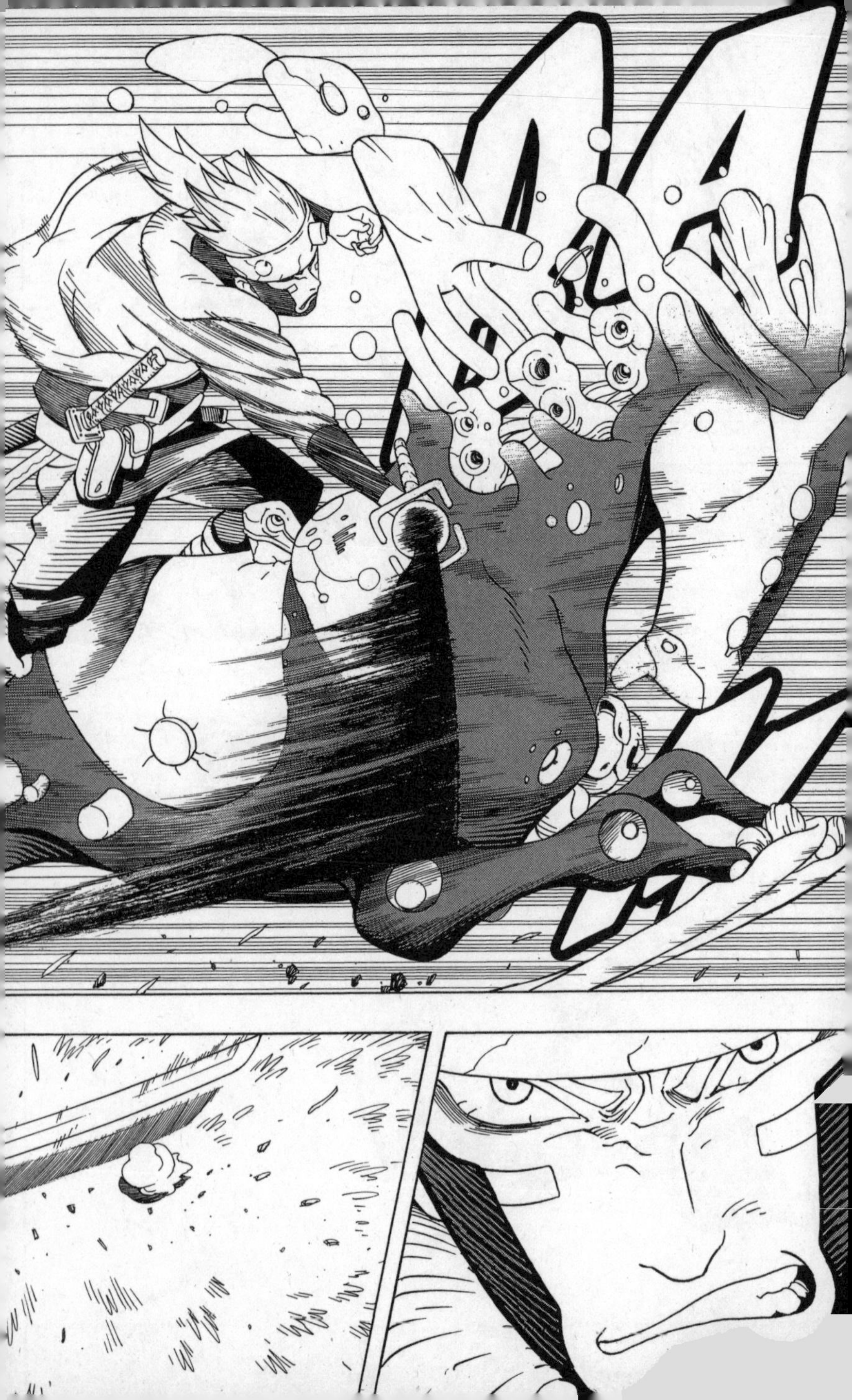

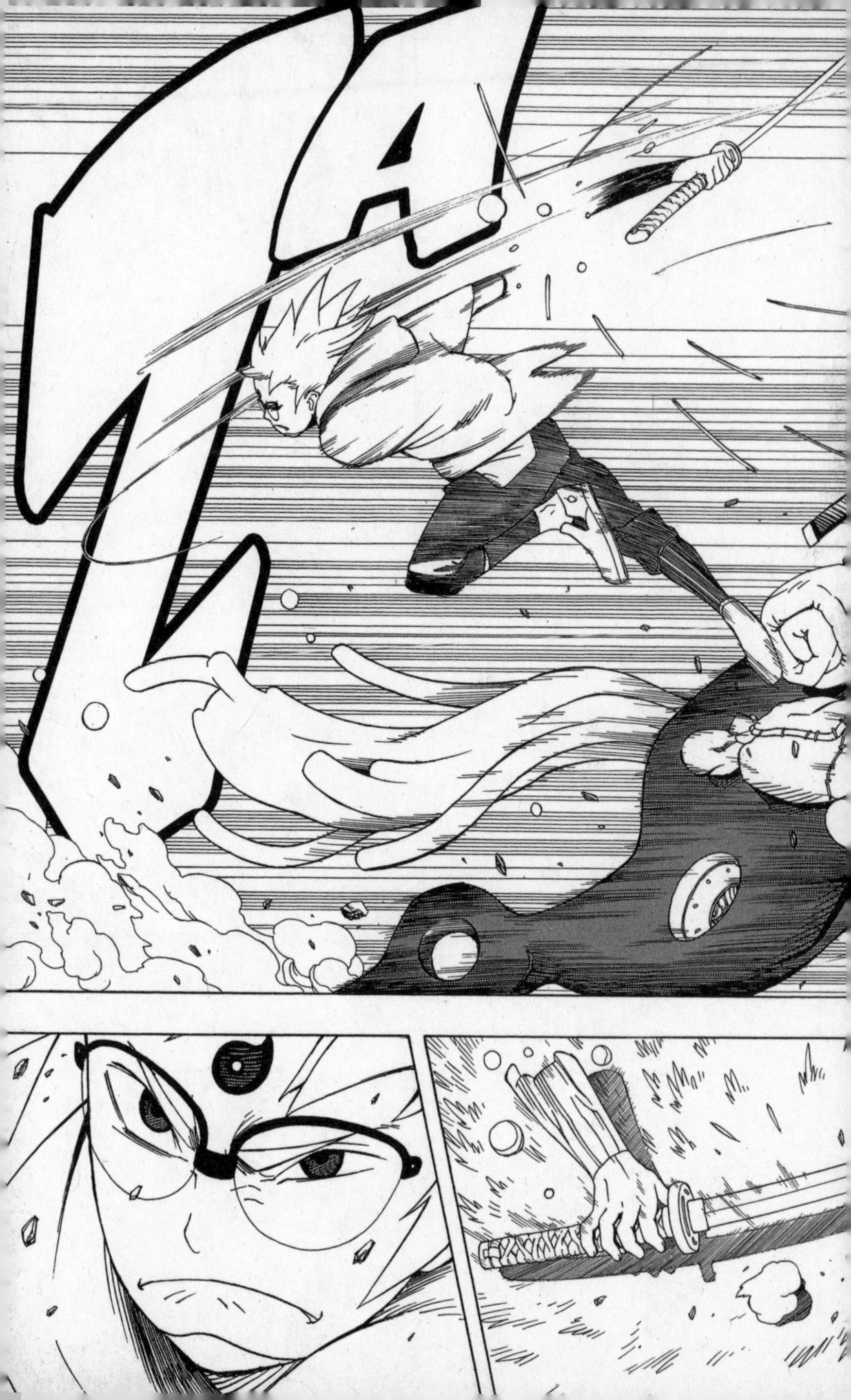
ZA

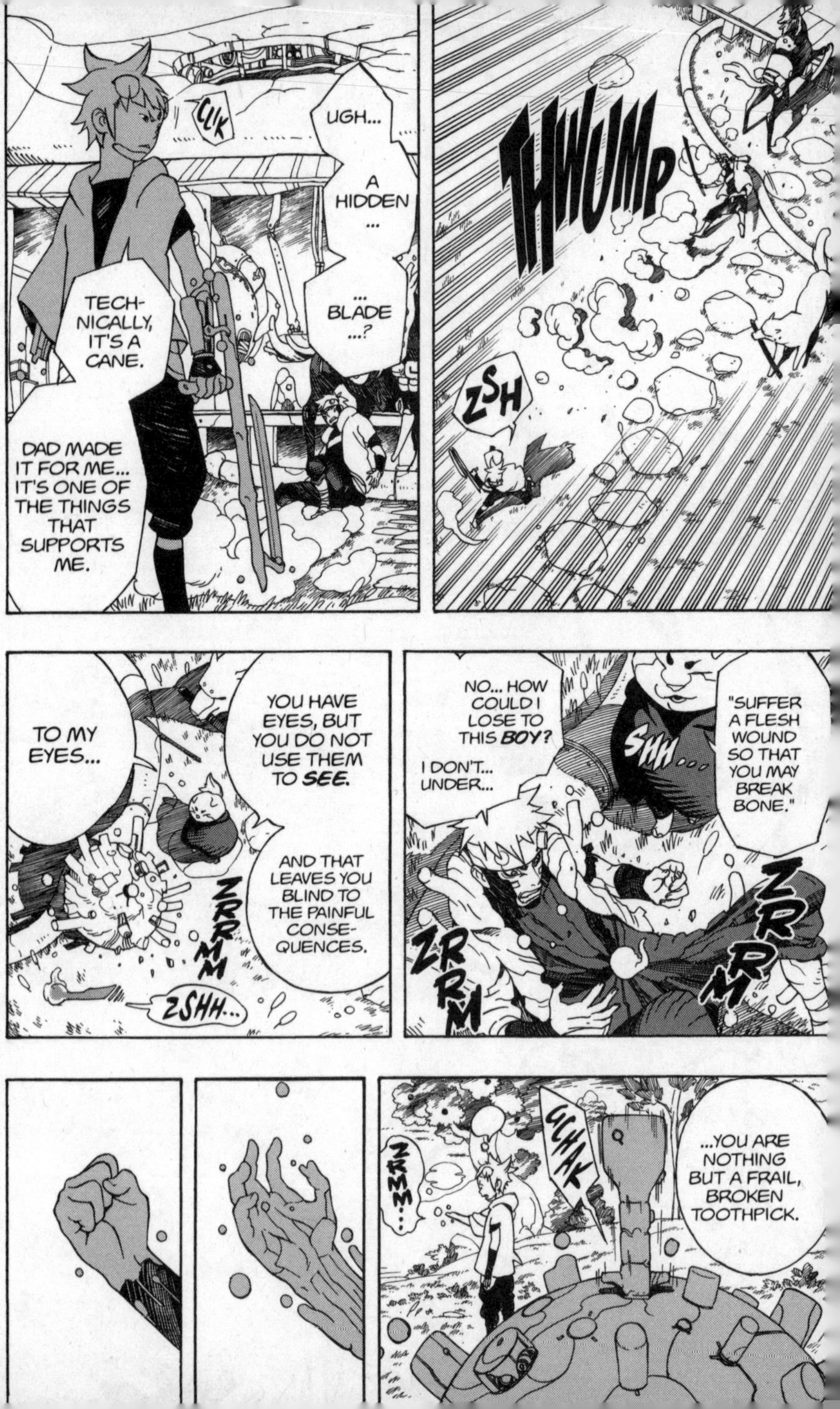
THWUMP
ZSH
UGH...
A HIDDEN ...
... BLADE ...?
CLIK
TECH-NICALLY, IT'S A CANE.
DAD MADE IT FOR ME... IT'S ONE OF THE THINGS THAT SUPPORTS ME.
"SUFFER A FLESH WOUND SO THAT YOU MAY BREAK BONE."
SHH...
NO... HOW COULD I LOSE TO THIS BOY?
I DON'T... UNDER...
ZRRM
ZRRM
YOU HAVE EYES, BUT YOU DO NOT USE THEM TO SEE.
AND THAT LEAVES YOU BLIND TO THE PAINFUL CONSE-QUENCES.
TO MY EYES...
ZRRMM
ZSHH...
...YOU ARE NOTHING BUT A FRAIL, BROKEN TOOTHPICK.
GCHAK
ZRMM...

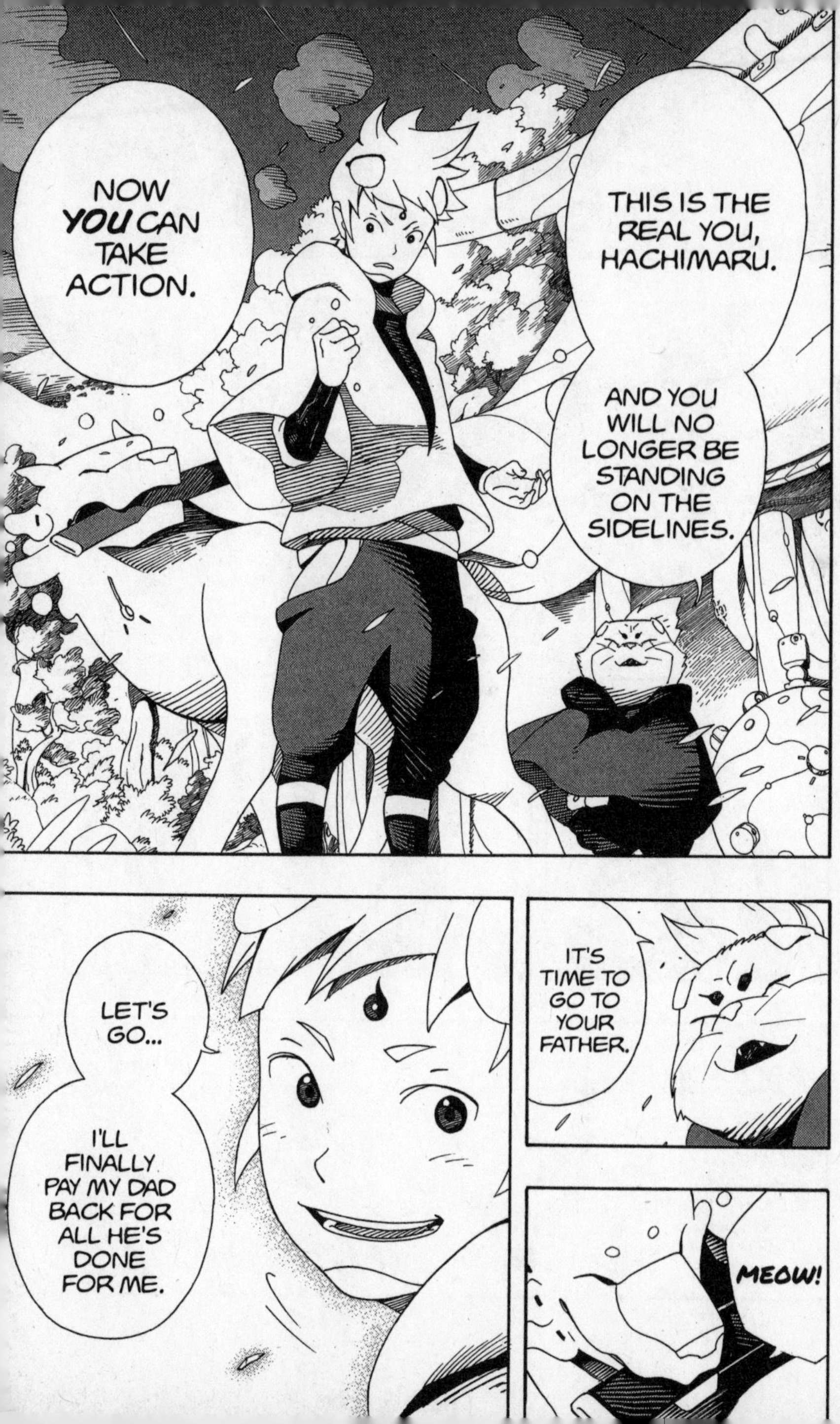
THIS IS THE REAL YOU, HACHIMARU.
AND YOU WILL NO LONGER BE STANDING ON THE SIDELINES.
NOW YOU CAN TAKE ACTION.
IT'S TIME TO GO TO YOUR FATHER.
MEOW!
LET'S GO...
I'LL FINALLY PAY MY DAD BACK FOR ALL HE'S DONE FOR ME.

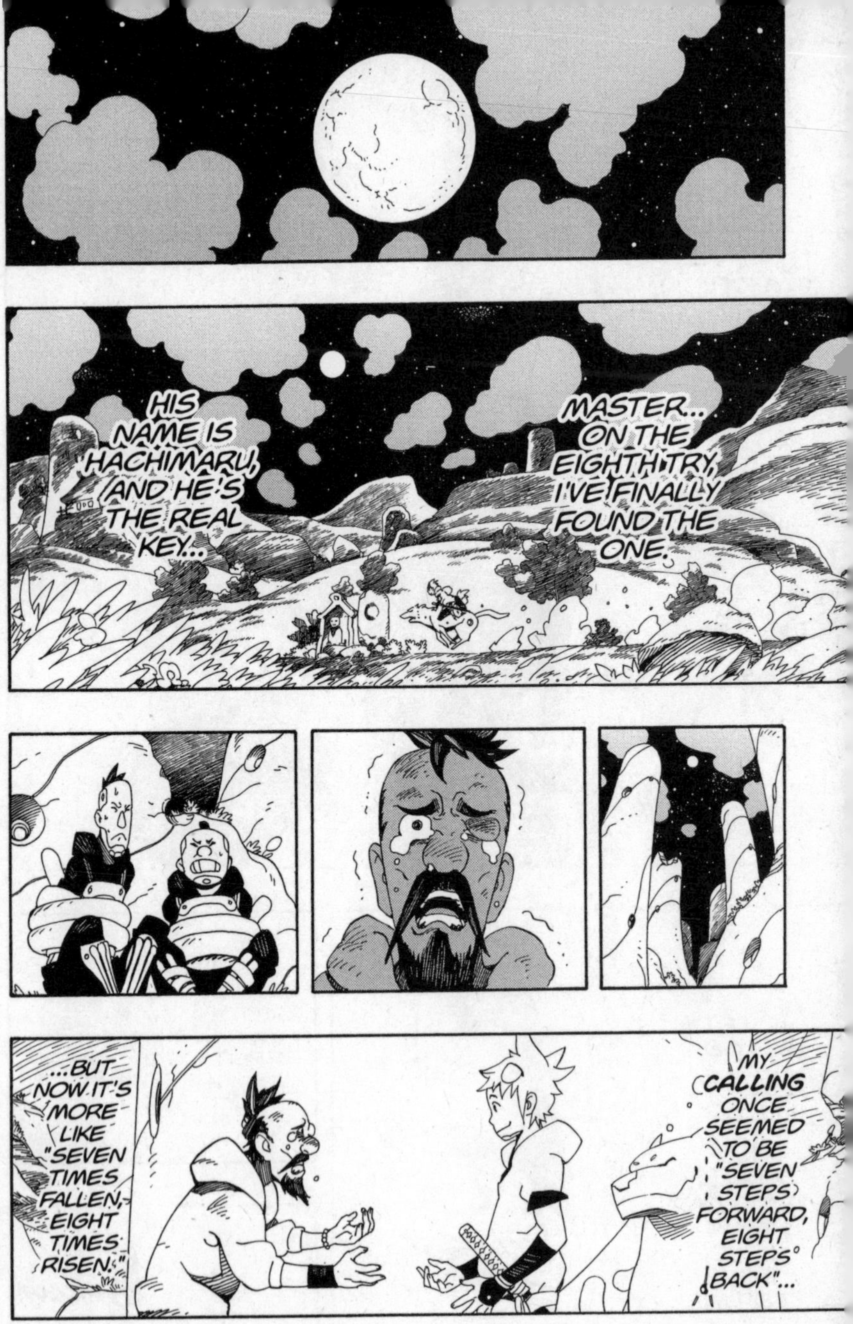
MASTER... ON THE EIGHTH TRY, I'VE FINALLY FOUND THE ONE.
HIS NAME IS HACHIMARU, AND HE'S THE REAL KEY...
MY **CALLING** ONCE SEEMED TO BE "SEVEN STEPS FORWARD, EIGHT STEPS BACK"...
...BUT NOW IT'S MORE LIKE "SEVEN TIMES FALLEN, EIGHT TIMES RISEN."

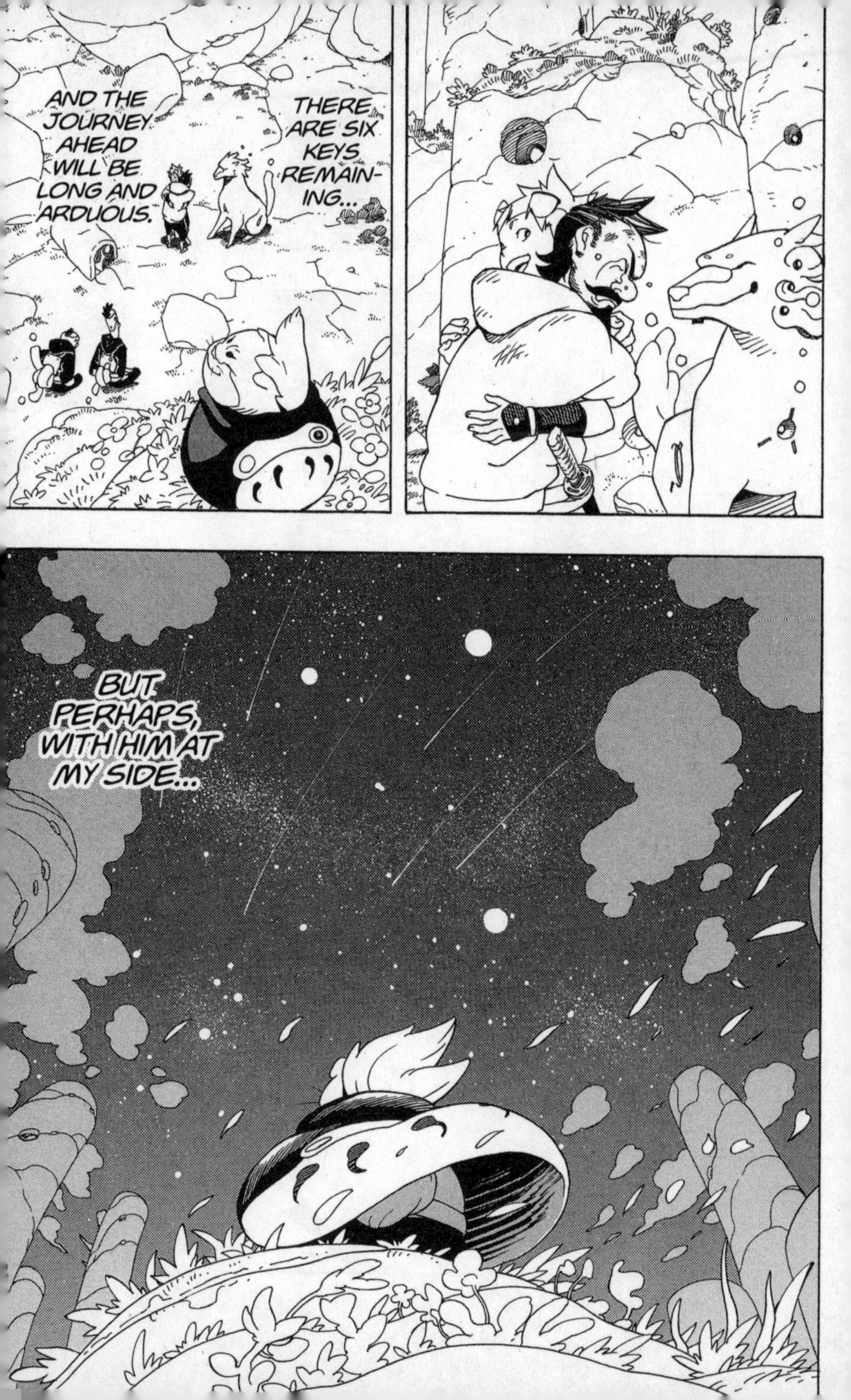
THERE ARE SIX KEYS REMAINING...
AND THE JOURNEY AHEAD WILL BE LONG AND ARDUOUS.
BUT PERHAPS, WITH HIM AT MY SIDE...

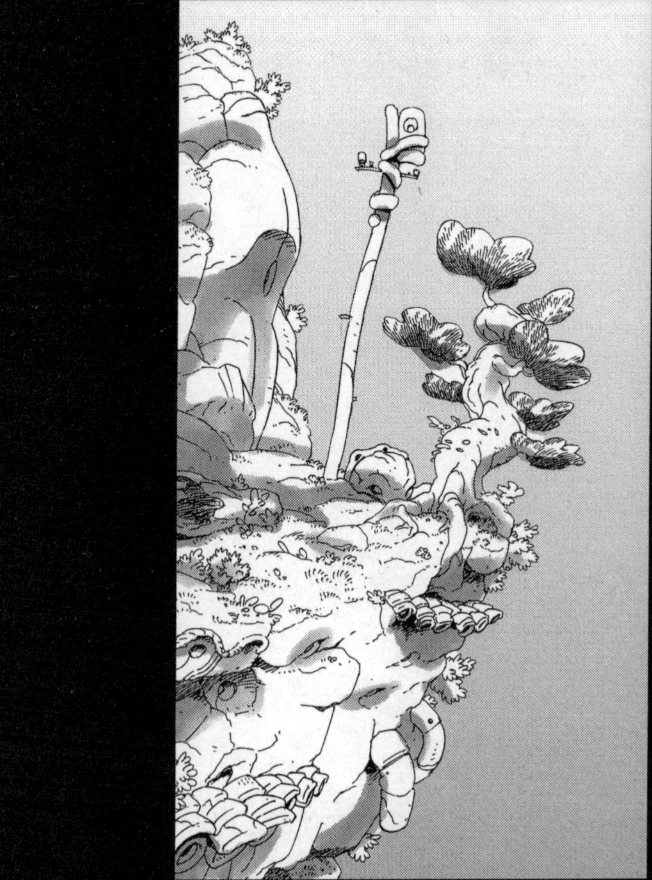

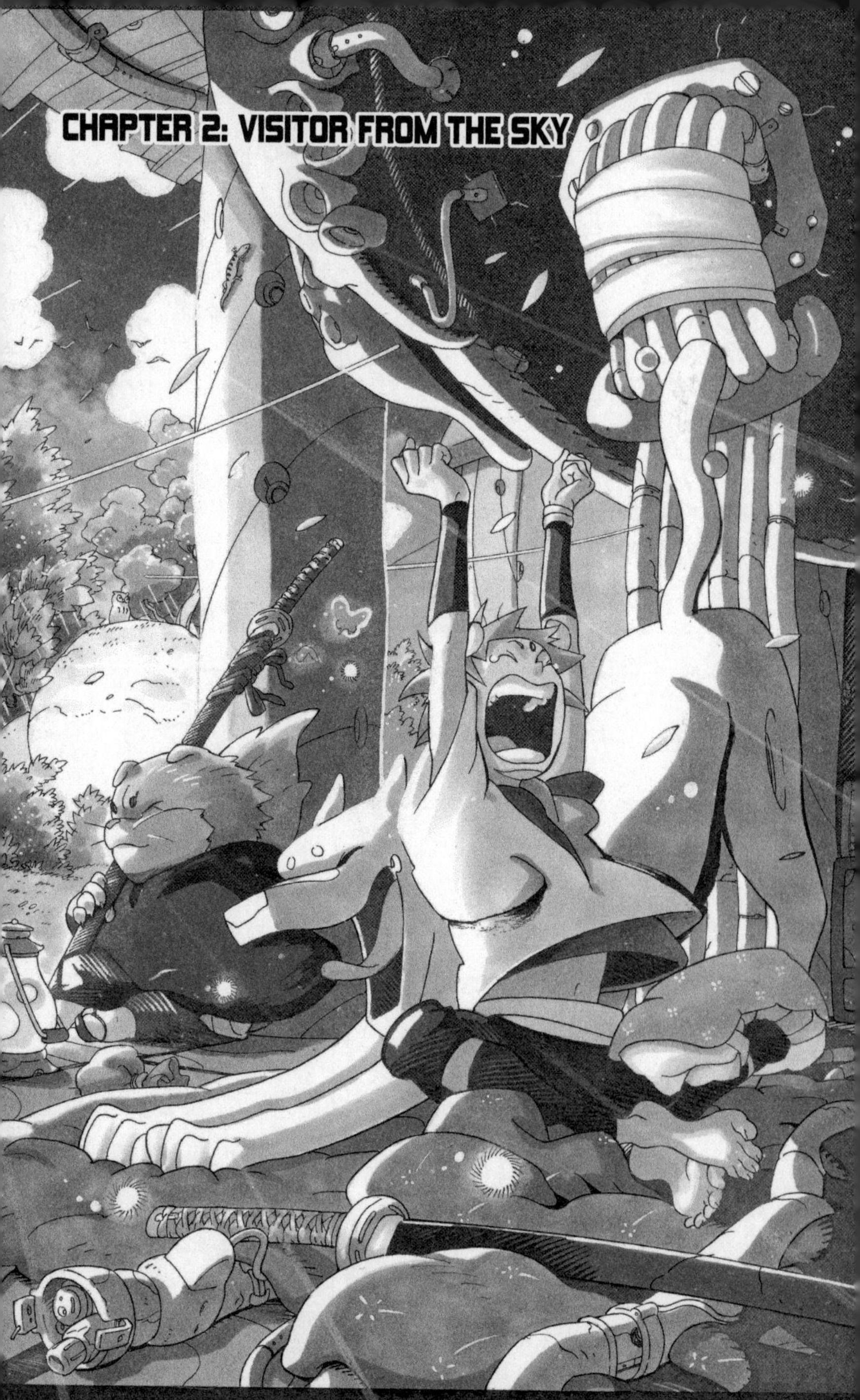
CHAPTER 2: VISITOR FROM THE SKY

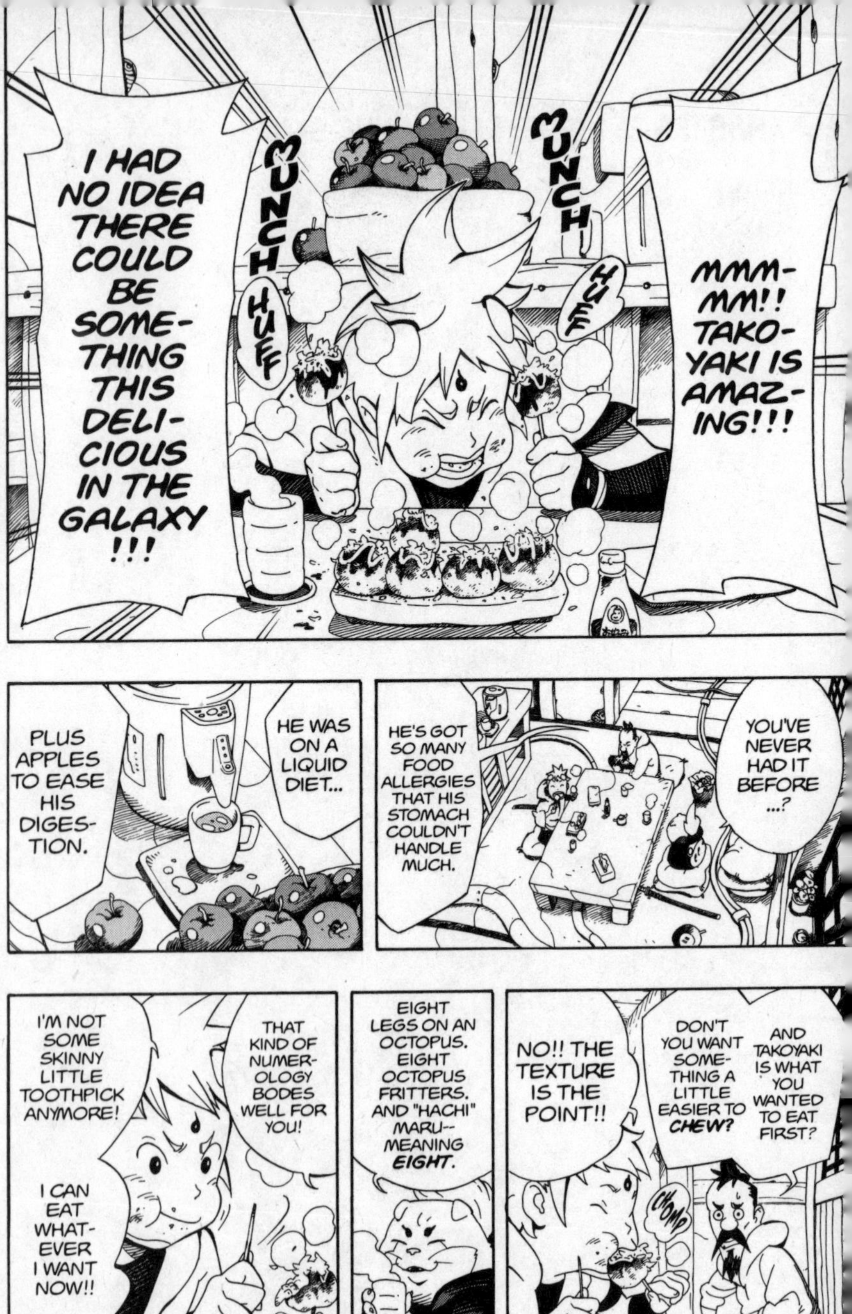
MMMM-MM!! TAKOYAKI IS AMAZING!!!
MUNCH
HUFF
MUNCH
HUFF
I HAD NO IDEA THERE COULD BE SOMETHING THIS DELICIOUS IN THE GALAXY!!!
YOU'VE NEVER HAD IT BEFORE ...?
HE'S GOT SO MANY FOOD ALLERGIES THAT HIS STOMACH COULDN'T HANDLE MUCH.
HE WAS ON A LIQUID DIET...
PLUS APPLES TO EASE HIS DIGESTION.
AND TAKOYAKI IS WHAT YOU WANTED TO EAT FIRST?
DON'T YOU WANT SOMETHING A LITTLE EASIER TO CHEW?
NO!! THE TEXTURE IS THE POINT!!
CHOMP
EIGHT LEGS ON AN OCTOPUS. EIGHT OCTOPUS FRITTERS. AND "HACHI" MARU--MEANING EIGHT.
THAT KIND OF NUMEROLOGY BODES WELL FOR YOU!
I'M NOT SOME SKINNY LITTLE TOOTHPICK ANYMORE!
I CAN EAT WHATEVER I WANT NOW!!

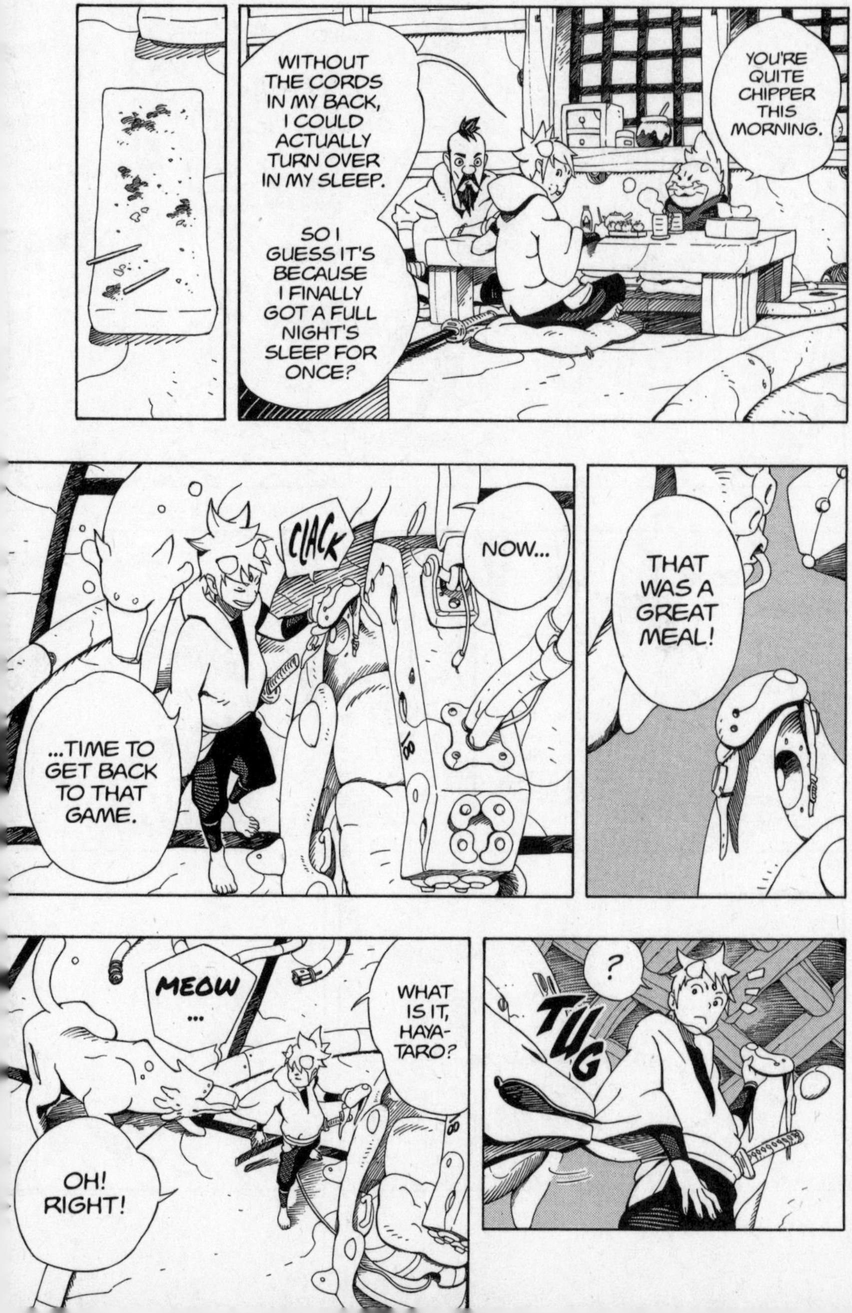

YOU'RE QUITE CHIPPER THIS MORNING.
WITHOUT THE CORDS IN MY BACK, I COULD ACTUALLY TURN OVER IN MY SLEEP.
SO I GUESS IT'S BECAUSE I FINALLY GOT A FULL NIGHT'S SLEEP FOR ONCE?
THAT WAS A GREAT MEAL!
NOW...
CLACK
...TIME TO GET BACK TO THAT GAME.
?
TUG
WHAT IS IT, HAYA-TARO?
MEOW ...
OH! RIGHT!

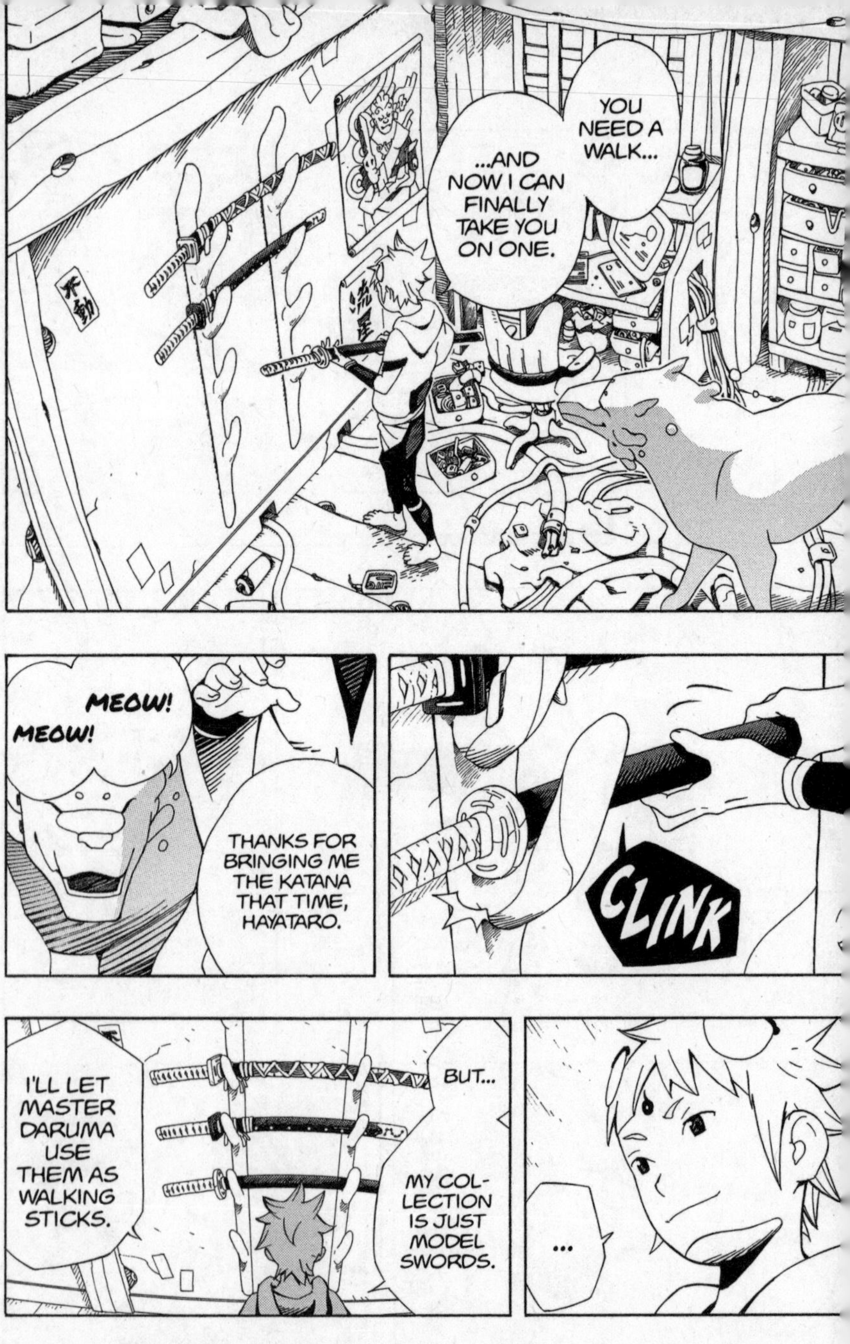
YOU NEED A WALK...
...AND NOW I CAN FINALLY TAKE YOU ON ONE.
CLINK
MEOW!
MEOW!
THANKS FOR BRINGING ME THE KATANA THAT TIME, HAYATARO.
...
BUT...
MY COL-LECTION IS JUST MODEL SWORDS.
I'LL LET MASTER DARUMA USE THEM AS WALKING STICKS.

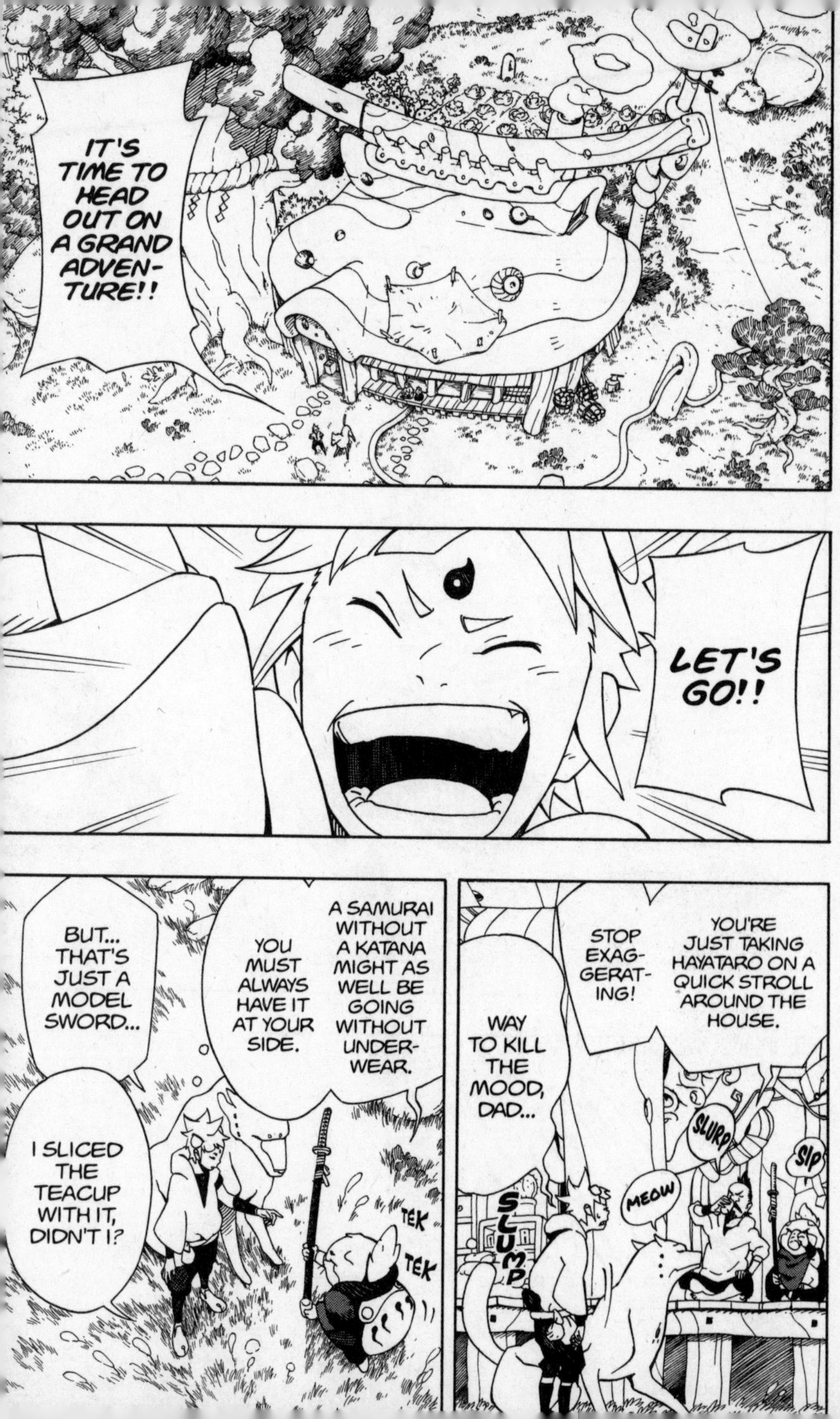
IT'S TIME TO HEAD OUT ON A GRAND ADVENTURE!!
LET'S GO!!
YOU'RE JUST TAKING HAYATARO ON A QUICK STROLL AROUND THE HOUSE.
STOP EXAGGERATING!
WAY TO KILL THE MOOD, DAD...
SLURP
SIP
MEOW
SLUMP
A SAMURAI WITHOUT A KATANA MIGHT AS WELL BE GOING WITHOUT UNDERWEAR.
YOU MUST ALWAYS HAVE IT AT YOUR SIDE.
BUT... THAT'S JUST A MODEL SWORD...
I SLICED THE TEACUP WITH IT, DIDN'T I?
TEK
TEK

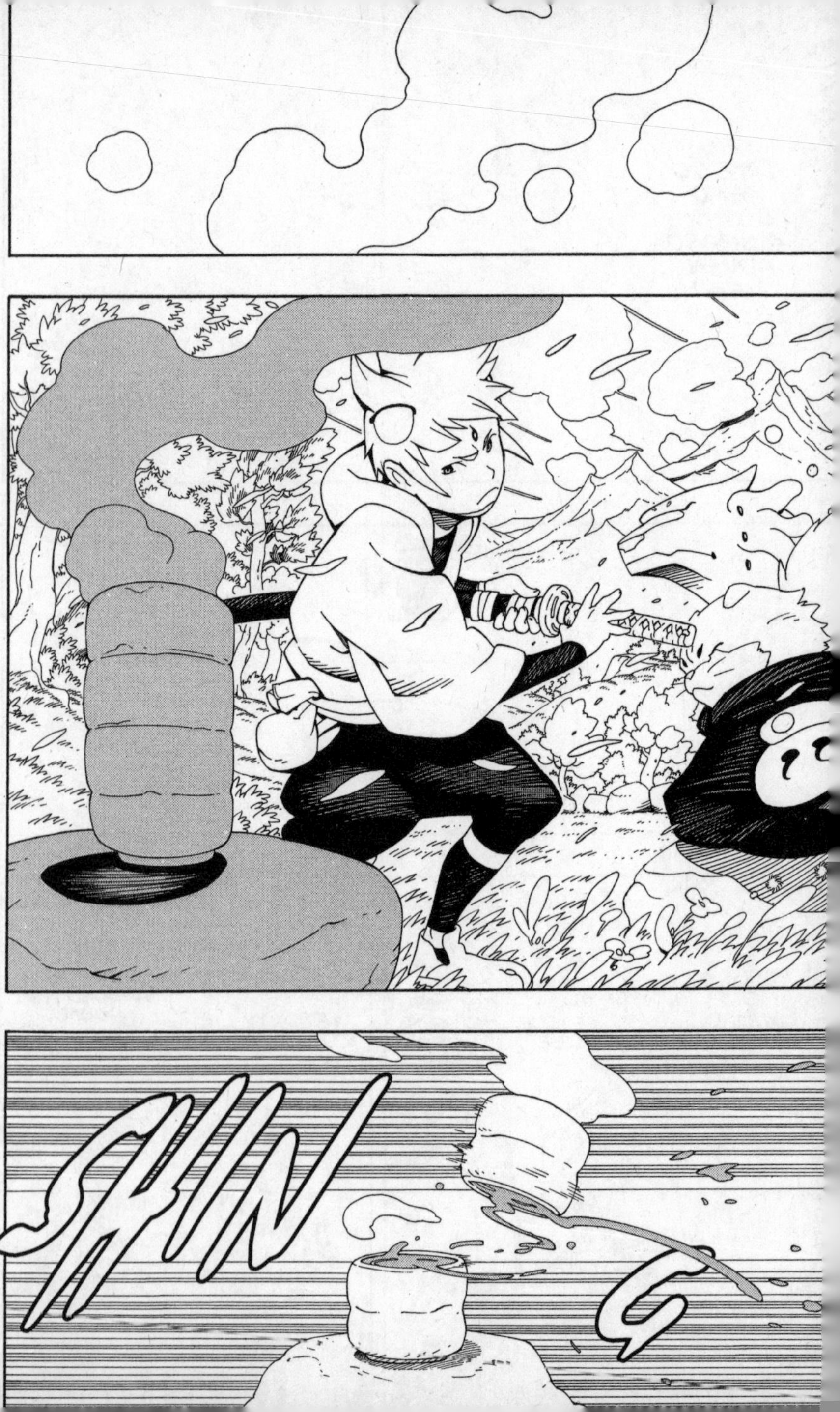
SHING

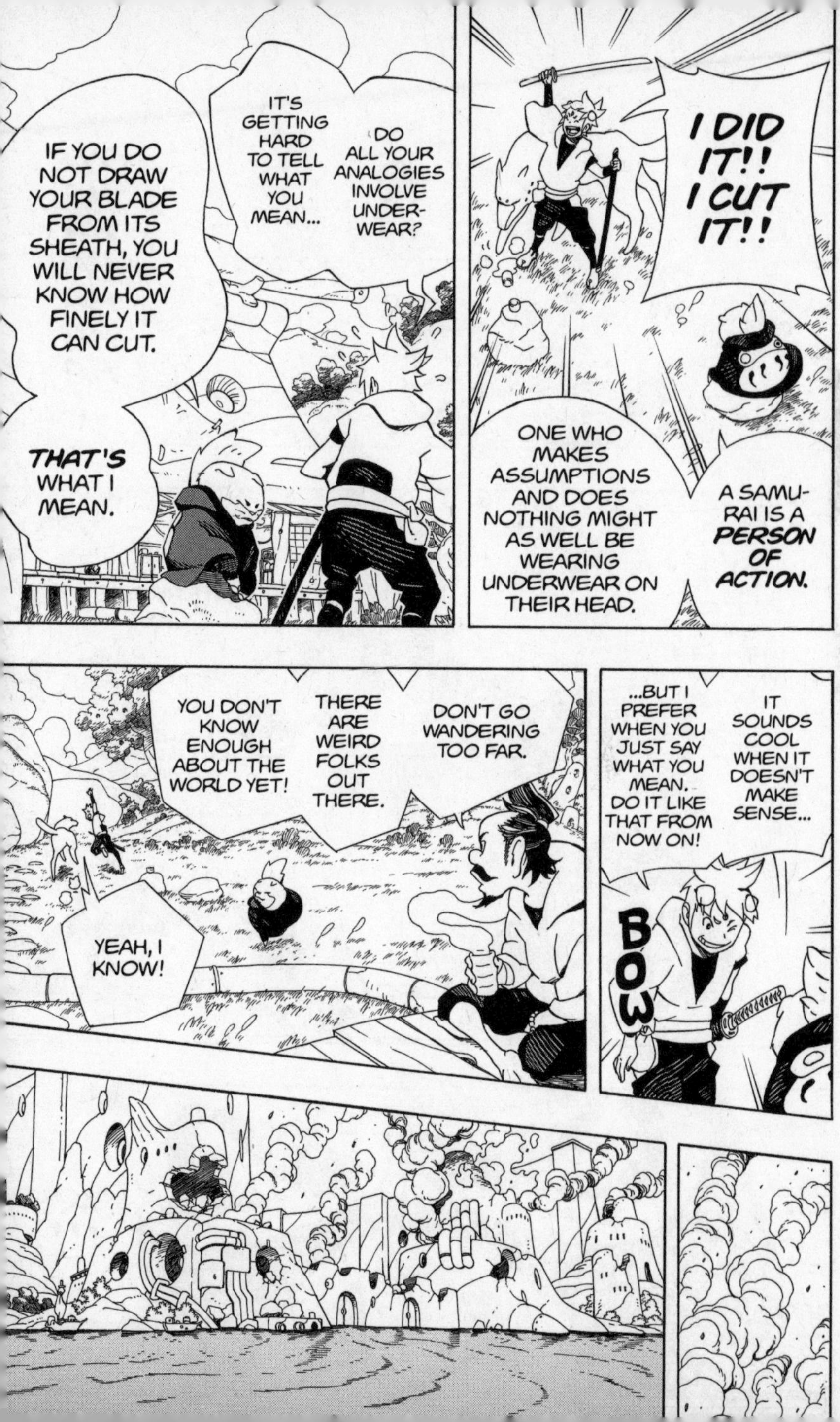
I DID IT!! I CUT IT!!
A SAMURAI IS A PERSON OF ACTION.
ONE WHO MAKES ASSUMPTIONS AND DOES NOTHING MIGHT AS WELL BE WEARING UNDERWEAR ON THEIR HEAD.
IT'S GETTING HARD TO TELL WHAT YOU MEAN...
DO ALL YOUR ANALOGIES INVOLVE UNDERWEAR?
IF YOU DO NOT DRAW YOUR BLADE FROM ITS SHEATH, YOU WILL NEVER KNOW HOW FINELY IT CAN CUT.
THAT'S WHAT I MEAN.
IT SOUNDS COOL WHEN IT DOESN'T MAKE SENSE...
...BUT I PREFER WHEN YOU JUST SAY WHAT YOU MEAN. DO IT LIKE THAT FROM NOW ON!
BOW
DON'T GO WANDERING TOO FAR.
THERE ARE WEIRD FOLKS OUT THERE.
YOU DON'T KNOW ENOUGH ABOUT THE WORLD YET!
YEAH, I KNOW!

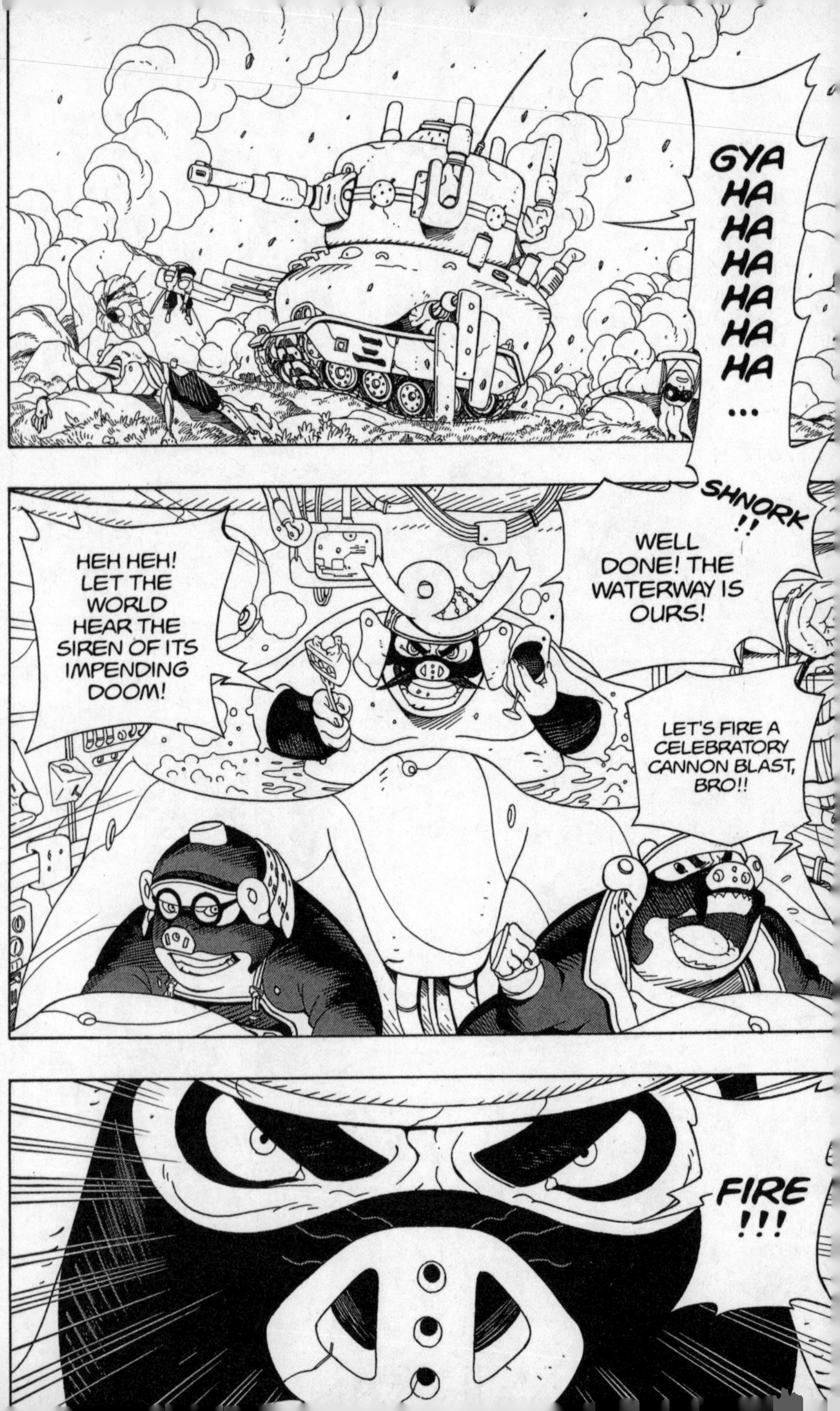
GYA HA HA HA HA HA HA...
SHNORK!!
WELL DONE! THE WATERWAY IS OURS!
HEH HEH! LET THE WORLD HEAR THE SIREN OF ITS IMPENDING DOOM!
LET'S FIRE A CELEBRATORY CANNON BLAST, BRO!!
FIRE!!!

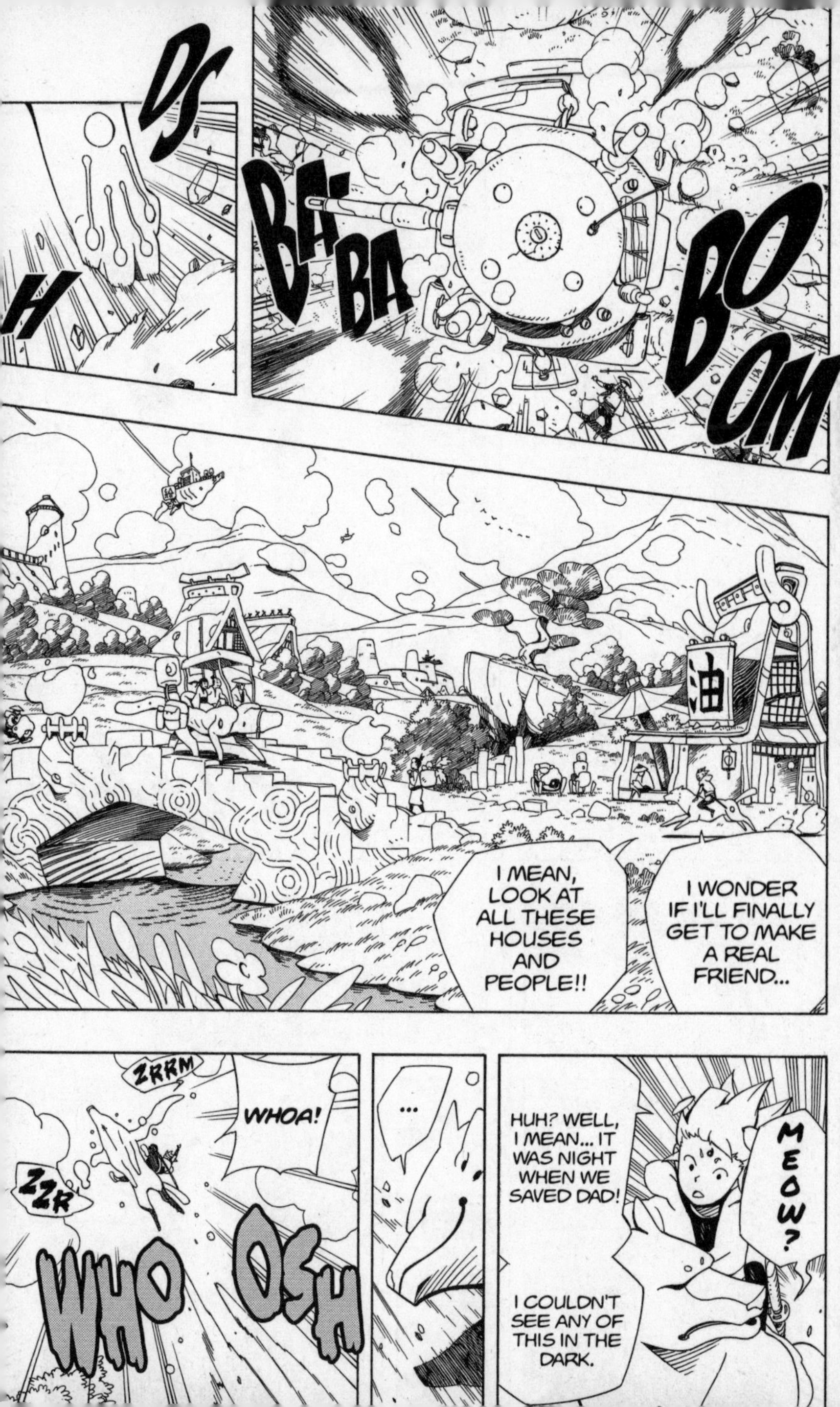
BA-BA
BOOM
DS
H
I WONDER IF I'LL FINALLY GET TO MAKE A REAL FRIEND...
I MEAN, LOOK AT ALL THESE HOUSES AND PEOPLE!!
MEOW?
HUH? WELL, I MEAN... IT WAS NIGHT WHEN WE SAVED DAD!
I COULDN'T SEE ANY OF THIS IN THE DARK.
...
WHOA!
ZRRM
ZZR
WHOOSH

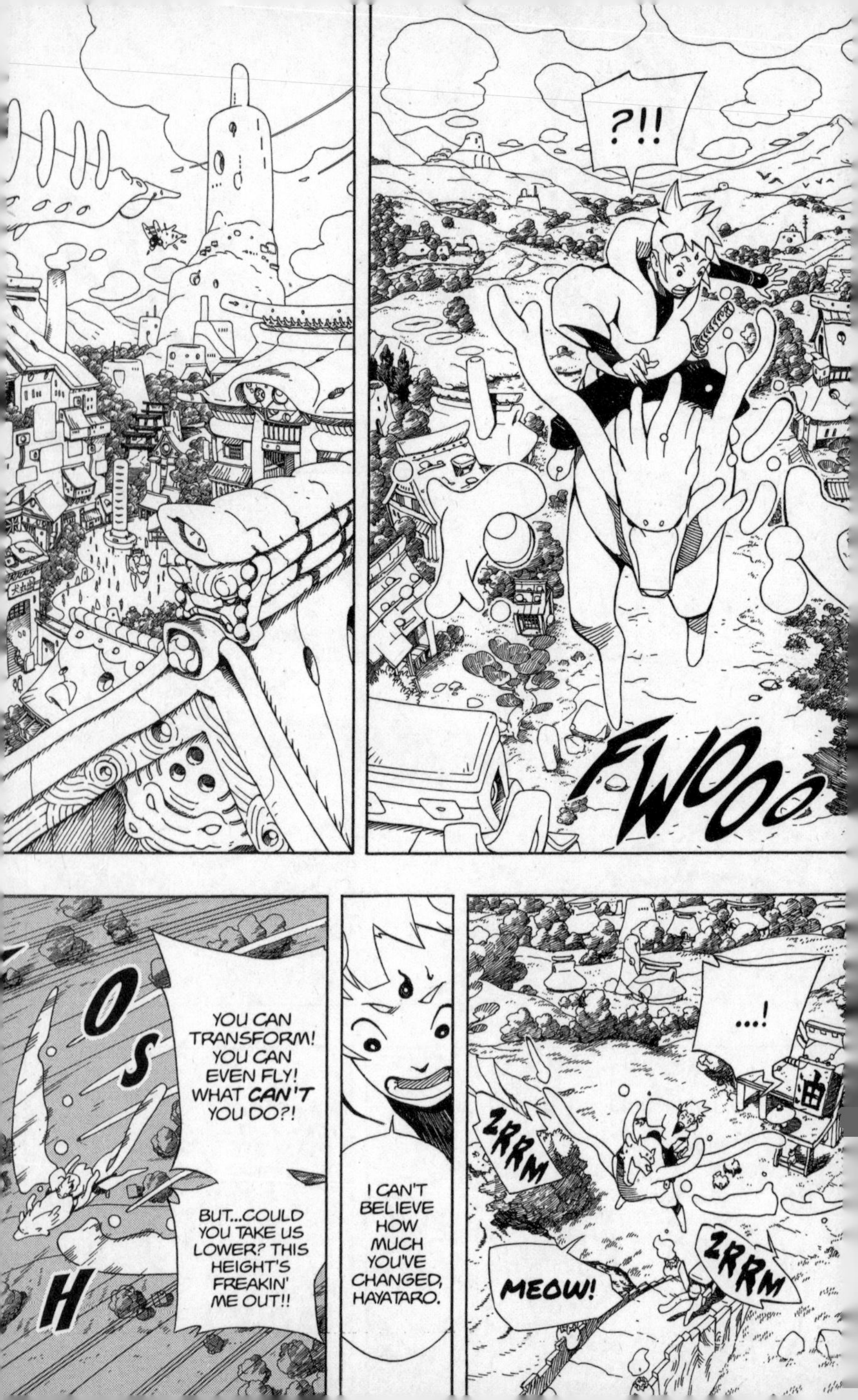
?!!
FWOOO
...!
ZRRM
ZRRM
MEOW!
I CAN'T BELIEVE HOW MUCH YOU'VE CHANGED, HAYATARO.
YOU CAN TRANSFORM! YOU CAN EVEN FLY! WHAT CAN'T YOU DO?!
BUT...COULD YOU TAKE US LOWER? THIS HEIGHT'S FREAKIN' ME OUT!!

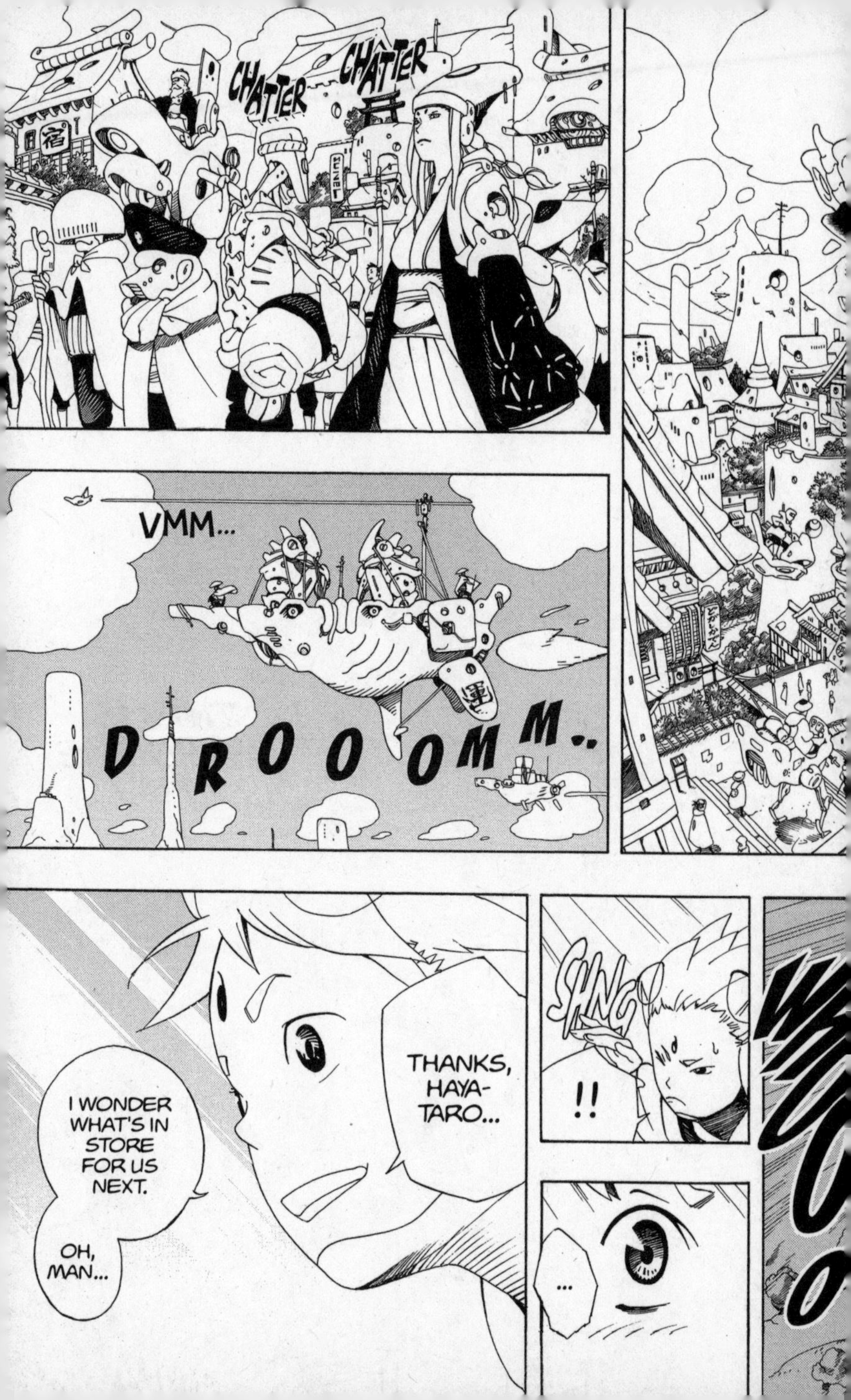

CHATTER CHATTER
VMM...
DROOOMM..
WHOOOO
SHING
!!
...
THANKS, HAYA-TARO...
I WONDER WHAT'S IN STORE FOR US NEXT.
OH, MAN...

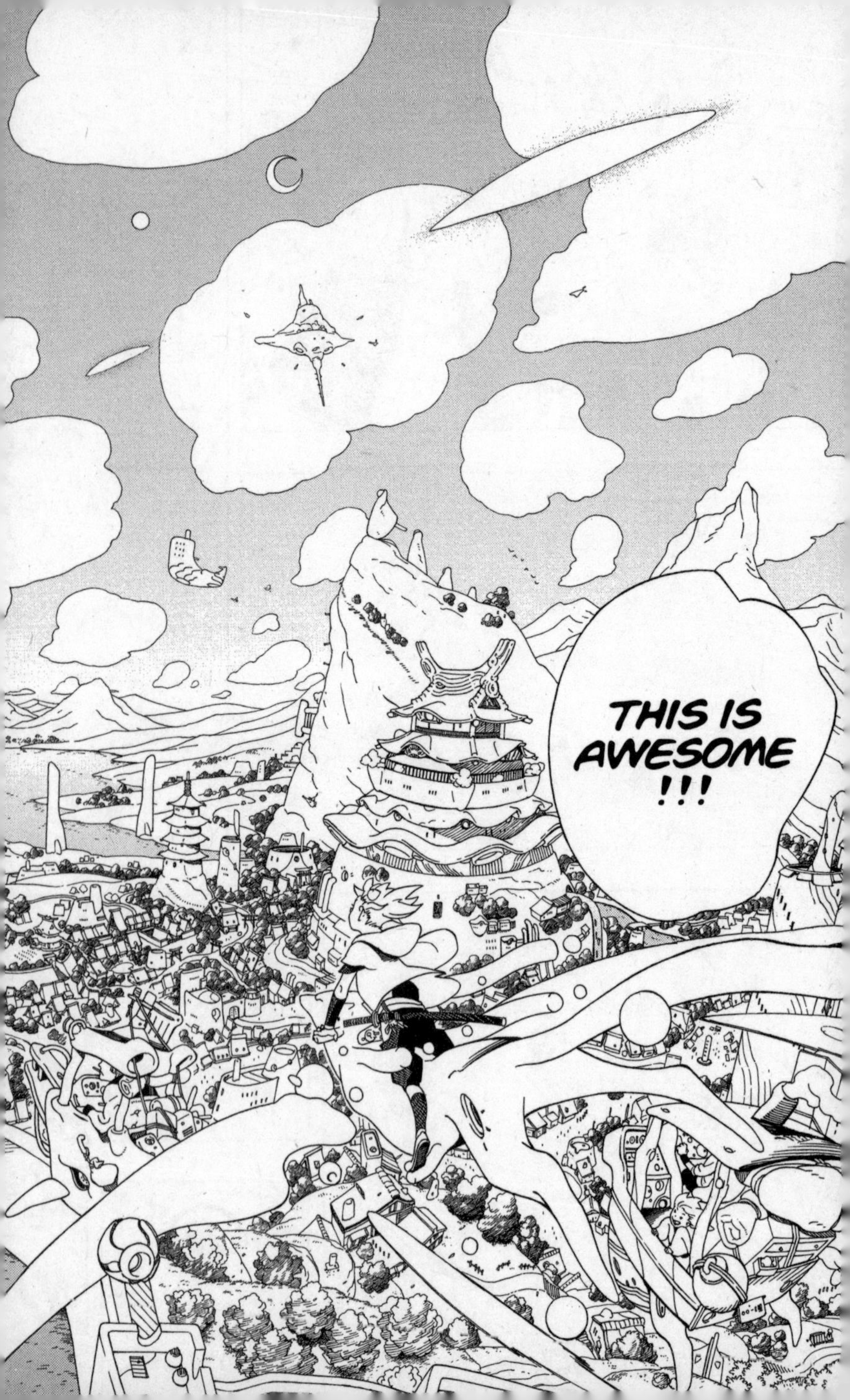
THIS IS AWESOME !!!

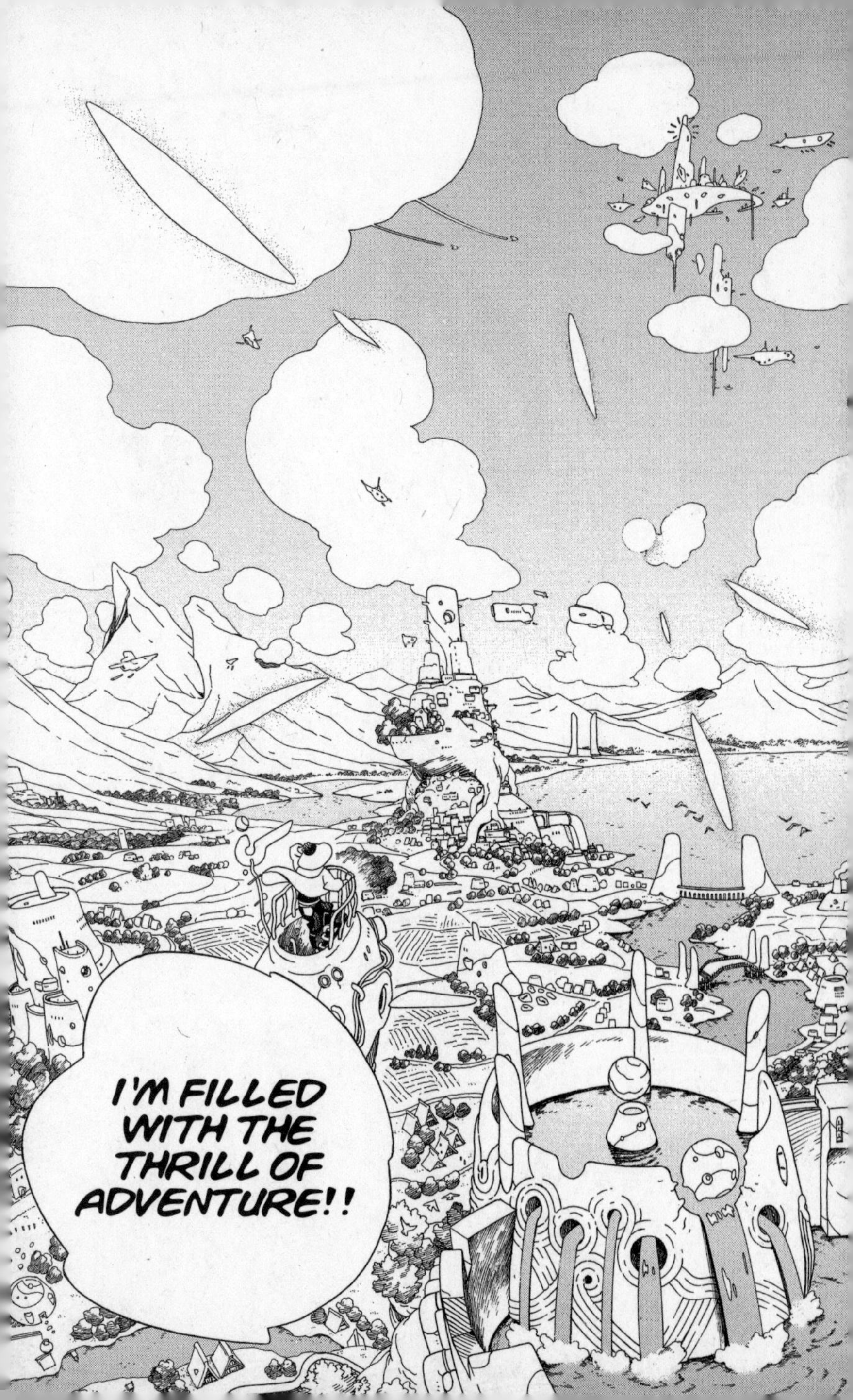
I'M FILLED WITH THE THRILL OF ADVENTURE!!

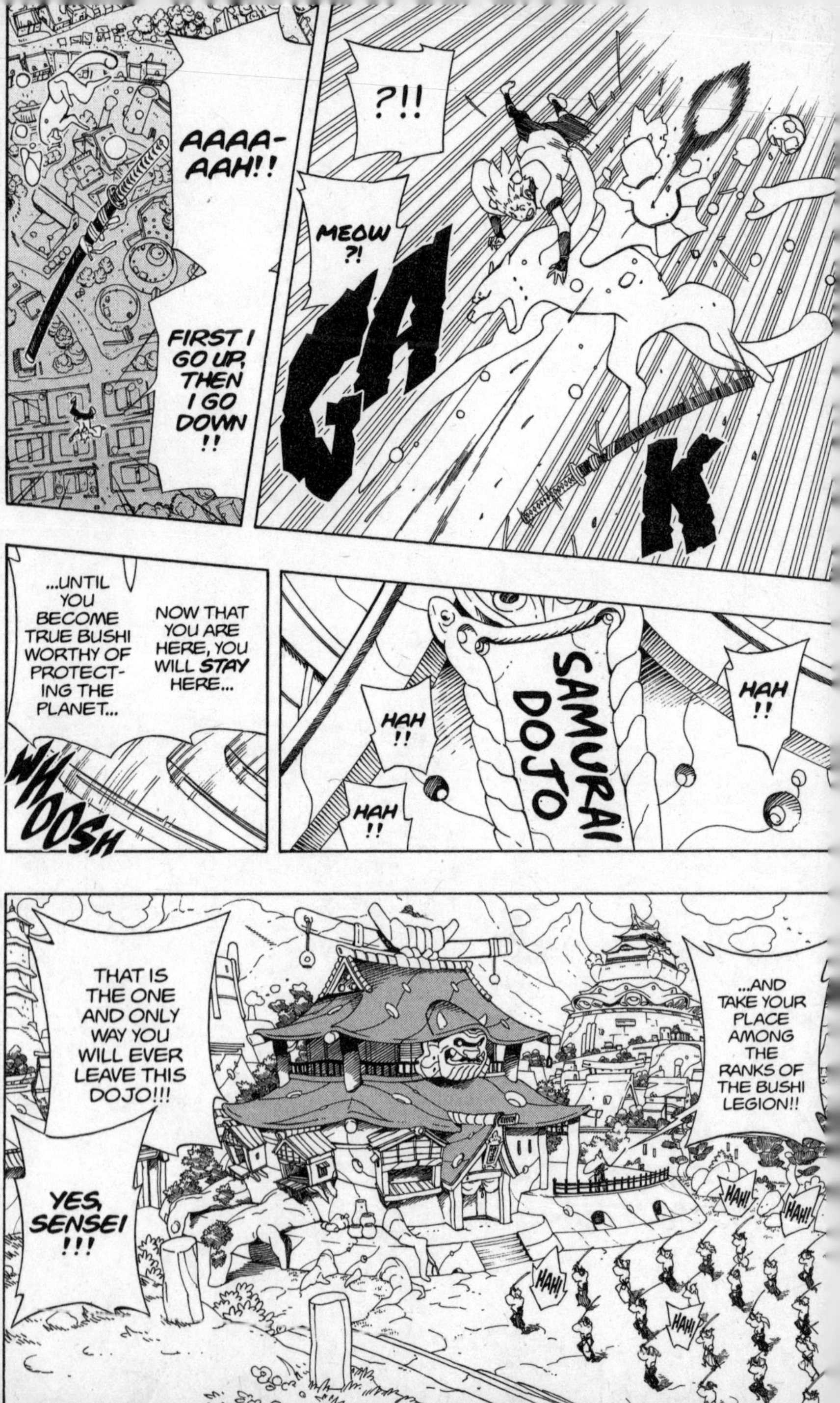
?!!
MEOW ?!
GAK
AAAA-AAH!!
FIRST I GO UP, THEN I GO DOWN!!
SAMURAI DOJO
HAH!!
HAH!!
HAH!!
NOW THAT YOU ARE HERE, YOU WILL STAY HERE...
...UNTIL YOU BECOME TRUE BUSHI WORTHY OF PROTECTING THE PLANET...
WHOOSH
...AND TAKE YOUR PLACE AMONG THE RANKS OF THE BUSHI LEGION!!
HAH!
HAH!
HAH!
HAH!
THAT IS THE ONE AND ONLY WAY YOU WILL EVER LEAVE THIS DOJO!!!
YES, SENSEI!!!

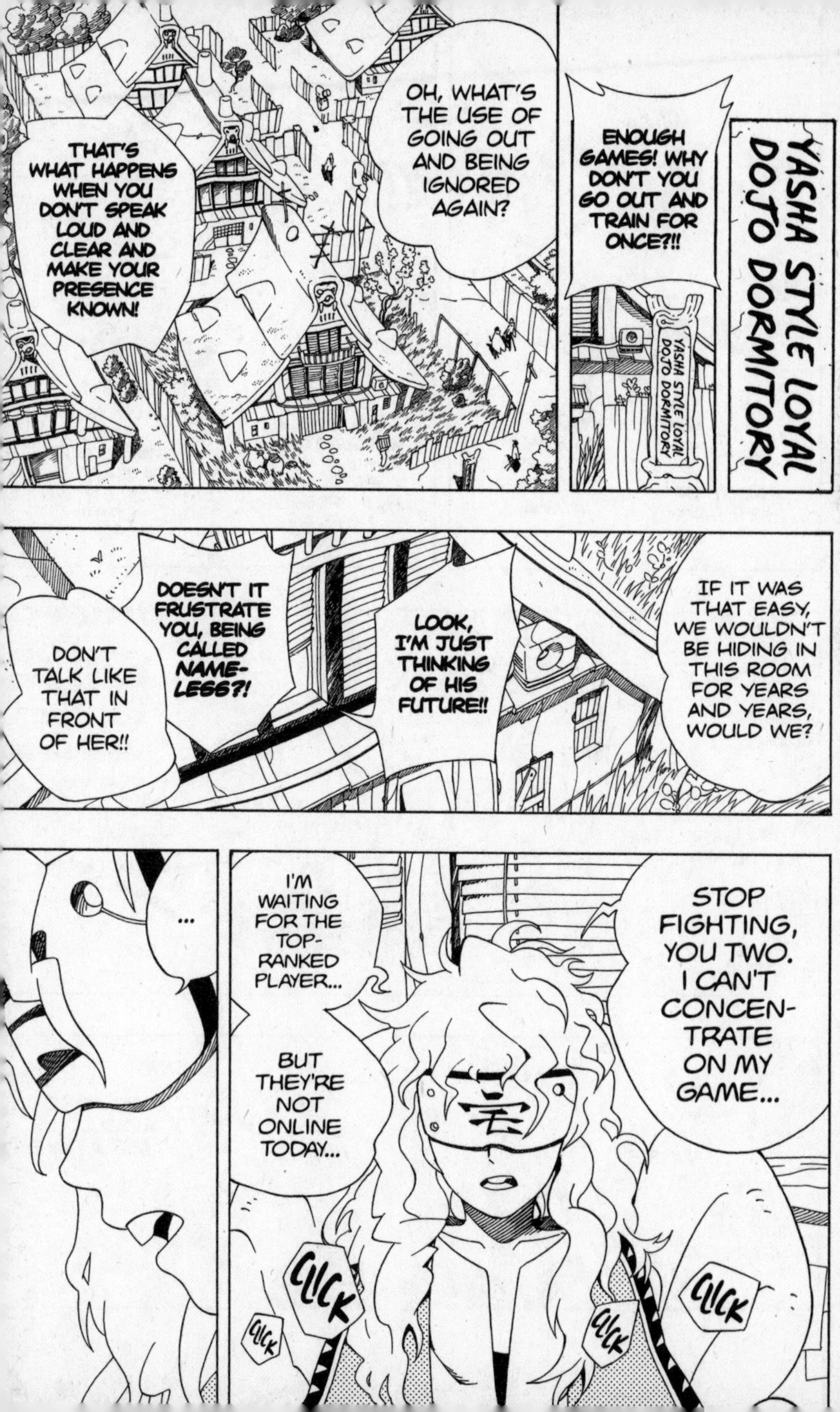
YASHA STYLE LOYAL DOJO DORMITORY
YASHA STYLE LOYAL DOJO DORMITORY
ENOUGH GAMES! WHY DON'T YOU GO OUT AND TRAIN FOR ONCE?!!
OH, WHAT'S THE USE OF GOING OUT AND BEING IGNORED AGAIN?
THAT'S WHAT HAPPENS WHEN YOU DON'T SPEAK LOUD AND CLEAR AND MAKE YOUR PRESENCE KNOWN!
IF IT WAS THAT EASY, WE WOULDN'T BE HIDING IN THIS ROOM FOR YEARS AND YEARS, WOULD WE?
LOOK, I'M JUST THINKING OF HIS FUTURE!!
DOESN'T IT FRUSTRATE YOU, BEING CALLED NAME-LESS?!
DON'T TALK LIKE THAT IN FRONT OF HER!!
STOP FIGHTING, YOU TWO. I CAN'T CONCENTRATE ON MY GAME...
I'M WAITING FOR THE TOP-RANKED PLAYER...
BUT THEY'RE NOT ONLINE TODAY...
CLICK
CLICK
CLICK
CLICK
...

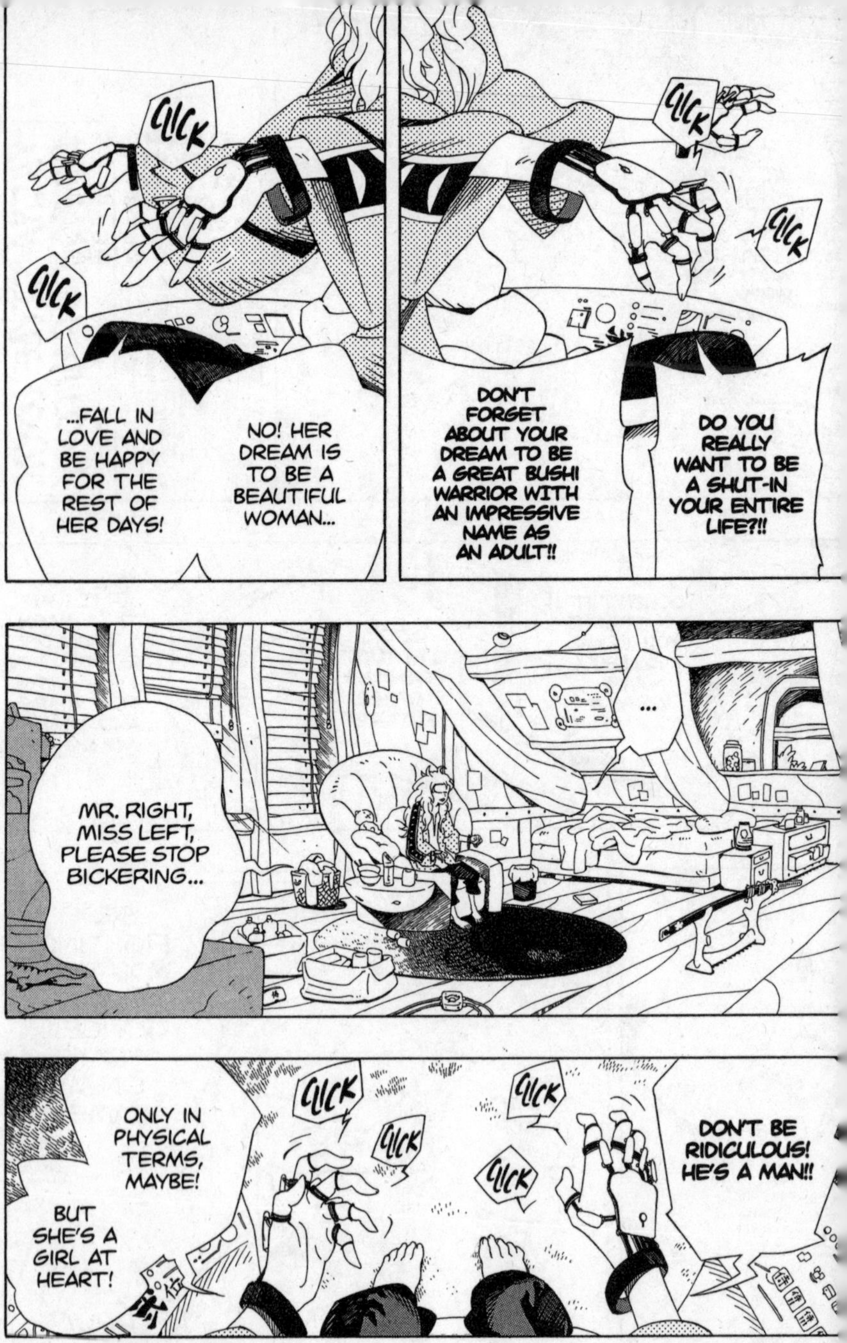
CLICK
CLICK
DO YOU REALLY WANT TO BE A SHUT-IN YOUR ENTIRE LIFE?!!
DON'T FORGET ABOUT YOUR DREAM TO BE A GREAT BUSHI WARRIOR WITH AN IMPRESSIVE NAME AS AN ADULT!!
CLICK
CLICK
NO! HER DREAM IS TO BE A BEAUTIFUL WOMAN...
...FALL IN LOVE AND BE HAPPY FOR THE REST OF HER DAYS!
...
MR. RIGHT, MISS LEFT, PLEASE STOP BICKERING...
DON'T BE RIDICULOUS! HE'S A MAN!!
CLICK
CLICK
CLICK
CLICK
ONLY IN PHYSICAL TERMS, MAYBE!
BUT SHE'S A GIRL AT HEART!

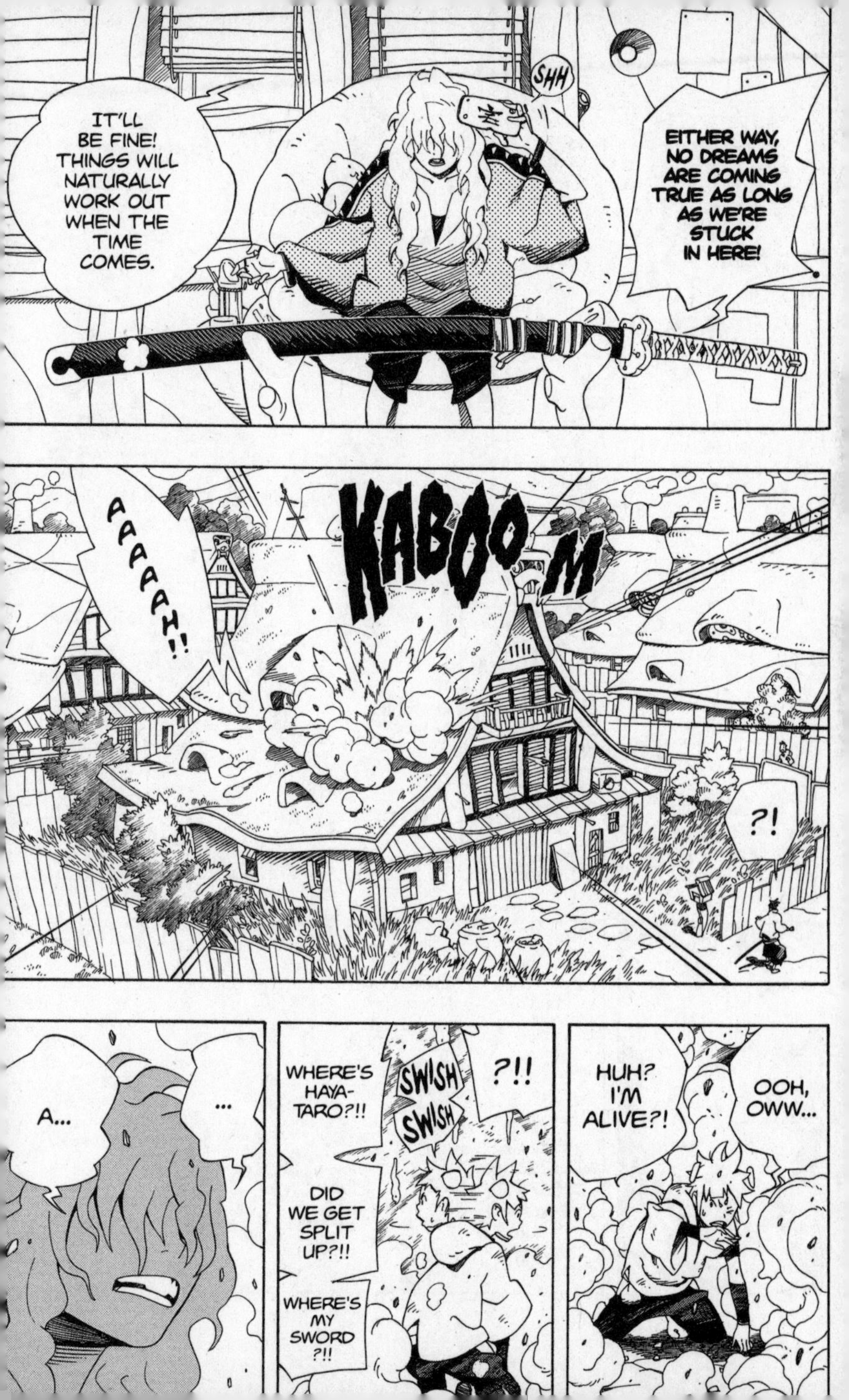
EITHER WAY, NO DREAMS ARE COMING TRUE AS LONG AS WE'RE STUCK IN HERE!
SHH
IT'LL BE FINE! THINGS WILL NATURALLY WORK OUT WHEN THE TIME COMES.
KABOOM
AAAAAH!!
?!
OOH, OWW...
HUH? I'M ALIVE?!
?!!
SWISH SWISH
WHERE'S HAYA-TARO?!!
DID WE GET SPLIT UP?!!
WHERE'S MY SWORD ?!!
...
A...

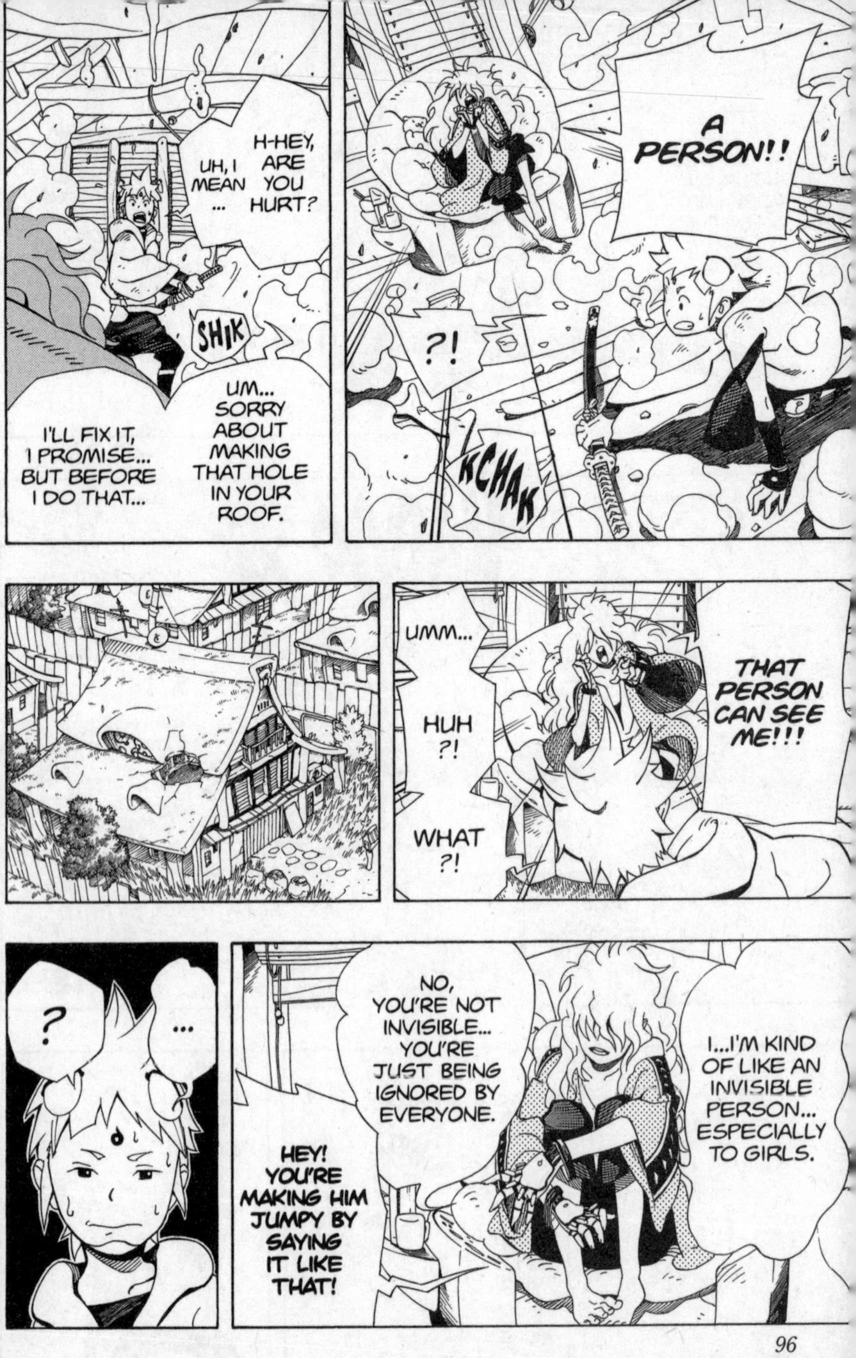
A PERSON!!
?!
KCHAK
H-HEY, ARE YOU HURT?
UH, I MEAN ...
SHIK
UM... SORRY ABOUT MAKING THAT HOLE IN YOUR ROOF.
I'LL FIX IT, I PROMISE... BUT BEFORE I DO THAT...
THAT PERSON CAN SEE ME!!!
UMM...
HUH ?!
WHAT ?!
I...I'M KIND OF LIKE AN INVISIBLE PERSON... ESPECIALLY TO GIRLS.
NO, YOU'RE NOT INVISIBLE... YOU'RE JUST BEING IGNORED BY EVERYONE.
HEY! YOU'RE MAKING HIM JUMPY BY SAYING IT LIKE THAT!
...
?

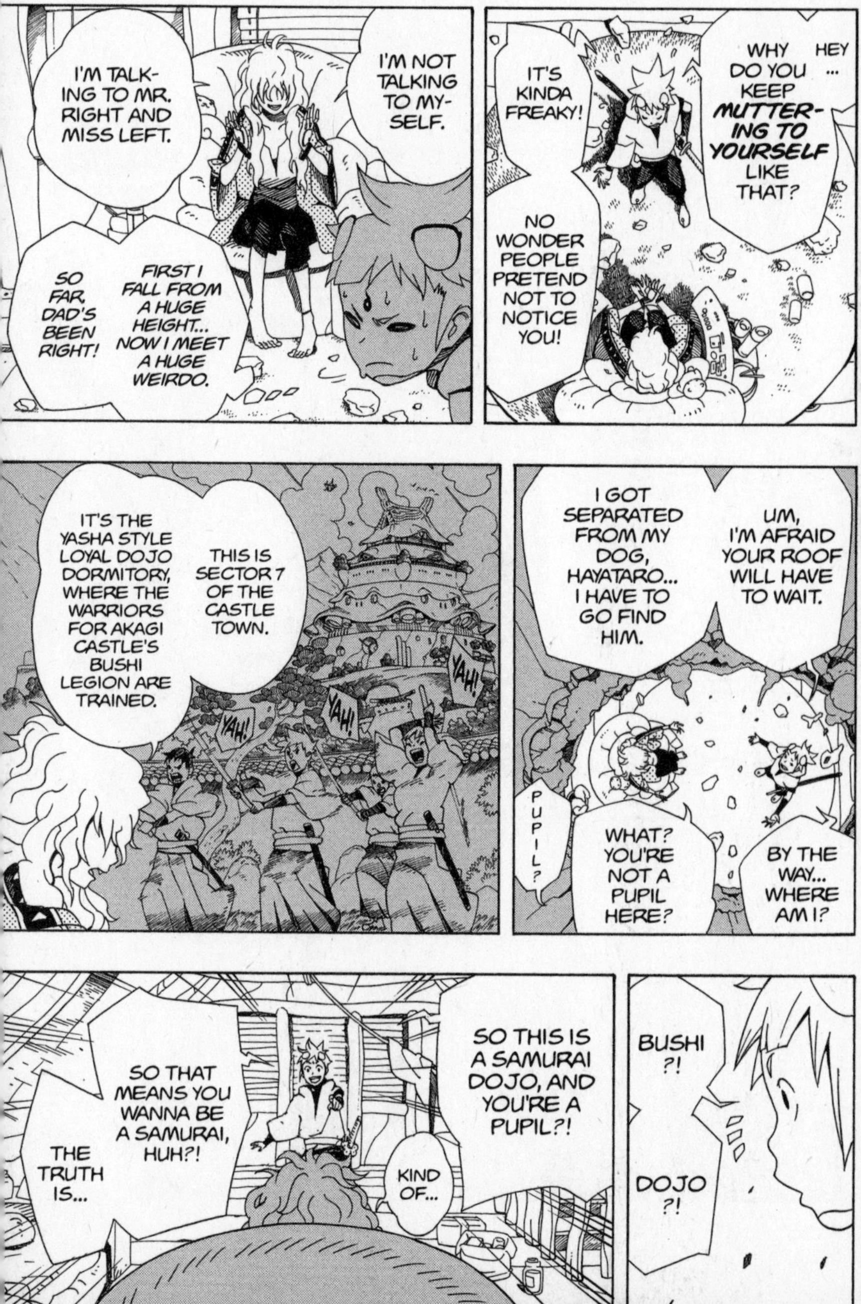
HEY ...
WHY DO YOU KEEP MUTTERING TO YOURSELF LIKE THAT?
IT'S KINDA FREAKY!
NO WONDER PEOPLE PRETEND NOT TO NOTICE YOU!
I'M NOT TALKING TO MYSELF.
I'M TALKING TO MR. RIGHT AND MISS LEFT.
FIRST I FALL FROM A HUGE HEIGHT... NOW I MEET A HUGE WEIRDO.
SO FAR, DAD'S BEEN RIGHT!
UM, I'M AFRAID YOUR ROOF WILL HAVE TO WAIT.
I GOT SEPARATED FROM MY DOG, HAYATARO... I HAVE TO GO FIND HIM.
BY THE WAY... WHERE AM I?
WHAT? YOU'RE NOT A PUPIL HERE?
PUPIL?
THIS IS SECTOR 7 OF THE CASTLE TOWN.
IT'S THE YASHA STYLE LOYAL DOJO DORMITORY, WHERE THE WARRIORS FOR AKAGI CASTLE'S BUSHI LEGION ARE TRAINED.
YAH!
YAH!
YAH!
BUSHI?!
DOJO?!
SO THIS IS A SAMURAI DOJO, AND YOU'RE A PUPIL?!
KIND OF...
SO THAT MEANS YOU WANNA BE A SAMURAI, HUH?!
THE TRUTH IS...

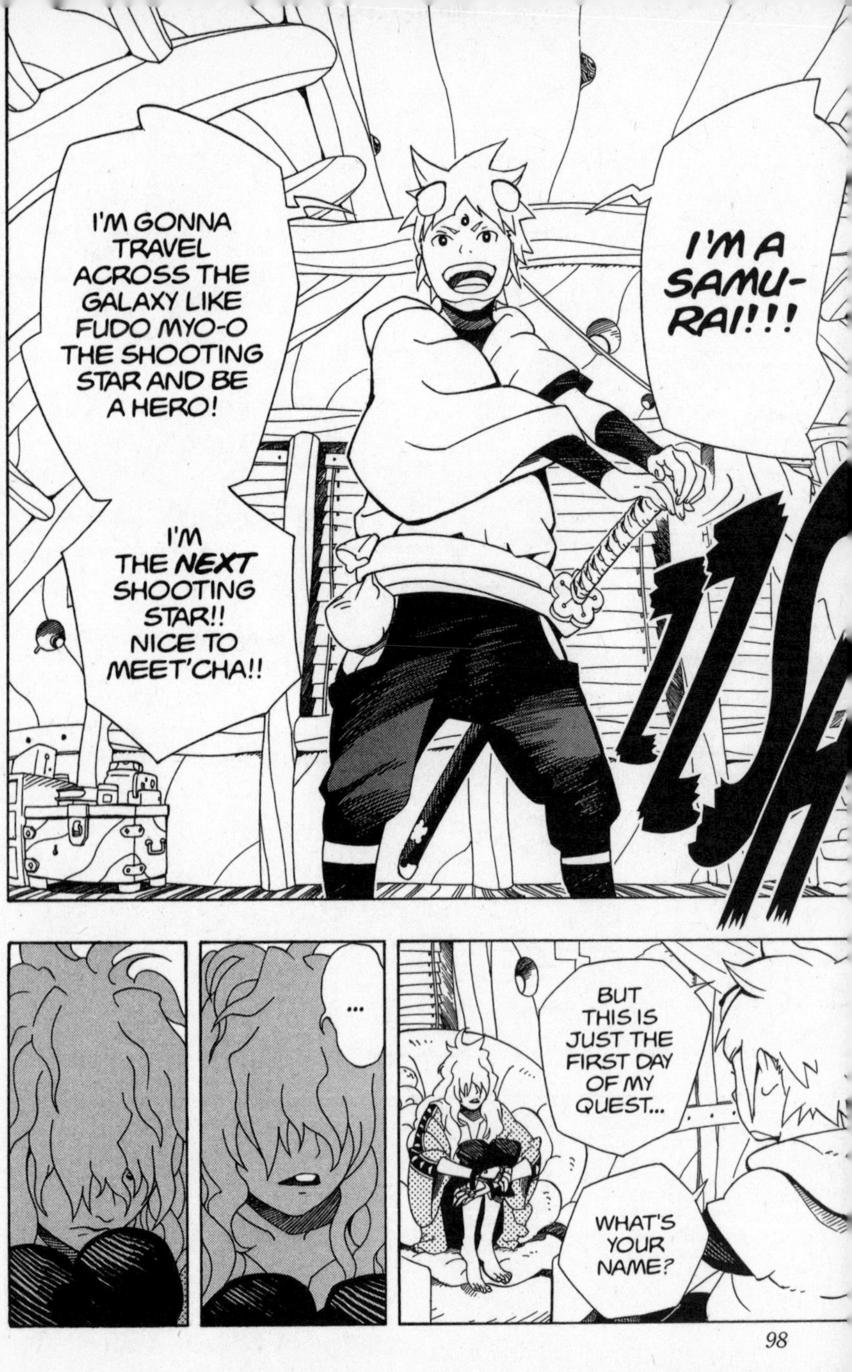
I'M A SAMURAI!!!
I'M GONNA TRAVEL ACROSS THE GALAXY LIKE FUDO MYO-O THE SHOOTING STAR AND BE A HERO!
I'M THE ***NEXT*** SHOOTING STAR!! NICE TO MEET'CHA!!
BUT THIS IS JUST THE FIRST DAY OF MY QUEST...
WHAT'S YOUR NAME?
...

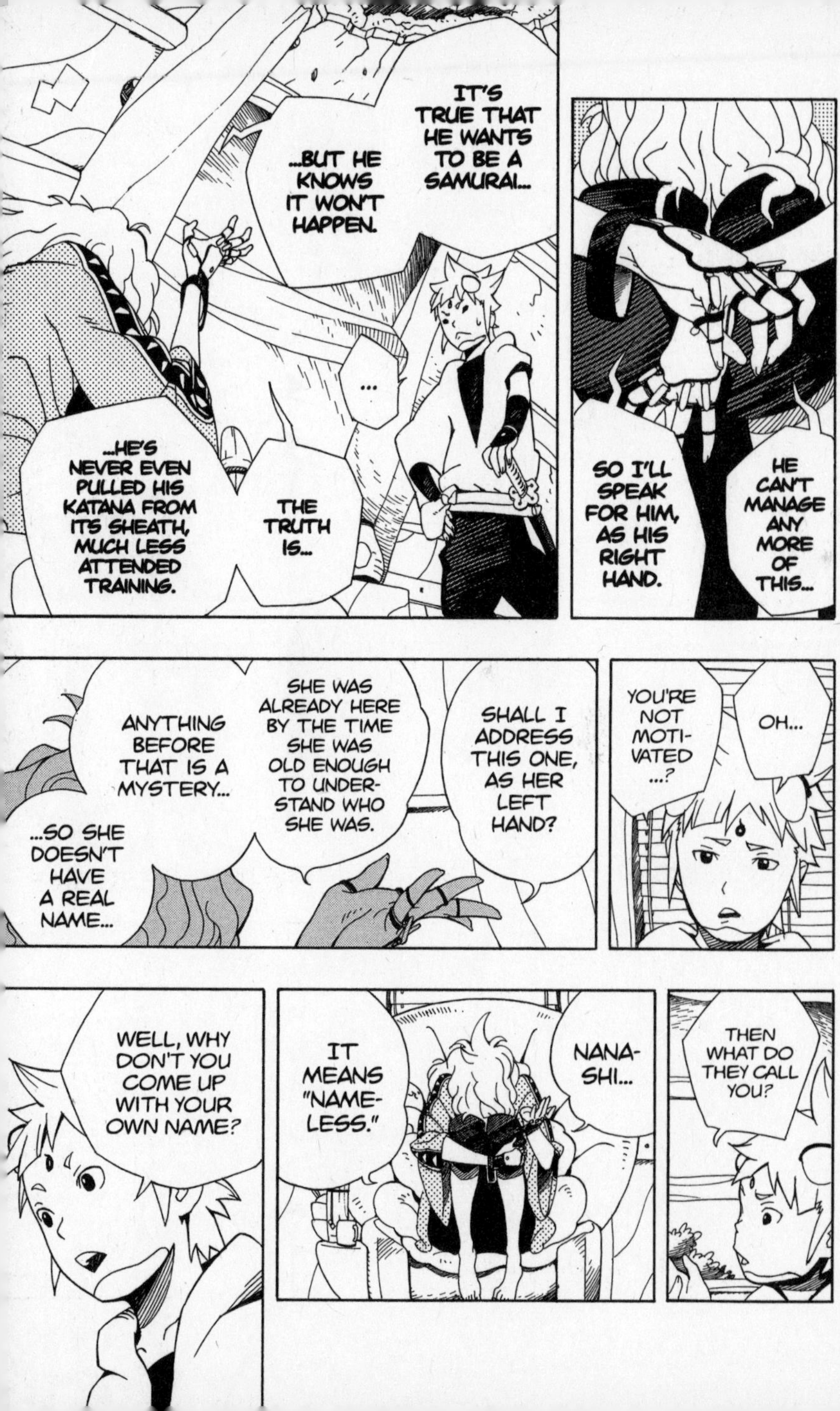
HE CAN'T MANAGE ANY MORE OF THIS...
SO I'LL SPEAK FOR HIM, AS HIS RIGHT HAND.
IT'S TRUE THAT HE WANTS TO BE A SAMURAI...
...BUT HE KNOWS IT WON'T HAPPEN.
...
THE TRUTH IS...
...HE'S NEVER EVEN PULLED HIS KATANA FROM ITS SHEATH, MUCH LESS ATTENDED TRAINING.
OH...
YOU'RE NOT MOTI-VATED ...?
SHALL I ADDRESS THIS ONE, AS HER LEFT HAND?
SHE WAS ALREADY HERE BY THE TIME SHE WAS OLD ENOUGH TO UNDER-STAND WHO SHE WAS.
ANYTHING BEFORE THAT IS A MYSTERY...
...SO SHE DOESN'T HAVE A REAL NAME...
THEN WHAT DO THEY CALL YOU?
NANA-SHI...
IT MEANS "NAME-LESS."
WELL, WHY DON'T YOU COME UP WITH YOUR OWN NAME?

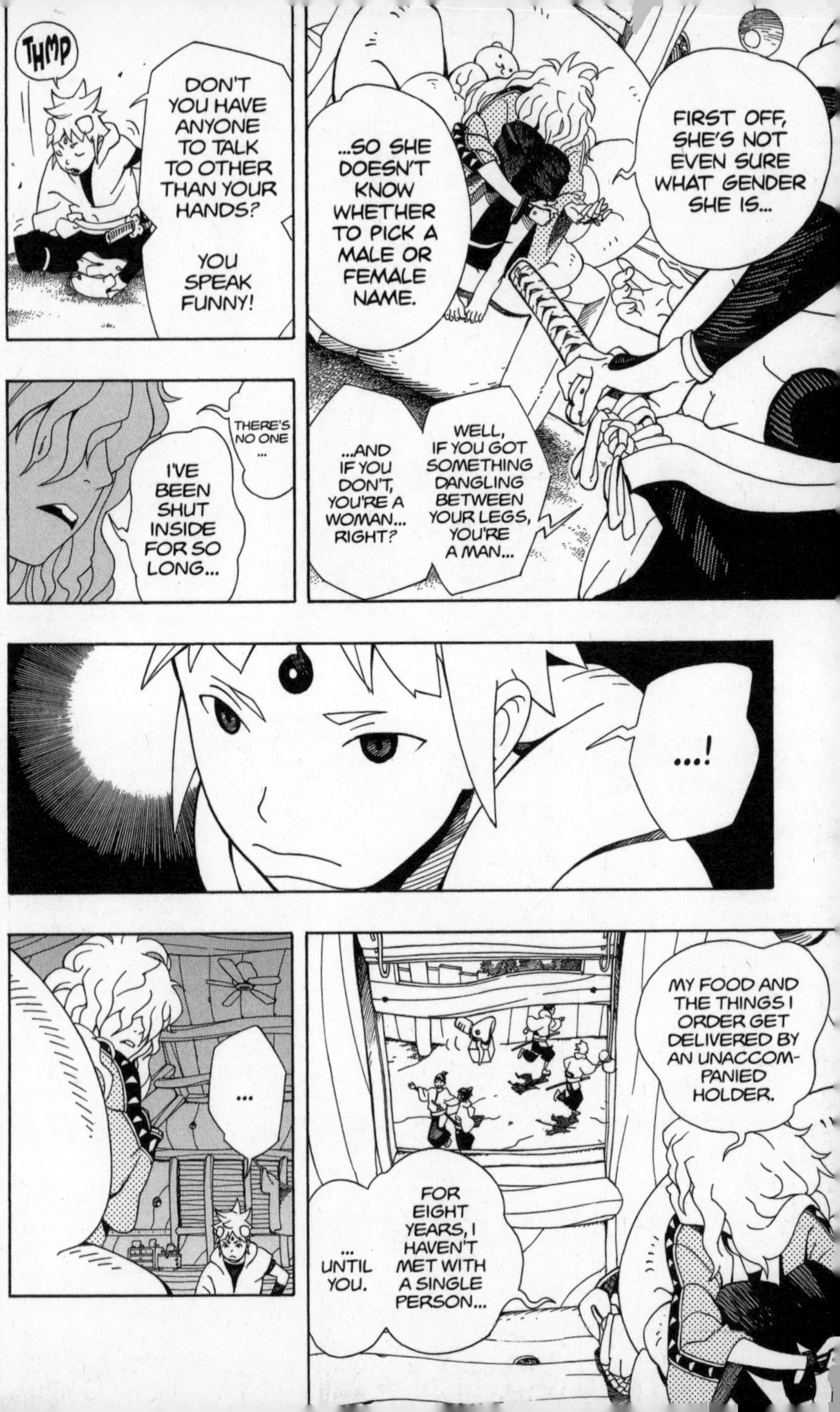
FIRST OFF, SHE'S NOT EVEN SURE WHAT GENDER SHE IS...
...SO SHE DOESN'T KNOW WHETHER TO PICK A MALE OR FEMALE NAME.
WELL, IF YOU GOT SOMETHING DANGLING BETWEEN YOUR LEGS, YOU'RE A MAN...
...AND IF YOU DON'T, YOU'RE A WOMAN... RIGHT?
THMP
DON'T YOU HAVE ANYONE TO TALK TO OTHER THAN YOUR HANDS?
YOU SPEAK FUNNY!
THERE'S NO ONE ...
I'VE BEEN SHUT INSIDE FOR SO LONG...
...!
MY FOOD AND THE THINGS I ORDER GET DELIVERED BY AN UNACCOM-PANIED HOLDER.
FOR EIGHT YEARS, I HAVEN'T MET WITH A SINGLE PERSON...
... UNTIL YOU.
...

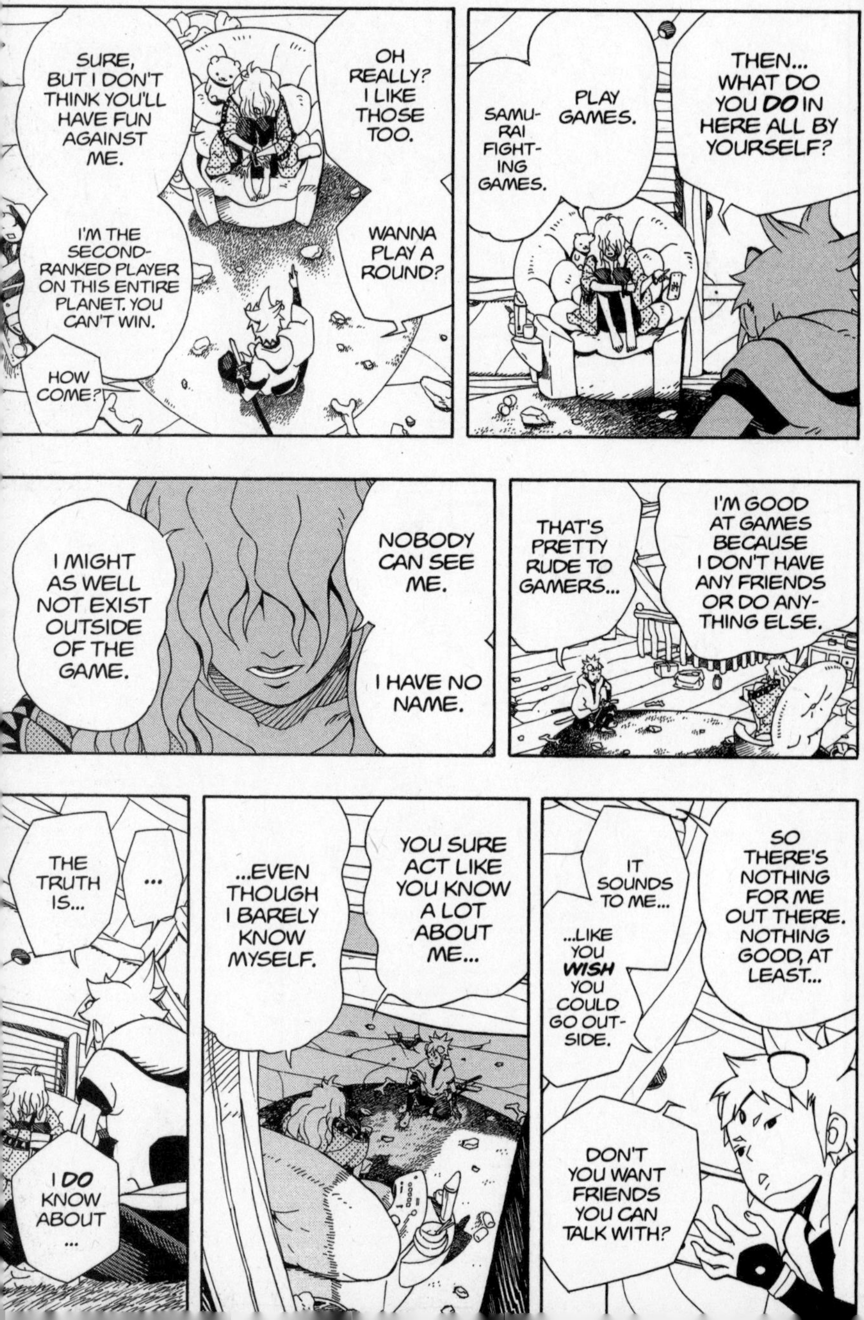
THEN... WHAT DO YOU *DO* IN HERE ALL BY YOURSELF?
PLAY GAMES.
SAMURAI FIGHTING GAMES.
OH REALLY? I LIKE THOSE TOO.
WANNA PLAY A ROUND?
SURE, BUT I DON'T THINK YOU'LL HAVE FUN AGAINST ME.
HOW COME?
I'M THE SECOND-RANKED PLAYER ON THIS ENTIRE PLANET. YOU CAN'T WIN.
I'M GOOD AT GAMES BECAUSE I DON'T HAVE ANY FRIENDS OR DO ANYTHING ELSE.
THAT'S PRETTY RUDE TO GAMERS...
NOBODY CAN SEE ME.
I HAVE NO NAME.
I MIGHT AS WELL NOT EXIST OUTSIDE OF THE GAME.
SO THERE'S NOTHING FOR ME OUT THERE. NOTHING GOOD, AT LEAST...
IT SOUNDS TO ME...
...LIKE YOU *WISH* YOU COULD GO OUTSIDE.
DON'T YOU WANT FRIENDS YOU CAN TALK WITH?
YOU SURE ACT LIKE YOU KNOW A LOT ABOUT ME...
...EVEN THOUGH I BARELY KNOW MYSELF.
...
THE TRUTH IS...
I *DO* KNOW ABOUT ...

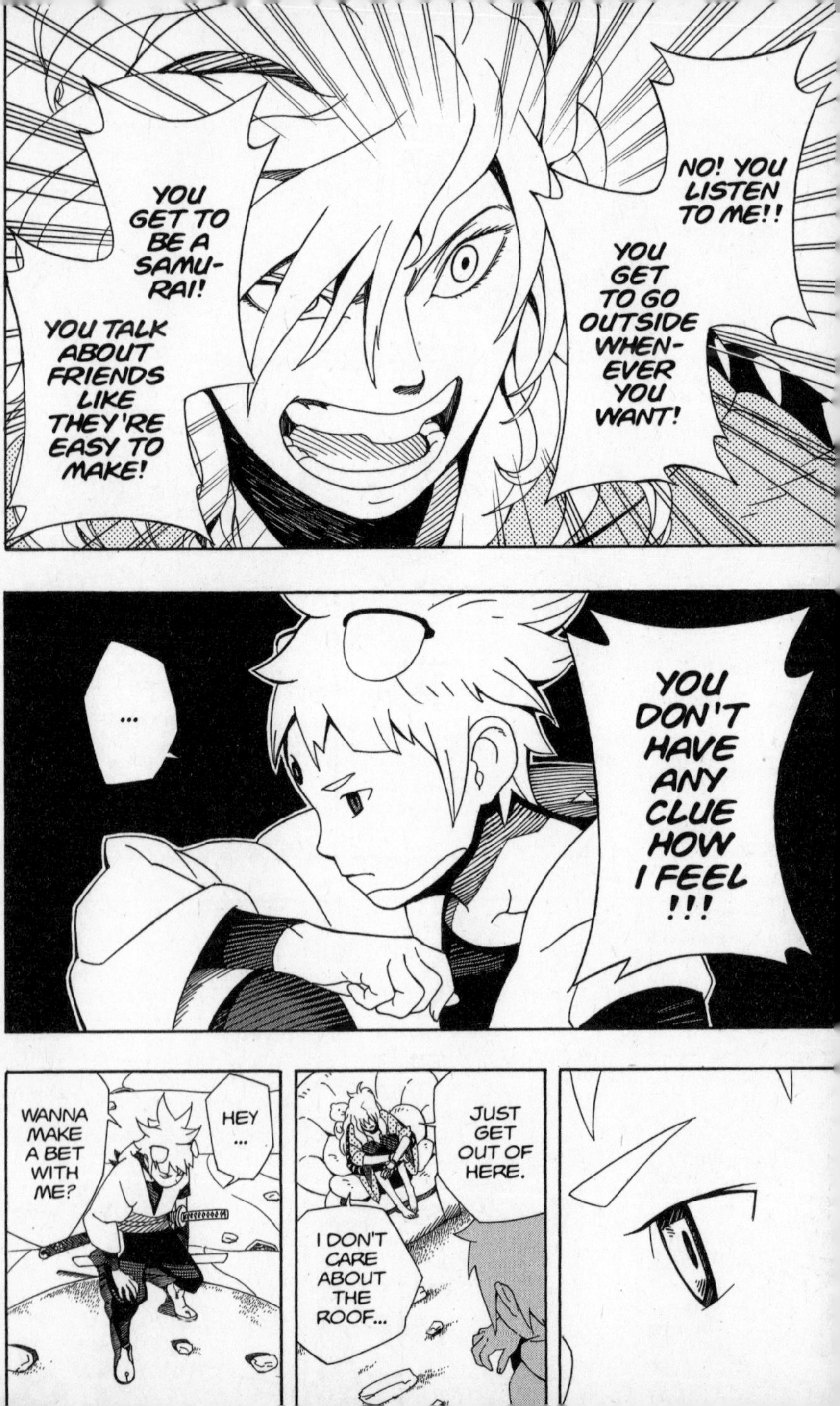
NO! YOU LISTEN TO ME!!
YOU GET TO GO OUTSIDE WHEN-EVER YOU WANT!
YOU GET TO BE A SAMU-RAI!
YOU TALK ABOUT FRIENDS LIKE THEY'RE EASY TO MAKE!
YOU DON'T HAVE ANY CLUE HOW I FEEL!!!
...
JUST GET OUT OF HERE.
I DON'T CARE ABOUT THE ROOF...
HEY...
WANNA MAKE A BET WITH ME?

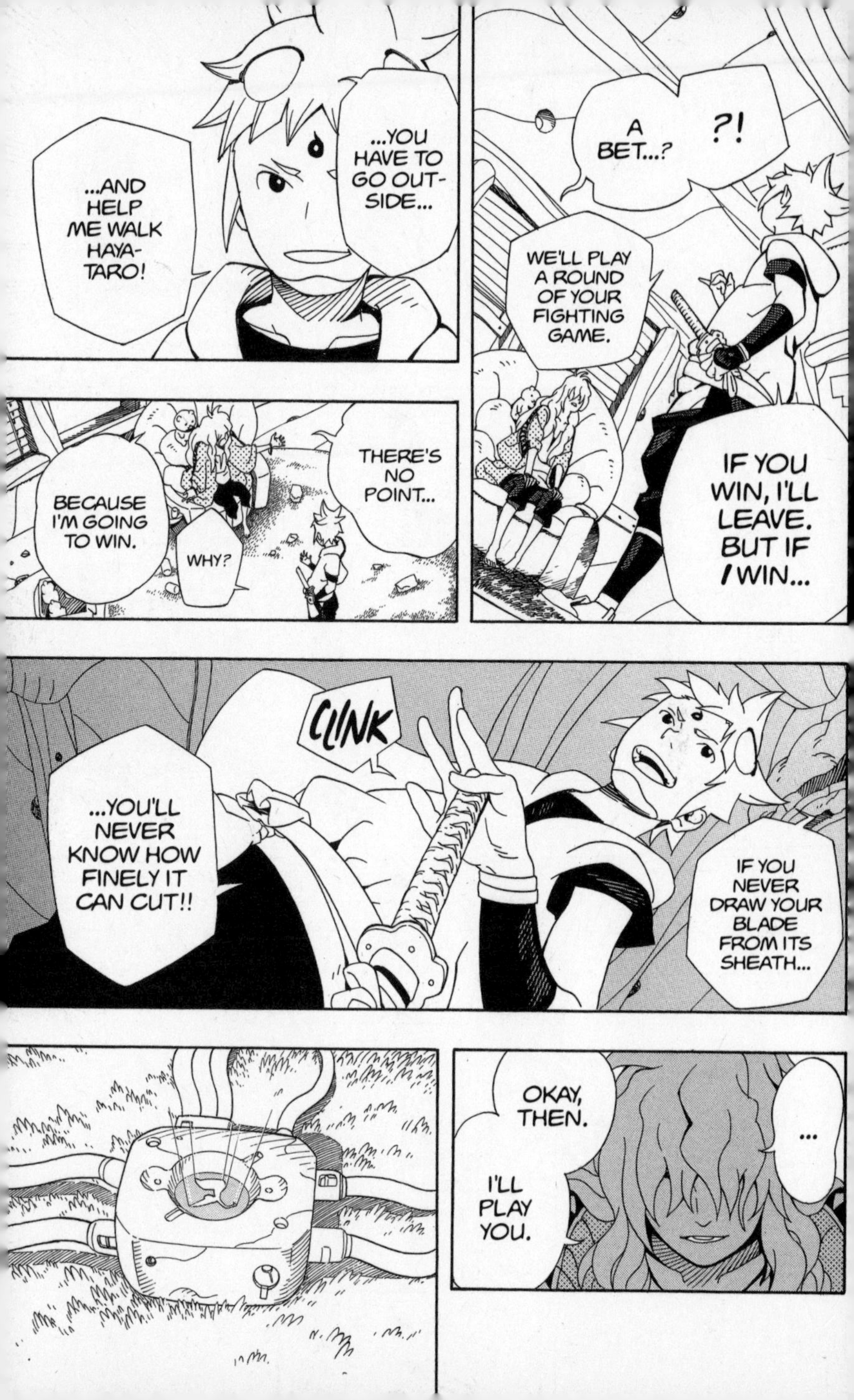
?!
A BET...?
WE'LL PLAY A ROUND OF YOUR FIGHTING GAME.
IF YOU WIN, I'LL LEAVE. BUT IF I WIN...
...YOU HAVE TO GO OUT-SIDE...
...AND HELP ME WALK HAYA-TARO!
THERE'S NO POINT...
WHY?
BECAUSE I'M GOING TO WIN.
IF YOU NEVER DRAW YOUR BLADE FROM ITS SHEATH...
CLINK
...YOU'LL NEVER KNOW HOW FINELY IT CAN CUT!!
...
OKAY, THEN.
I'LL PLAY YOU.

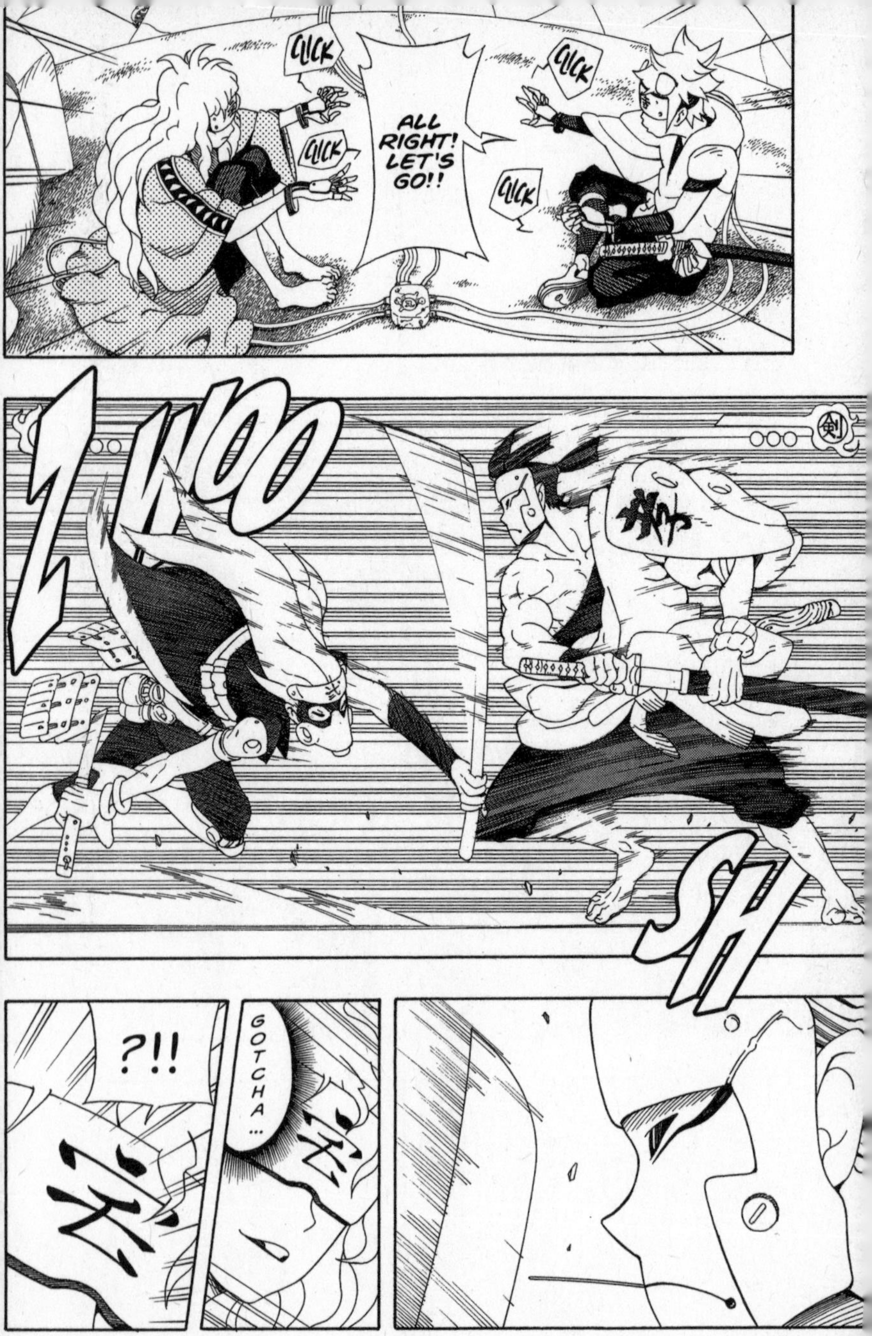
CLICK
CLICK
ALL RIGHT! LET'S GO!!
CLICK
CLICK
ZWOO
SH
GOTCHA...
?!!

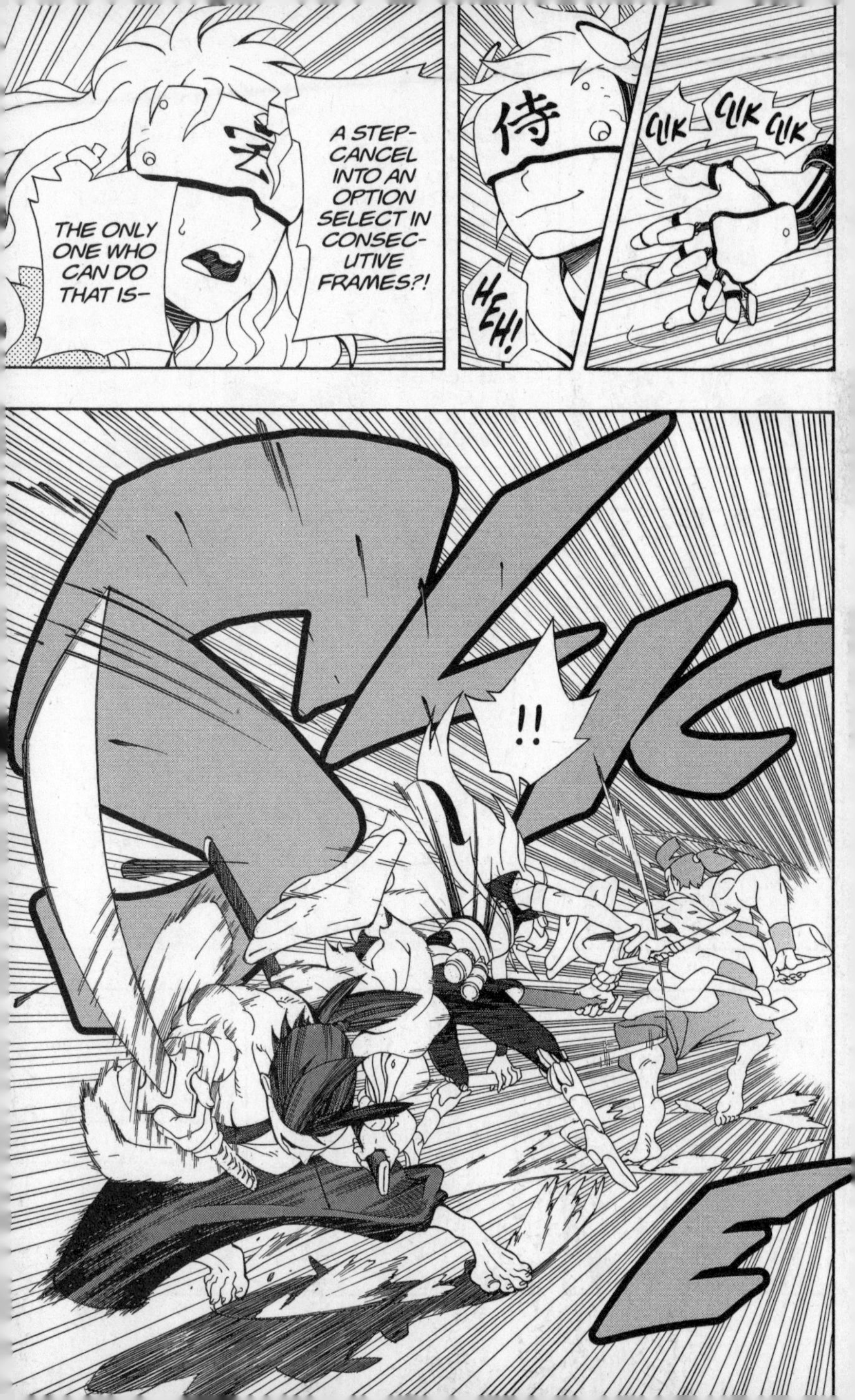
CLIK CLIK CLIK CLIK
侍
HEH!
A STEP-CANCEL INTO AN OPTION SELECT IN CONSECUTIVE FRAMES?!
THE ONLY ONE WHO CAN DO THAT IS-
!!

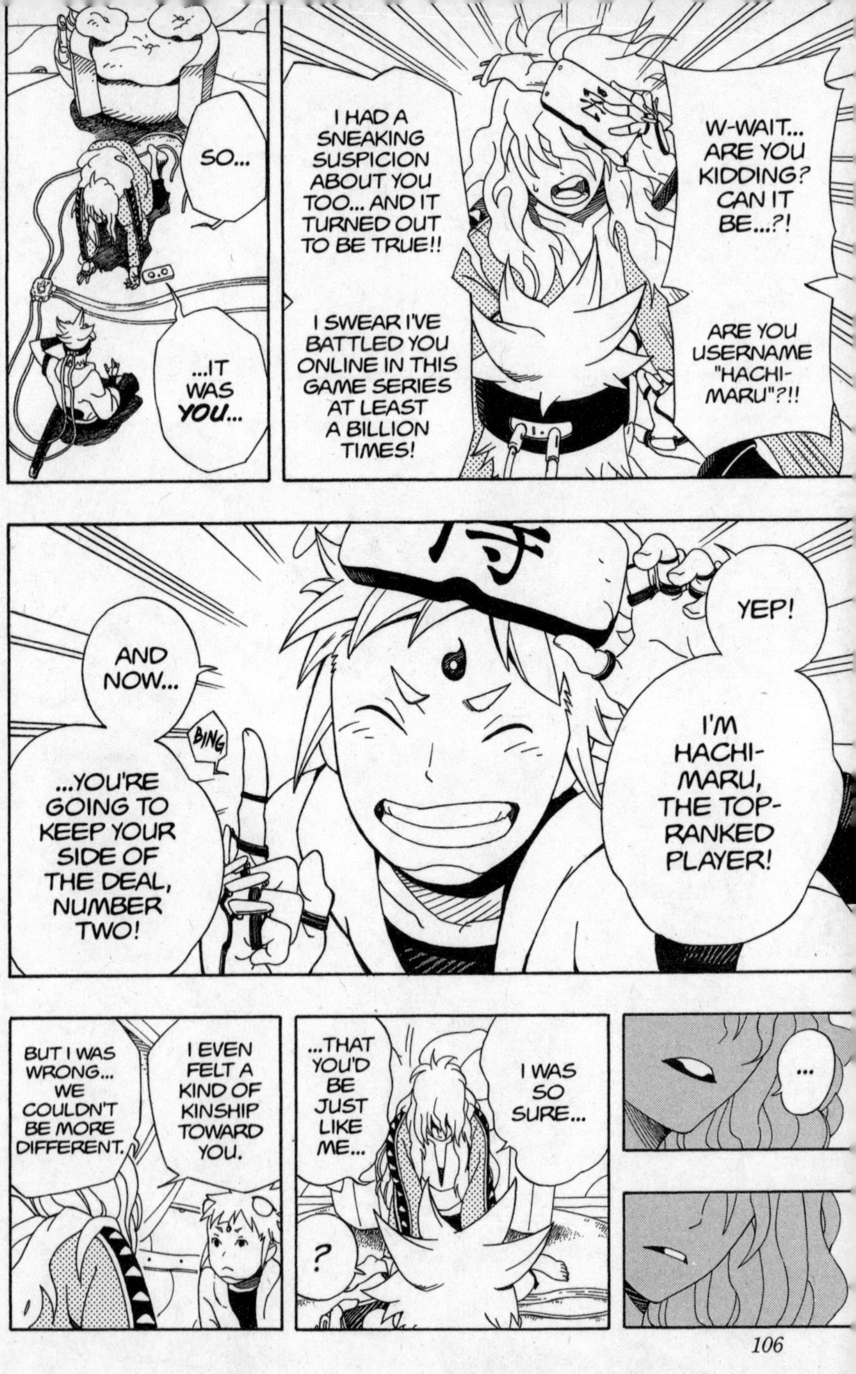
W-WAIT... ARE YOU KIDDING? CAN IT BE...?!
ARE YOU USERNAME "HACHI-MARU"?!!
I HAD A SNEAKING SUSPICION ABOUT YOU TOO... AND IT TURNED OUT TO BE TRUE!!
I SWEAR I'VE BATTLED YOU ONLINE IN THIS GAME SERIES AT LEAST A BILLION TIMES!
SO...
...IT WAS *YOU*...
YEP!
I'M HACHI-MARU, THE TOP-RANKED PLAYER!
AND NOW...
...YOU'RE GOING TO KEEP YOUR SIDE OF THE DEAL, NUMBER TWO!
BING
...
I WAS SO SURE...
...THAT YOU'D BE JUST LIKE ME...
?
I EVEN FELT A KIND OF KINSHIP TOWARD YOU.
BUT I WAS WRONG... WE COULDN'T BE MORE DIFFERENT.

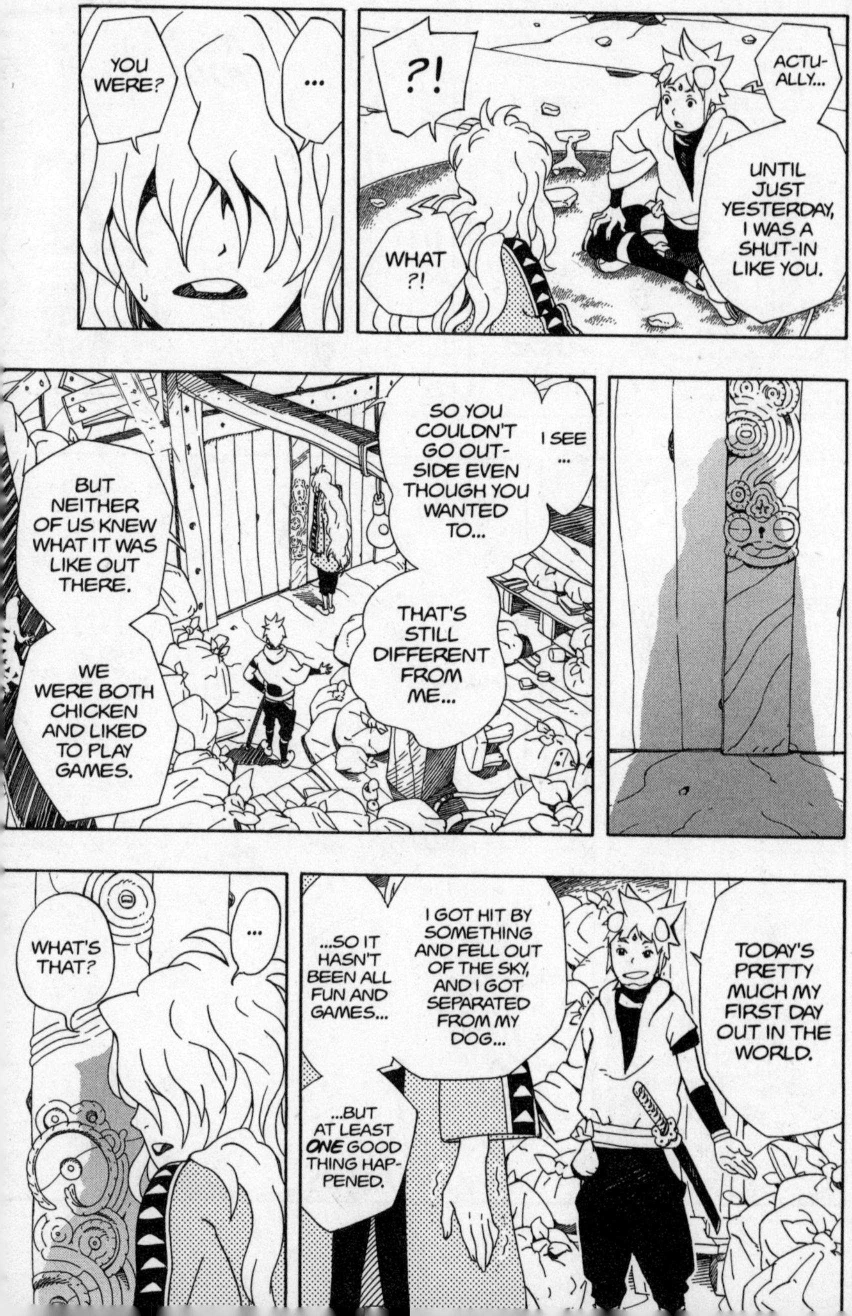
ACTU-ALLY...
?!
UNTIL JUST YESTERDAY, I WAS A SHUT-IN LIKE YOU.
WHAT ?!
...
YOU WERE?
I SEE ...
SO YOU COULDN'T GO OUT-SIDE EVEN THOUGH YOU WANTED TO...
THAT'S STILL DIFFERENT FROM ME...
BUT NEITHER OF US KNEW WHAT IT WAS LIKE OUT THERE.
WE WERE BOTH CHICKEN AND LIKED TO PLAY GAMES.
TODAY'S PRETTY MUCH MY FIRST DAY OUT IN THE WORLD.
I GOT HIT BY SOMETHING AND FELL OUT OF THE SKY, AND I GOT SEPARATED FROM MY DOG...
...SO IT HASN'T BEEN ALL FUN AND GAMES...
...BUT AT LEAST *ONE* GOOD THING HAP-PENED.
...
WHAT'S THAT?

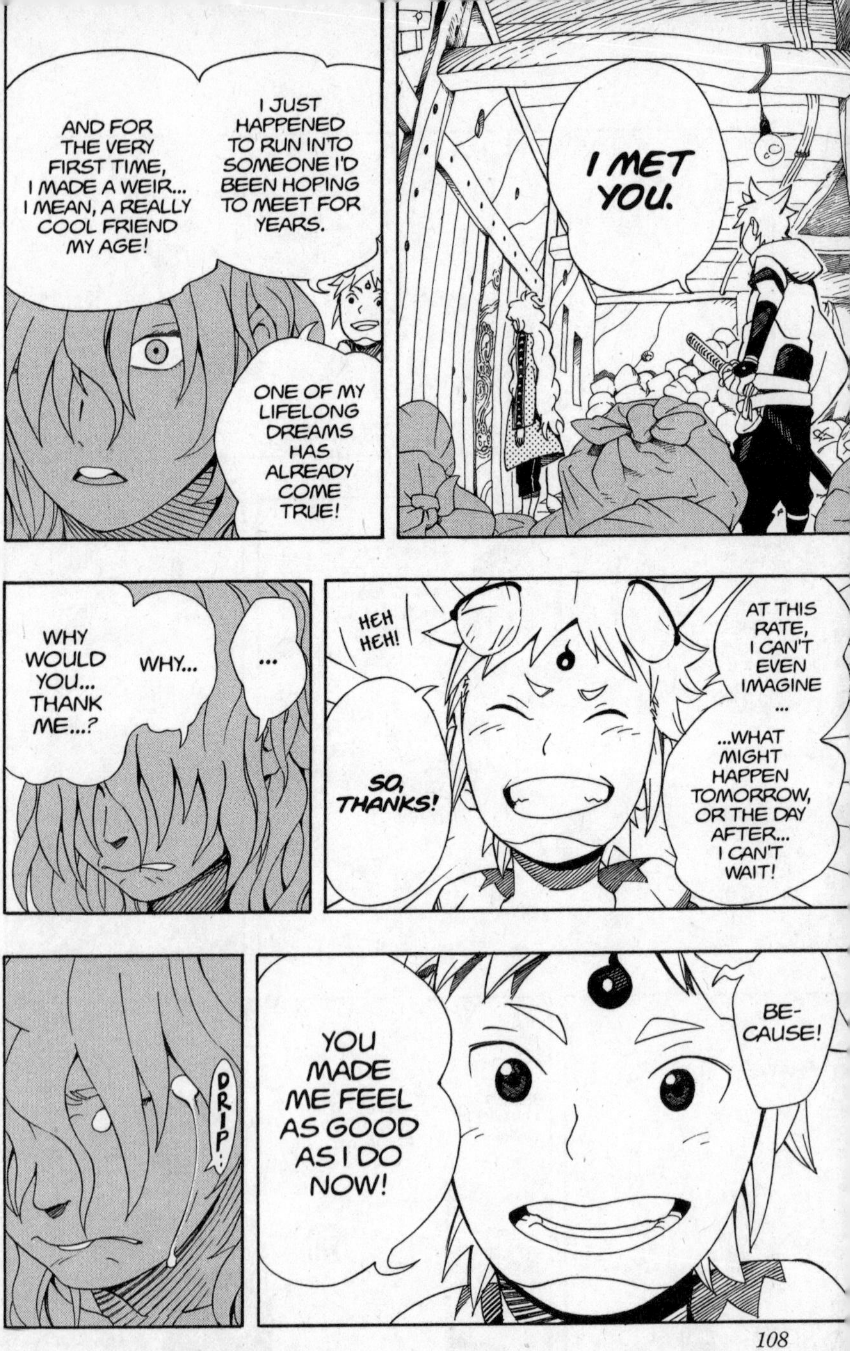
I MET YOU.
I JUST HAPPENED TO RUN INTO SOMEONE I'D BEEN HOPING TO MEET FOR YEARS.
AND FOR THE VERY FIRST TIME, I MADE A WEIR... I MEAN, A REALLY COOL FRIEND MY AGE!
ONE OF MY LIFELONG DREAMS HAS ALREADY COME TRUE!
AT THIS RATE, I CAN'T EVEN IMAGINE...
...WHAT MIGHT HAPPEN TOMORROW, OR THE DAY AFTER... I CAN'T WAIT!
HEH HEH!
SO, THANKS!
...
WHY...
WHY WOULD YOU... THANK ME...?
BE-CAUSE!
YOU MADE ME FEEL AS GOOD AS I DO NOW!
DRIP...

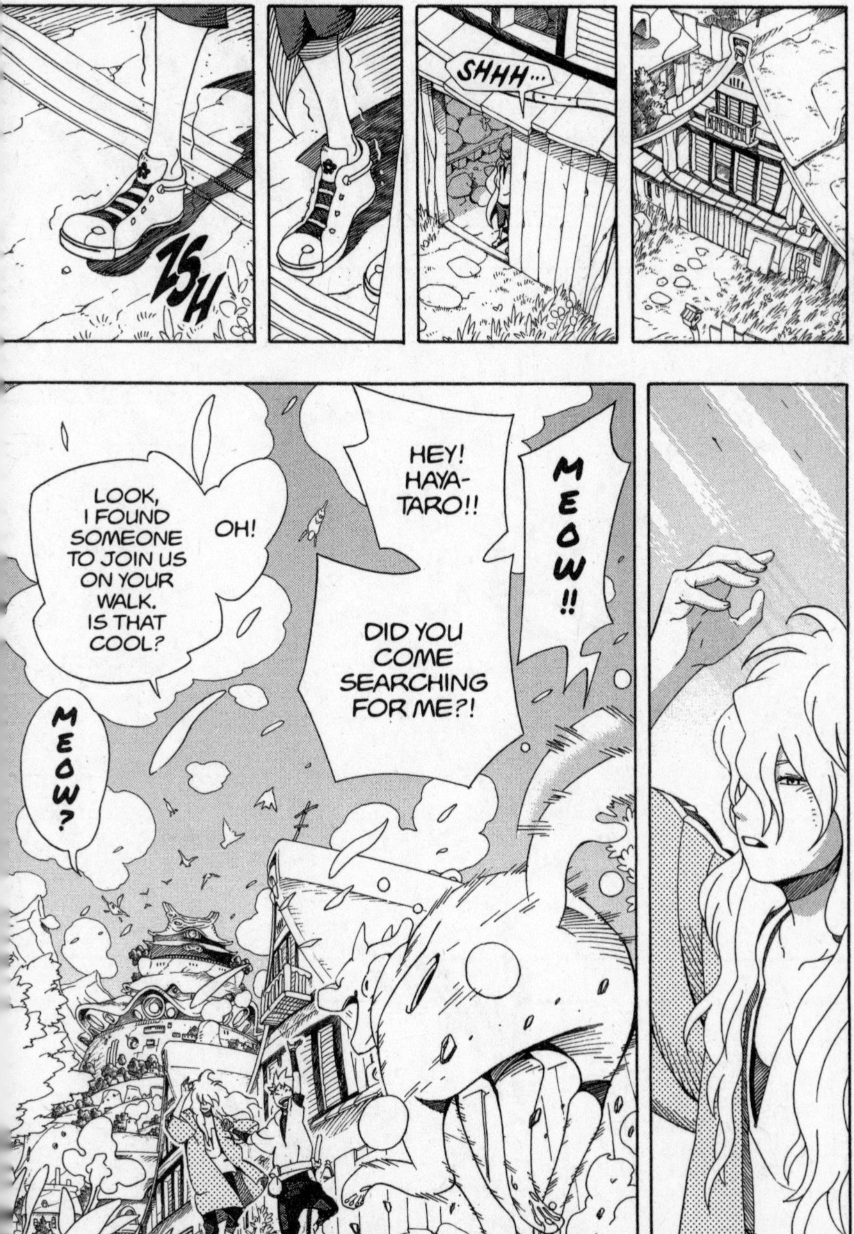
SHHH...
ZSH
MEOW!!
HEY! HAYA-TARO!!
DID YOU COME SEARCHING FOR ME?!
OH!
LOOK, I FOUND SOMEONE TO JOIN US ON YOUR WALK. IS THAT COOL?
MEOW?

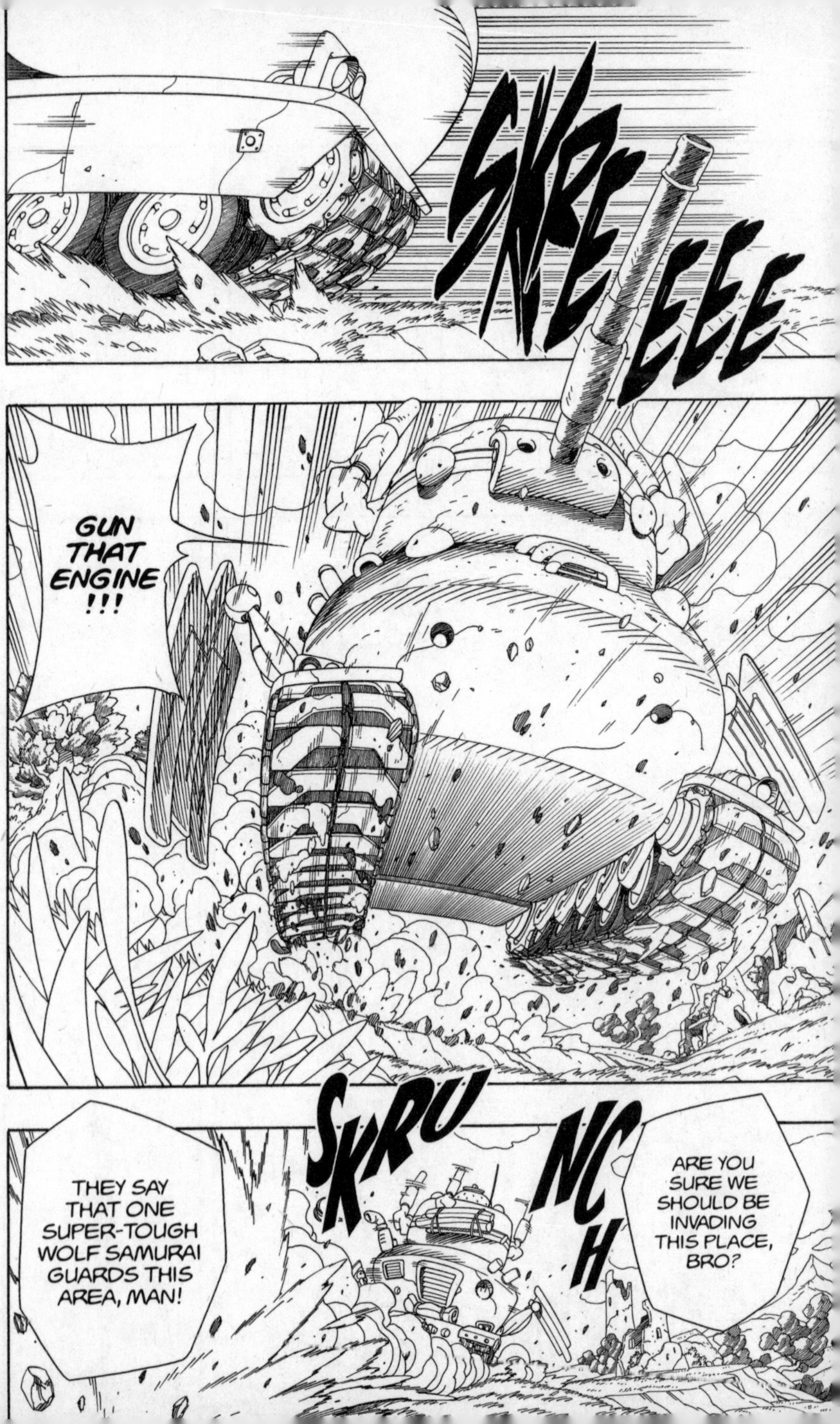
SKREEEEE
GUN THAT ENGINE!!!
SKRUNCH
ARE YOU SURE WE SHOULD BE INVADING THIS PLACE, BRO?
THEY SAY THAT ONE SUPER-TOUGH WOLF SAMURAI GUARDS THIS AREA, MAN!

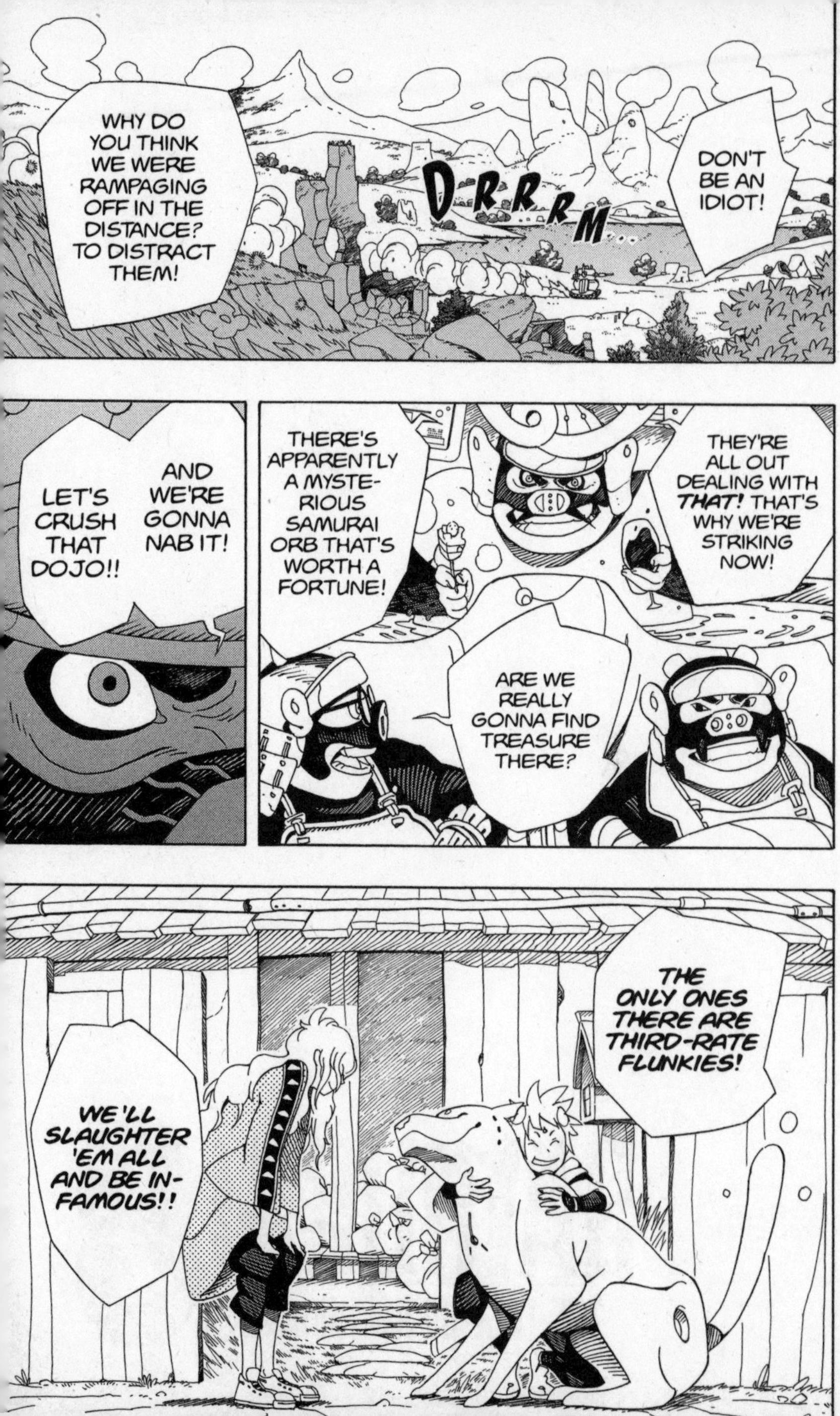
DON'T BE AN IDIOT!
WHY DO YOU THINK WE WERE RAMPAGING OFF IN THE DISTANCE? TO DISTRACT THEM!
DRRRRM
THEY'RE ALL OUT DEALING WITH THAT! THAT'S WHY WE'RE STRIKING NOW!
THERE'S APPARENTLY A MYSTE-RIOUS SAMURAI ORB THAT'S WORTH A FORTUNE!
ARE WE REALLY GONNA FIND TREASURE THERE?
AND WE'RE GONNA NAB IT!
LET'S CRUSH THAT DOJO!!
THE ONLY ONES THERE ARE THIRD-RATE FLUNKIES!
WE'LL SLAUGHTER 'EM ALL AND BE IN-FAMOUS!!

SAMURAI 8
THE TALE OF HACHIMARU

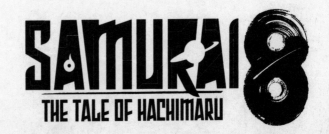

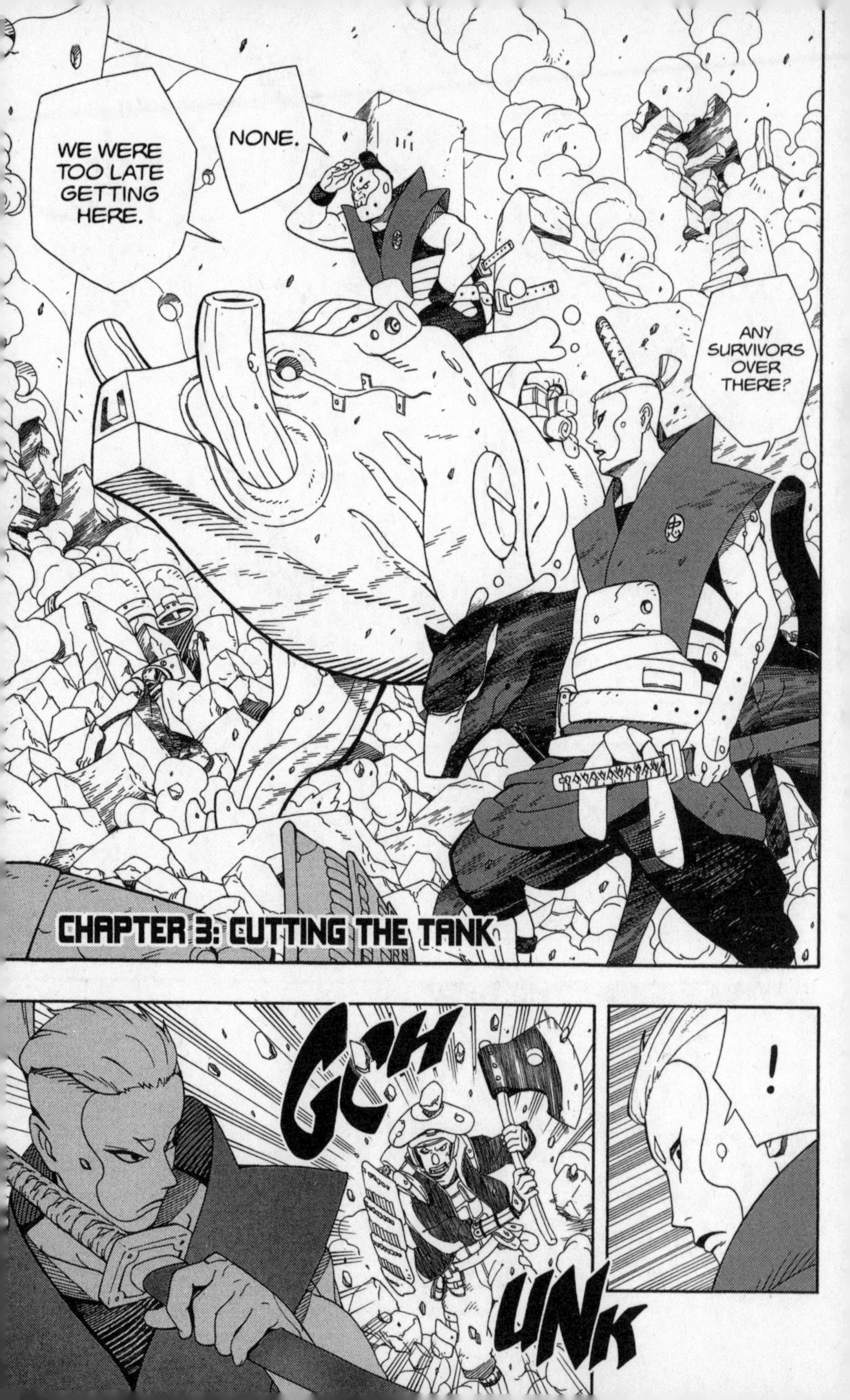
ANY SURVIVORS OVER THERE?
NONE.
WE WERE TOO LATE GETTING HERE.
CHAPTER 3: CUTTING THE TANK
!
GCH
UNK

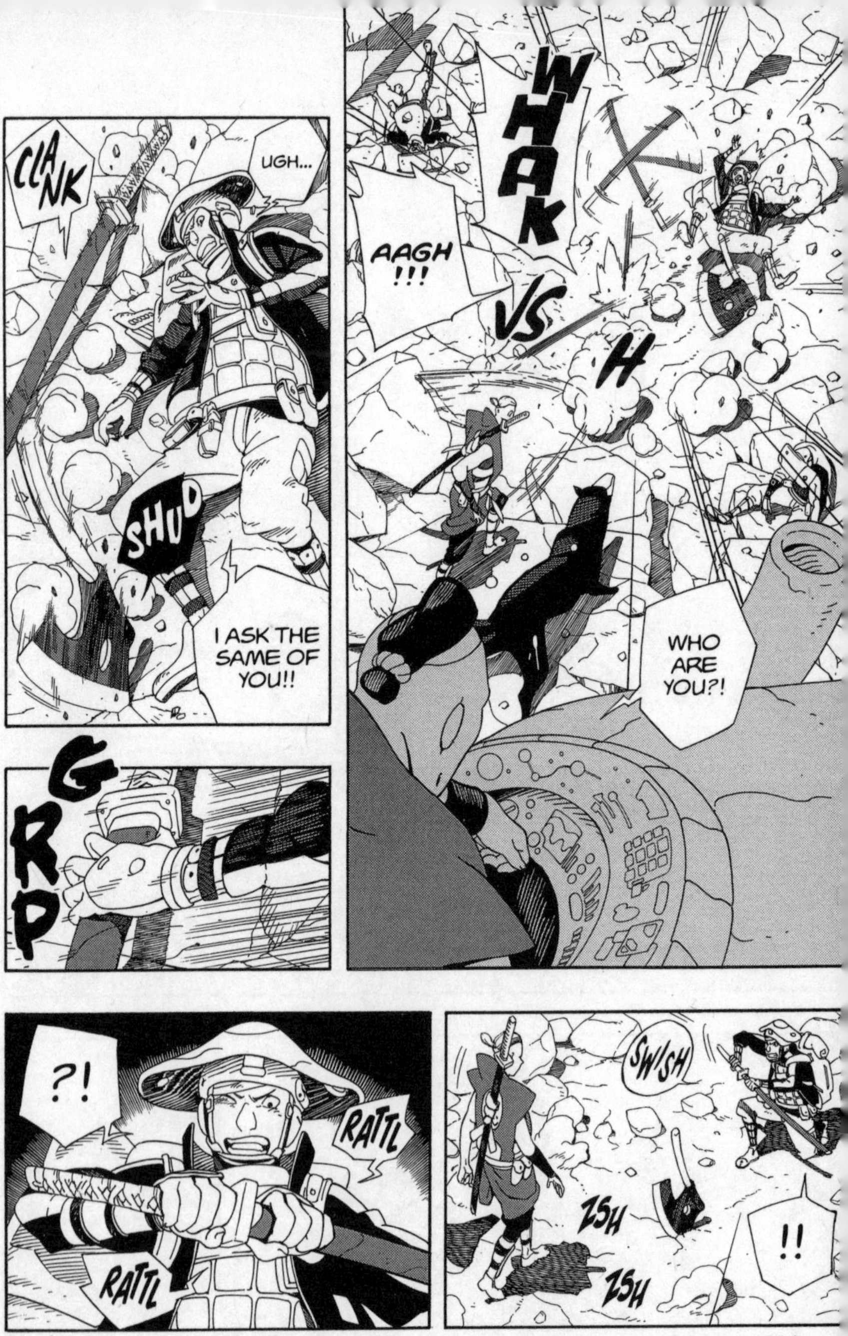
WHAK
AAGH!!!
VSH
WHO ARE YOU?!
UGH...
CLANK
SHUD
I ASK THE SAME OF YOU!!
GRP
SWISH
!!
ZSH
ZSH
?!
RATTL
RATTL

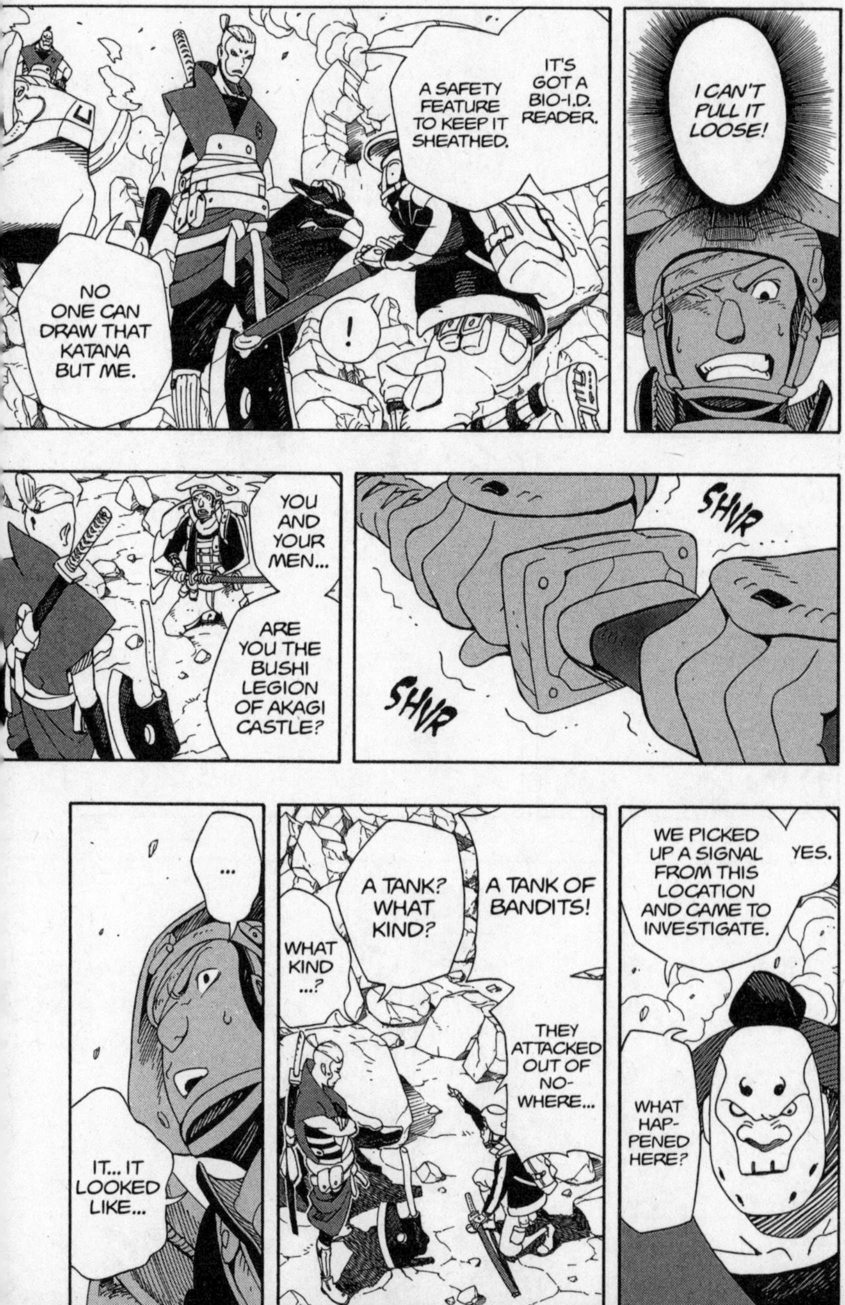

I CAN'T PULL IT LOOSE!
IT'S GOT A BIO-I.D. READER.
A SAFETY FEATURE TO KEEP IT SHEATHED.
!
NO ONE CAN DRAW THAT KATANA BUT ME.
SHVR
SHVR
YOU AND YOUR MEN...
ARE YOU THE BUSHI LEGION OF AKAGI CASTLE?
YES.
WE PICKED UP A SIGNAL FROM THIS LOCATION AND CAME TO INVESTIGATE.
WHAT HAPPENED HERE?
A TANK OF BANDITS!
A TANK? WHAT KIND?
WHAT KIND ...?
THEY ATTACKED OUT OF NO-WHERE...
...
IT... IT LOOKED LIKE...

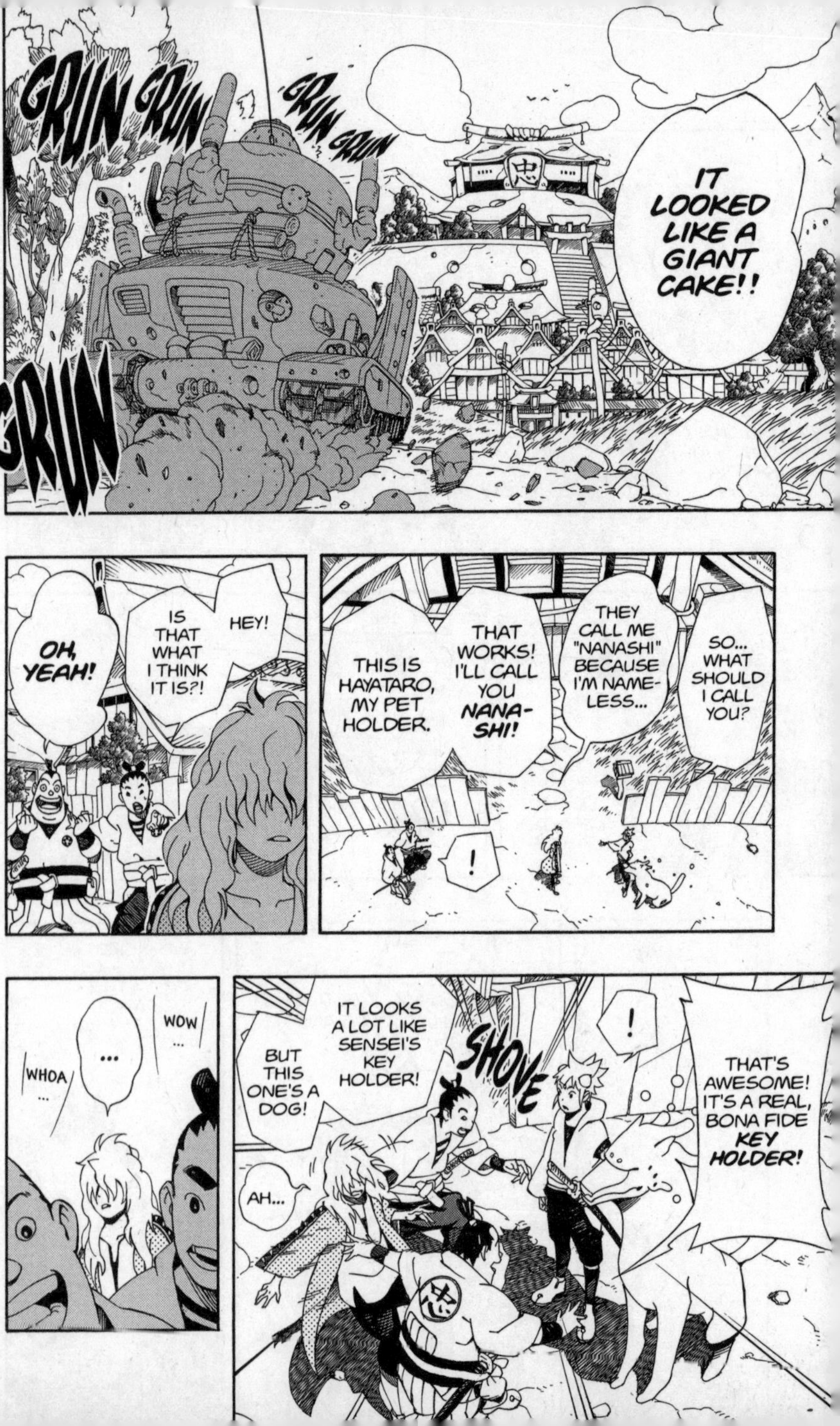
IT LOOKED LIKE A GIANT CAKE!!
GRUN GRUN
GRUN GRUN
GRUN
SO... WHAT SHOULD I CALL YOU?
THEY CALL ME "NANASHI" BECAUSE I'M NAME-LESS...
THAT WORKS! I'LL CALL YOU NANA-SHI!
THIS IS HAYATARO, MY PET HOLDER.
!
HEY!
IS THAT WHAT I THINK IT IS?!
OH, YEAH!
THAT'S AWESOME! IT'S A REAL, BONA FIDE KEY HOLDER!
!
SHOVE
IT LOOKS A LOT LIKE SENSEI'S KEY HOLDER!
BUT THIS ONE'S A DOG!
AH...
WOW ...
...
WHOA ...

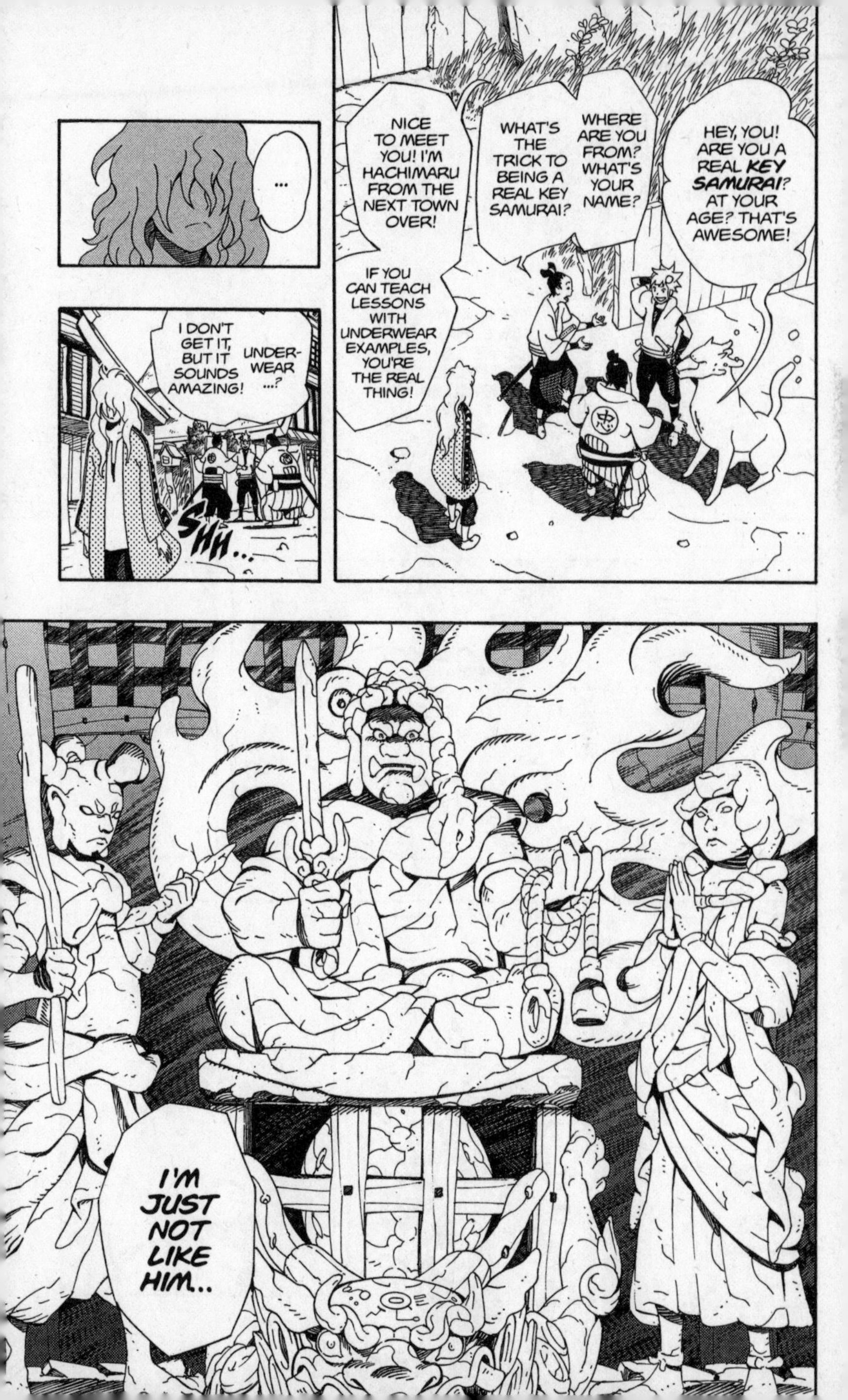
HEY, YOU! ARE YOU A REAL KEY SAMURAI? AT YOUR AGE? THAT'S AWESOME!
WHERE ARE YOU FROM? WHAT'S YOUR NAME?
WHAT'S THE TRICK TO BEING A REAL KEY SAMURAI?
NICE TO MEET YOU! I'M HACHIMARU FROM THE NEXT TOWN OVER!
IF YOU CAN TEACH LESSONS WITH UNDERWEAR EXAMPLES, YOU'RE THE REAL THING!
...
UNDER-WEAR ...?
I DON'T GET IT, BUT IT SOUNDS AMAZING!
SHH...
I'M JUST NOT LIKE HIM...

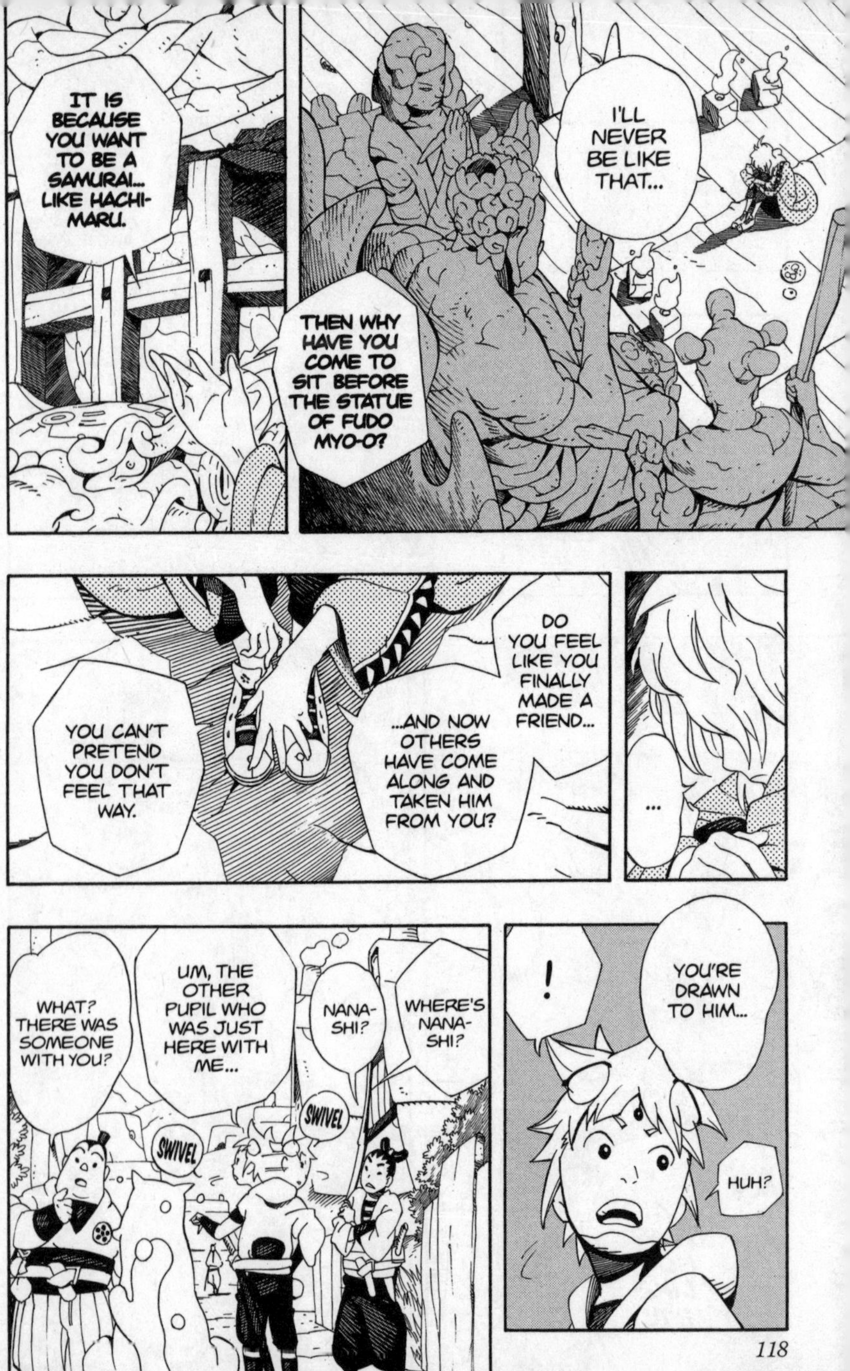
I'LL NEVER BE LIKE THAT...
THEN WHY HAVE YOU COME TO SIT BEFORE THE STATUE OF FUDO MYO-O?
IT IS BECAUSE YOU WANT TO BE A SAMURAI... LIKE HACHI-MARU.
...
DO YOU FEEL LIKE YOU FINALLY MADE A FRIEND...
...AND NOW OTHERS HAVE COME ALONG AND TAKEN HIM FROM YOU?
YOU CAN'T PRETEND YOU DON'T FEEL THAT WAY.
YOU'RE DRAWN TO HIM...
!
HUH?
WHERE'S NANA-SHI?
NANA-SHI?
SWIVEL
UM, THE OTHER PUPIL WHO WAS JUST HERE WITH ME...
SWIVEL
WHAT? THERE WAS SOMEONE WITH YOU?

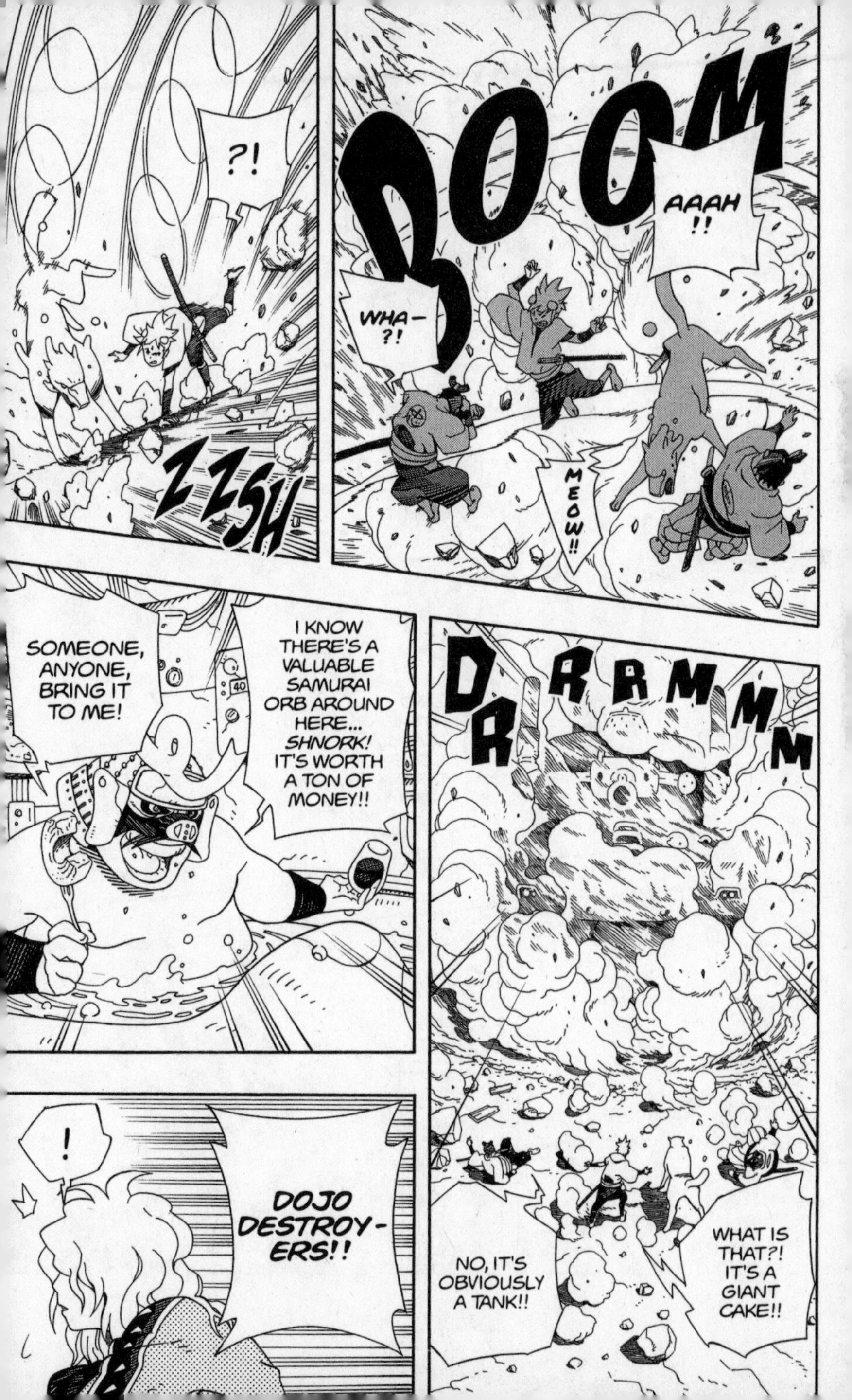
BOOM
AAAH!!
WHA-?!
MEOW!!
?!
ZZSH
DRRRMMMM
WHAT IS THAT?! IT'S A GIANT CAKE!!
NO, IT'S OBVIOUSLY A TANK!!
I KNOW THERE'S A VALUABLE SAMURAI ORB AROUND HERE... SHNORK! IT'S WORTH A TON OF MONEY!!
SOMEONE, ANYONE, BRING IT TO ME!
DOJO DESTROYERS!!
!

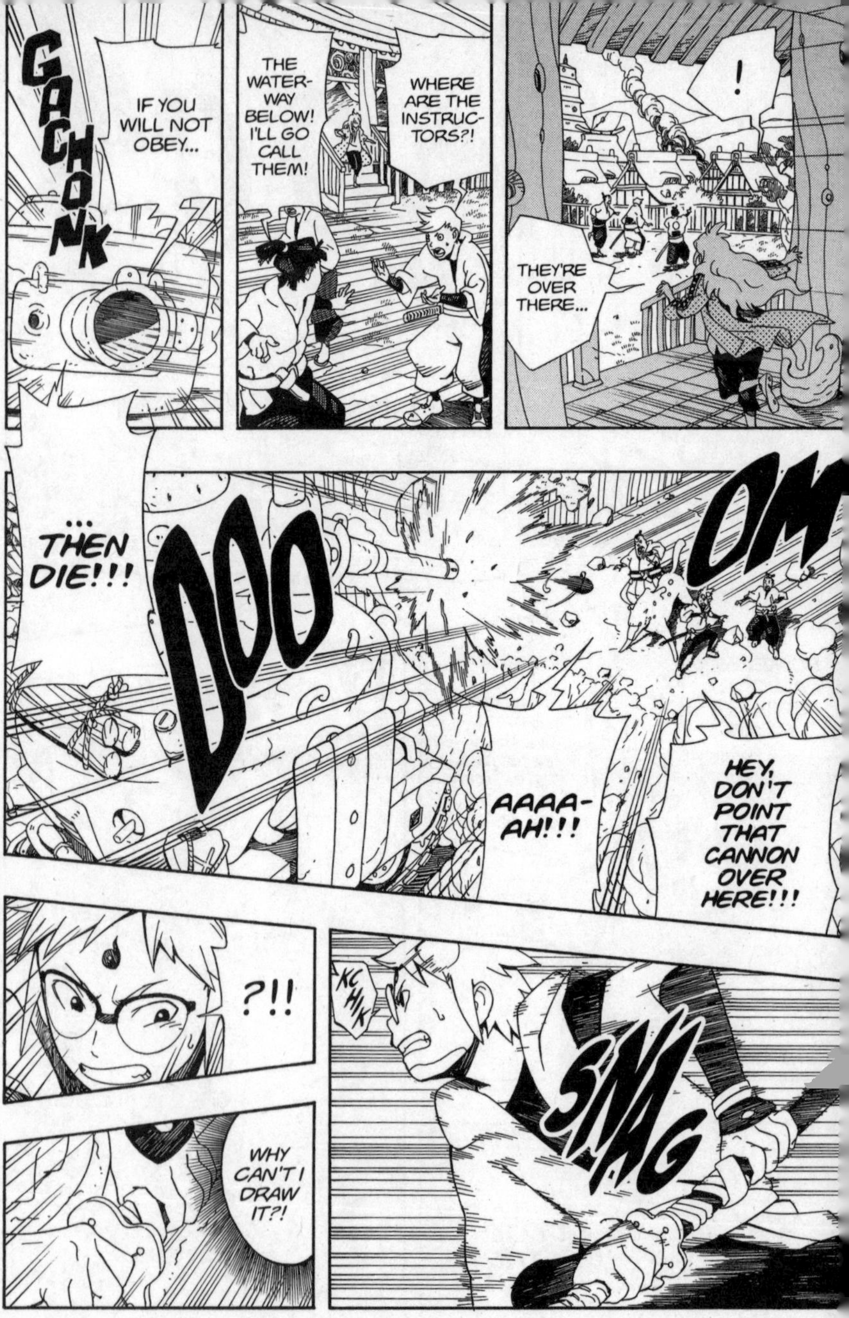
!
THEY'RE OVER THERE...
WHERE ARE THE INSTRUCTORS?!
THE WATER-WAY BELOW! I'LL GO CALL THEM!
IF YOU WILL NOT OBEY...
GACHONK
...THEN DIE!!!
DOOOM
HEY, DON'T POINT THAT CANNON OVER HERE!!!
AAAA-AH!!!
KCHIK
SHING
?!!
WHY CAN'T I DRAW IT?!

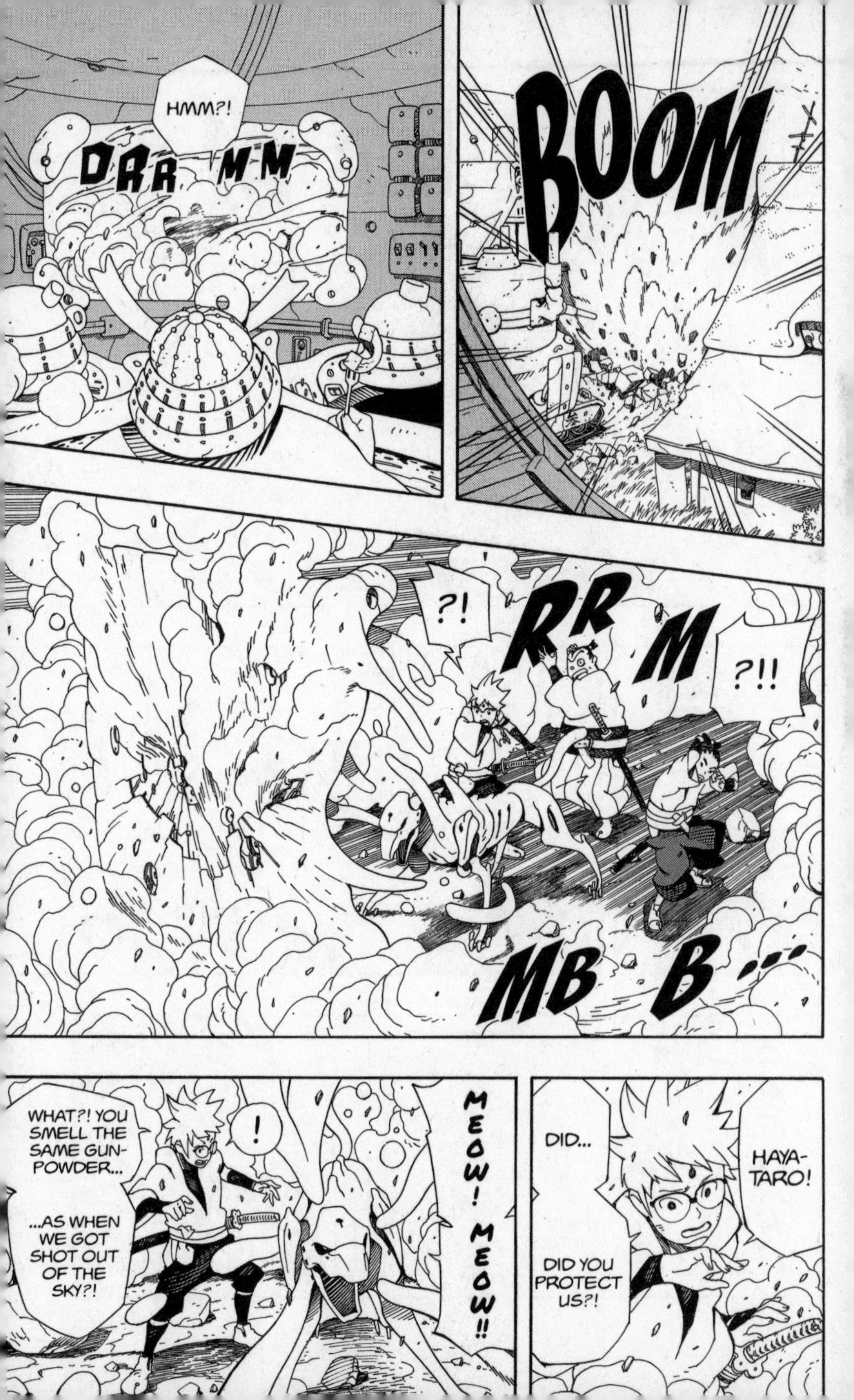
BOOM
HMM?!
DRR MM
?!!
RR M
?!
MB B...
HAYA-TARO!
DID...
DID YOU PROTECT US?!
MEOW! MEOW!!
!
WHAT?! YOU SMELL THE SAME GUN-POWDER...
...AS WHEN WE GOT SHOT OUT OF THE SKY?!

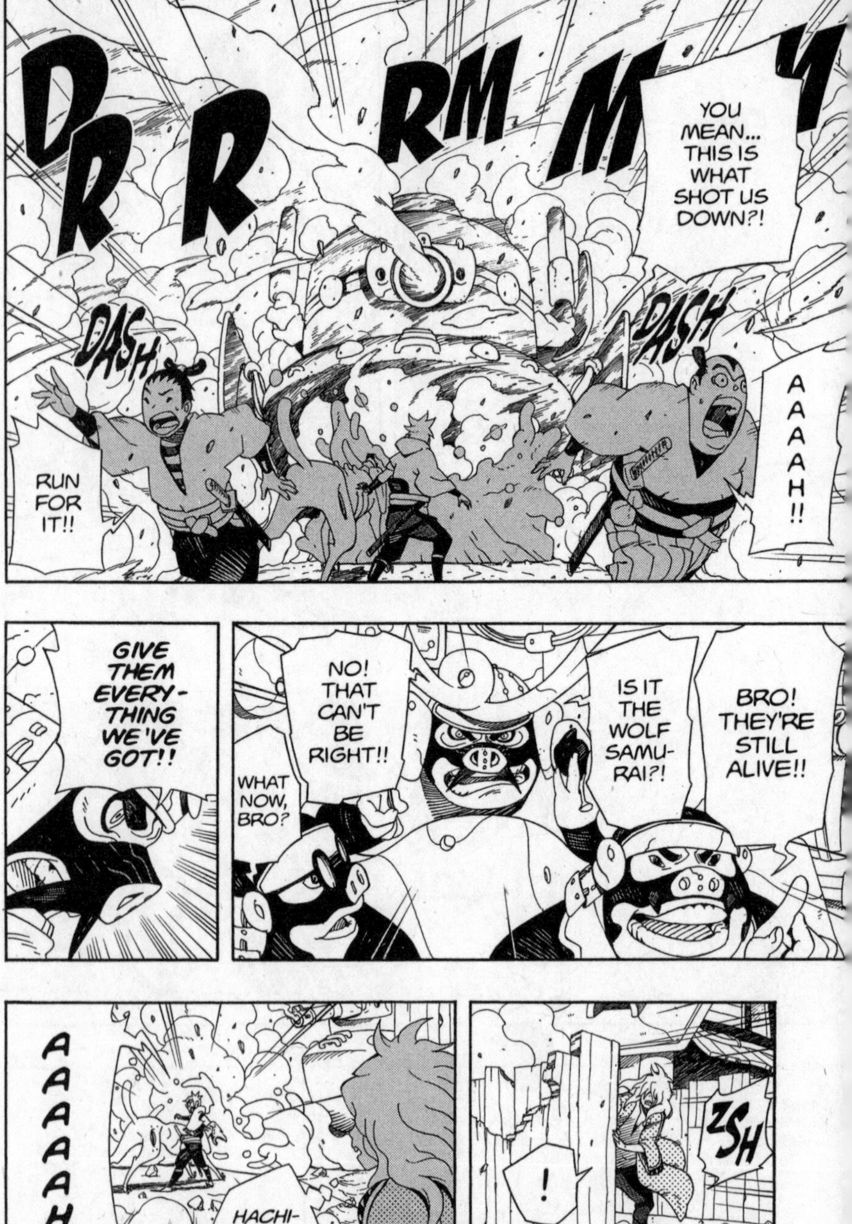
YOU MEAN... THIS IS WHAT SHOT US DOWN?!
DRRRMM
DASH
AAAAAH!!
DASH
RUN FOR IT!!
BRO! THEY'RE STILL ALIVE!!
IS IT THE WOLF SAMURAI?!
NO! THAT CAN'T BE RIGHT!!
WHAT NOW, BRO?
GIVE THEM EVERYTHING WE'VE GOT!!
ZSH
!
HACHIMARU...?
AAAAAAH!!

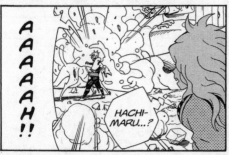

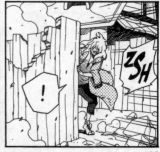

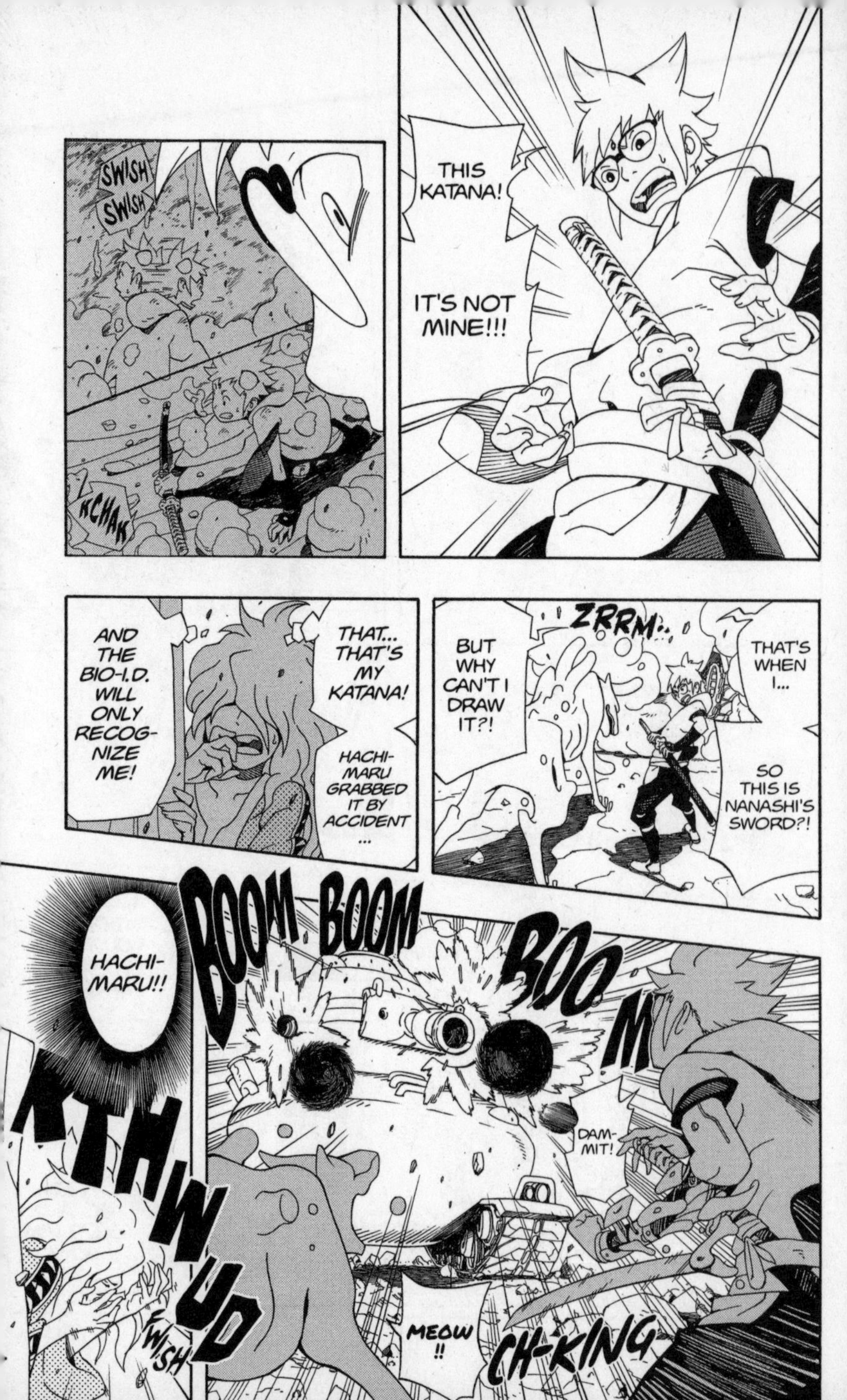
THIS KATANA!
IT'S NOT MINE!!!
SWISH SWISH
KCHAK
THAT'S WHEN I...
SO THIS IS NANASHI'S SWORD?!
ZRRM...
BUT WHY CAN'T I DRAW IT?!
THAT... THAT'S MY KATANA!
HACHIMARU GRABBED IT BY ACCIDENT...
AND THE BIO-I.D. WILL ONLY RECOGNIZE ME!
BOOM BOOM
BOOOM
DAMMIT!
HACHIMARU!!
KTHWUD
FWISH
MEOW!!
CH-KING

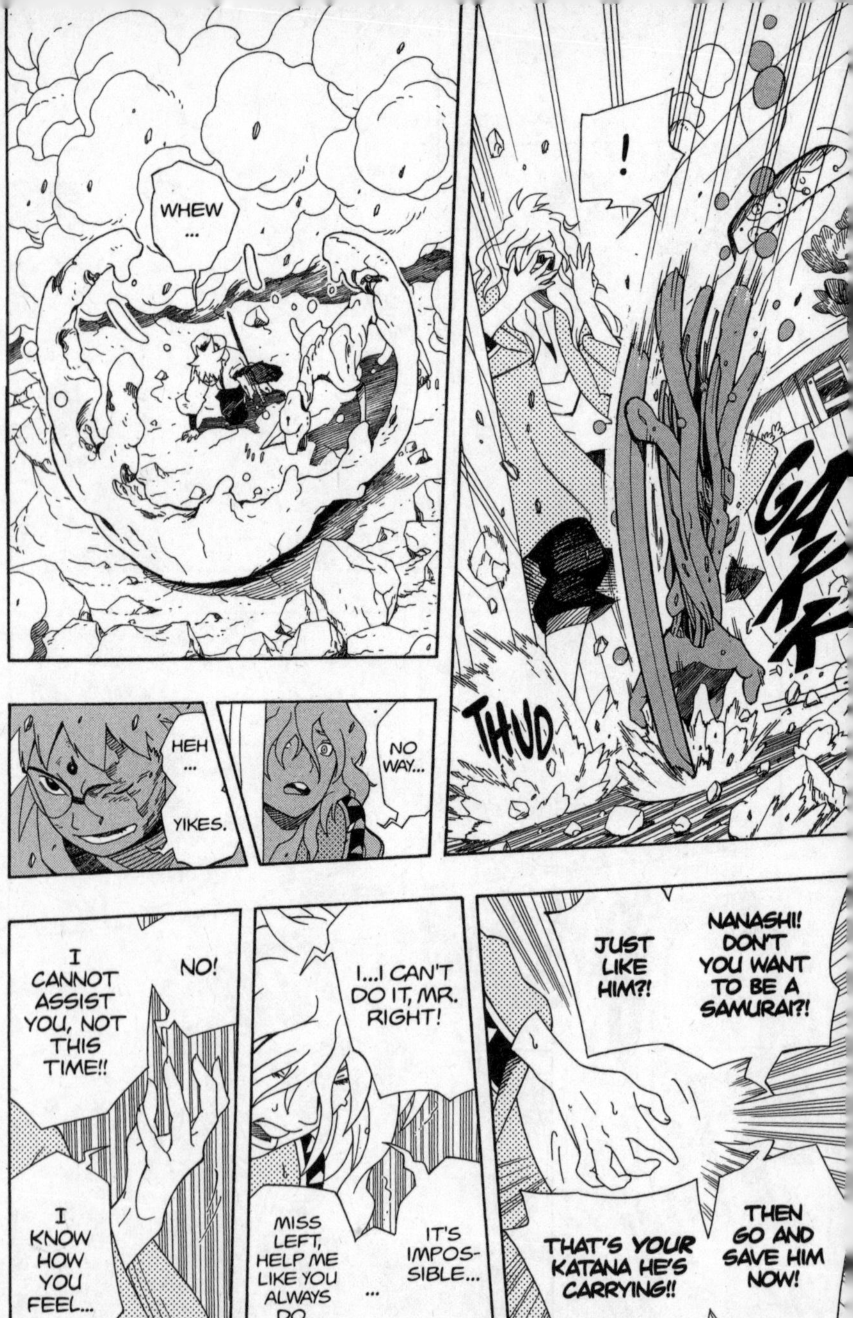
!
GAKK
THUD
WHEW ...
NO WAY...
HEH ... YIKES.
NANASHI! DON'T YOU WANT TO BE A SAMURAI?!
JUST LIKE HIM?!
THEN GO AND SAVE HIM NOW!
THAT'S YOUR KATANA HE'S CARRYING!!
I...I CAN'T DO IT, MR. RIGHT!
IT'S IMPOSSIBLE...
...
MISS LEFT, HELP ME LIKE YOU ALWAYS DO...
NO!
I CANNOT ASSIST YOU, NOT THIS TIME!!
I KNOW HOW YOU FEEL...

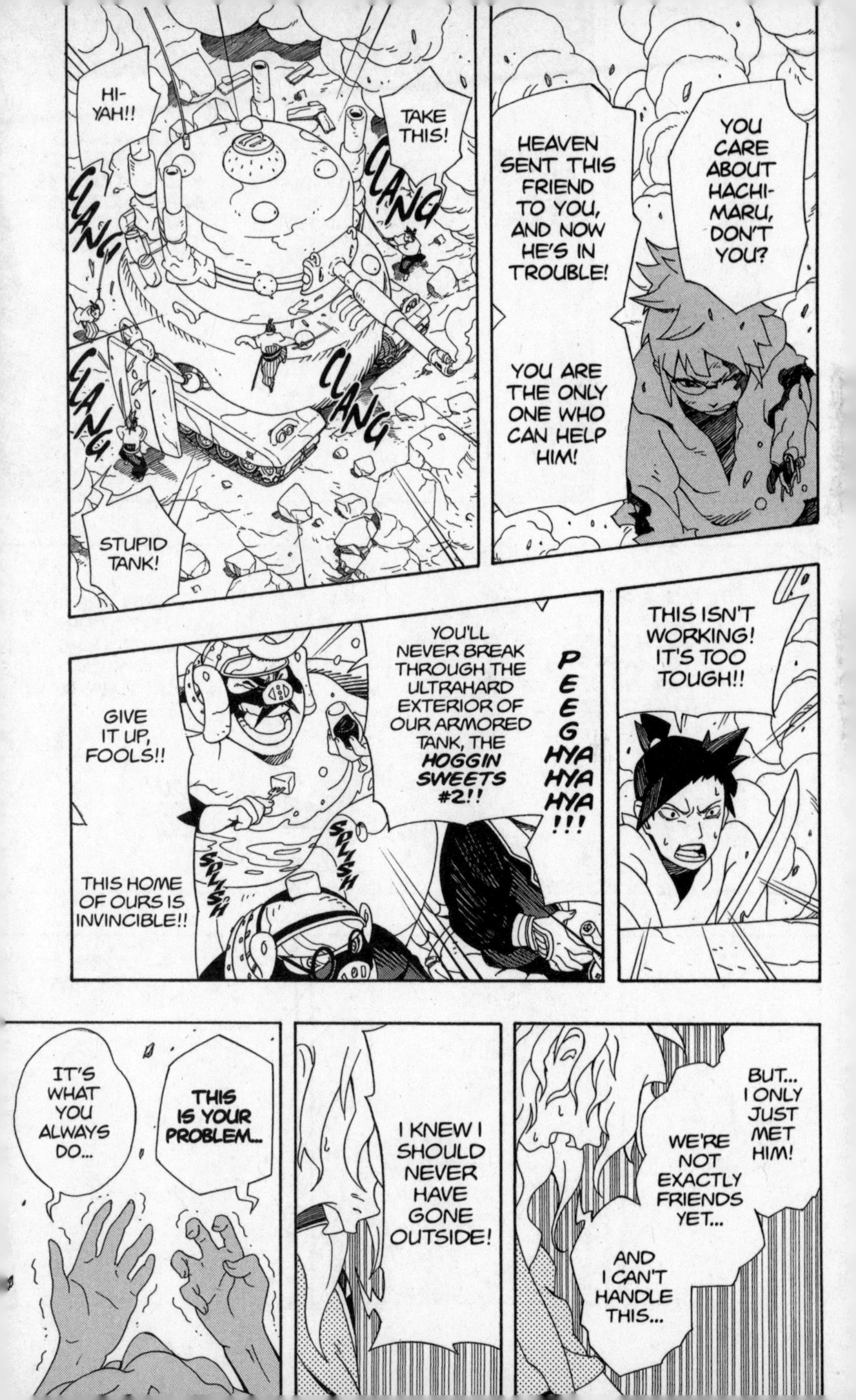
YOU CARE ABOUT HACHIMARU, DON'T YOU?
HEAVEN SENT THIS FRIEND TO YOU, AND NOW HE'S IN TROUBLE!
YOU ARE THE ONLY ONE WHO CAN HELP HIM!
TAKE THIS!
CLANG
HI-YAH!!
CLANG
CLANG
CLANG
STUPID TANK!
THIS ISN'T WORKING! IT'S TOO TOUGH!!
PEEGHYAHYAHYA!!!
YOU'LL NEVER BREAK THROUGH THE ULTRAHARD EXTERIOR OF OUR ARMORED TANK, THE HOGGIN SWEETS #2!!
GIVE IT UP, FOOLS!!
SPLISH
SPLISH
THIS HOME OF OURS IS INVINCIBLE!!
BUT... I ONLY JUST MET HIM!
WE'RE NOT EXACTLY FRIENDS YET...
AND I CAN'T HANDLE THIS...
I KNEW I SHOULD NEVER HAVE GONE OUTSIDE!
THIS IS YOUR PROBLEM...
IT'S WHAT YOU ALWAYS DO...

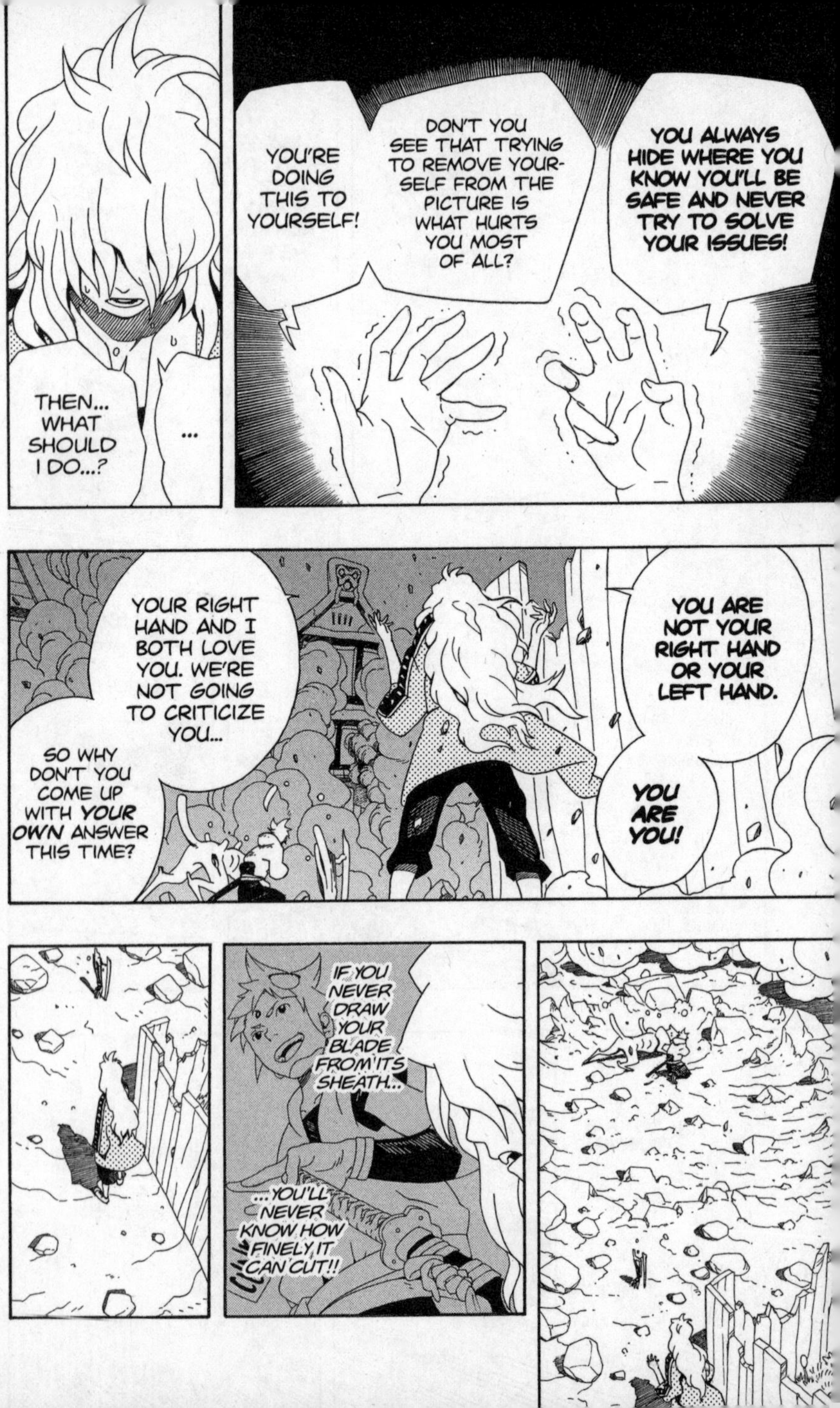
YOU ALWAYS HIDE WHERE YOU KNOW YOU'LL BE SAFE AND NEVER TRY TO SOLVE YOUR ISSUES!
DON'T YOU SEE THAT TRYING TO REMOVE YOURSELF FROM THE PICTURE IS WHAT HURTS YOU MOST OF ALL?
YOU'RE DOING THIS TO YOURSELF!
...
THEN... WHAT SHOULD I DO...?
YOU ARE NOT YOUR RIGHT HAND OR YOUR LEFT HAND.
YOU ARE YOU!
YOUR RIGHT HAND AND I BOTH LOVE YOU. WE'RE NOT GOING TO CRITICIZE YOU...
SO WHY DON'T YOU COME UP WITH YOUR OWN ANSWER THIS TIME?
IF YOU NEVER DRAW YOUR BLADE FROM ITS SHEATH...
...YOU'LL NEVER KNOW HOW FINELY IT CAN CUT!!

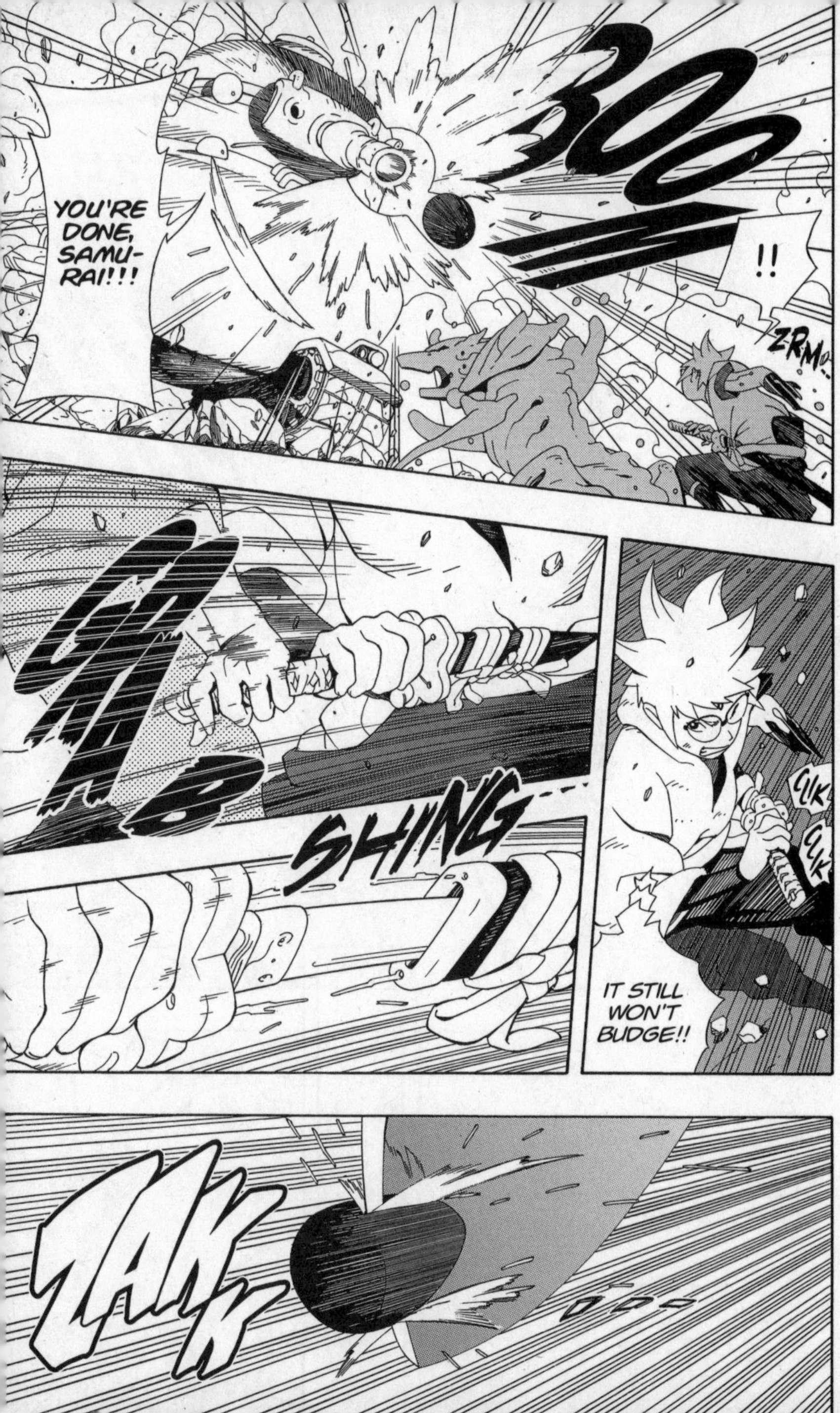
BOOM
!!
ZRM...
YOU'RE DONE, SAMURAI!!!
CLIK
CLIK
IT STILL WON'T BUDGE!!
GRAB
SHING
TAK

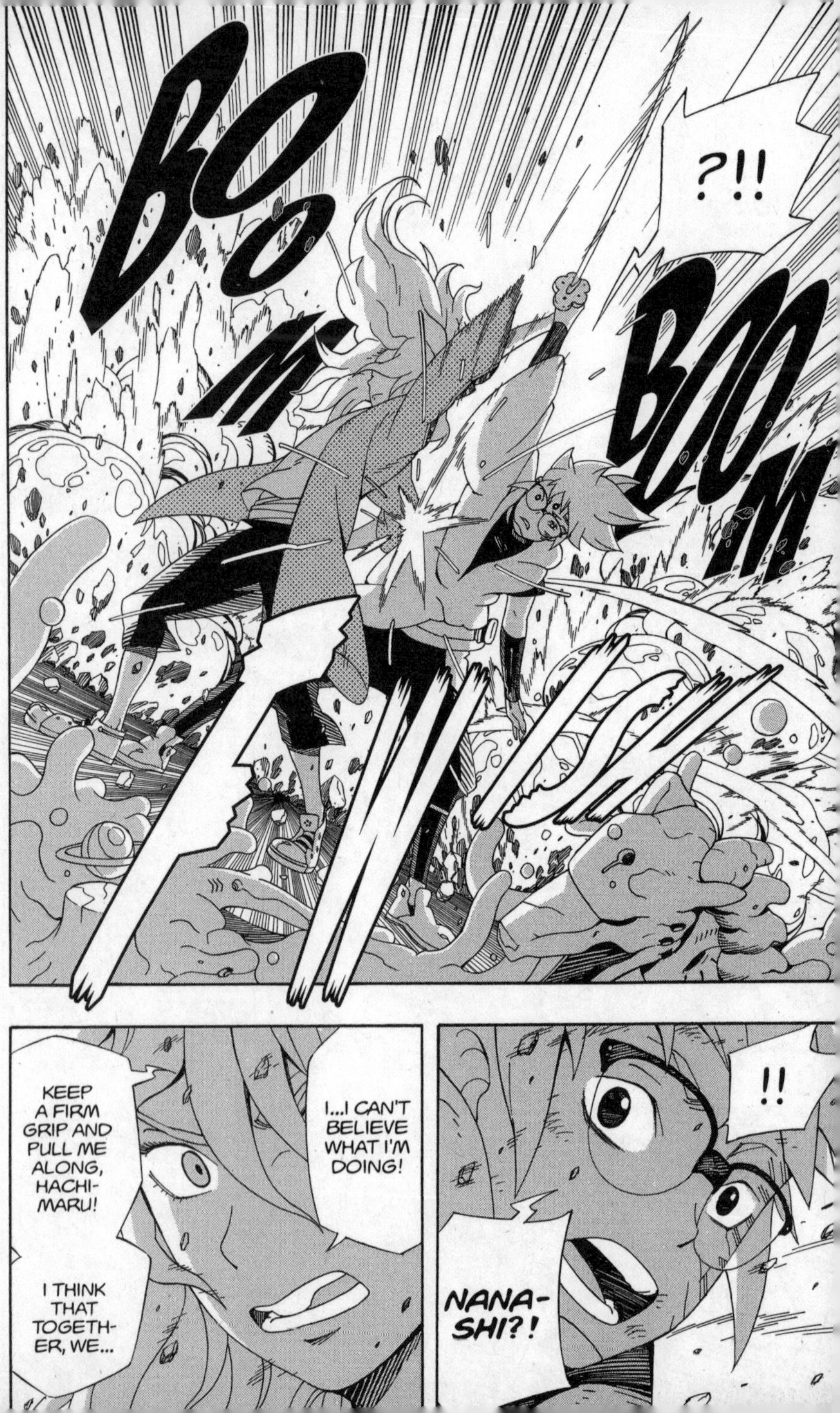
?!!
BOOM
BOOM
!!
NANA-SHI?!
I...I CAN'T BELIEVE WHAT I'M DOING!
KEEP A FIRM GRIP AND PULL ME ALONG, HACHI-MARU!
I THINK THAT TOGETH-ER, WE...

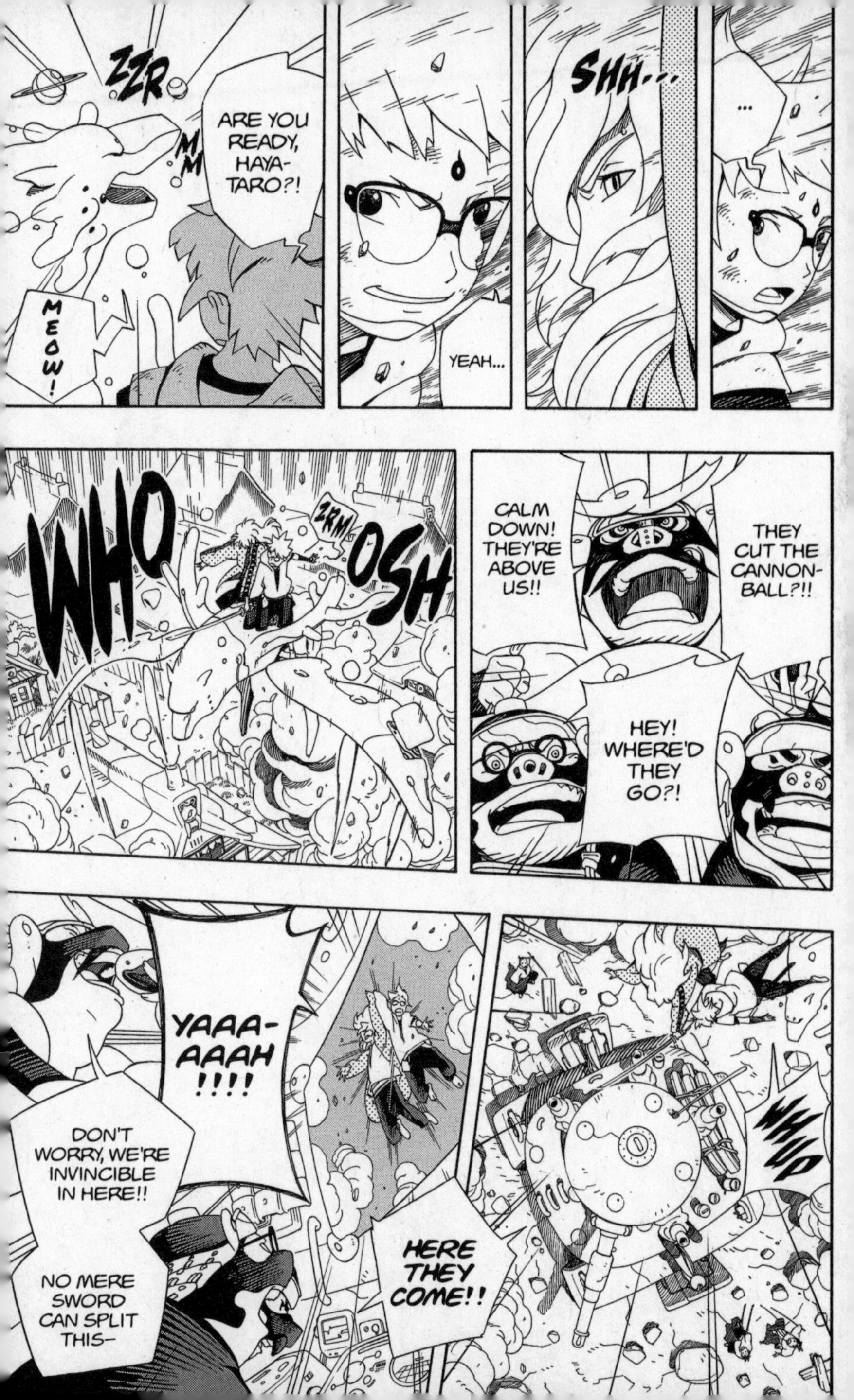
...
SHH...
YEAH...
ZZR
MM
ARE YOU READY, HAYA-TARO?!
MEOW!
THEY CUT THE CANNON-BALL?!!
CALM DOWN! THEY'RE ABOVE US!!
HEY! WHERE'D THEY GO?!
ZRM
WHO OSH
WHUP
YAAAA-AAAH!!!!
HERE THEY COME!!
DON'T WORRY, WE'RE INVINCIBLE IN HERE!!
NO MERE SWORD CAN SPLIT THIS–

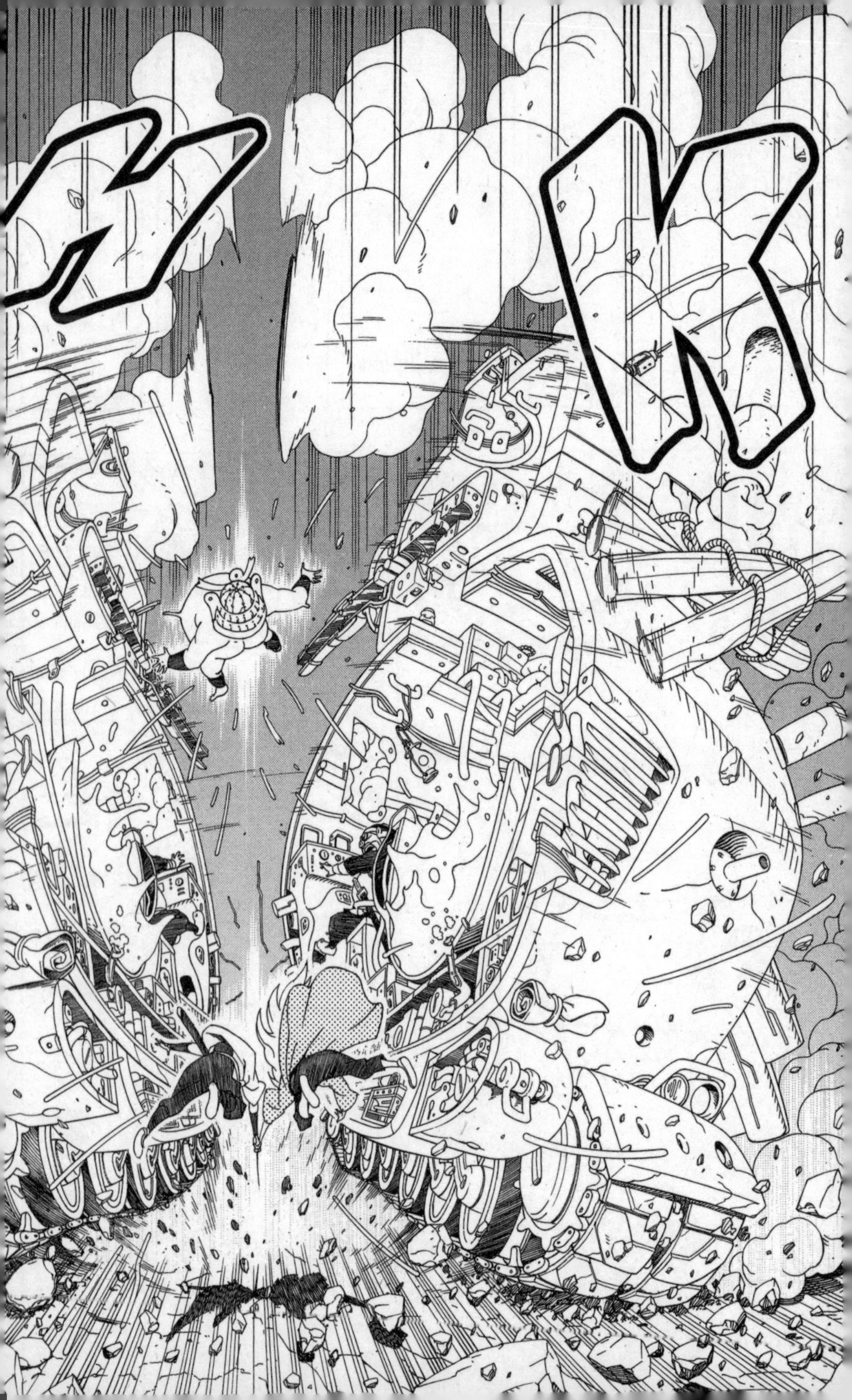

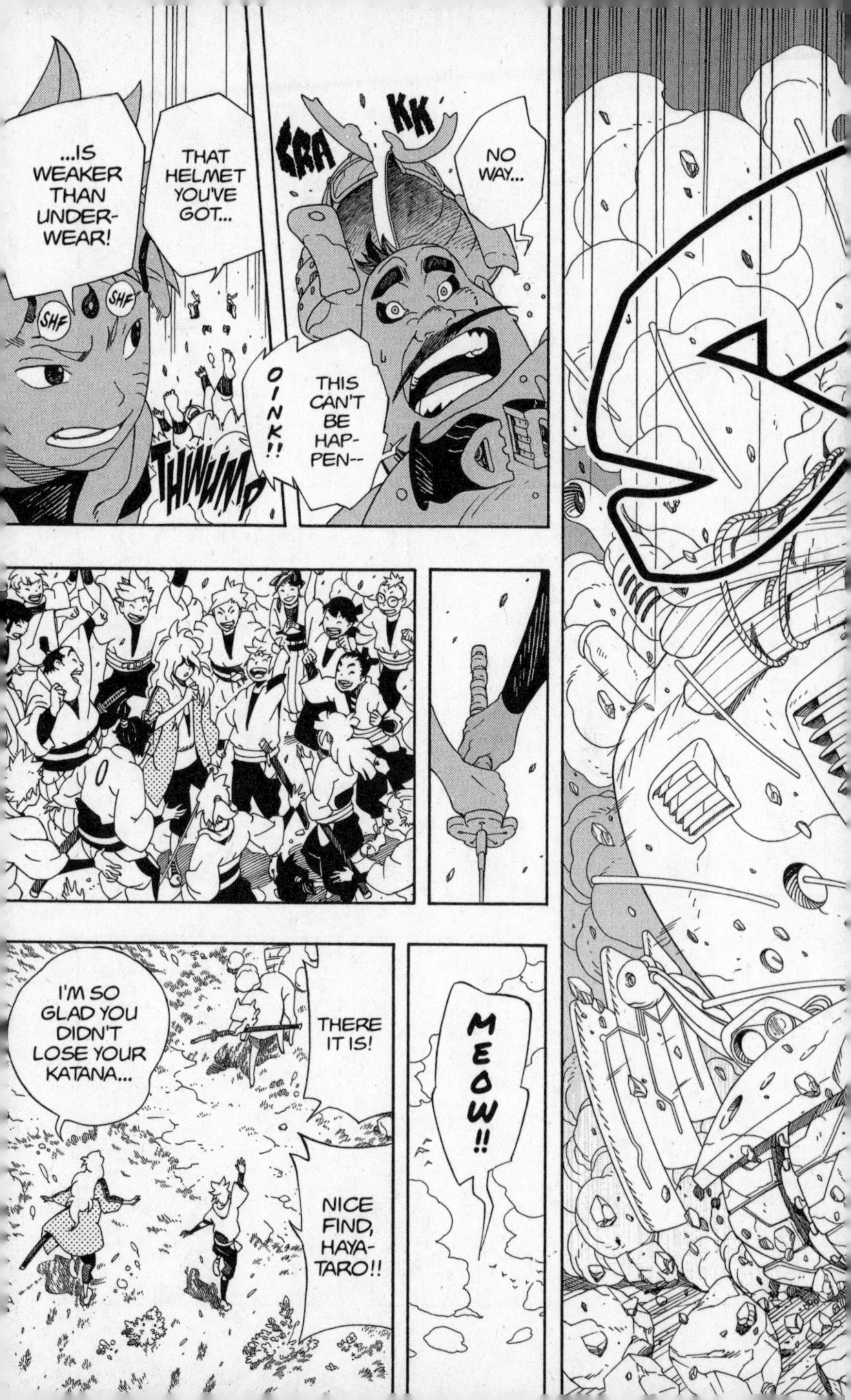
NO WAY...
CRAKK
THAT HELMET YOU'VE GOT...
...IS WEAKER THAN UNDER-WEAR!
SHF
SHF
THIS CAN'T BE HAP-PEN--
OINK!!
THWUMP
MEOW!!
THERE IT IS!
I'M SO GLAD YOU DIDN'T LOSE YOUR KATANA...
NICE FIND, HAYA-TARO!!

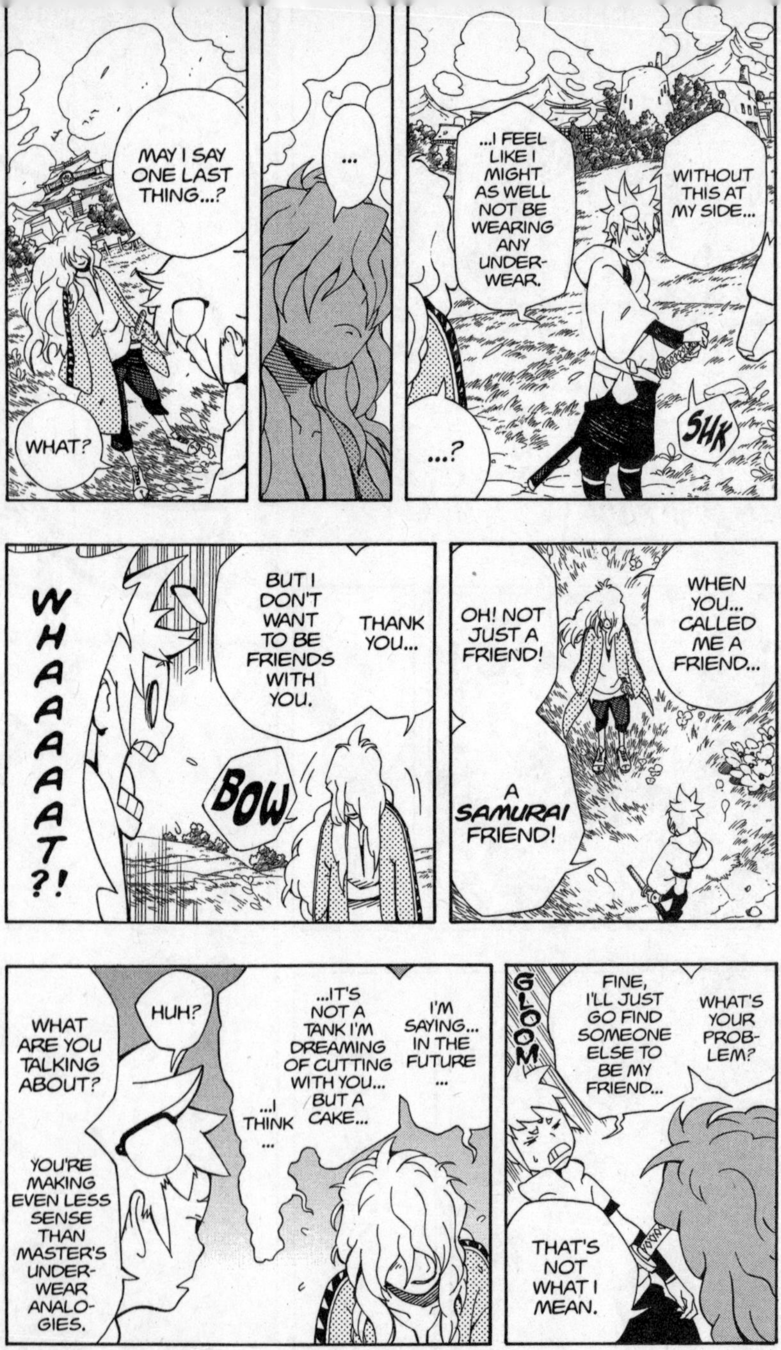
WITHOUT THIS AT MY SIDE...
...I FEEL LIKE I MIGHT AS WELL NOT BE WEARING ANY UNDERWEAR.
SHK
...?
...
MAY I SAY ONE LAST THING...?
WHAT?
WHEN YOU... CALLED ME A FRIEND...
OH! NOT JUST A FRIEND!
A SAMURAI FRIEND!
THANK YOU...
BUT I DON'T WANT TO BE FRIENDS WITH YOU.
BOW
WHAAAAAAAT?!
WHAT'S YOUR PROBLEM?
FINE, I'LL JUST GO FIND SOMEONE ELSE TO BE MY FRIEND...
GLOOM
THAT'S NOT WHAT I MEAN.
I'M SAYING... IN THE FUTURE...
...IT'S NOT A TANK I'M DREAMING OF CUTTING WITH YOU... BUT A CAKE...
...I THINK...
HUH?
WHAT ARE YOU TALKING ABOUT?
YOU'RE MAKING EVEN LESS SENSE THAN MASTER'S UNDER-WEAR ANALO-GIES.

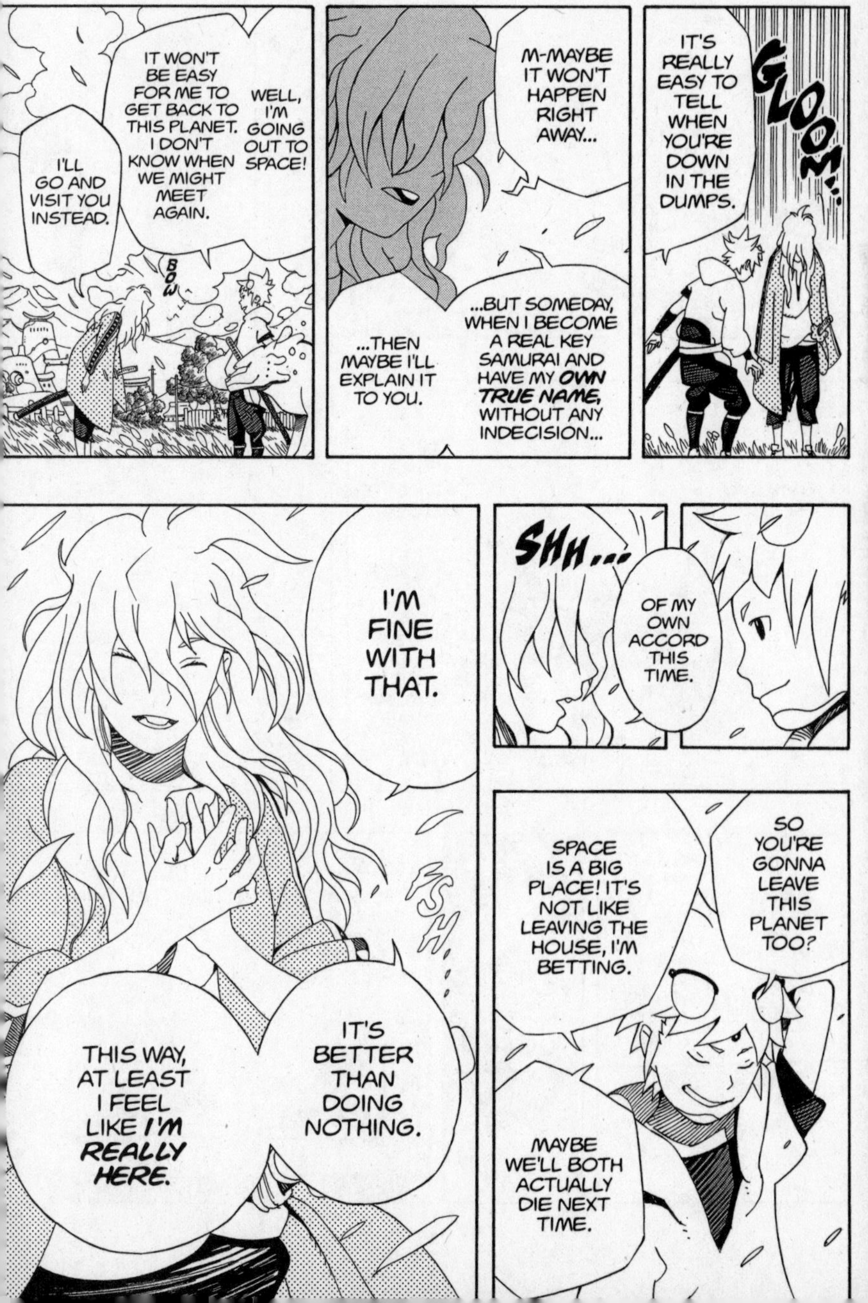
IT'S REALLY EASY TO TELL WHEN YOU'RE DOWN IN THE DUMPS.
GLOOM...
M-MAYBE IT WON'T HAPPEN RIGHT AWAY...
...BUT SOMEDAY, WHEN I BECOME A REAL KEY SAMURAI AND HAVE MY **OWN TRUE NAME,** WITHOUT ANY INDECISION...
...THEN MAYBE I'LL EXPLAIN IT TO YOU.
WELL, I'M GOING OUT TO SPACE!
IT WON'T BE EASY FOR ME TO GET BACK TO THIS PLANET. I DON'T KNOW WHEN WE MIGHT MEET AGAIN.
BOW
I'LL GO AND VISIT YOU INSTEAD.
OF MY OWN ACCORD THIS TIME.
SHH...
SO YOU'RE GONNA LEAVE THIS PLANET TOO?
SPACE IS A BIG PLACE! IT'S NOT LIKE LEAVING THE HOUSE, I'M BETTING.
MAYBE WE'LL BOTH ACTUALLY DIE NEXT TIME.
I'M FINE WITH THAT.
FSH...
IT'S BETTER THAN DOING NOTHING.
THIS WAY, AT LEAST I FEEL LIKE ***I'M REALLY HERE.***

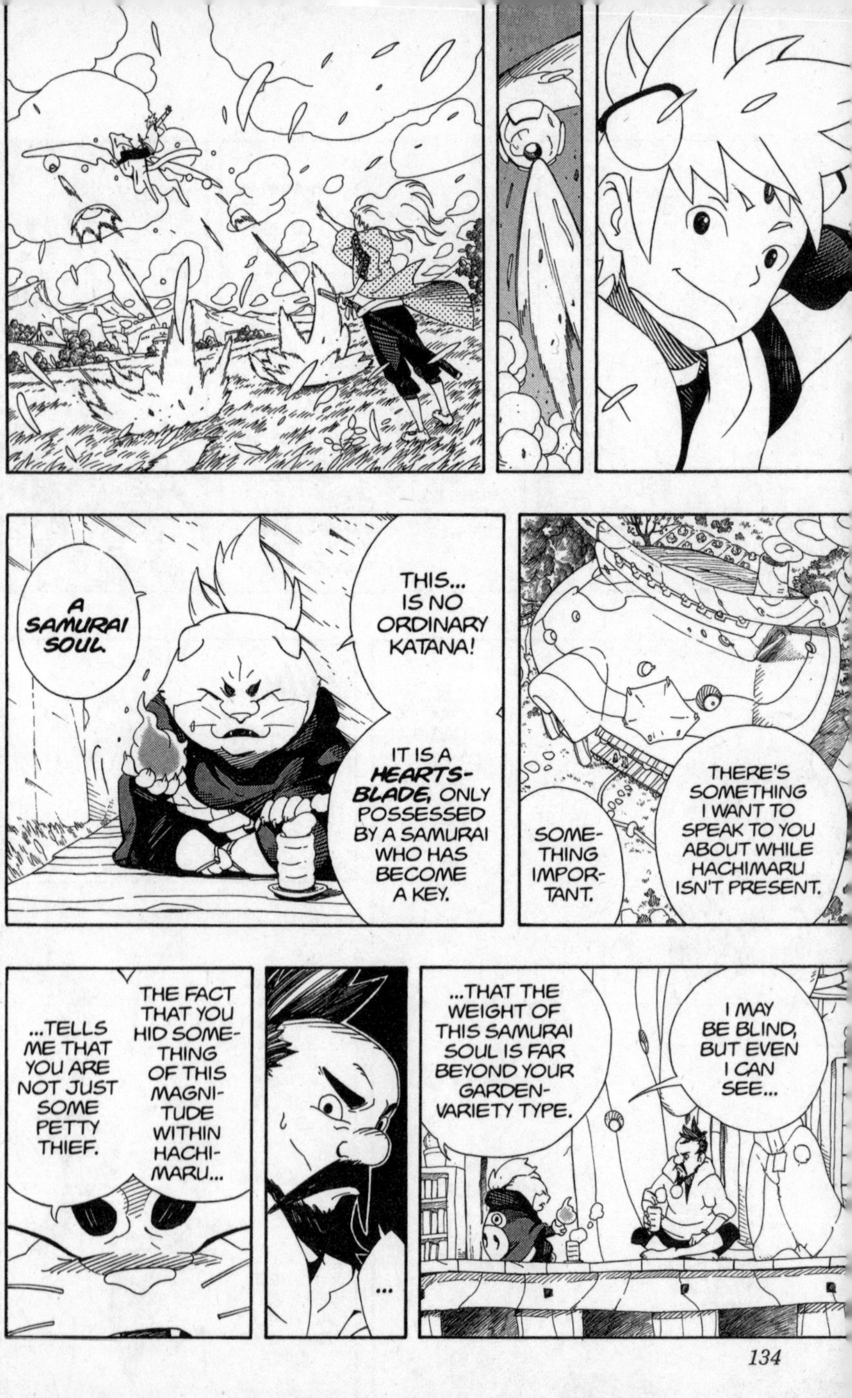
THERE'S SOMETHING I WANT TO SPEAK TO YOU ABOUT WHILE HACHIMARU ISN'T PRESENT.
SOMETHING IMPORTANT.
THIS... IS NO ORDINARY KATANA!
IT IS A HEARTS-BLADE, ONLY POSSESSED BY A SAMURAI WHO HAS BECOME A KEY.
A SAMURAI SOUL.
I MAY BE BLIND, BUT EVEN I CAN SEE...
...THAT THE WEIGHT OF THIS SAMURAI SOUL IS FAR BEYOND YOUR GARDEN-VARIETY TYPE.
...
THE FACT THAT YOU HID SOMETHING OF THIS MAGNITUDE WITHIN HACHIMARU...
...TELLS ME THAT YOU ARE NOT JUST SOME PETTY THIEF.

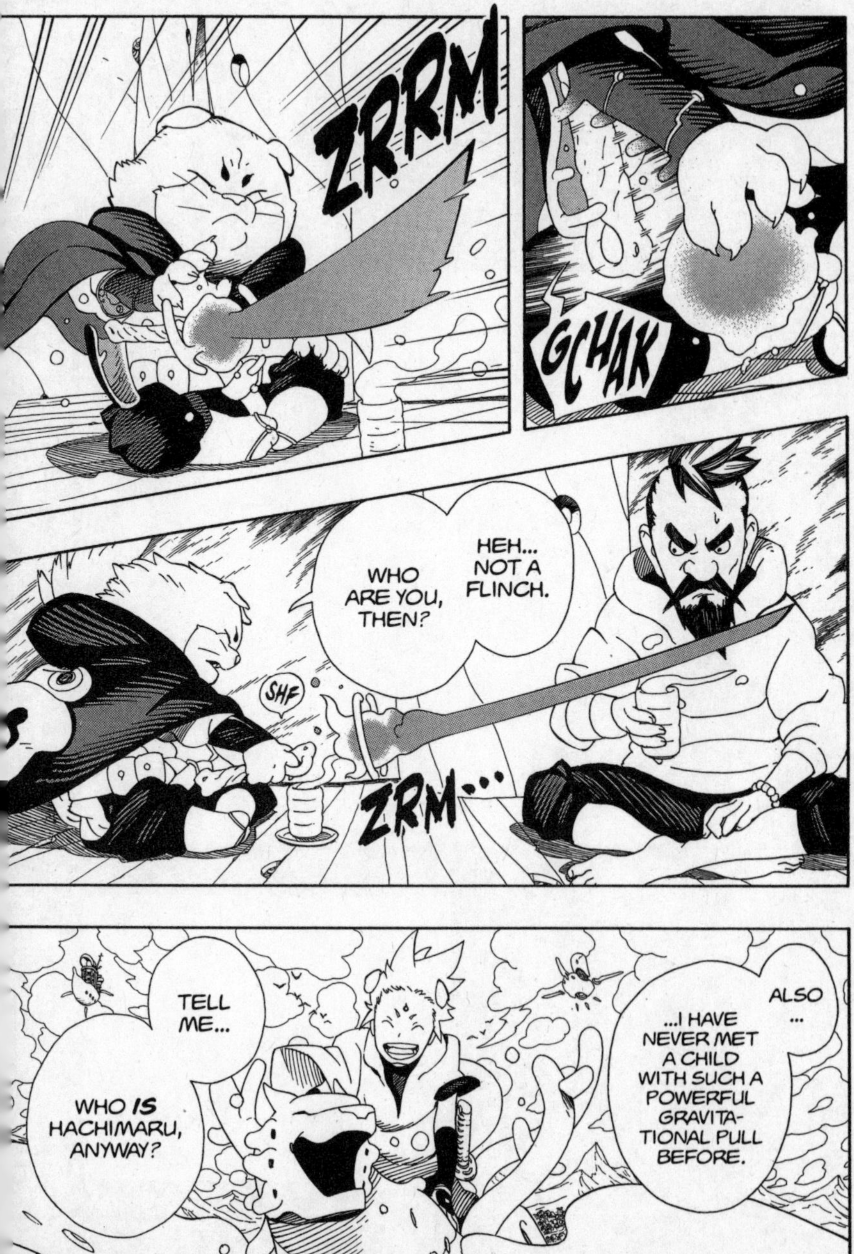
GCHAK
ZRRM
HEH... NOT A FLINCH.
WHO ARE YOU, THEN?
SHF
ZRM...
ALSO...
...I HAVE NEVER MET A CHILD WITH SUCH A POWERFUL GRAVITA-TIONAL PULL BEFORE.
TELL ME...
WHO *IS* HACHIMARU, ANYWAY?

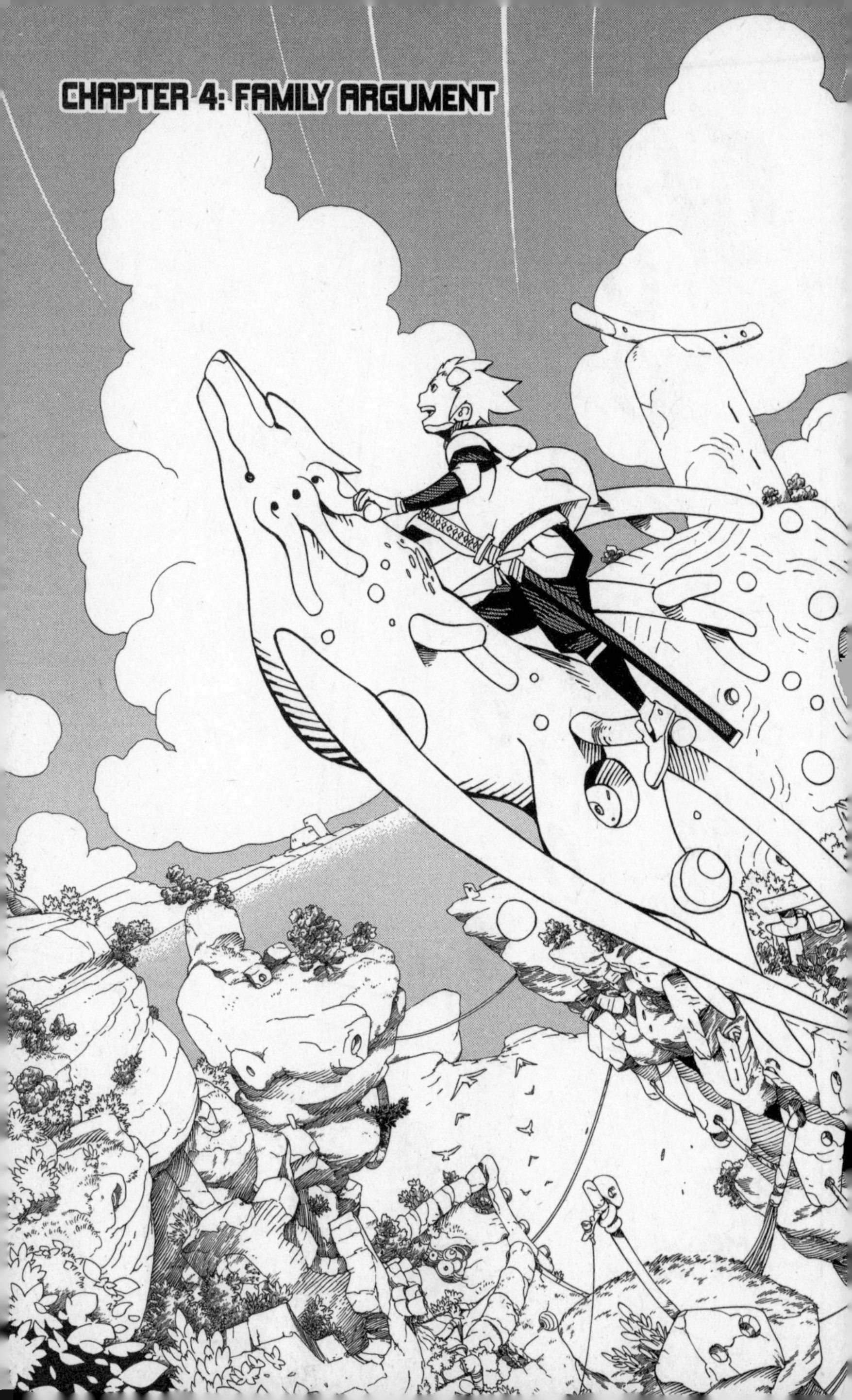
CHAPTER 4: FAMILY ARGUMENT

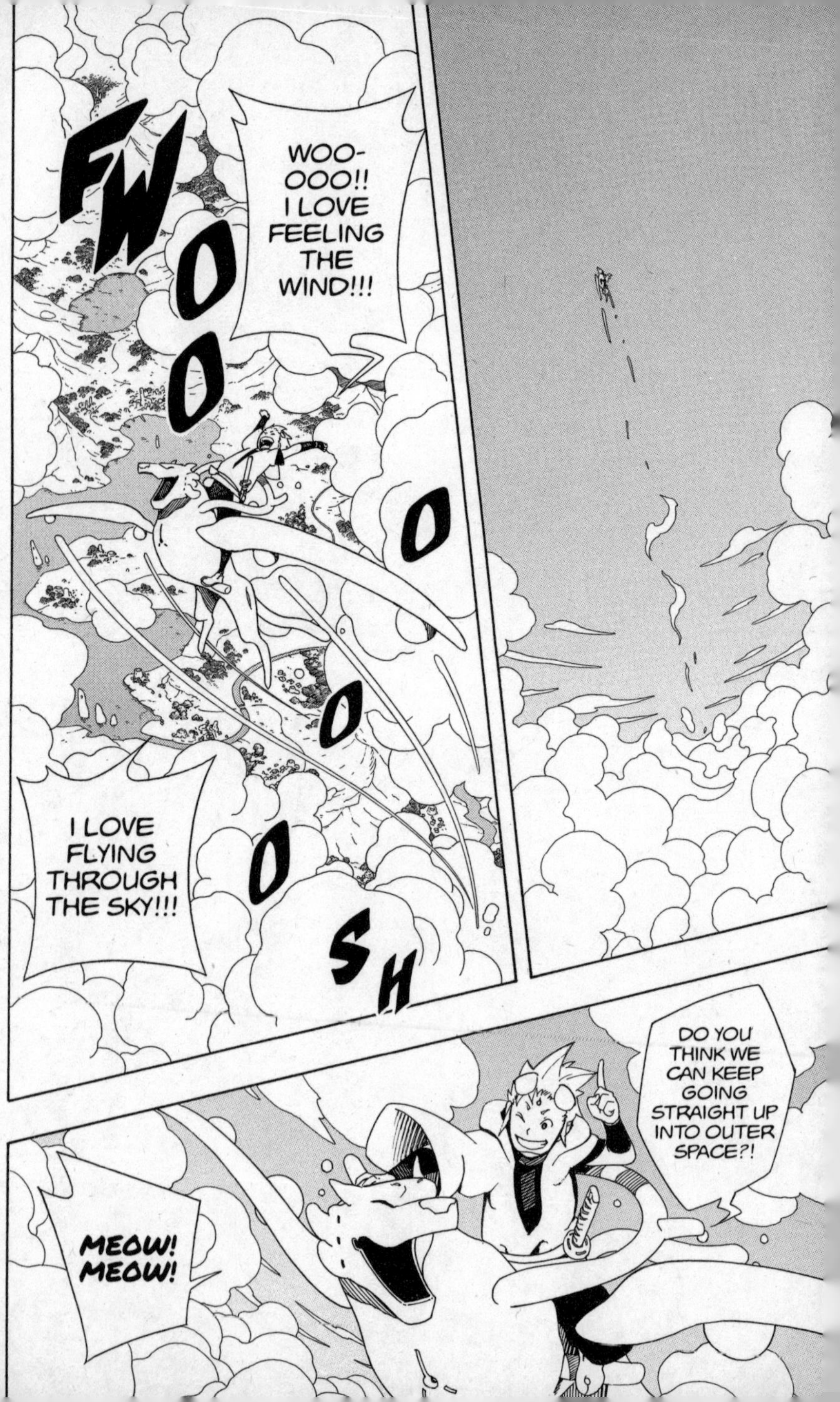
FWOOOOOOSH
WOO-OOO!! I LOVE FEELING THE WIND!!!
I LOVE FLYING THROUGH THE SKY!!!
DO YOU THINK WE CAN KEEP GOING STRAIGHT UP INTO OUTER SPACE?!
MEOW! MEOW!

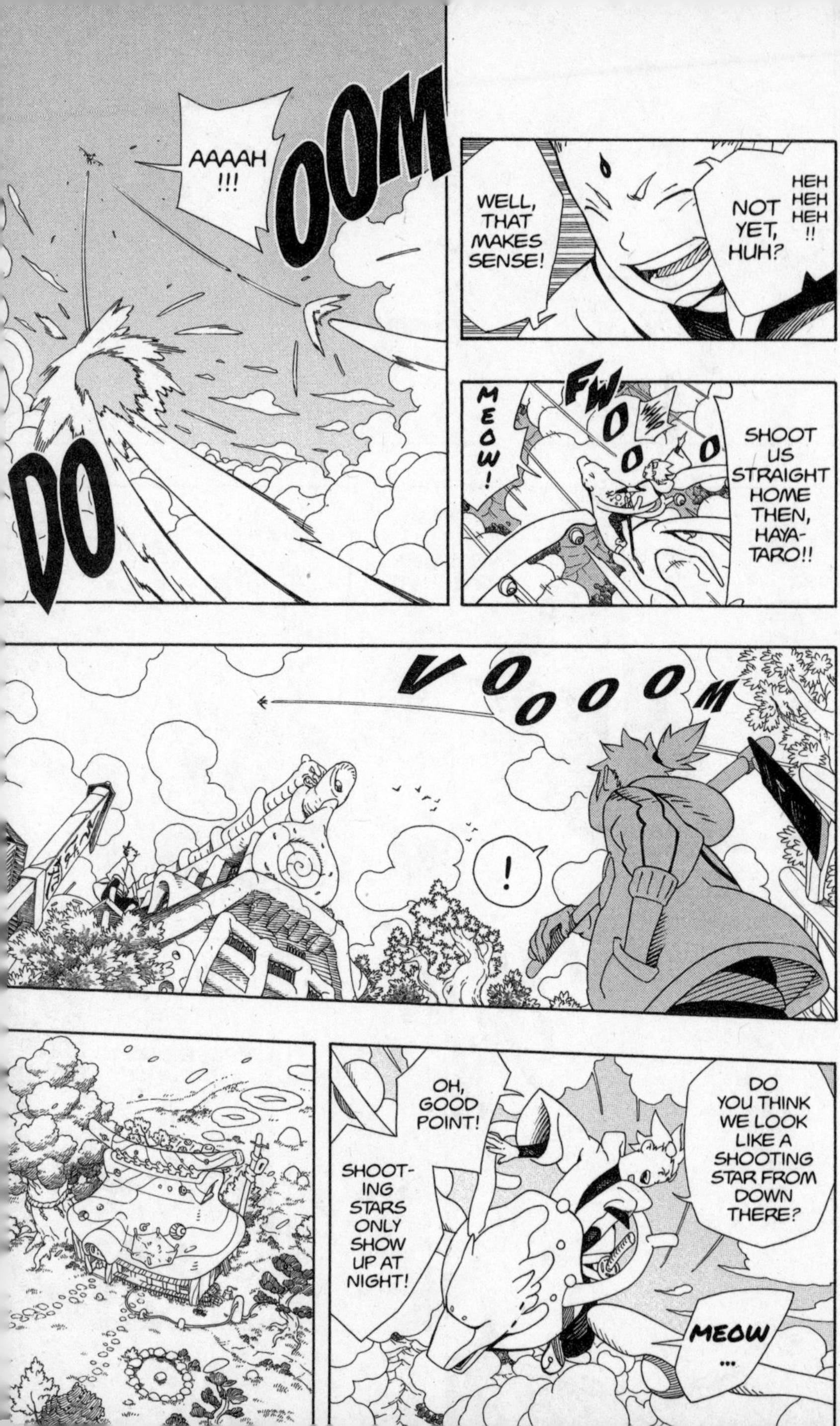
HEH HEH HEH !!
NOT YET, HUH?
WELL, THAT MAKES SENSE!
SHOOT US STRAIGHT HOME THEN, HAYA-TARO!!
FWOOOO
MEOW!
OOM
AAAAH !!!
DO
VOOOOM
!
DO YOU THINK WE LOOK LIKE A SHOOTING STAR FROM DOWN THERE?
OH, GOOD POINT!
SHOOT-ING STARS ONLY SHOW UP AT NIGHT!
MEOW ...

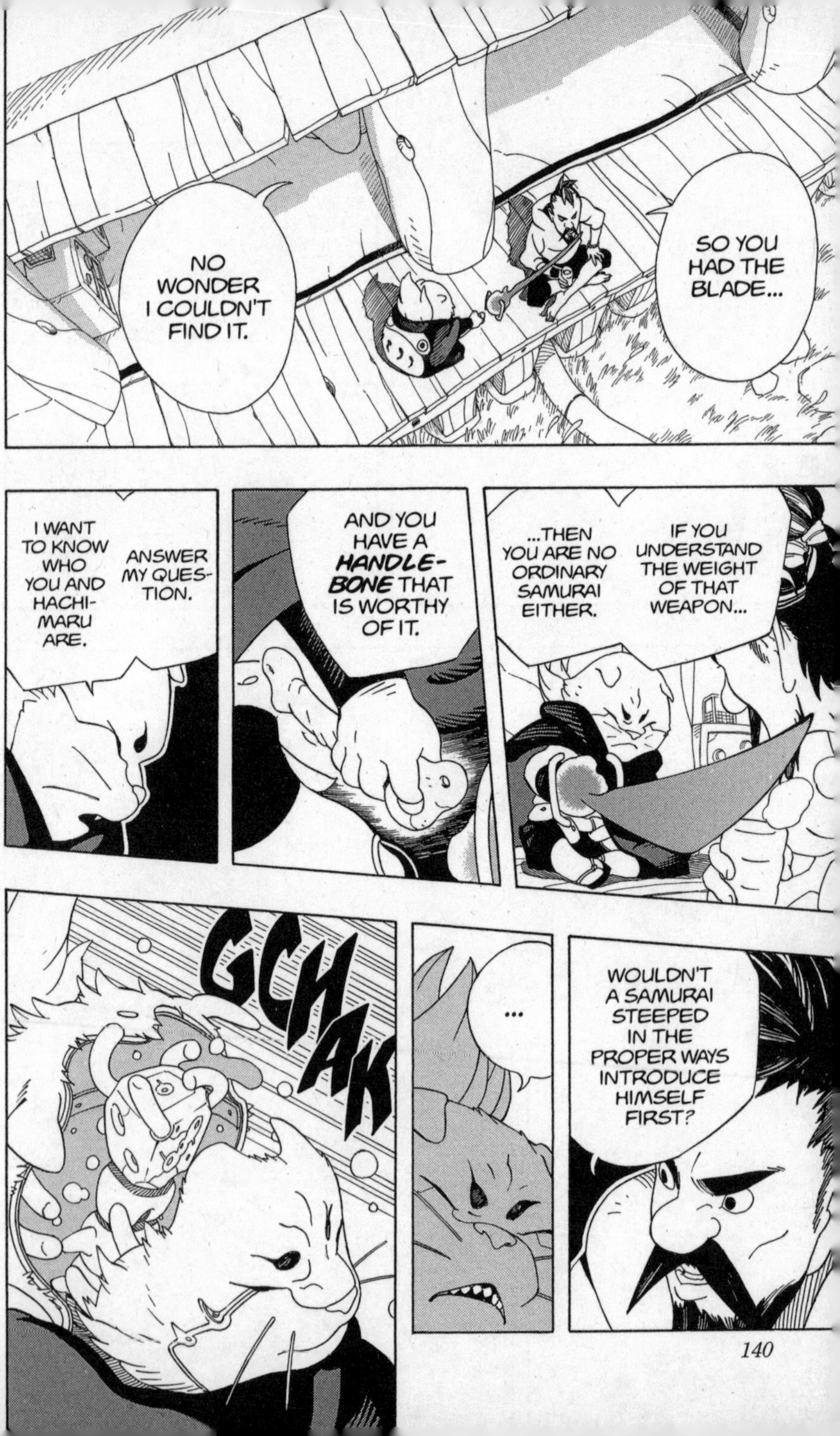
SO YOU HAD THE BLADE...
NO WONDER I COULDN'T FIND IT.
IF YOU UNDERSTAND THE WEIGHT OF THAT WEAPON...
...THEN YOU ARE NO ORDINARY SAMURAI EITHER.
AND YOU HAVE A ***HANDLE-BONE*** THAT IS WORTHY OF IT.
ANSWER MY QUESTION.
I WANT TO KNOW WHO YOU AND HACHIMARU ARE.
WOULDN'T A SAMURAI STEEPED IN THE PROPER WAYS INTRODUCE HIMSELF FIRST?
...
GCHAK

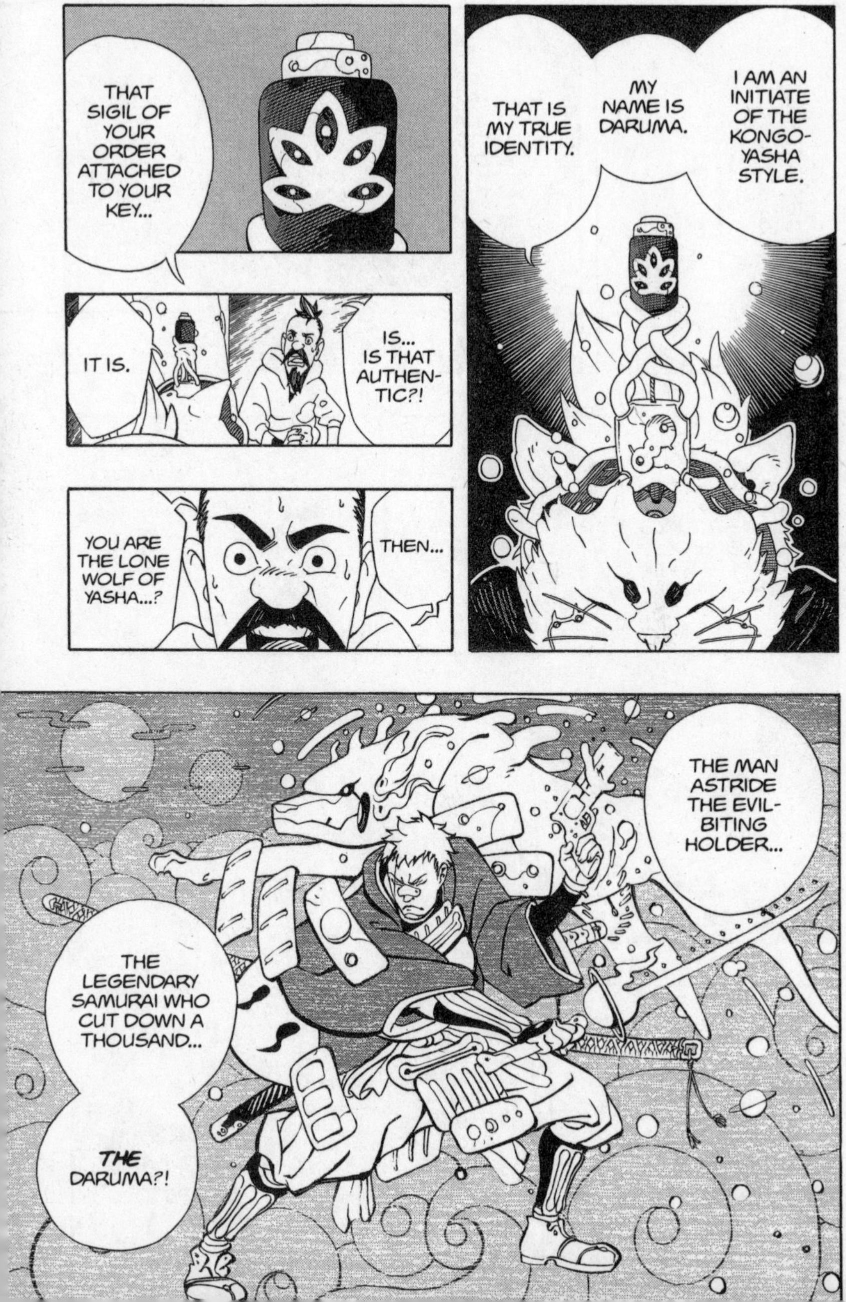
I AM AN INITIATE OF THE KONGO-YASHA STYLE.
MY NAME IS DARUMA.
THAT IS MY TRUE IDENTITY.
THAT SIGIL OF YOUR ORDER ATTACHED TO YOUR KEY...
IS... IS THAT AUTHENTIC?!
IT IS.
THEN...
YOU ARE THE LONE WOLF OF YASHA...?
THE MAN ASTRIDE THE EVIL-BITING HOLDER...
THE LEGENDARY SAMURAI WHO CUT DOWN A THOUSAND...
THE DARUMA?!

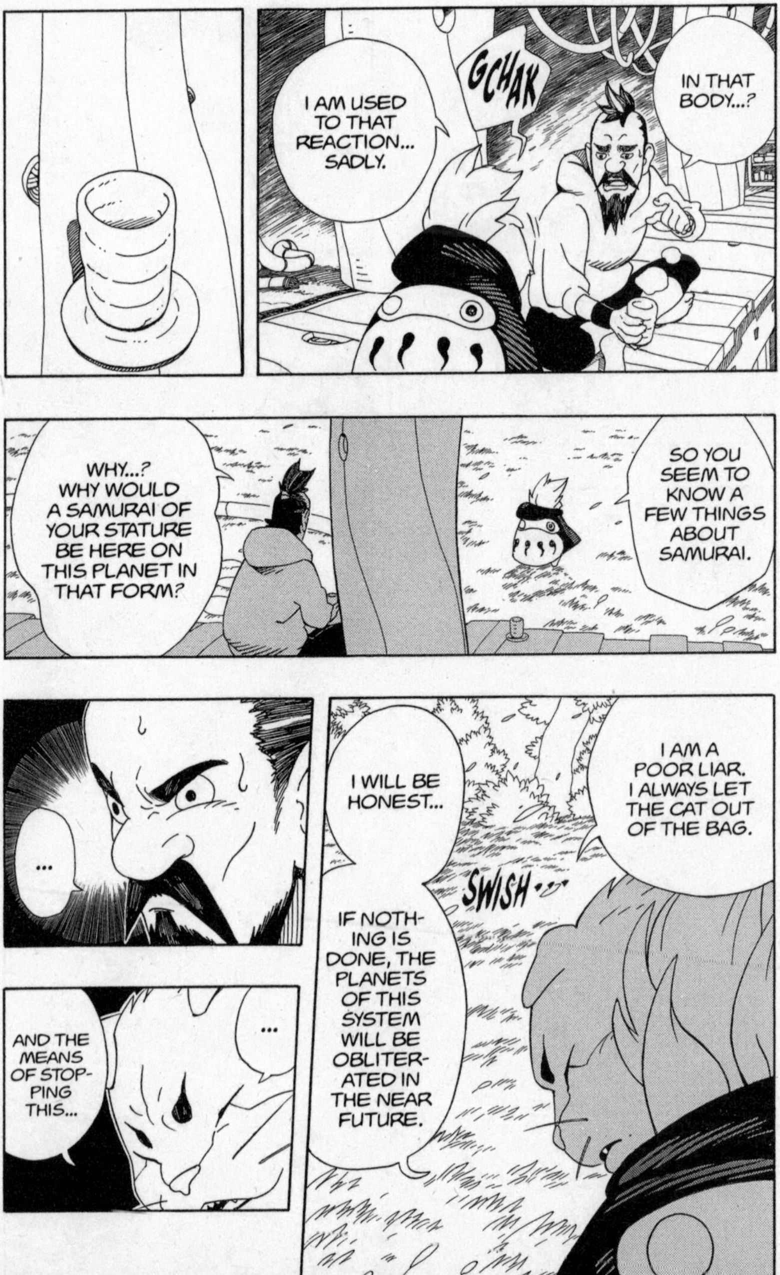
IN THAT BODY...?
GCHAK
I AM USED TO THAT REACTION... SADLY.
SO YOU SEEM TO KNOW A FEW THINGS ABOUT SAMURAI.
WHY...? WHY WOULD A SAMURAI OF YOUR STATURE BE HERE ON THIS PLANET IN THAT FORM?
I AM A POOR LIAR. I ALWAYS LET THE CAT OUT OF THE BAG.
SWISH
I WILL BE HONEST...
IF NOTH-ING IS DONE, THE PLANETS OF THIS SYSTEM WILL BE OBLITER-ATED IN THE NEAR FUTURE.
...
...
AND THE MEANS OF STOP-PING THIS...

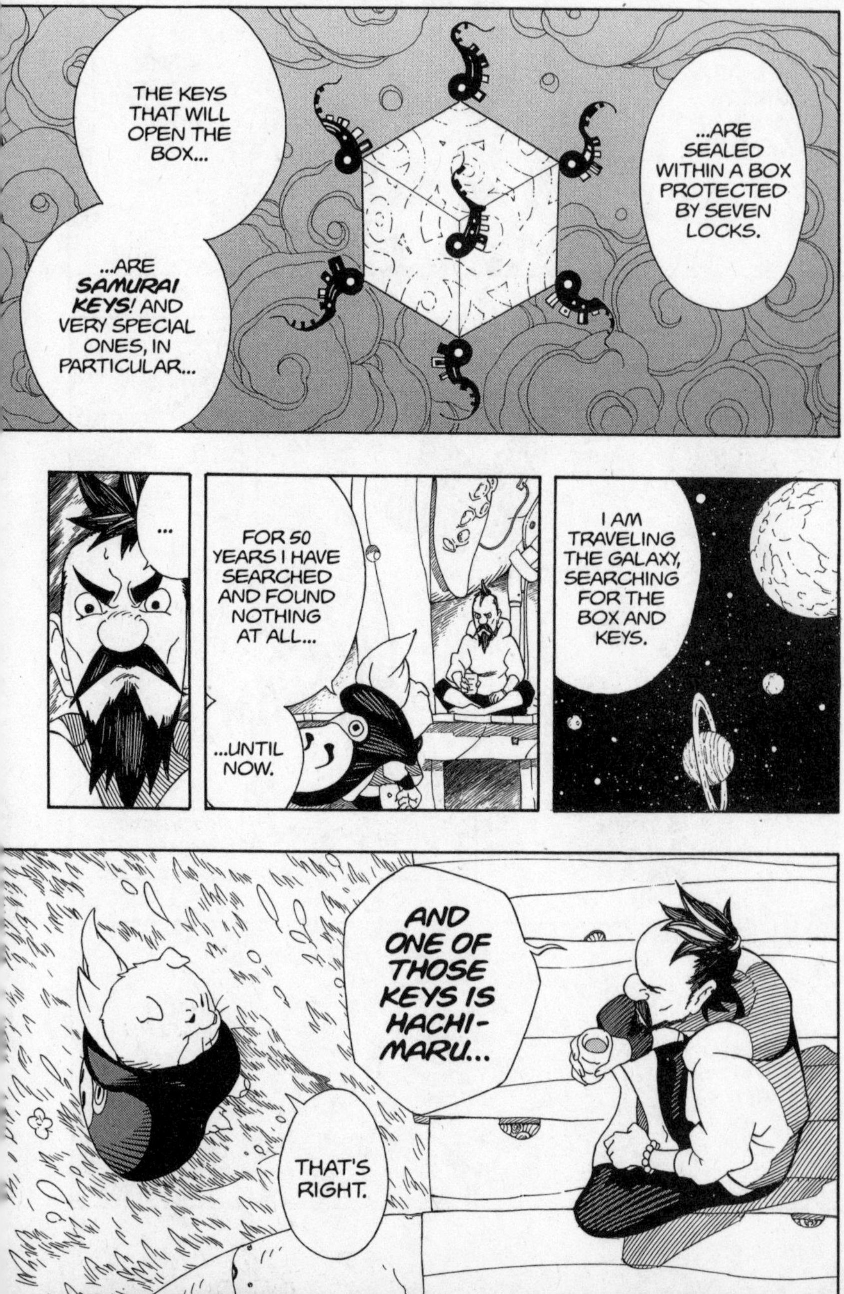
...ARE SEALED WITHIN A BOX PROTECTED BY SEVEN LOCKS.
THE KEYS THAT WILL OPEN THE BOX...
...ARE ***SAMURAI KEYS!*** AND VERY SPECIAL ONES, IN PARTICULAR...
I AM TRAVELING THE GALAXY, SEARCHING FOR THE BOX AND KEYS.
FOR 50 YEARS I HAVE SEARCHED AND FOUND NOTHING AT ALL...
...UNTIL NOW.
...
AND ONE OF THOSE KEYS IS HACHI-MARU...
THAT'S RIGHT.

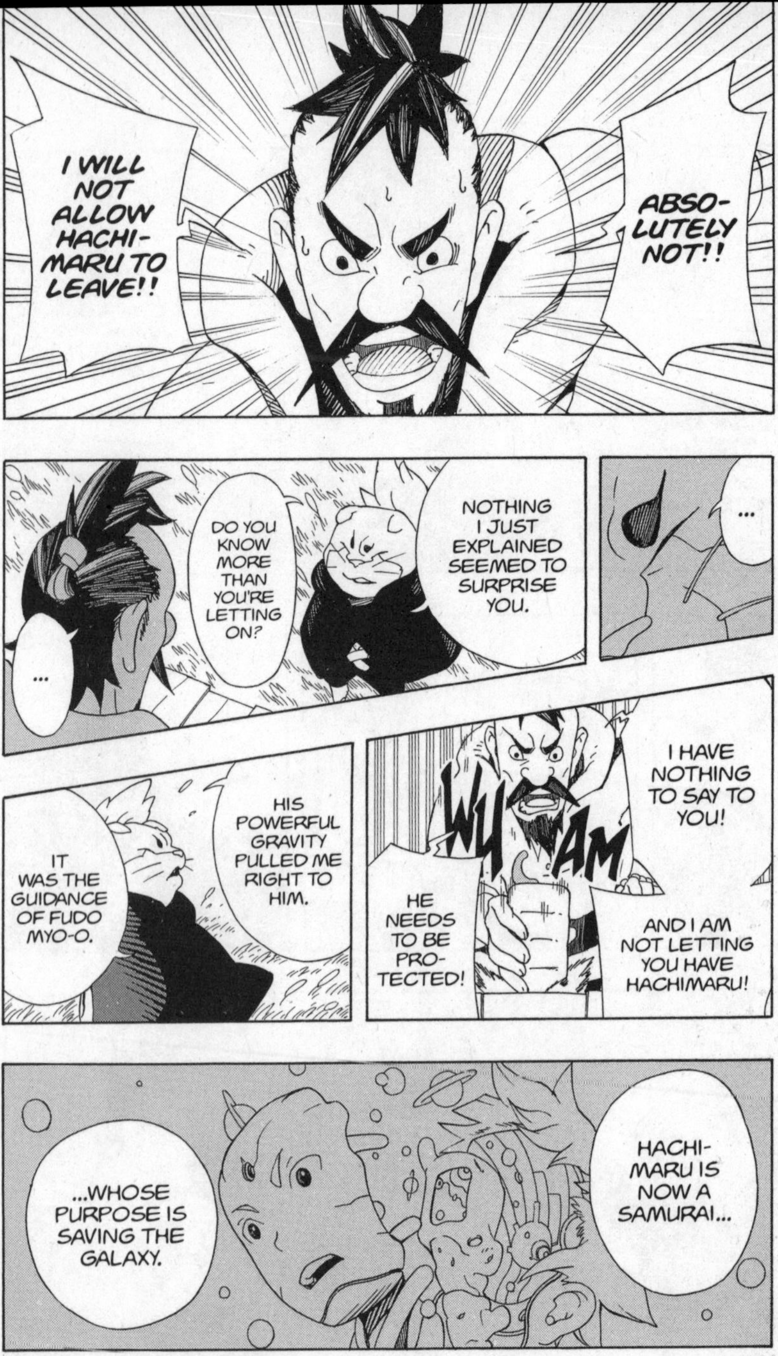
I WILL NOT ALLOW HACHI-MARU TO LEAVE!!
ABSO-LUTELY NOT!!
...
NOTHING I JUST EXPLAINED SEEMED TO SURPRISE YOU.
DO YOU KNOW MORE THAN YOU'RE LETTING ON?
...
I HAVE NOTHING TO SAY TO YOU!
WHAM
AND I AM NOT LETTING YOU HAVE HACHIMARU!
HE NEEDS TO BE PRO-TECTED!
HIS POWERFUL GRAVITY PULLED ME RIGHT TO HIM.
IT WAS THE GUIDANCE OF FUDO MYO-O.
HACHI-MARU IS NOW A SAMURAI...
...WHOSE PURPOSE IS SAVING THE GALAXY.

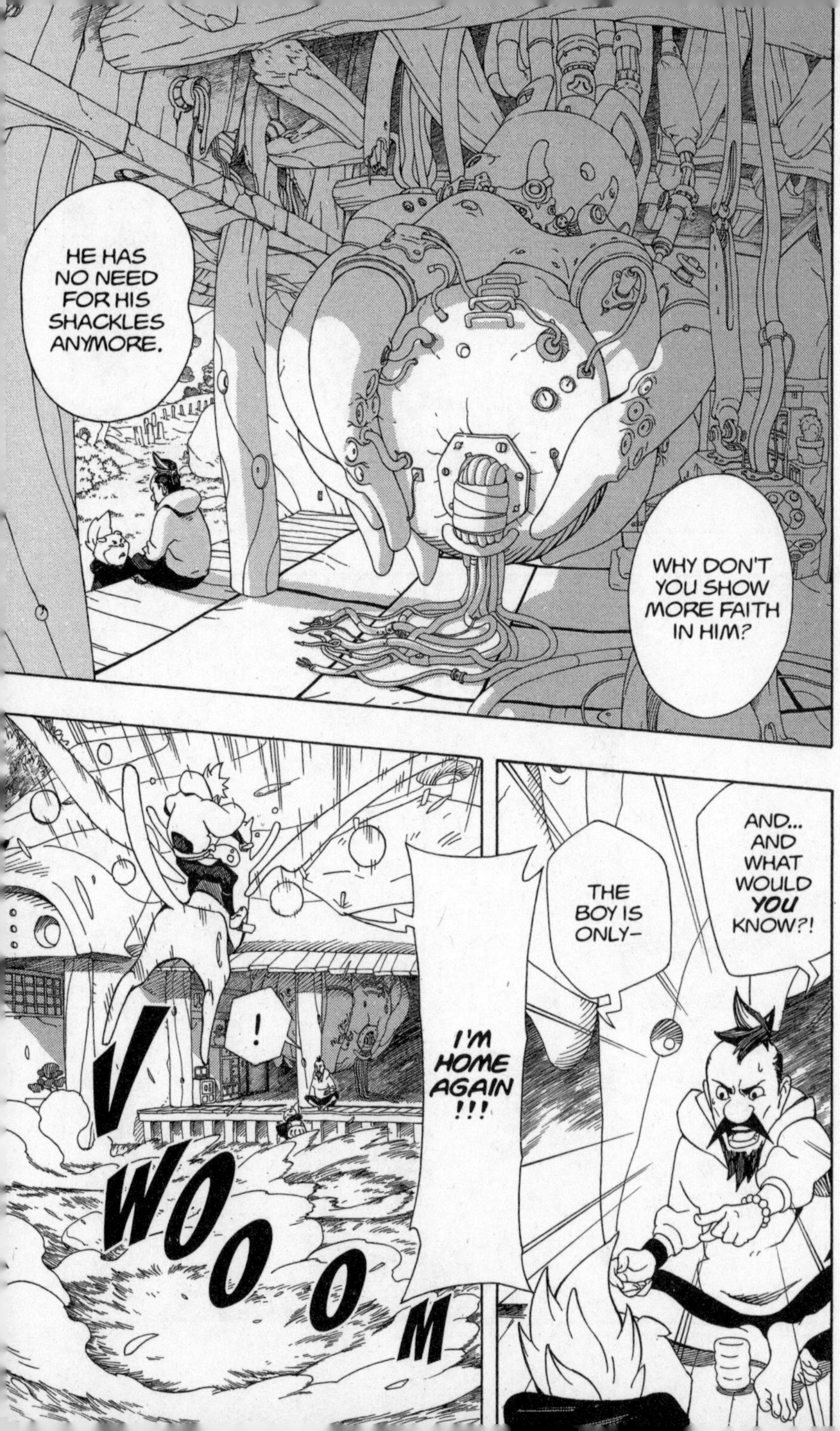
WHY DON'T YOU SHOW MORE FAITH IN HIM?
HE HAS NO NEED FOR HIS SHACKLES ANYMORE.
AND... AND WHAT WOULD *YOU* KNOW?!
THE BOY IS ONLY-
I'M HOME AGAIN!!!
!
VWOOOOM

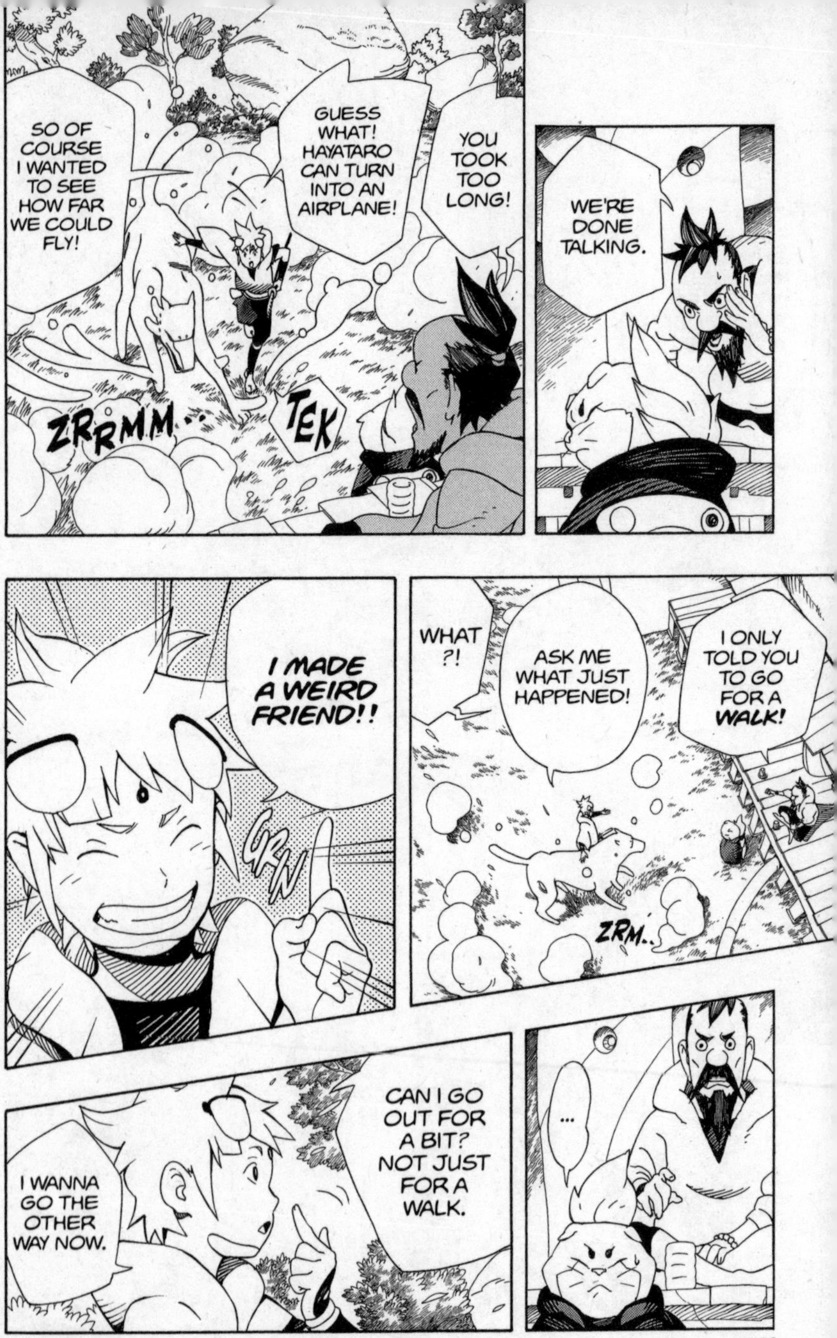
WE'RE DONE TALKING.
YOU TOOK TOO LONG!
GUESS WHAT! HAYATARO CAN TURN INTO AN AIRPLANE!
SO OF COURSE I WANTED TO SEE HOW FAR WE COULD FLY!
TEK
ZRRMM...
I ONLY TOLD YOU TO GO FOR A WALK!
ASK ME WHAT JUST HAPPENED!
WHAT?!
ZRM..
I MADE A WEIRD FRIEND!!
GRN
...
CAN I GO OUT FOR A BIT? NOT JUST FOR A WALK.
I WANNA GO THE OTHER WAY NOW.

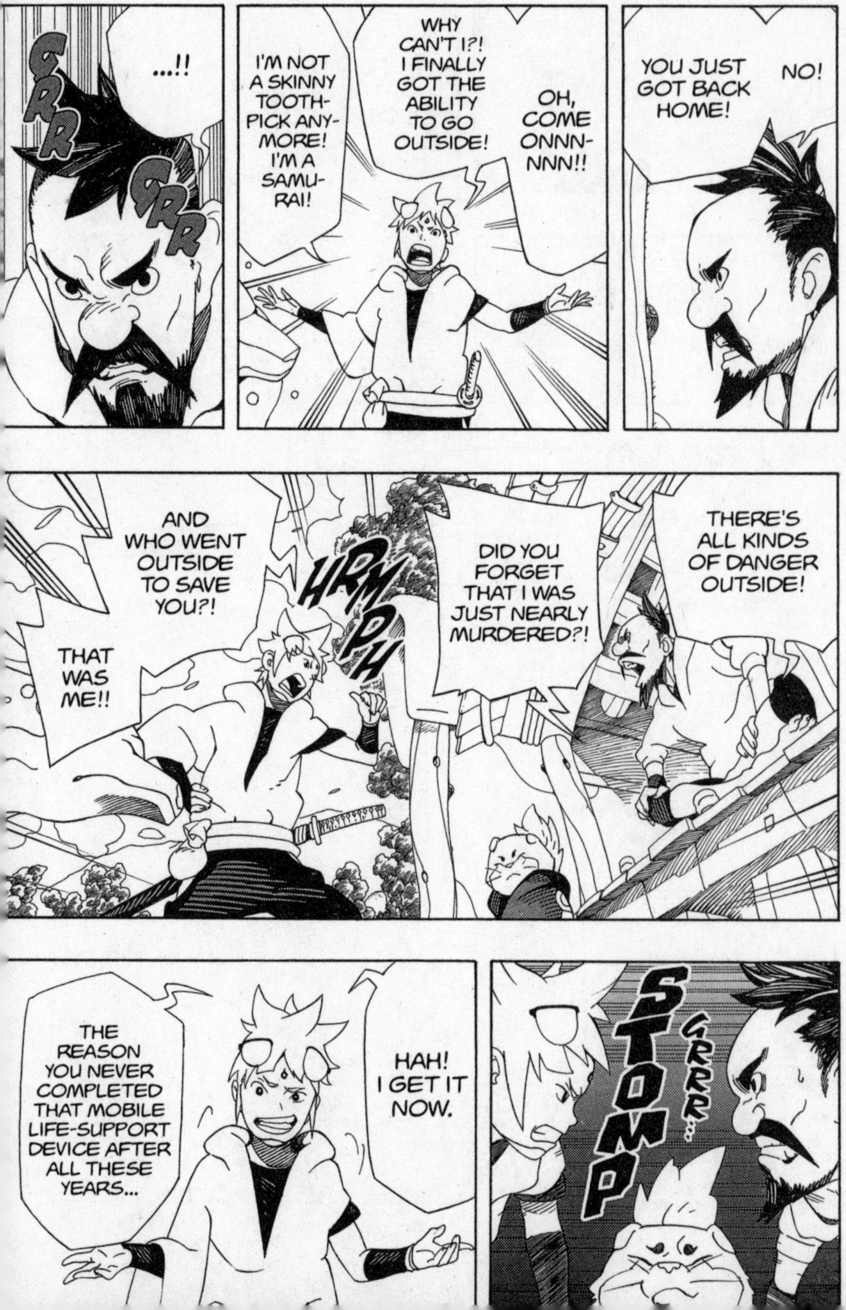
NO!
YOU JUST GOT BACK HOME!
OH, COME ONNN-NNN!!
WHY CAN'T I?! I FINALLY GOT THE ABILITY TO GO OUTSIDE!
I'M NOT A SKINNY TOOTH-PICK ANY-MORE! I'M A SAMU-RAI!
GRR GRR
...!!
THERE'S ALL KINDS OF DANGER OUTSIDE!
DID YOU FORGET THAT I WAS JUST NEARLY MURDERED?!
HRMPH
AND WHO WENT OUTSIDE TO SAVE YOU?!
THAT WAS ME!!
GRRR...
STOMP
HAH! I GET IT NOW.
THE REASON YOU NEVER COMPLETED THAT MOBILE LIFE-SUPPORT DEVICE AFTER ALL THESE YEARS...

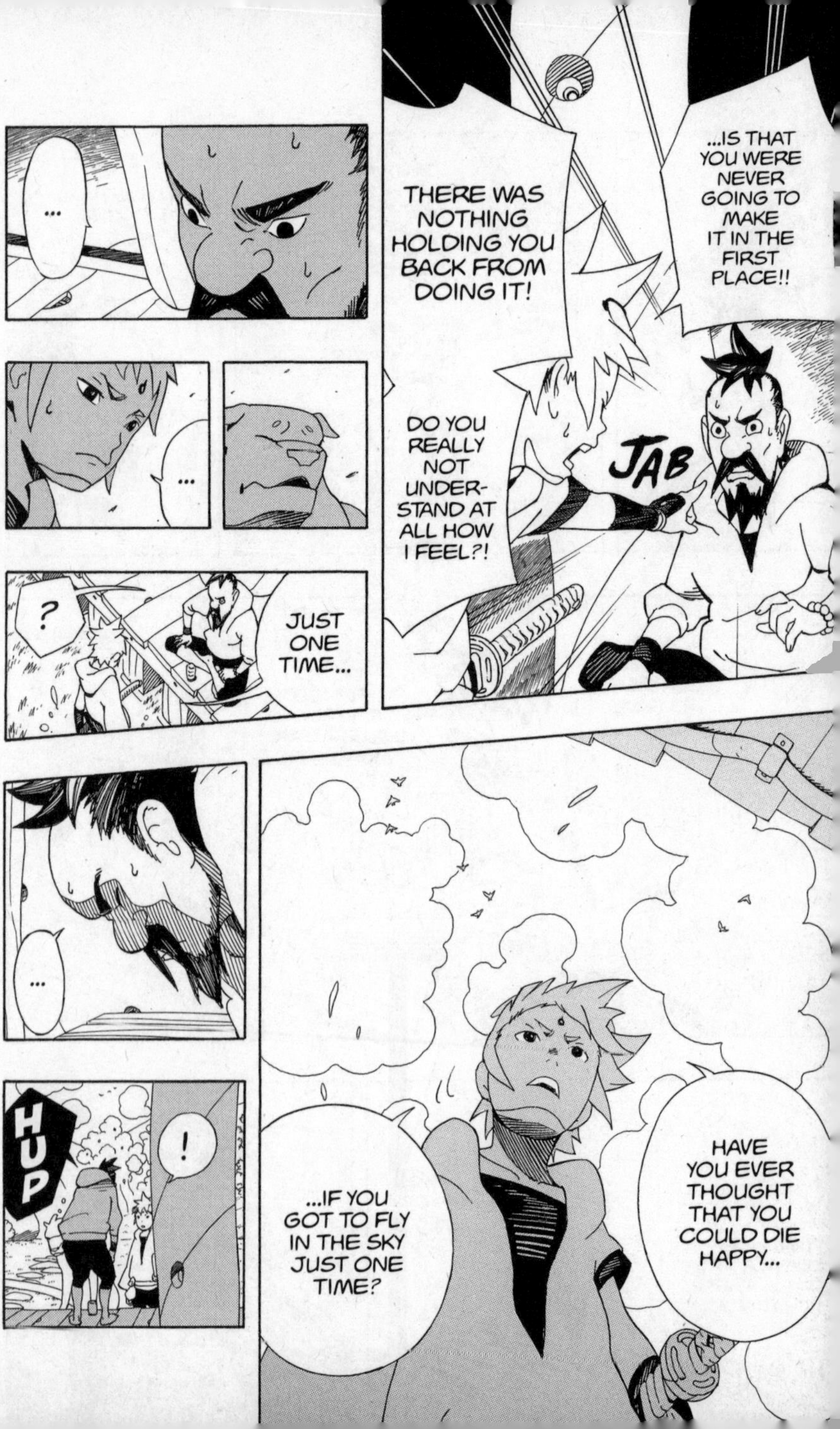
...IS THAT YOU WERE NEVER GOING TO MAKE IT IN THE FIRST PLACE!!
THERE WAS NOTHING HOLDING YOU BACK FROM DOING IT!
DO YOU REALLY NOT UNDER-STAND AT ALL HOW I FEEL?!
JAB
...
...
?
JUST ONE TIME...
HAVE YOU EVER THOUGHT THAT YOU COULD DIE HAPPY...
...IF YOU GOT TO FLY IN THE SKY JUST ONE TIME?
...
!
HUP

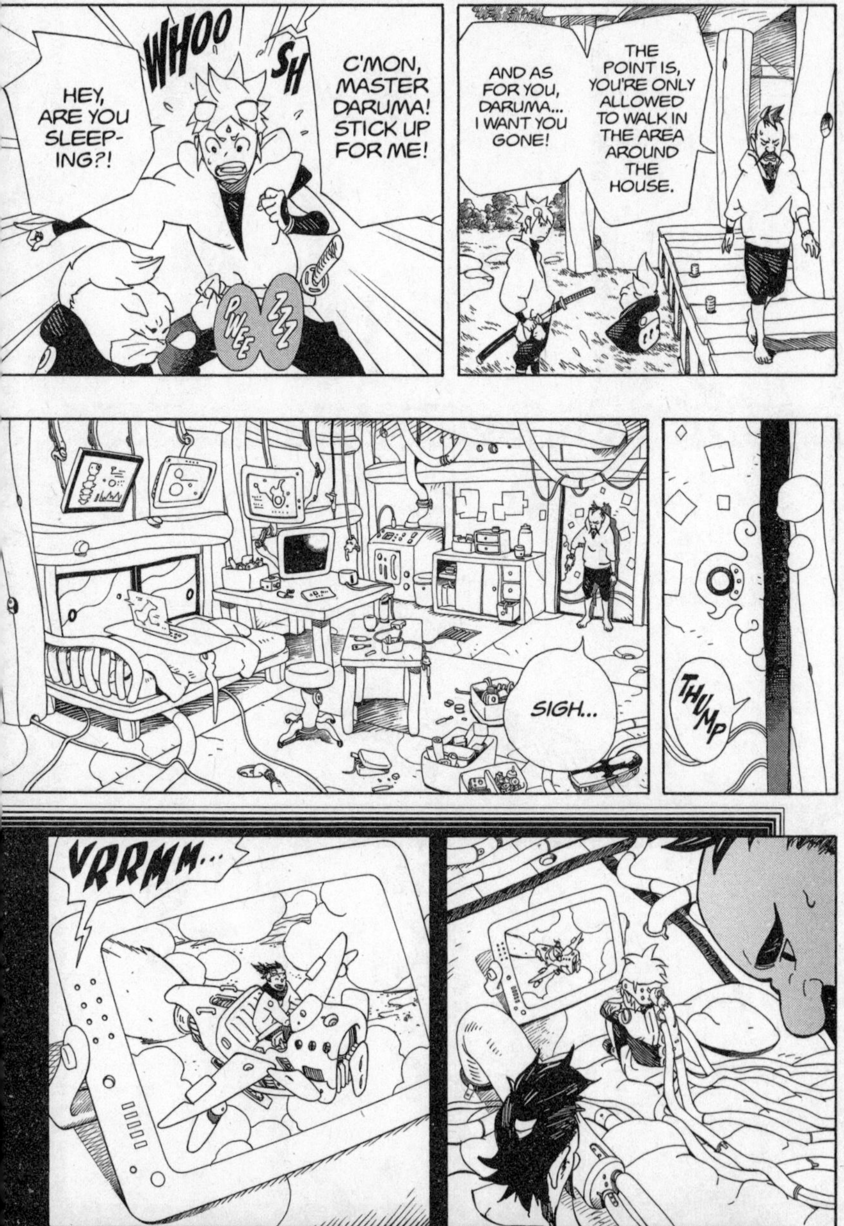
THE POINT IS, YOU'RE ONLY ALLOWED TO WALK IN THE AREA AROUND THE HOUSE.
AND AS FOR YOU, DARUMA... I WANT YOU GONE!
C'MON, MASTER DARUMA! STICK UP FOR ME!
WHOOSH
HEY, ARE YOU SLEEP-ING?!
PWEE
ZZZ
THUMP
SIGH...
VRRMM...

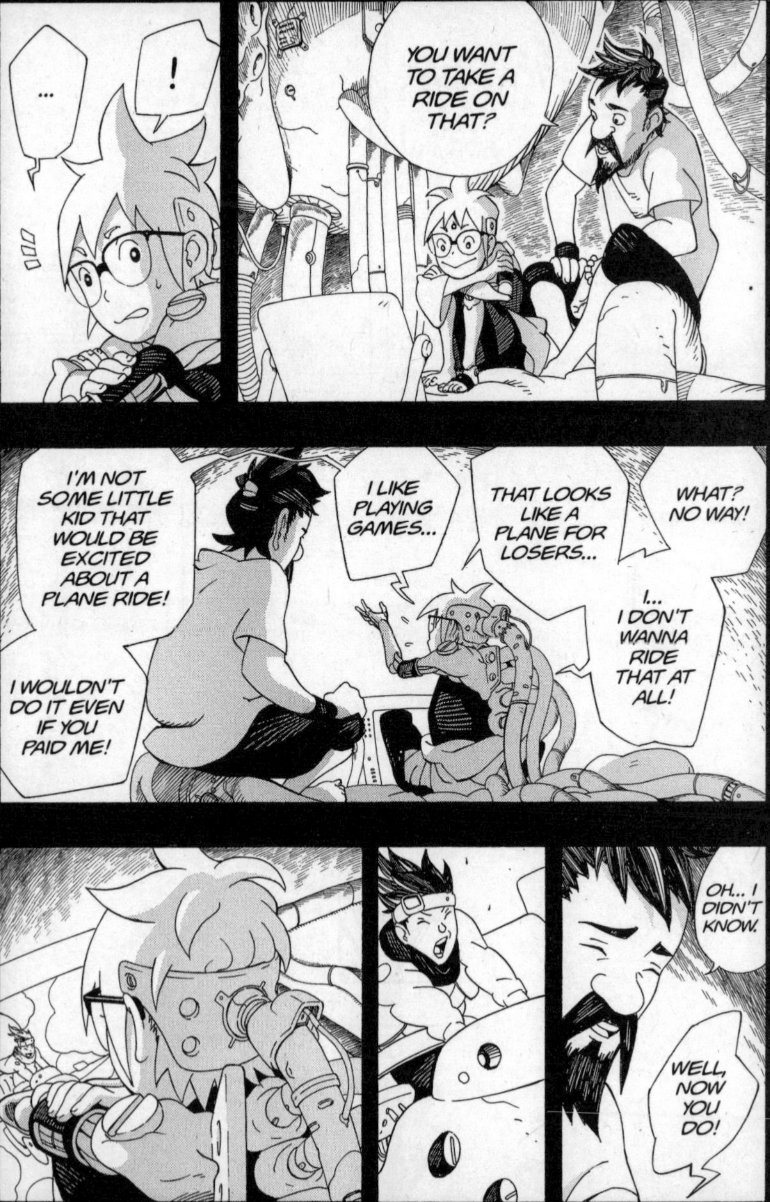
YOU WANT TO TAKE A RIDE ON THAT?
!
...
WHAT? NO WAY!
THAT LOOKS LIKE A PLANE FOR LOSERS...
I LIKE PLAYING GAMES...
I'M NOT SOME LITTLE KID THAT WOULD BE EXCITED ABOUT A PLANE RIDE!
I... I DON'T WANNA RIDE THAT AT ALL!
I WOULDN'T DO IT EVEN IF YOU PAID ME!
OH... I DIDN'T KNOW.
WELL, NOW YOU DO!

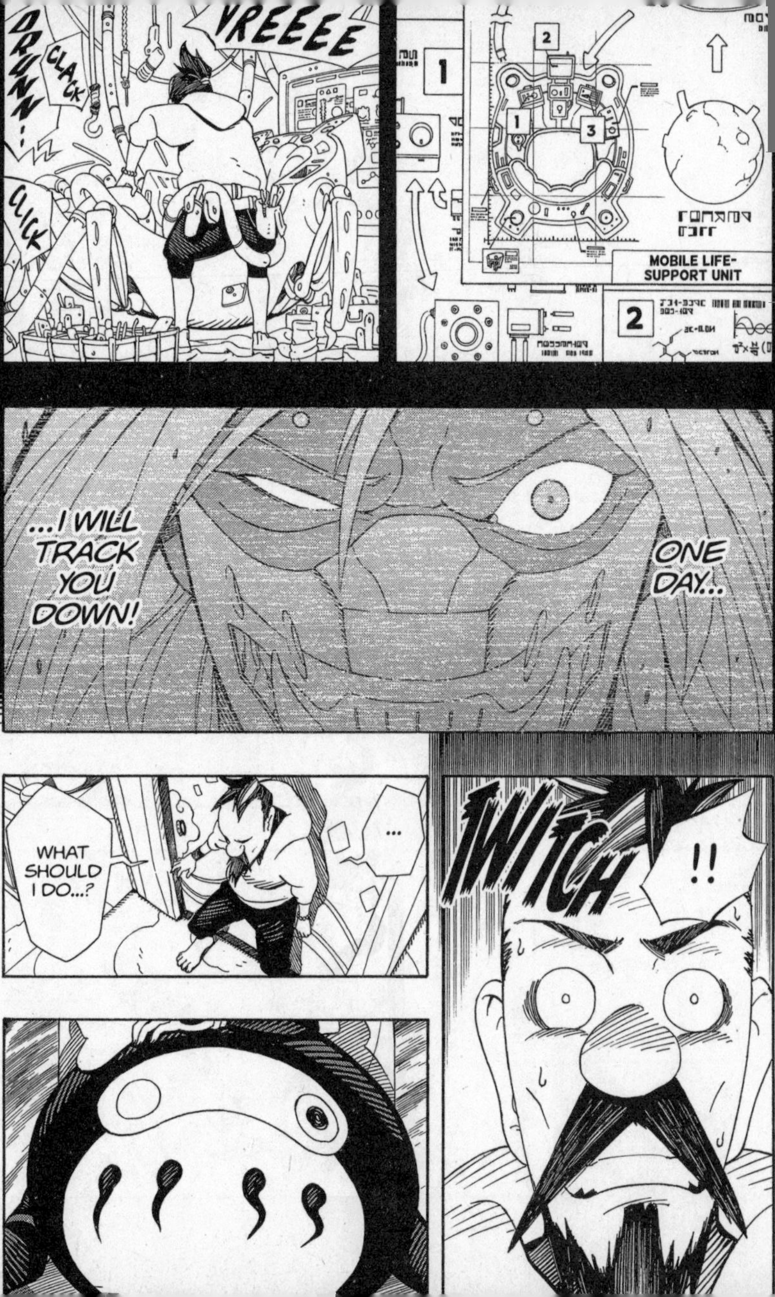

1
2
3
MOBILE LIFE-SUPPORT UNIT
2
VREEEE
DRUNN..
CLACK
CLICK
ONE DAY...
...I WILL TRACK YOU DOWN!
TWITCH
!!
...
WHAT SHOULD I DO...?

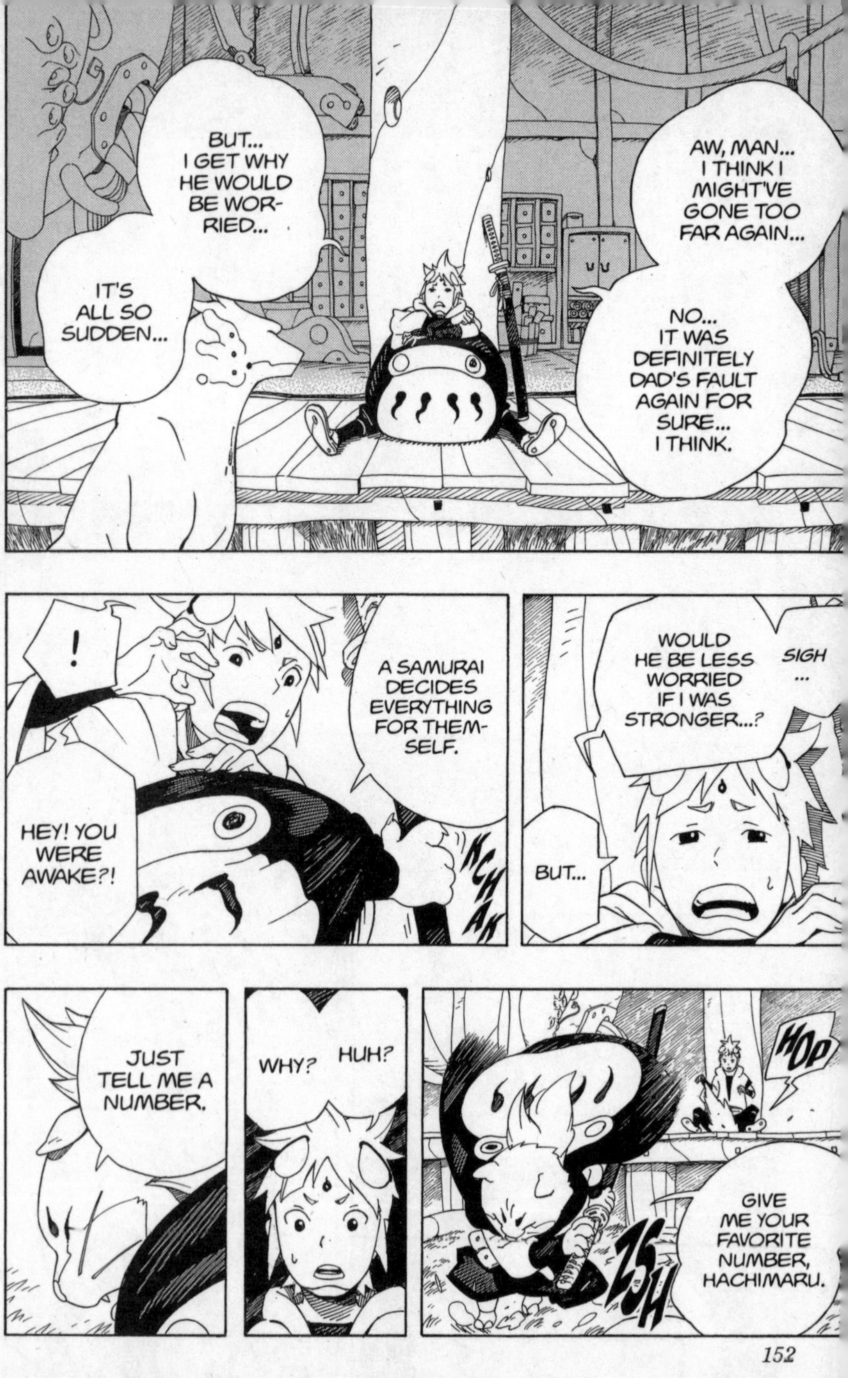
AW, MAN... I THINK I MIGHT'VE GONE TOO FAR AGAIN...
NO... IT WAS DEFINITELY DAD'S FAULT AGAIN FOR SURE... I THINK.
BUT... I GET WHY HE WOULD BE WOR-RIED...
IT'S ALL SO SUDDEN...
SIGH...
WOULD HE BE LESS WORRIED IF I WAS STRONGER...?
BUT...
A SAMURAI DECIDES EVERYTHING FOR THEM-SELF.
KCHAK
!
HEY! YOU WERE AWAKE?!
HOP
GIVE ME YOUR FAVORITE NUMBER, HACHIMARU.
ZSH
HUH?
WHY?
JUST TELL ME A NUMBER.

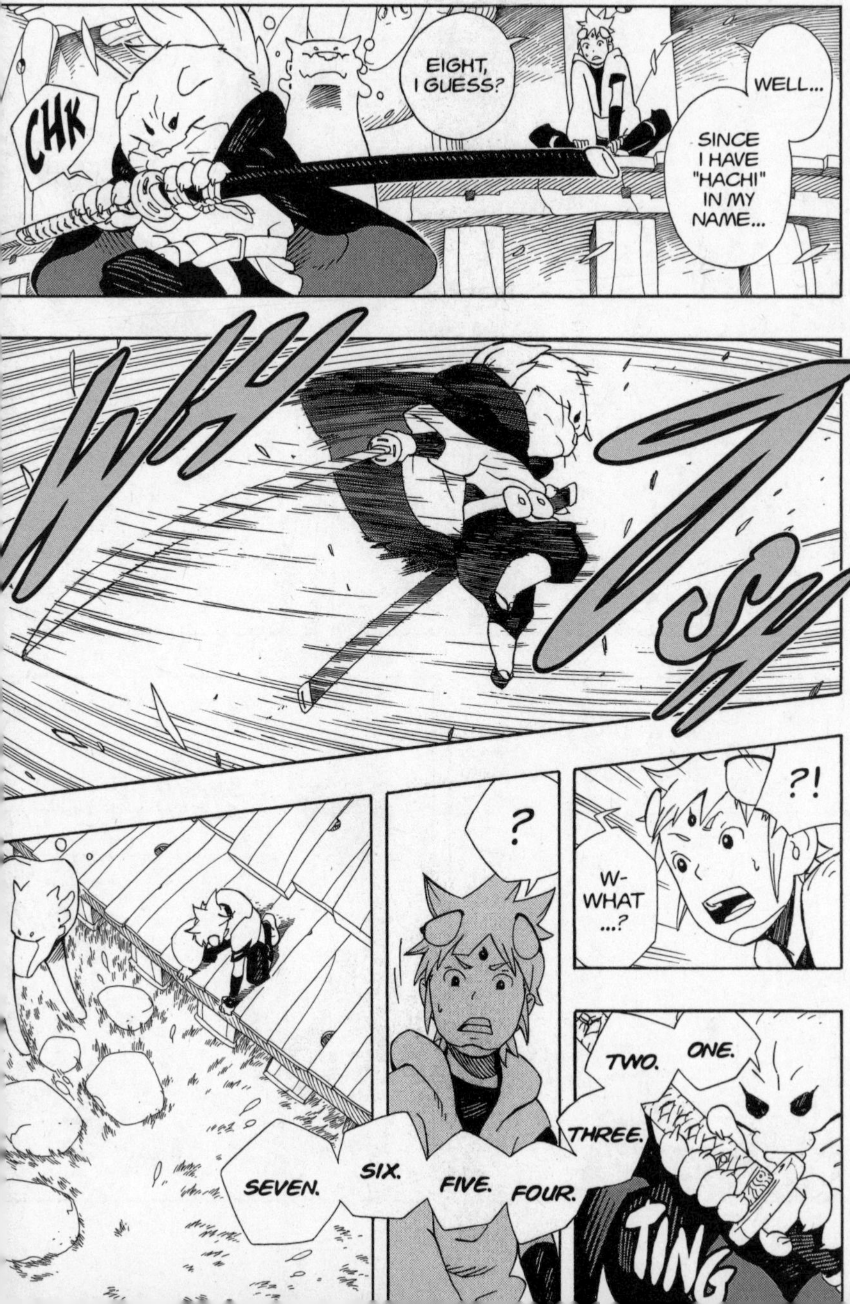
WELL...
SINCE I HAVE "HACHI" IN MY NAME...
EIGHT, I GUESS?
CHK
?!
W-WHAT ...?
?
SEVEN.
SIX.
FIVE.
FOUR.
THREE.
TWO.
ONE.
TING

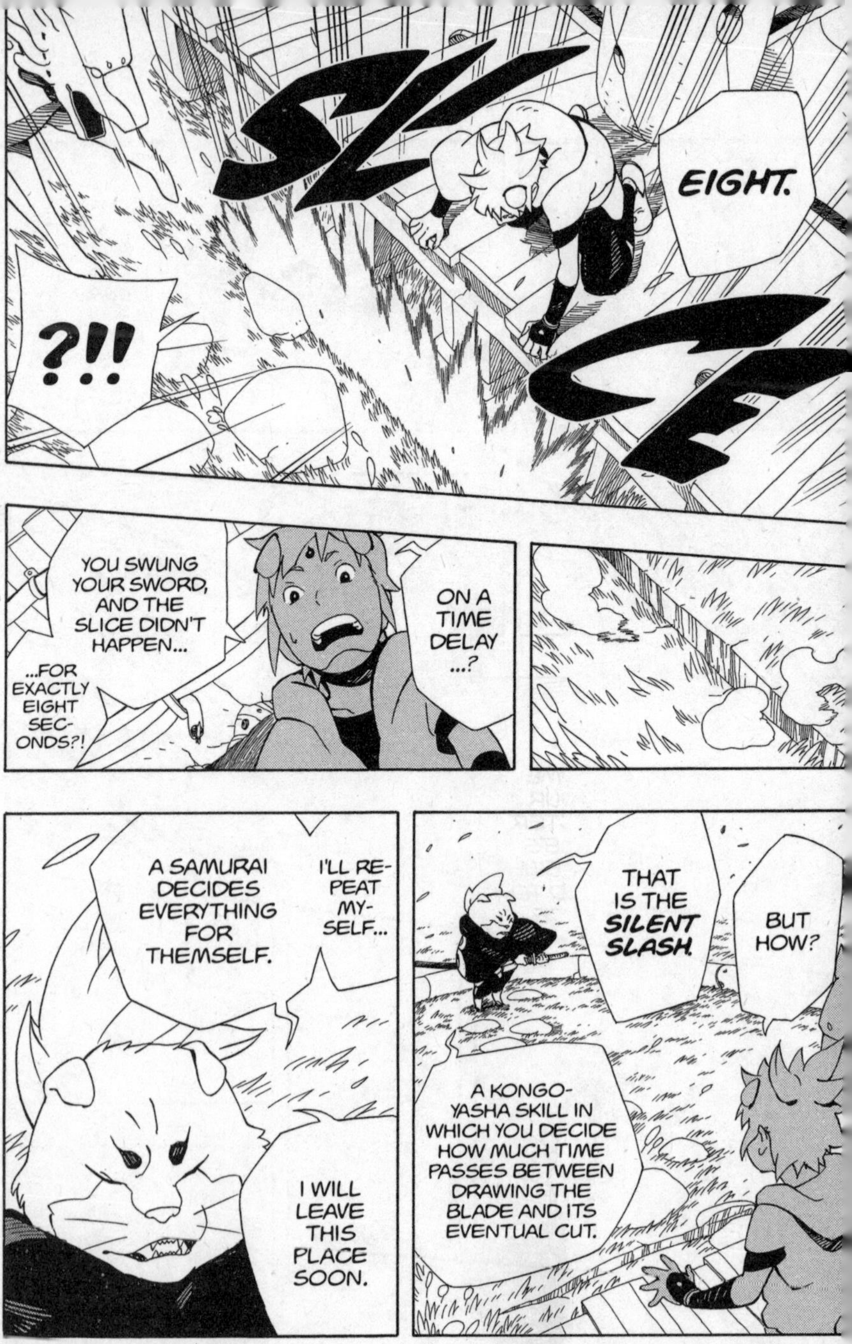
EIGHT.
?!!
ON A TIME DELAY ...?
YOU SWUNG YOUR SWORD, AND THE SLICE DIDN'T HAPPEN...
...FOR EXACTLY EIGHT SEC-ONDS?!
BUT HOW?
THAT IS THE SILENT SLASH.
A KONGO-YASHA SKILL IN WHICH YOU DECIDE HOW MUCH TIME PASSES BETWEEN DRAWING THE BLADE AND ITS EVENTUAL CUT.
I'LL RE-PEAT MY-SELF...
A SAMURAI DECIDES EVERYTHING FOR THEMSELF.
I WILL LEAVE THIS PLACE SOON.

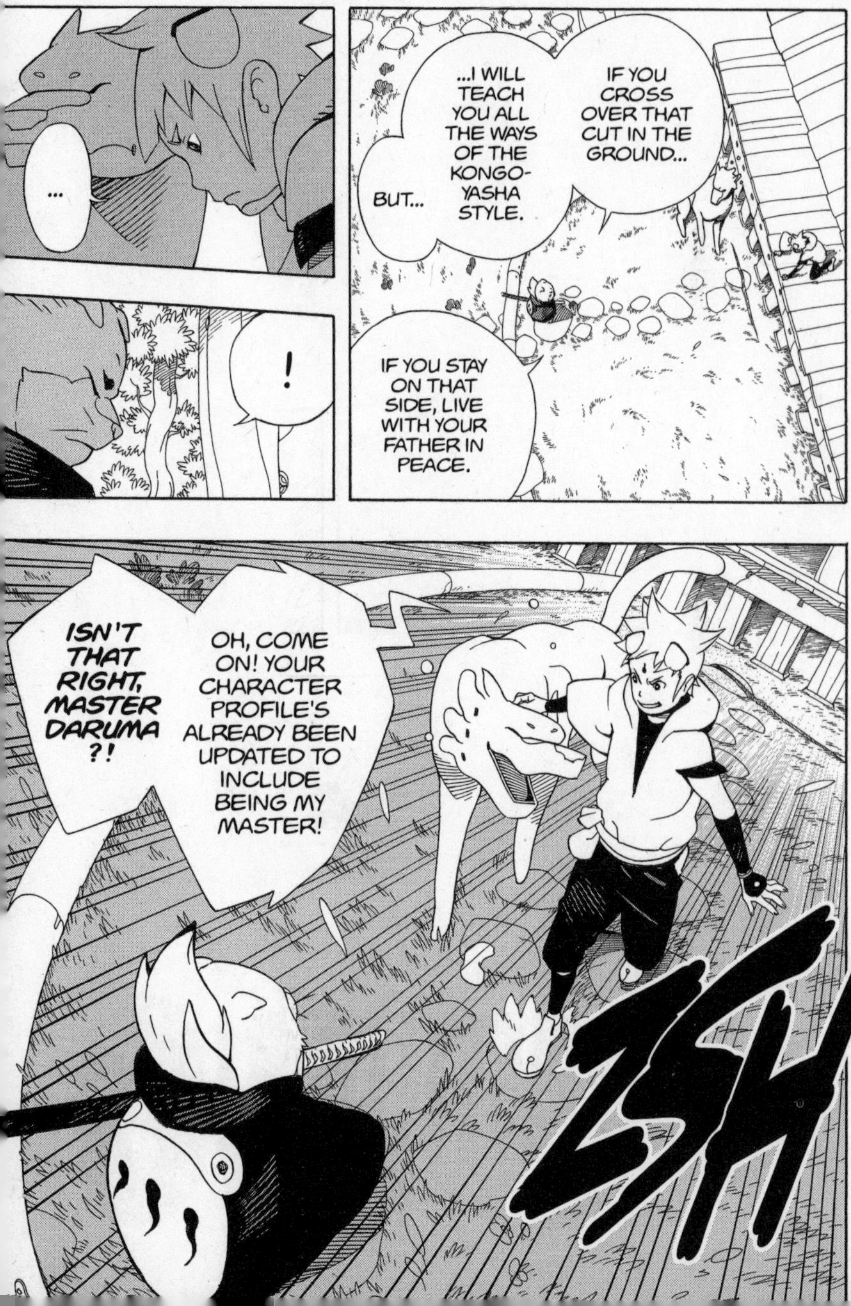
IF YOU CROSS OVER THAT CUT IN THE GROUND...
...I WILL TEACH YOU ALL THE WAYS OF THE KONGO-YASHA STYLE.
BUT...
IF YOU STAY ON THAT SIDE, LIVE WITH YOUR FATHER IN PEACE.
...
!
OH, COME ON! YOUR CHARACTER PROFILE'S ALREADY BEEN UPDATED TO INCLUDE BEING MY MASTER!
ISN'T THAT RIGHT, MASTER DARUMA?!
ZSH

SAMURAI 8
THE TALE OF HACHIMARU

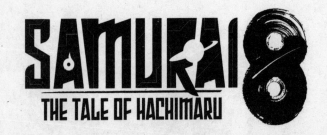

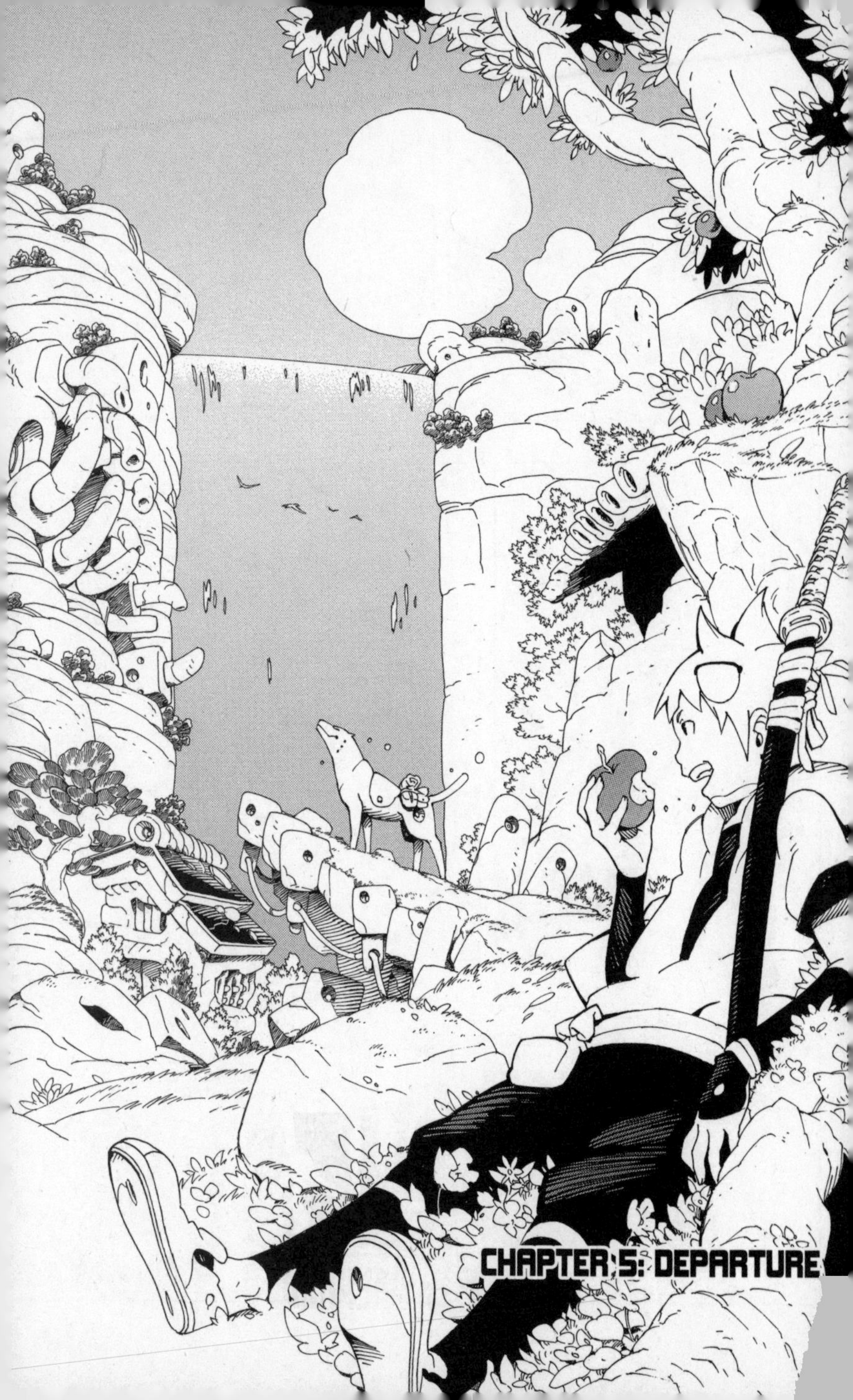
CHAPTER 5: DEPARTURE

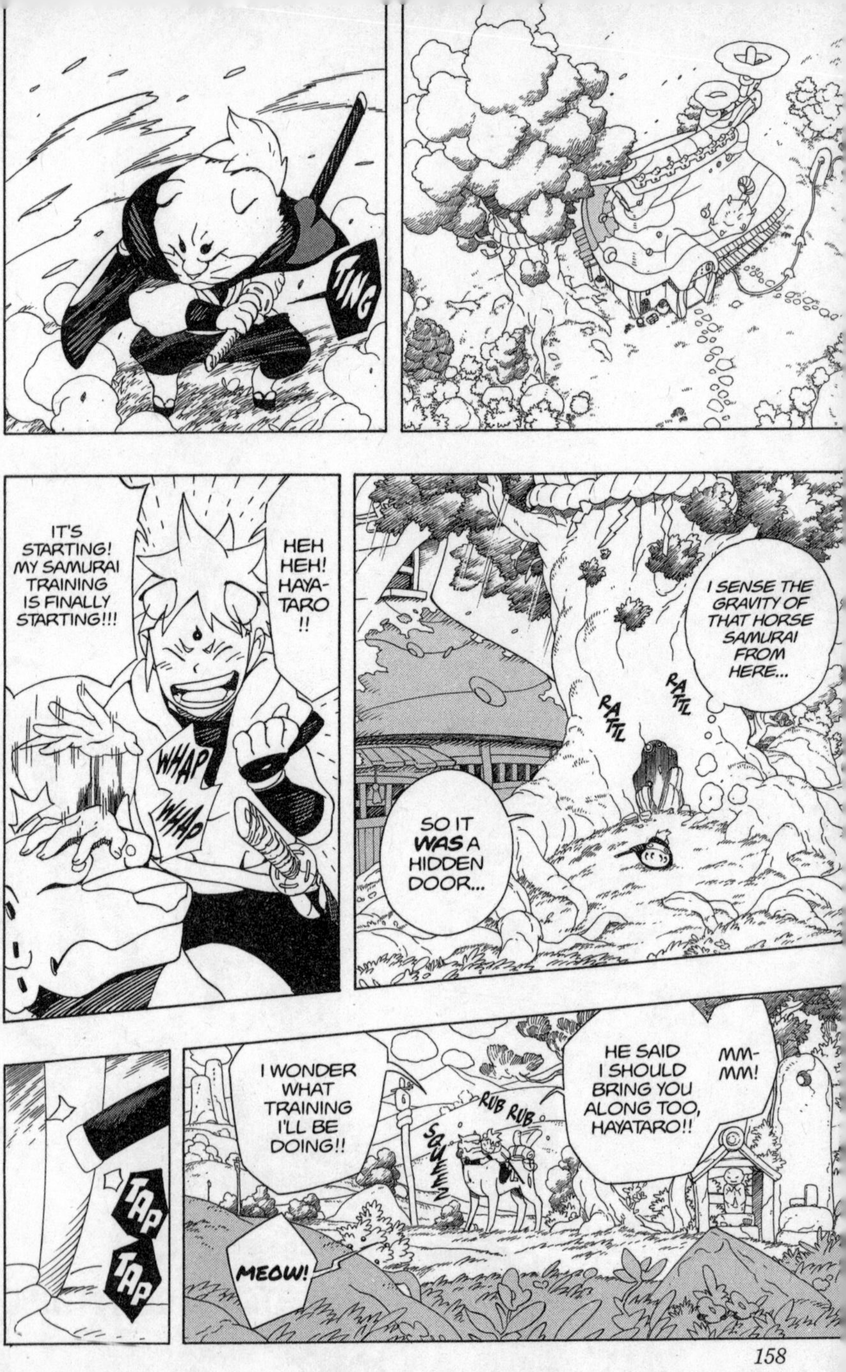
TING
I SENSE THE GRAVITY OF THAT HORSE SAMURAI FROM HERE...
RATTL
RATTL
SO IT WAS A HIDDEN DOOR...
HEH HEH! HAYA-TARO!!
IT'S STARTING! MY SAMURAI TRAINING IS FINALLY STARTING!!!
WHAP
WHAP
MM-MM!
HE SAID I SHOULD BRING YOU ALONG TOO, HAYATARO!!
RUB RUB
SQUEEZ
I WONDER WHAT TRAINING I'LL BE DOING!!
MEOW!
TAP
TAP

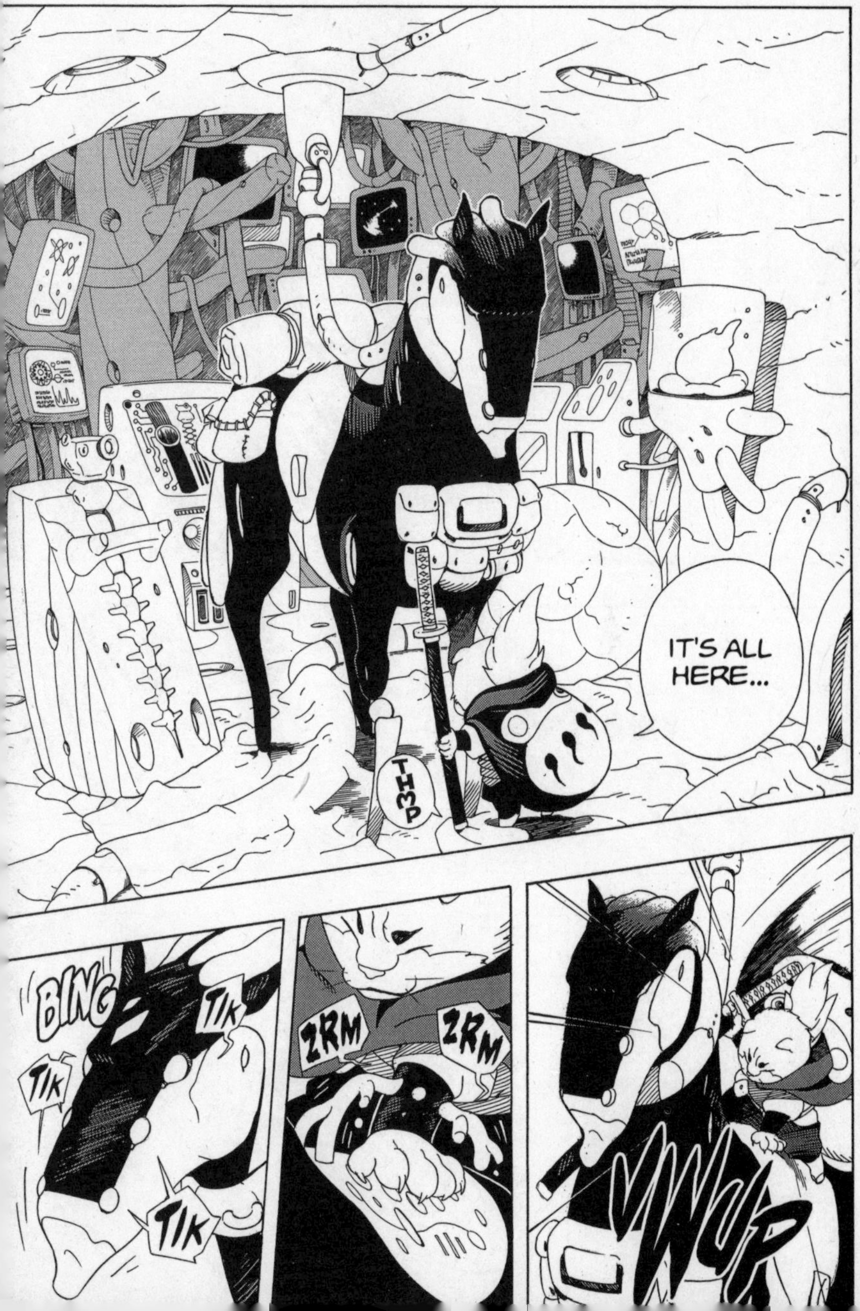
IT'S ALL HERE...
THMP
VWUP
ZRM
ZRM
BING
TIK
TIK
TIK

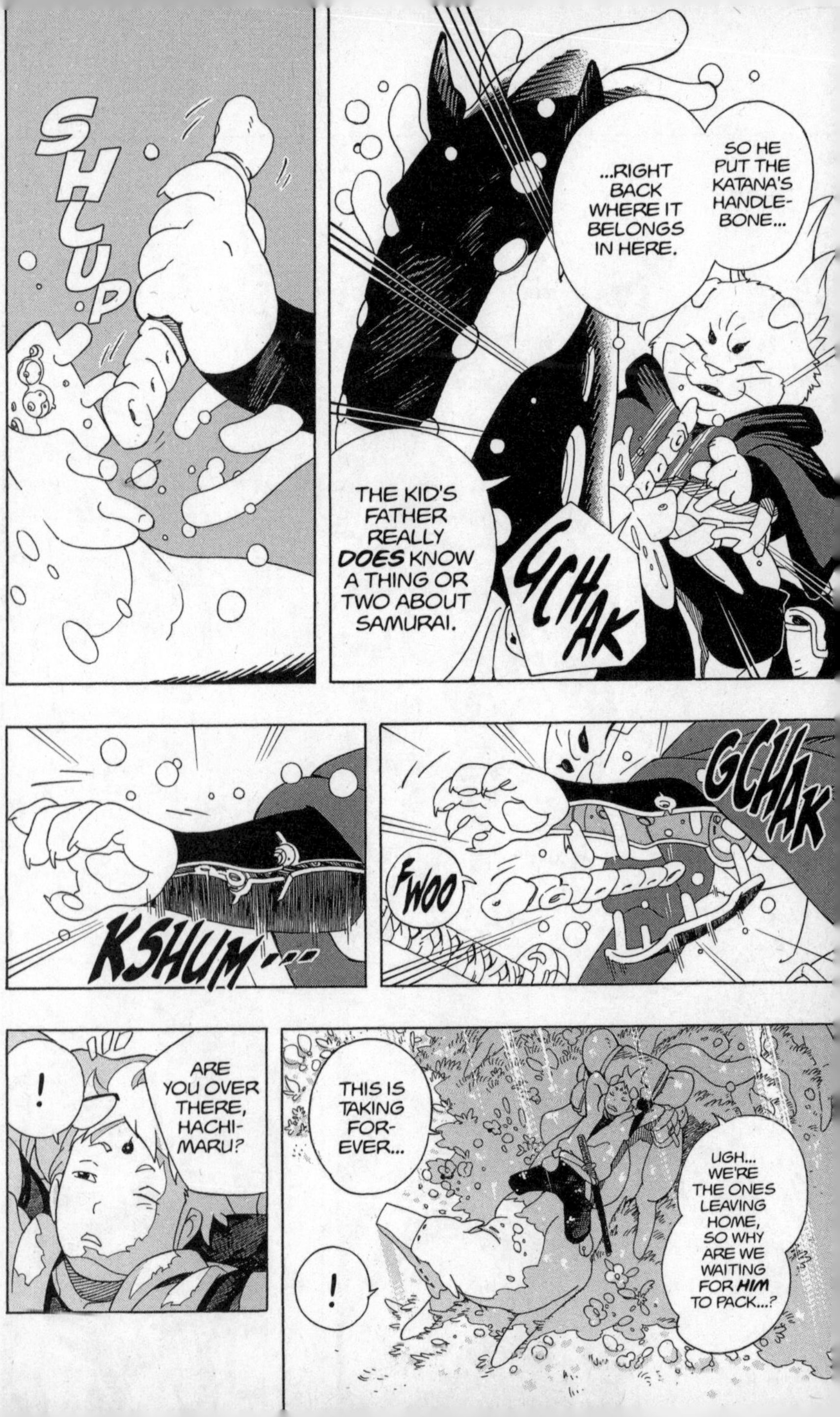
SO HE PUT THE KATANA'S HANDLE-BONE...
...RIGHT BACK WHERE IT BELONGS IN HERE.
THE KID'S FATHER REALLY **DOES** KNOW A THING OR TWO ABOUT SAMURAI.
GCHAK
SHLUP
GCHAK
FWOO
KSHUM...
UGH... WE'RE THE ONES LEAVING HOME, SO WHY ARE WE WAITING FOR **HIM** TO PACK...?
THIS IS TAKING FOR-EVER...
!
ARE YOU OVER THERE, HACHI-MARU?
!

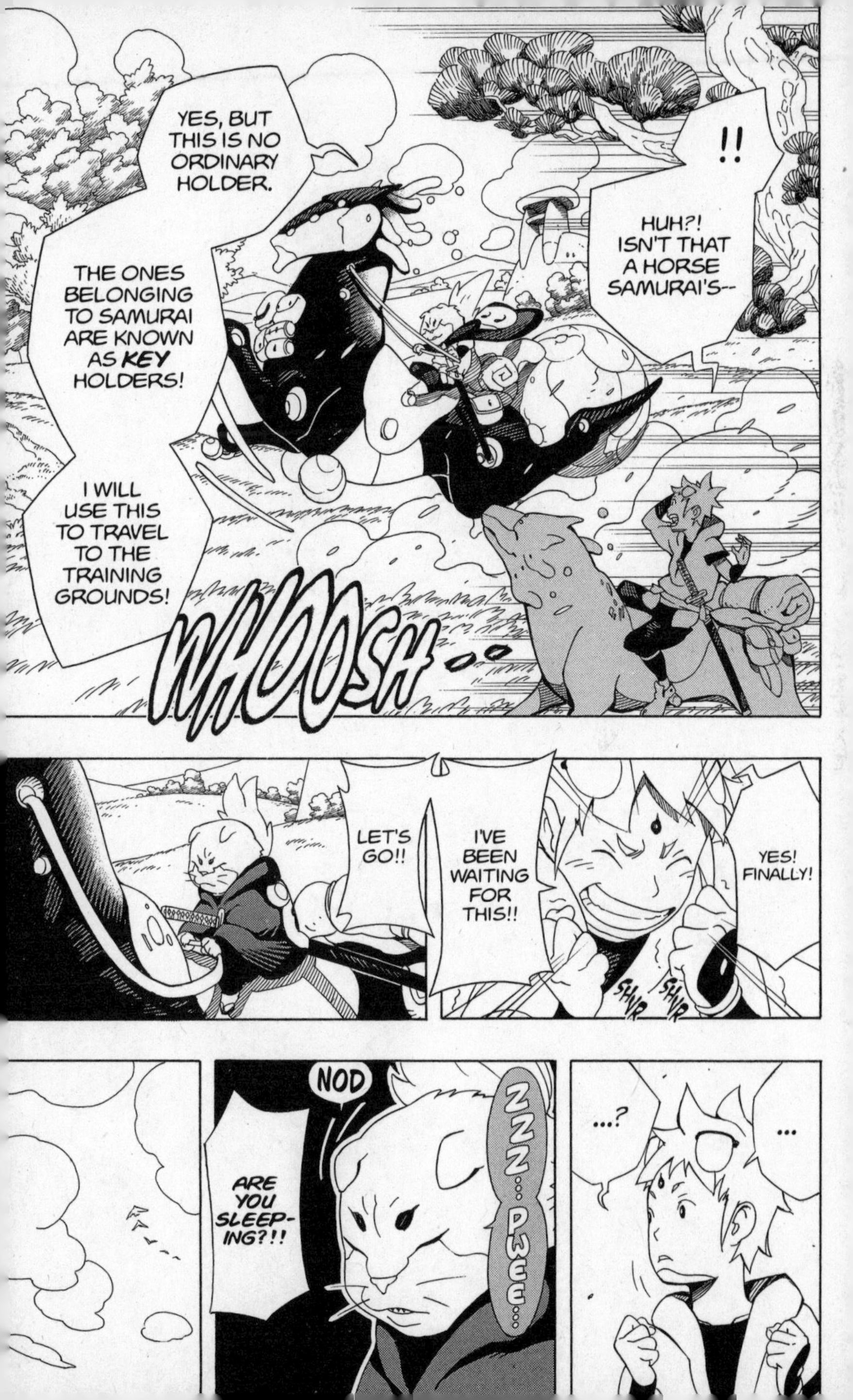
!!
HUH?! ISN'T THAT A HORSE SAMURAI'S--
YES, BUT THIS IS NO ORDINARY HOLDER.
THE ONES BELONGING TO SAMURAI ARE KNOWN AS **KEY** HOLDERS!
I WILL USE THIS TO TRAVEL TO THE TRAINING GROUNDS!
WHOOSH..
YES! FINALLY!
I'VE BEEN WAITING FOR THIS!!
SHVR
SHVR
LET'S GO!!
...
...?
NOD
ZZZ... PWEE...
ARE YOU SLEEPING?!!

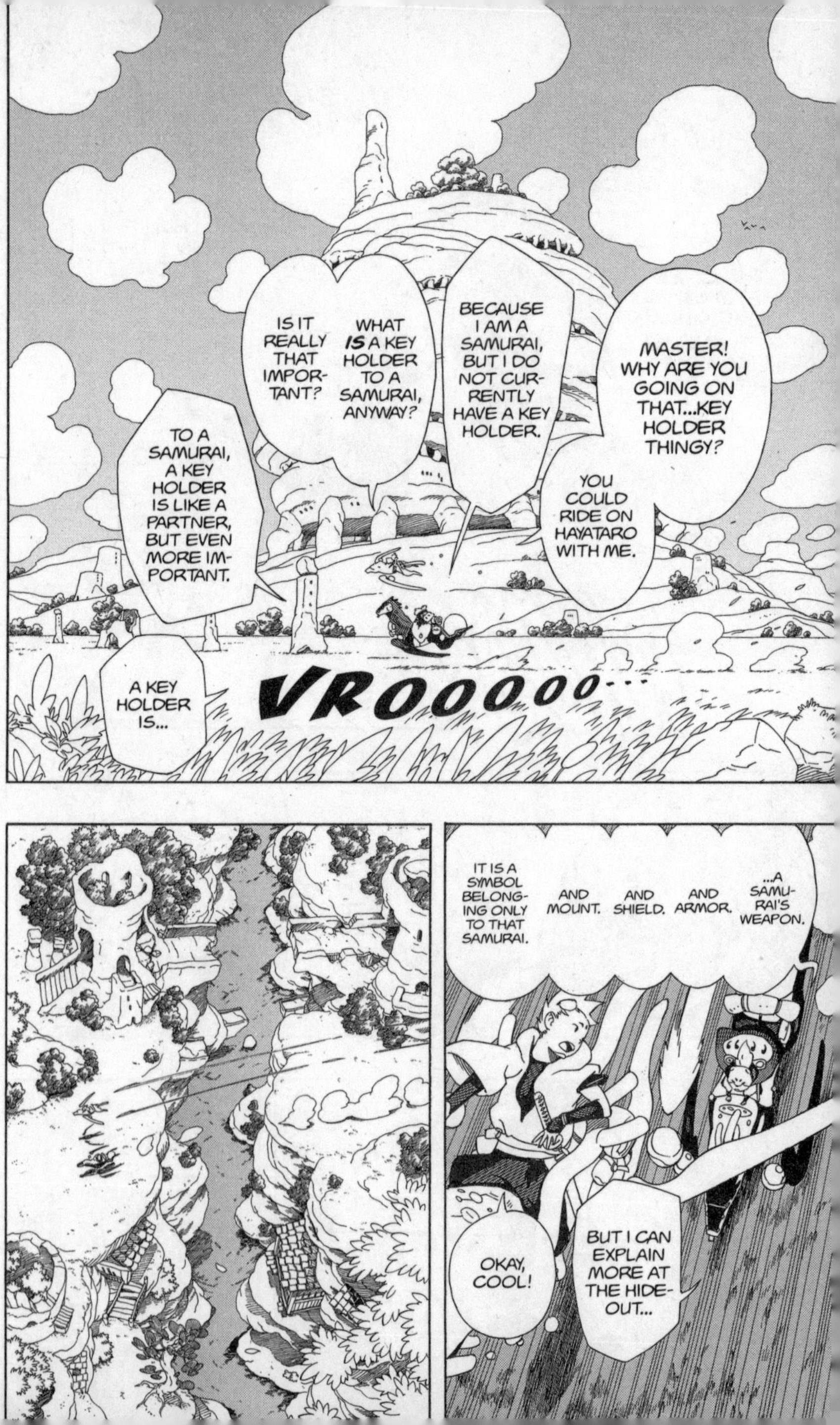
MASTER! WHY ARE YOU GOING ON THAT...KEY HOLDER THINGY?
YOU COULD RIDE ON HAYATARO WITH ME.
BECAUSE I AM A SAMURAI, BUT I DO NOT CURRENTLY HAVE A KEY HOLDER.
WHAT *IS* A KEY HOLDER TO A SAMURAI, ANYWAY?
IS IT REALLY THAT IMPORTANT?
TO A SAMURAI, A KEY HOLDER IS LIKE A PARTNER, BUT EVEN MORE IMPORTANT.
A KEY HOLDER IS...
VROOOOO...
...A SAMURAI'S WEAPON.
AND ARMOR.
AND SHIELD.
AND MOUNT.
IT IS A SYMBOL BELONGING ONLY TO THAT SAMURAI.
BUT I CAN EXPLAIN MORE AT THE HIDEOUT...
OKAY, COOL!

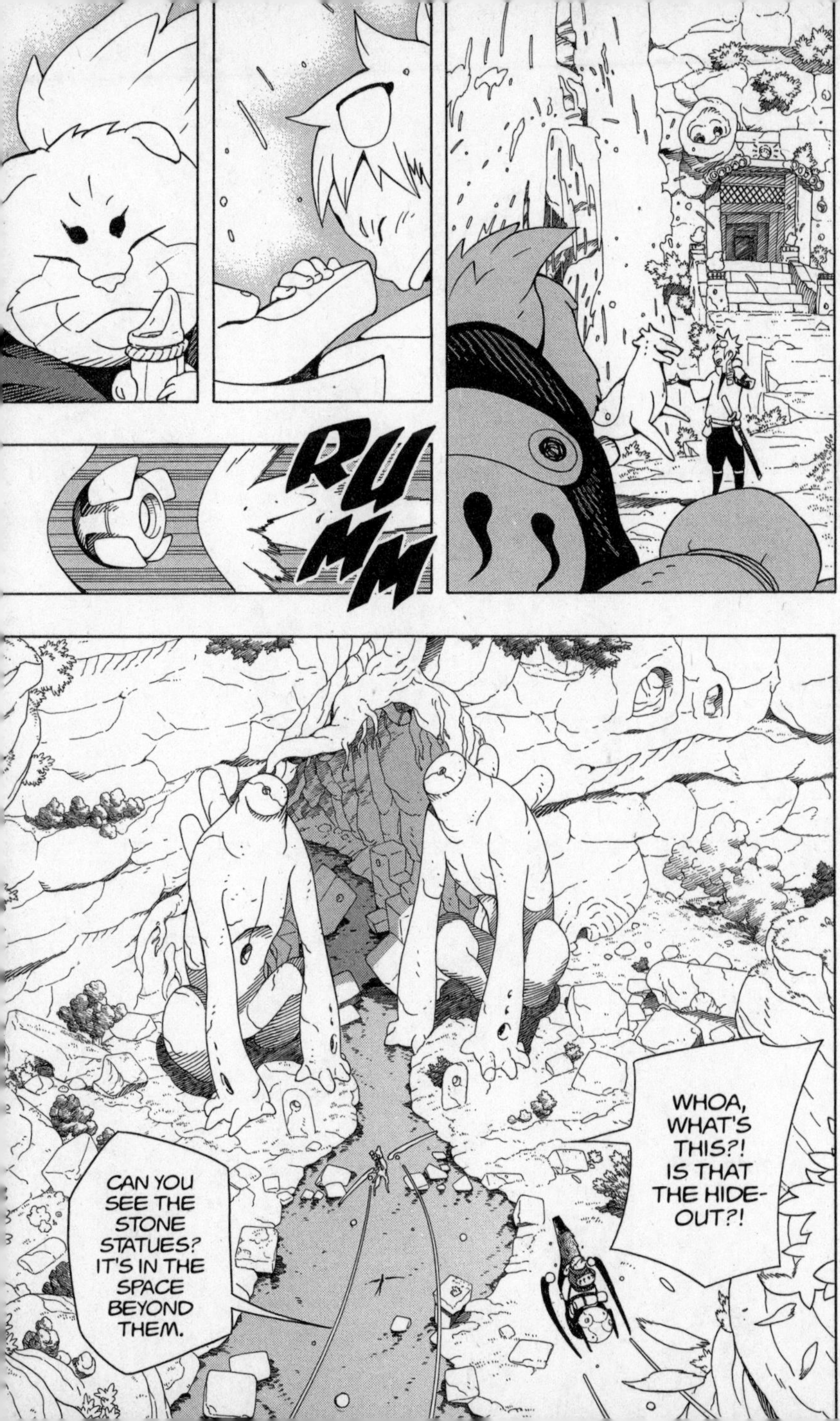
RUMM
WHOA, WHAT'S THIS?! IS THAT THE HIDE-OUT?!
CAN YOU SEE THE STONE STATUES? IT'S IN THE SPACE BEYOND THEM.

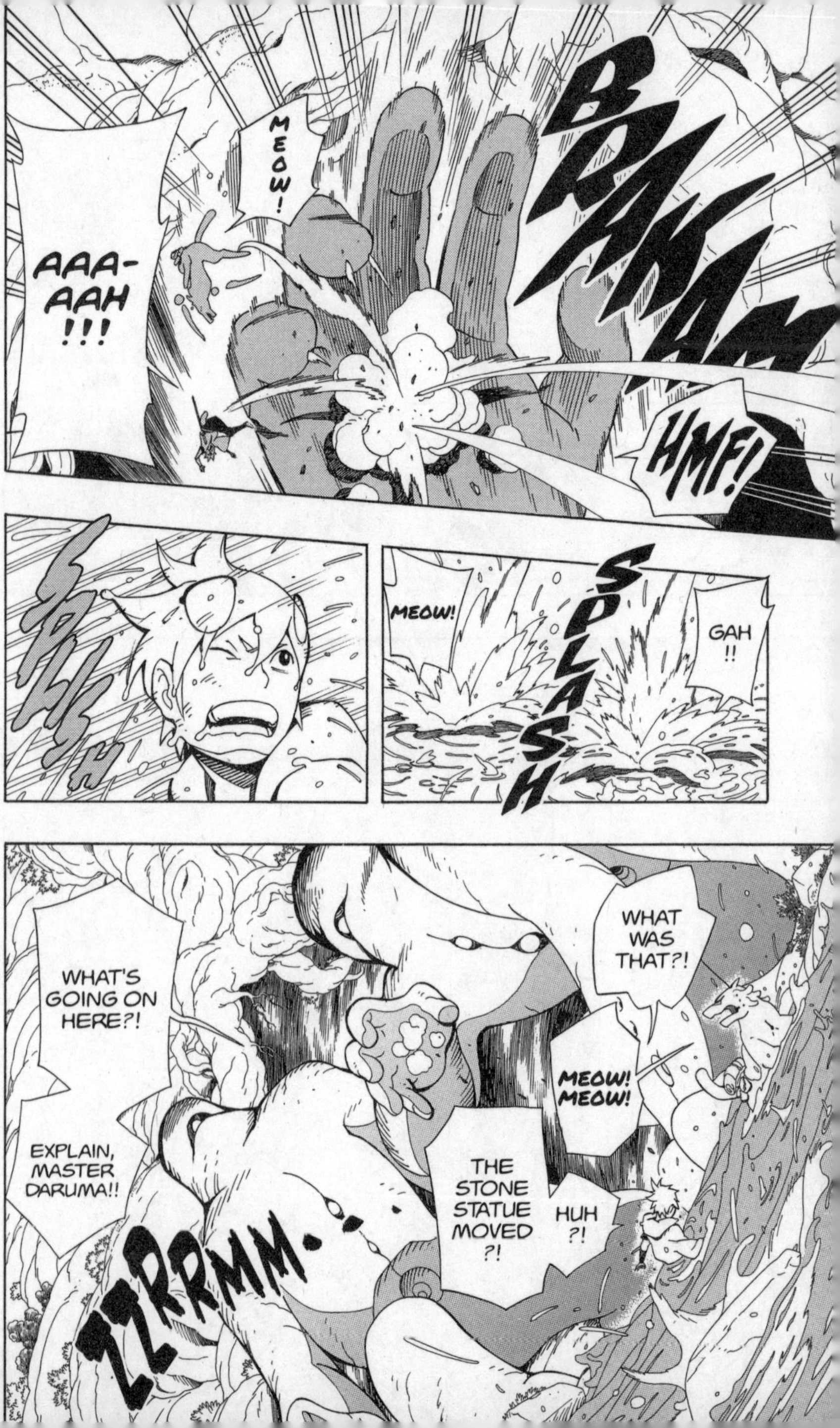
HMF!
MEOW!
AAA-AAH!!!
GAH!!
SPLASH
MEOW!
WHAT WAS THAT?!
WHAT'S GOING ON HERE?!
MEOW! MEOW!
HUH?!
THE STONE STATUE MOVED?!
EXPLAIN, MASTER DARUMA!!
ZZRRMM

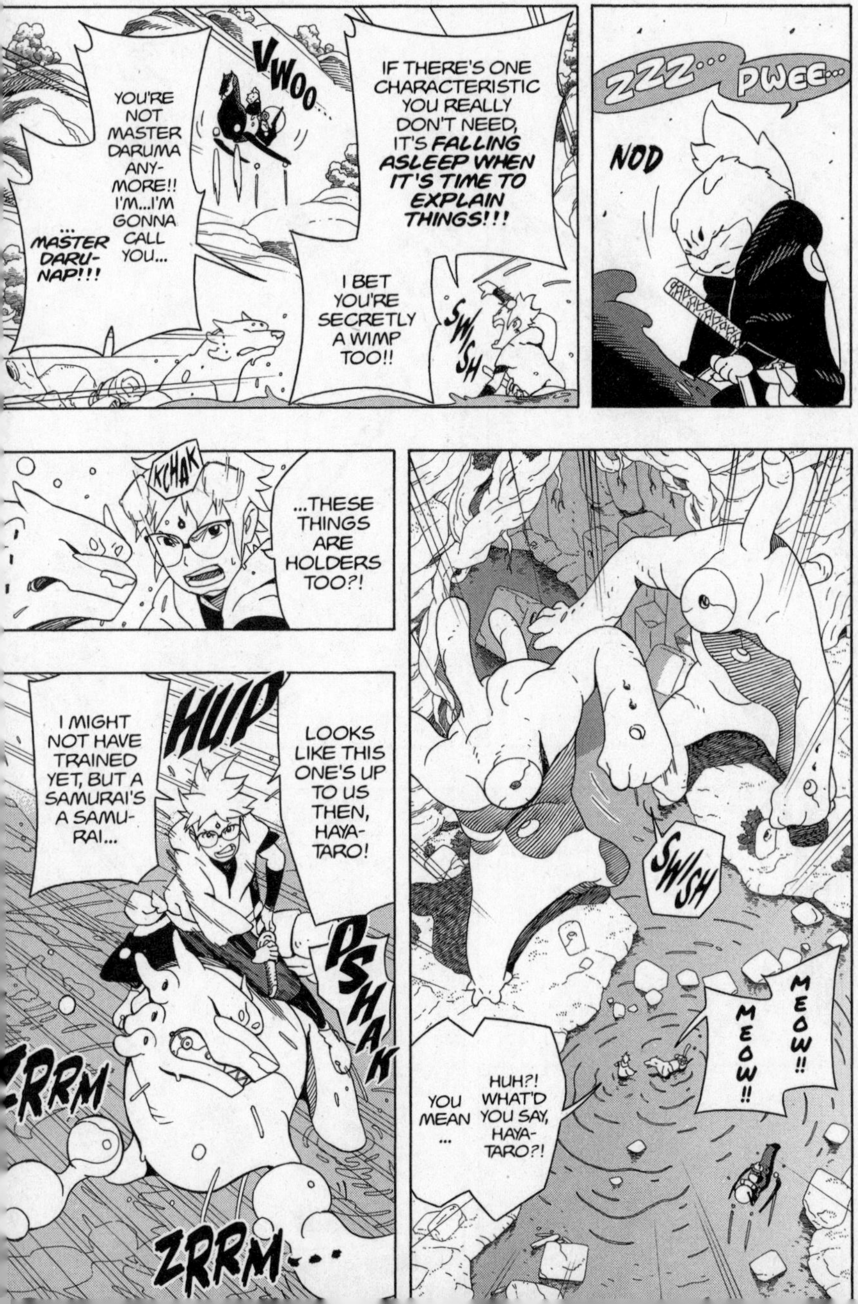
ZZZ...
PWEE...
NOD
IF THERE'S ONE CHARACTERISTIC YOU REALLY DON'T NEED, IT'S FALLING ASLEEP WHEN IT'S TIME TO EXPLAIN THINGS!!!
VWOO
YOU'RE NOT MASTER DARUMA ANYMORE!! I'M...I'M GONNA CALL YOU...
...MASTER DARU-NAP!!!
I BET YOU'RE SECRETLY A WIMP TOO!!
SWISH
SWISH
MEOW!!
MEOW!!
HUH?! WHAT'D YOU SAY, HAYATARO?!
YOU MEAN...
KCHAK
...THESE THINGS ARE HOLDERS TOO?!
LOOKS LIKE THIS ONE'S UP TO US THEN, HAYATARO!
HUP
I MIGHT NOT HAVE TRAINED YET, BUT A SAMURAI'S A SAMURAI...
PSHAK
ZRRM
ZRRM...

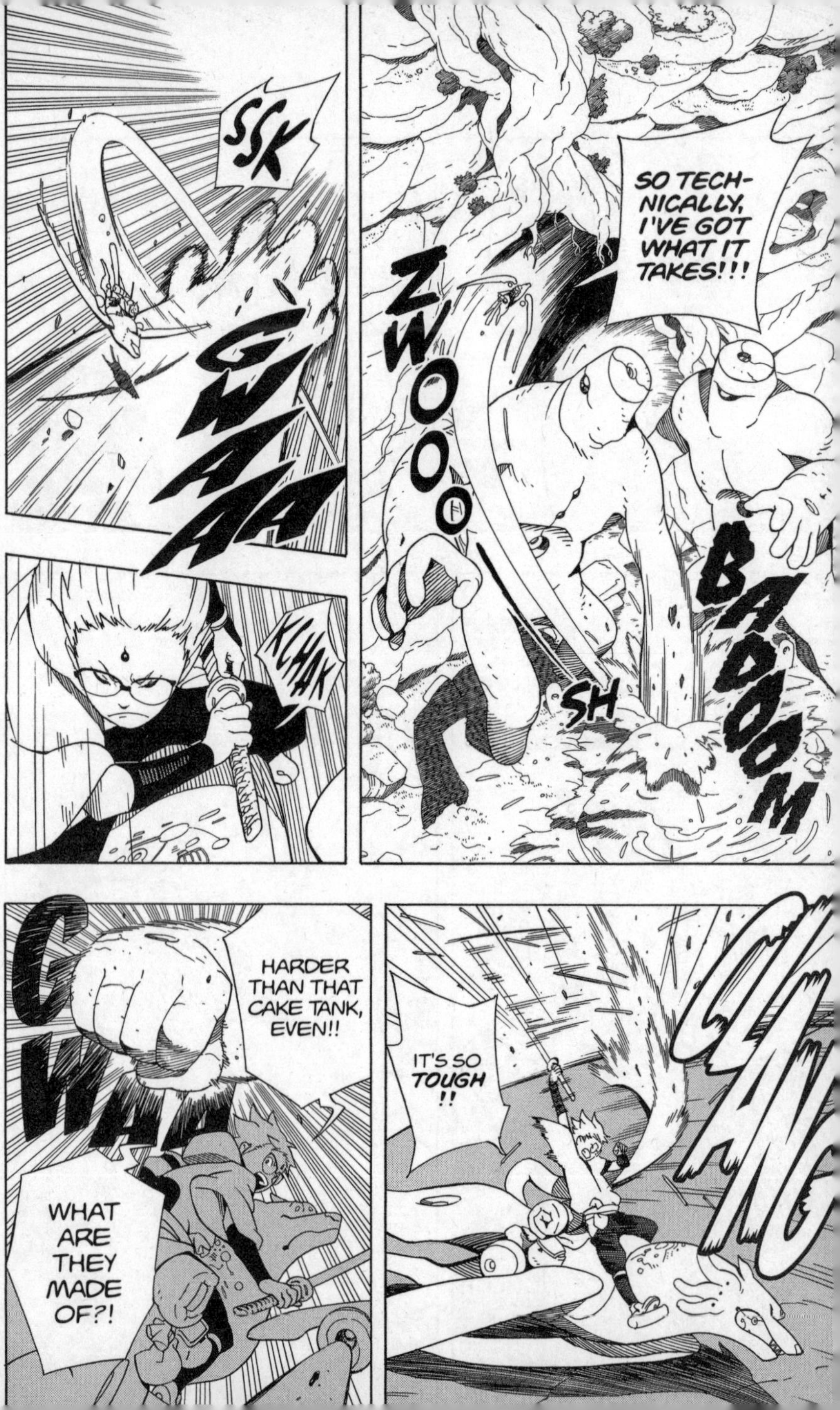
SO TECHNICALLY, I'VE GOT WHAT IT TAKES!!!
ZWOOOH
SH
BADOOM
SSK
GWAAA
KCHAK
CLANG
IT'S SO TOUGH!!
GWAA
HARDER THAN THAT CAKE TANK, EVEN!!
WHAT ARE THEY MADE OF?!

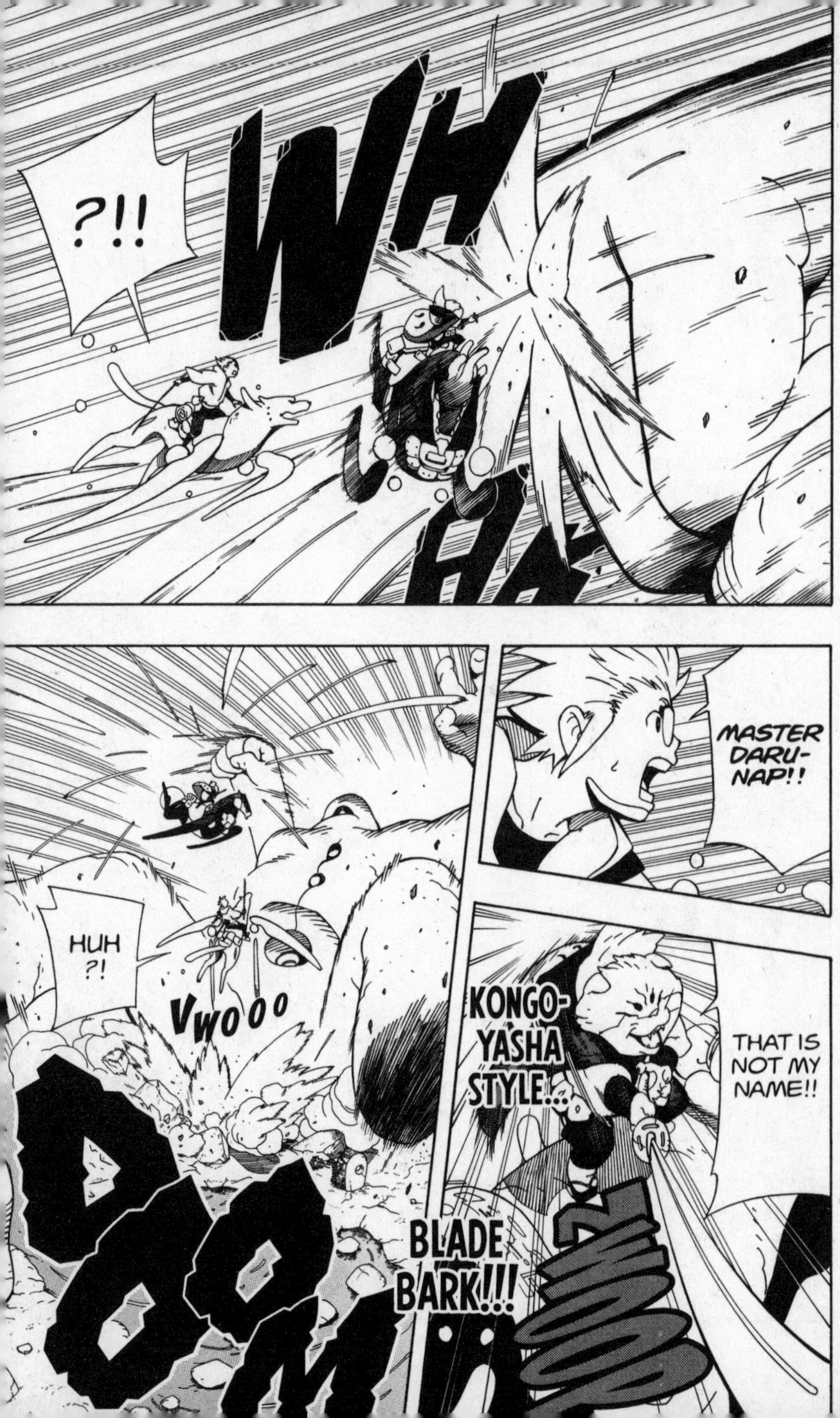
?!!
WH
MASTER DARU-NAP!!
THAT IS NOT MY NAME!!
KONGO-YASHA STYLE...
BLADE BARK!!!
HUH ?!
VWOOO
BOOM

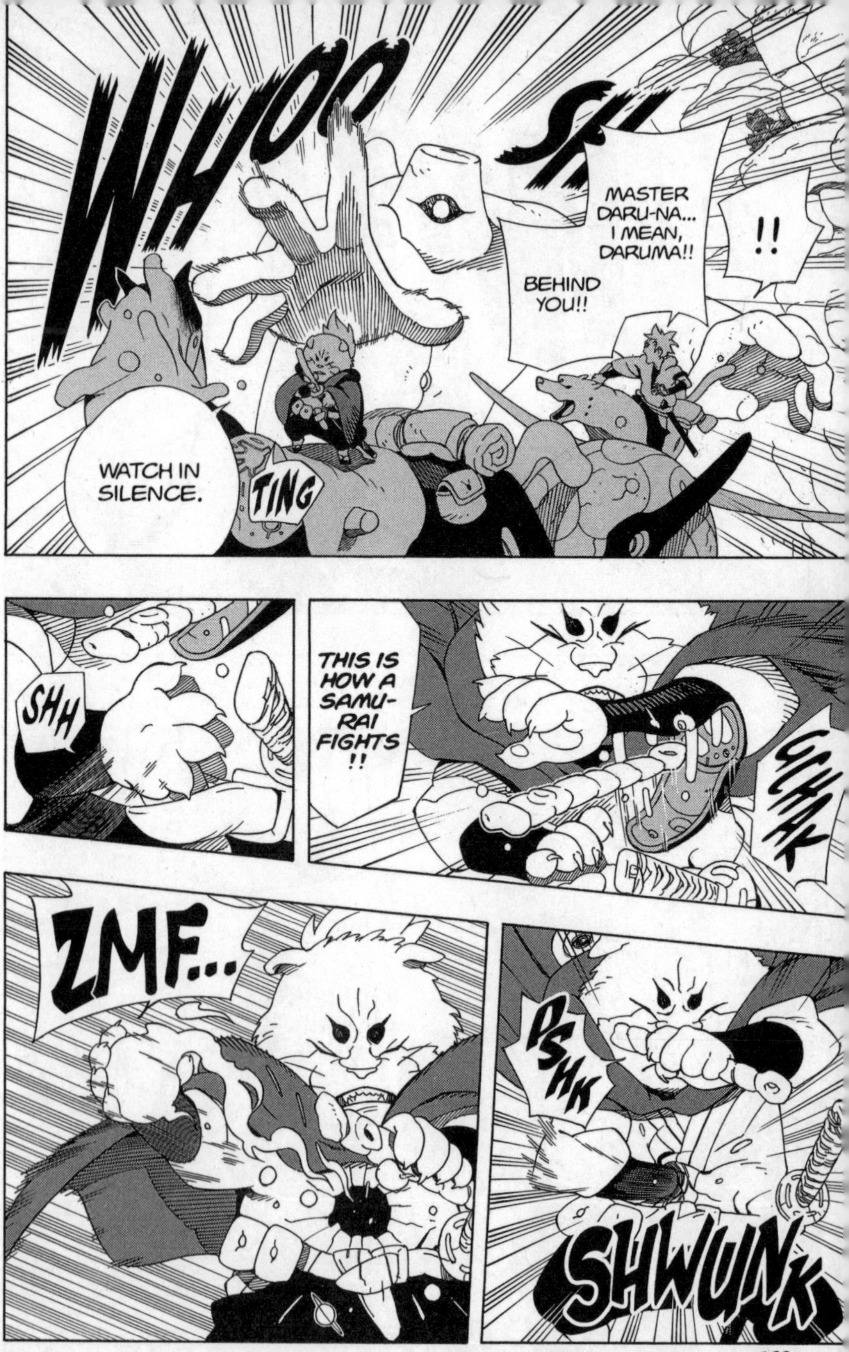
!!
MASTER DARU-NA... I MEAN, DARUMA!!
BEHIND YOU!!
WHOOSH
TING
WATCH IN SILENCE.
UCHAK
THIS IS HOW A SAMURAI FIGHTS!!
SHH
DSHK
SHWUNK
ZMF...

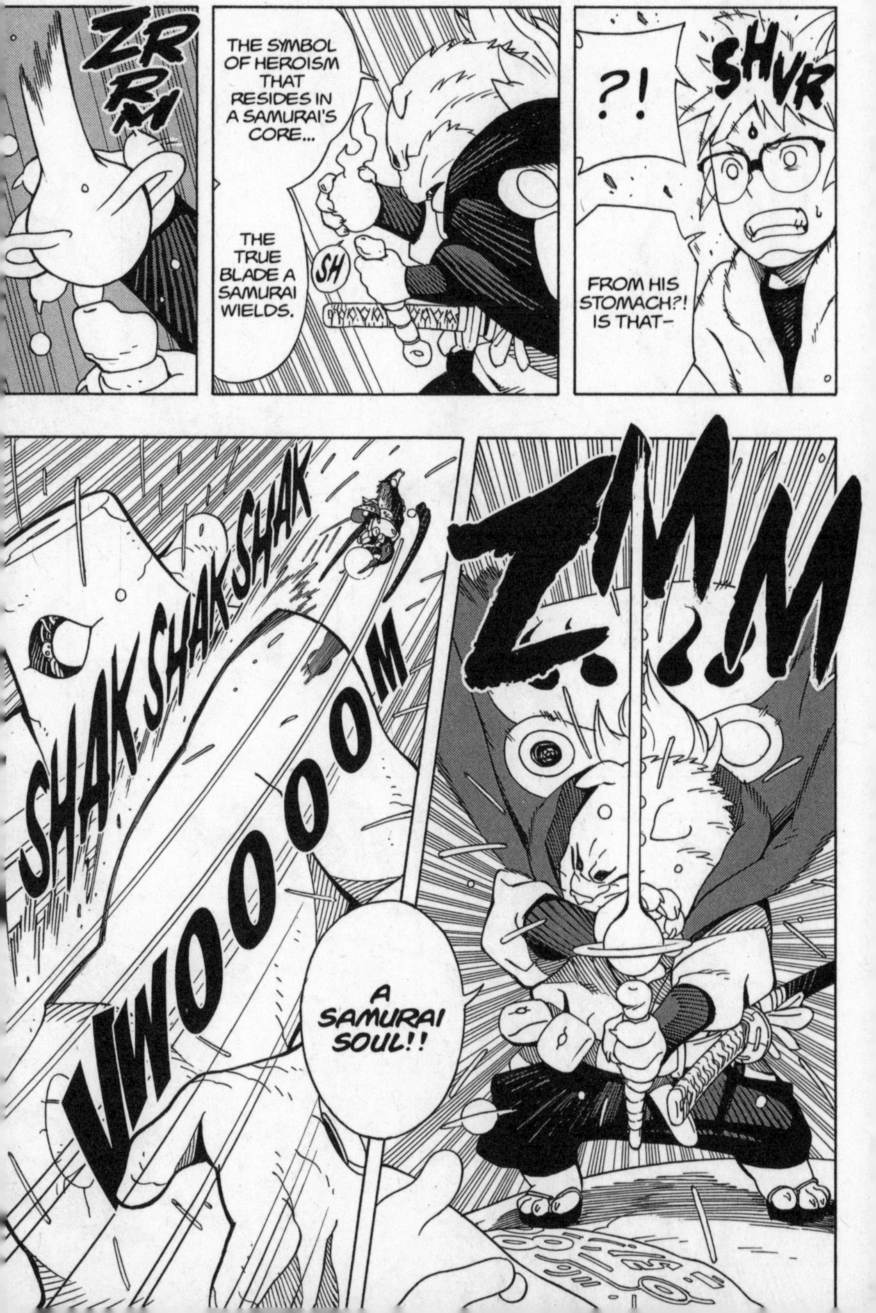
?!
SHVR
FROM HIS STOMACH?! IS THAT–
THE SYMBOL OF HEROISM THAT RESIDES IN A SAMURAI'S CORE...
THE TRUE BLADE A SAMURAI WIELDS.
SH
ZRRM
ZMM
A SAMURAI SOUL!!
SHAKSHAKSHAK
VWOOOOOM

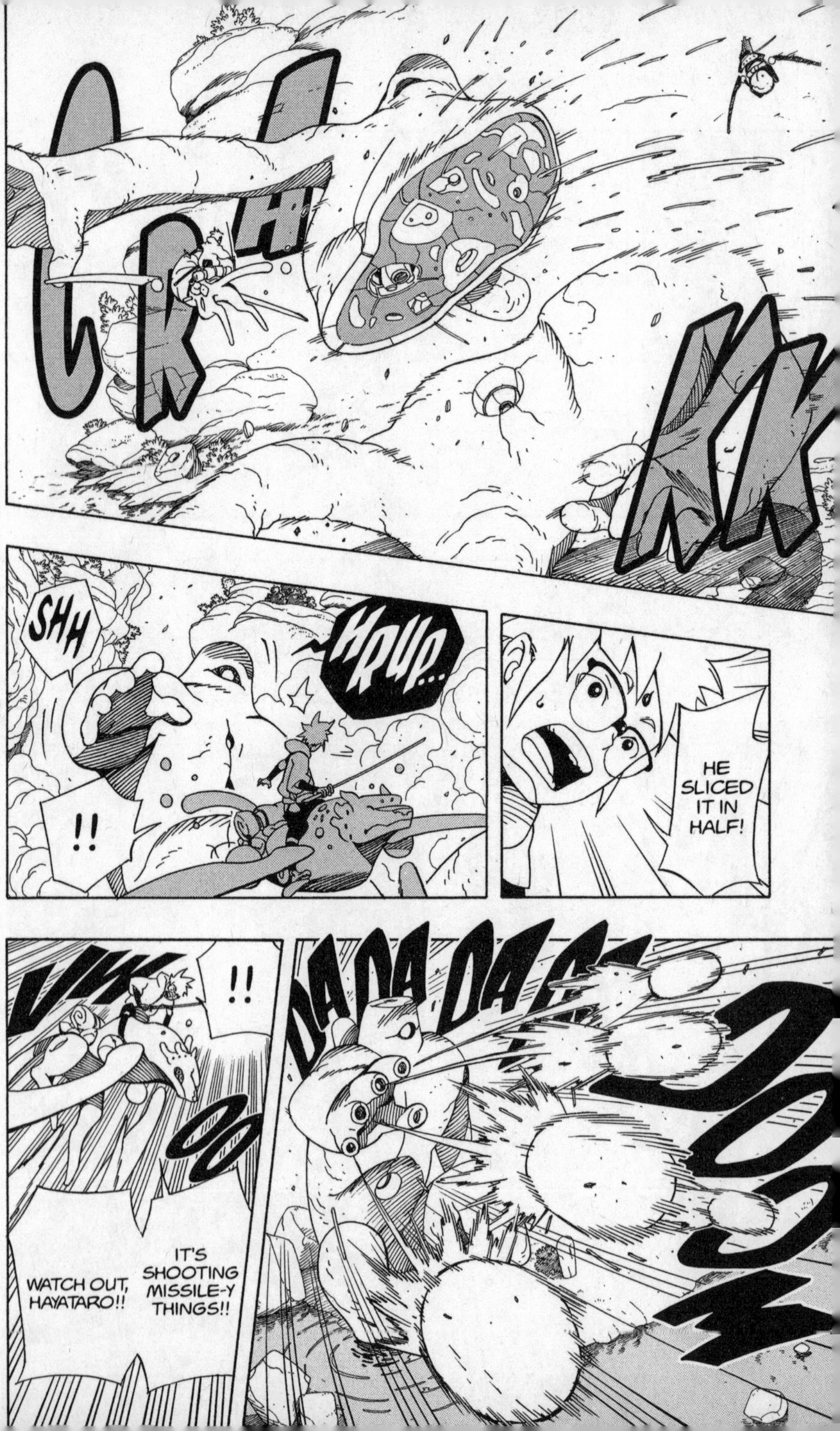
HE SLICED IT IN HALF!
HRUP...
SHH
!!
!!
IT'S SHOOTING MISSILE-Y THINGS!!
WATCH OUT, HAYATARO!!

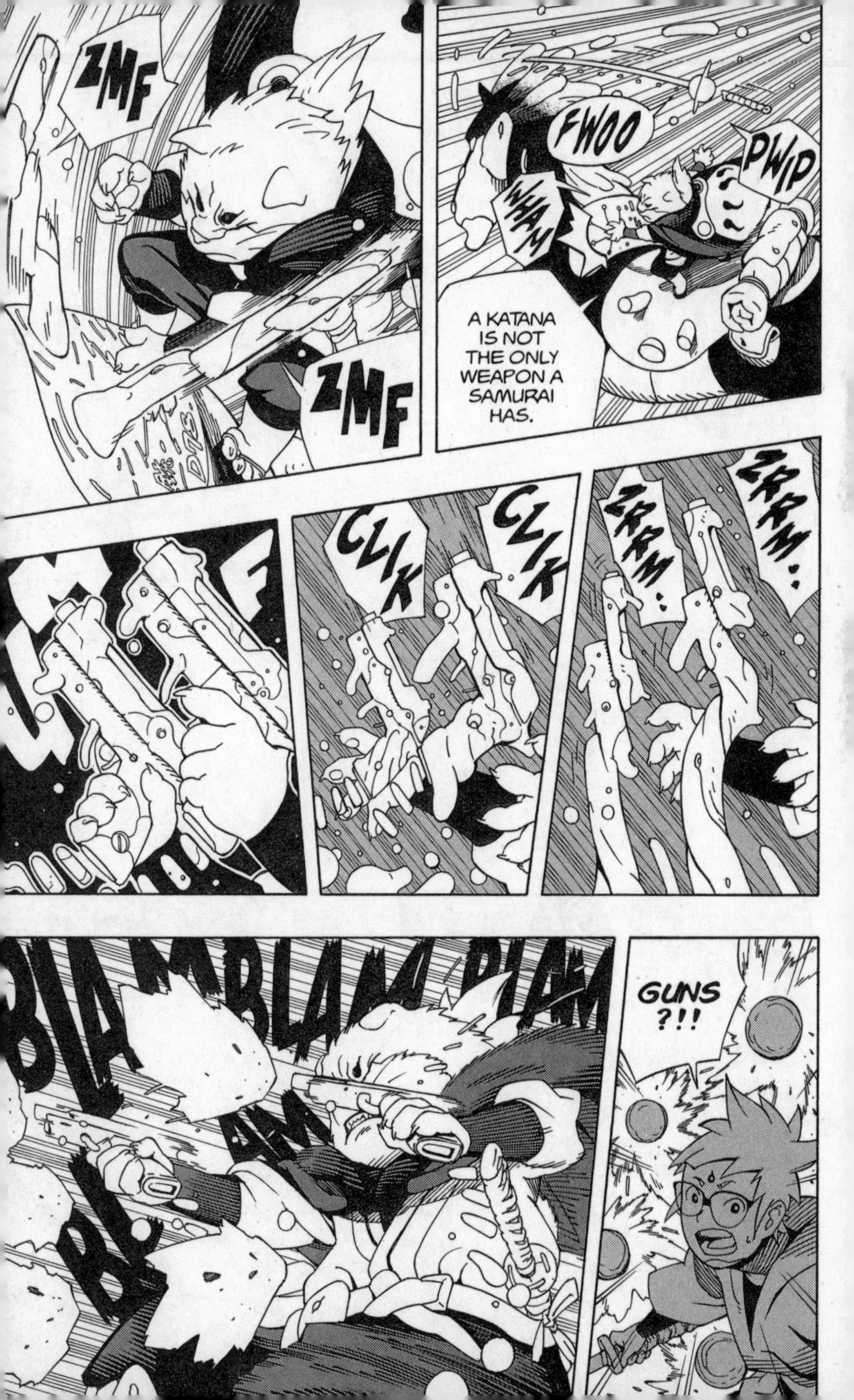
PWIP
FWOO
WHAM
A KATANA IS NOT THE ONLY WEAPON A SAMURAI HAS.
ZMF
ZMF
ZRRM..
ZRRM..
CLIK
CLIK
GUNS ?!!
BLAM
BLAM

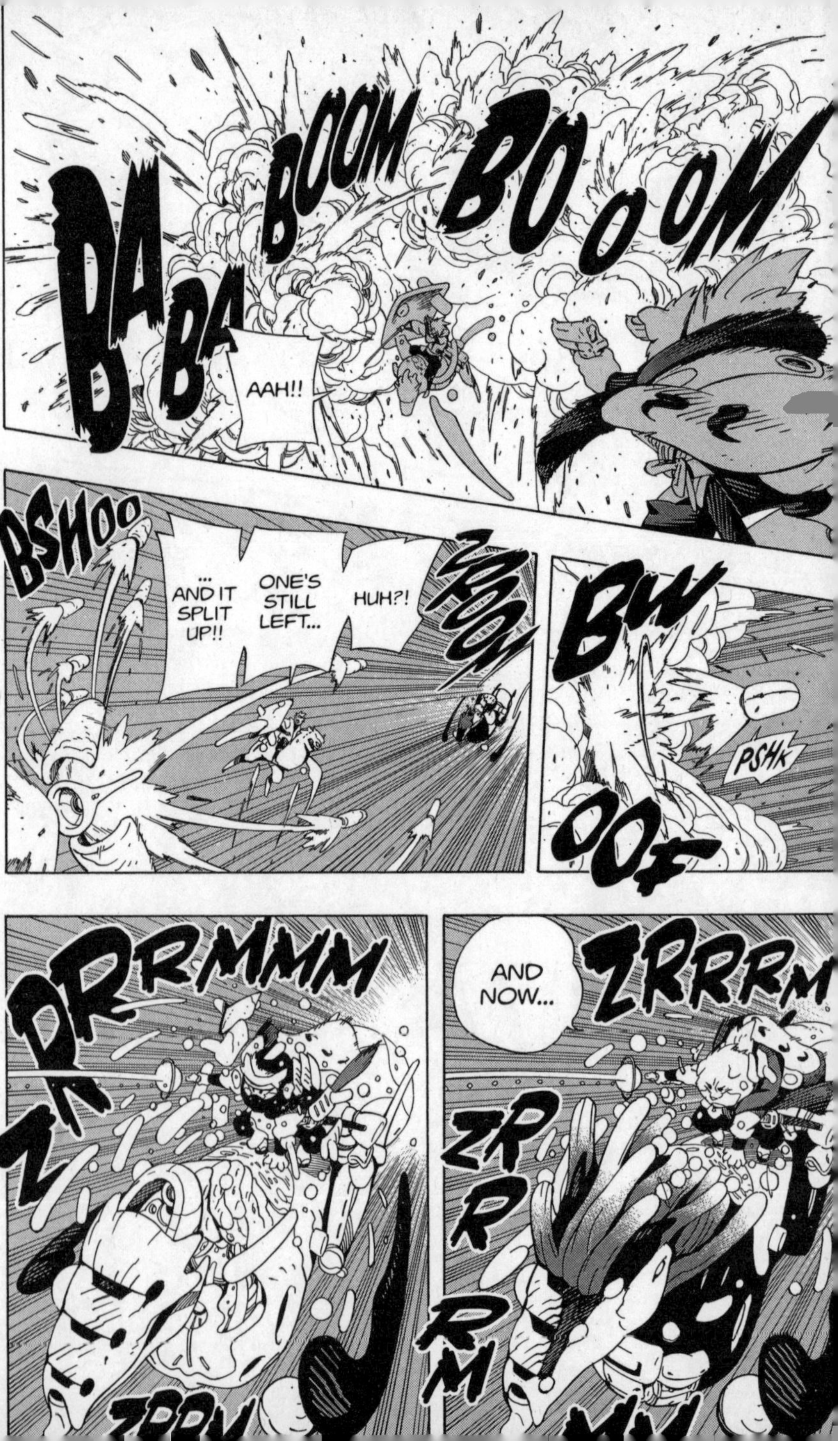
BA BA BOOM BOOOOM
AAH!!
BW
PSHK
OOF
HUH?!
ONE'S STILL LEFT...
...AND IT SPLIT UP!!
ZOOOM
BSHOO
AND NOW...
ZRRRM
ZRRRM
VRRMMMM

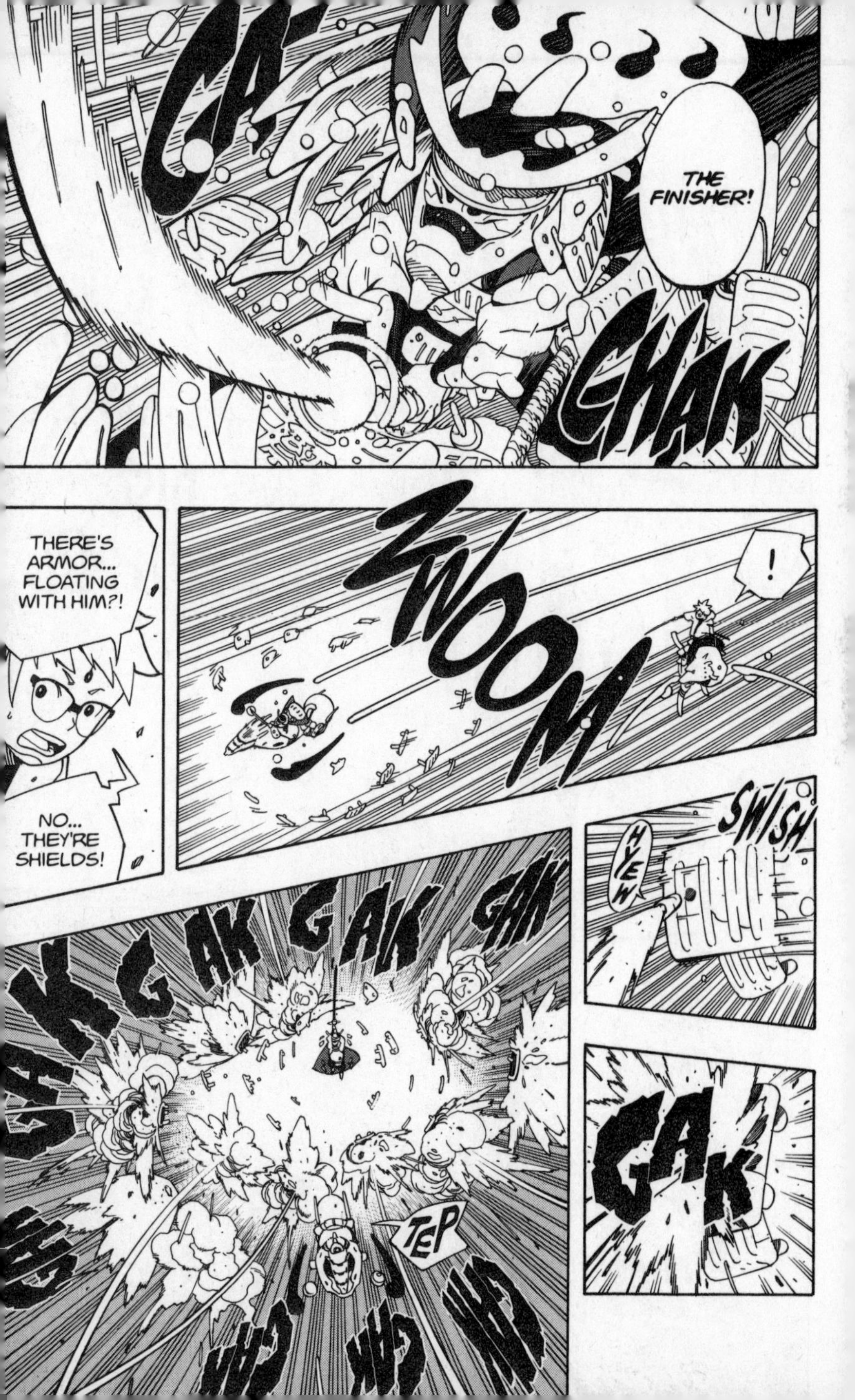

CA-
CHAK
THE FINISHER!
ZWOOM
!
THERE'S ARMOR... FLOATING WITH HIM?!
NO... THEY'RE SHIELDS!
SWISH
HYEW
GAK
GAK GAK GAK
TEP
CHAK

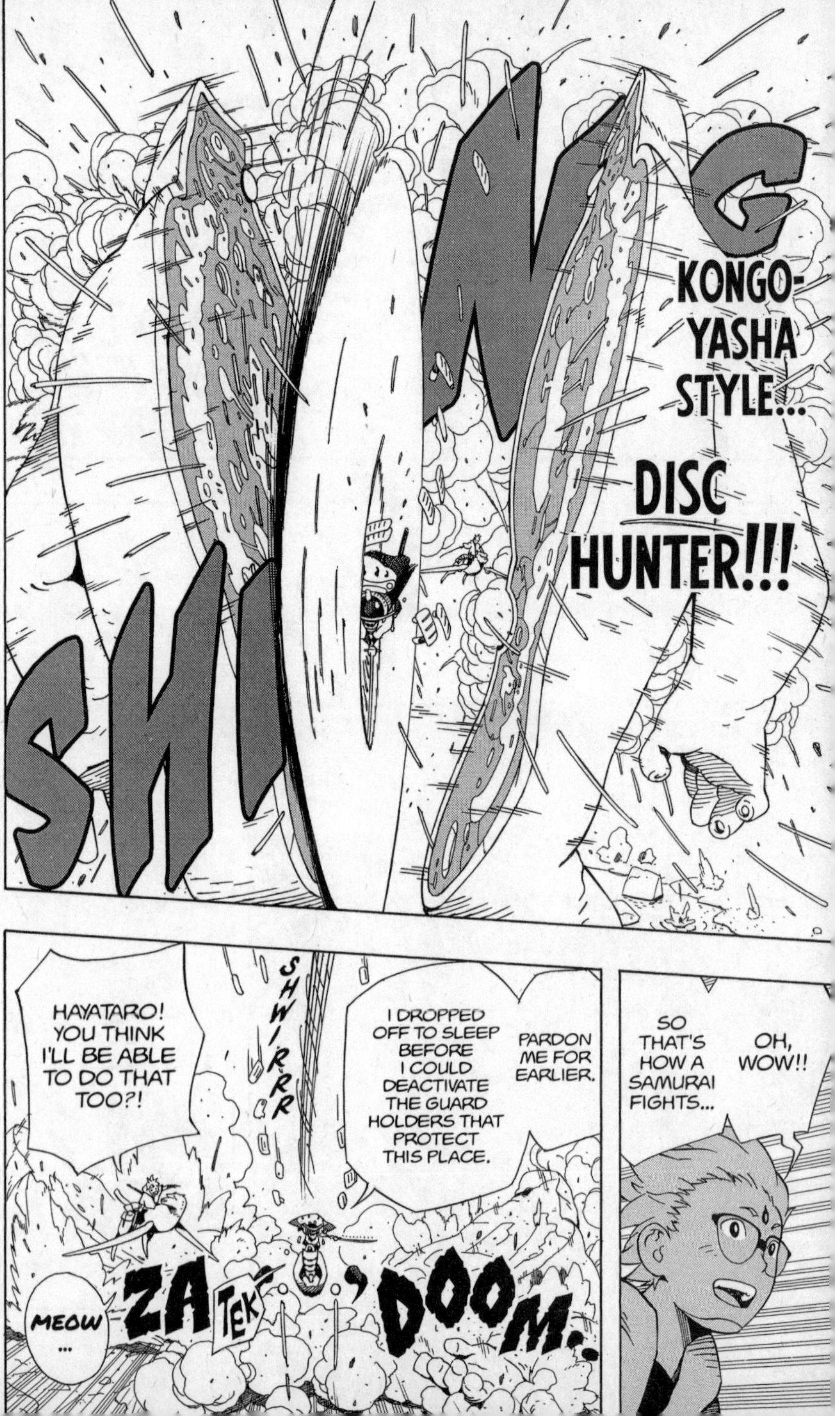
SHING
KONGO-YASHA STYLE...
DISC HUNTER!!!
OH, WOW!!
SO THAT'S HOW A SAMURAI FIGHTS...
PARDON ME FOR EARLIER.
I DROPPED OFF TO SLEEP BEFORE I COULD DEACTIVATE THE GUARD HOLDERS THAT PROTECT THIS PLACE.
SHWIRRR
HAYATARO! YOU THINK I'LL BE ABLE TO DO THAT TOO?!
DOOM
TEK
ZA
MEOW ...

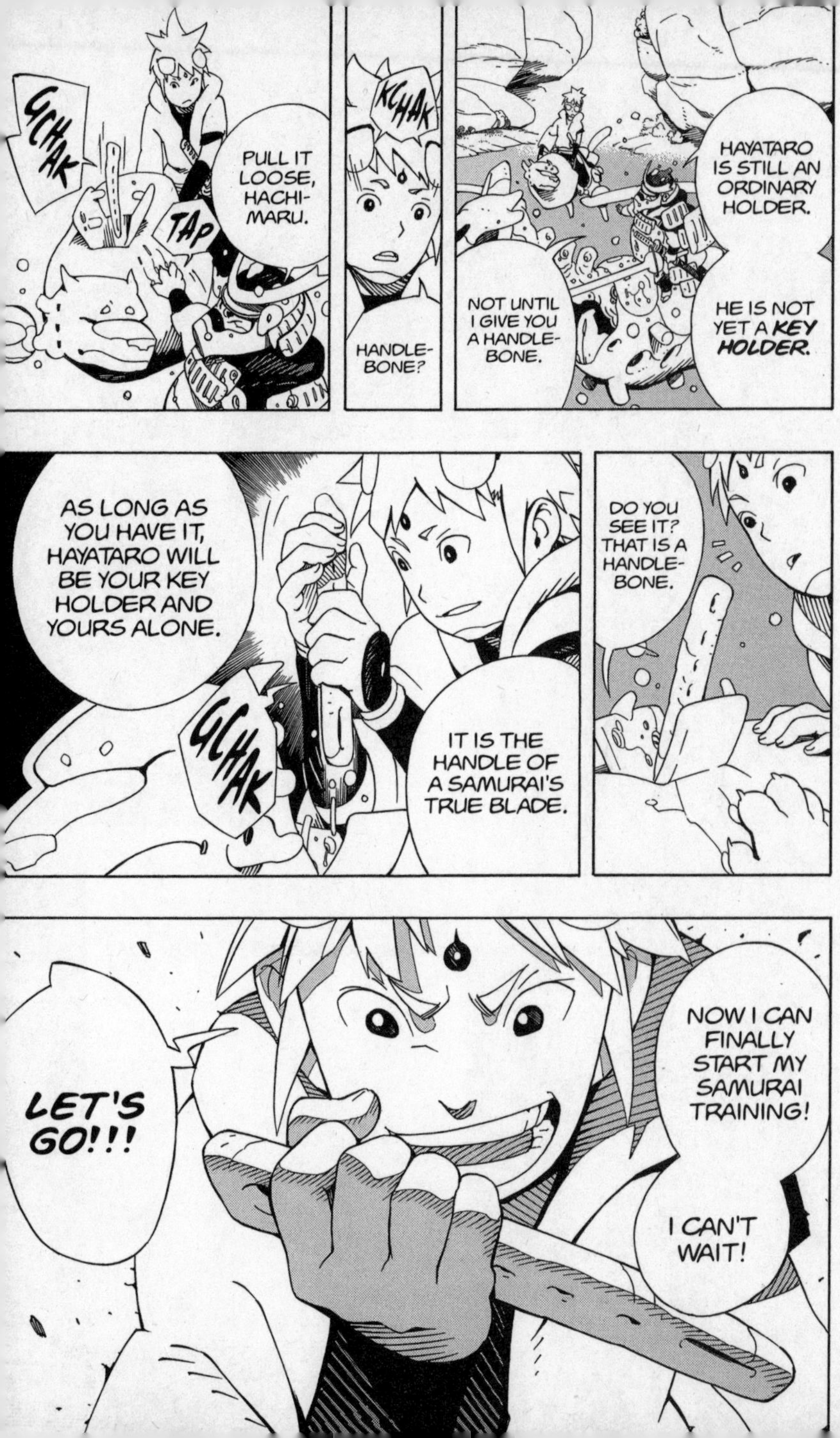
HAYATARO IS STILL AN ORDINARY HOLDER.
HE IS NOT YET A **KEY HOLDER.**
NOT UNTIL I GIVE YOU A HANDLE-BONE.
KCHAK
HANDLE-BONE?
PULL IT LOOSE, HACHI-MARU.
UCHAK
TAP
DO YOU SEE IT? THAT IS A HANDLE-BONE.
IT IS THE HANDLE OF A SAMURAI'S TRUE BLADE.
AS LONG AS YOU HAVE IT, HAYATARO WILL BE YOUR KEY HOLDER AND YOURS ALONE.
UCHAK
NOW I CAN FINALLY START MY SAMURAI TRAINING!
I CAN'T WAIT!
LET'S GO!!!

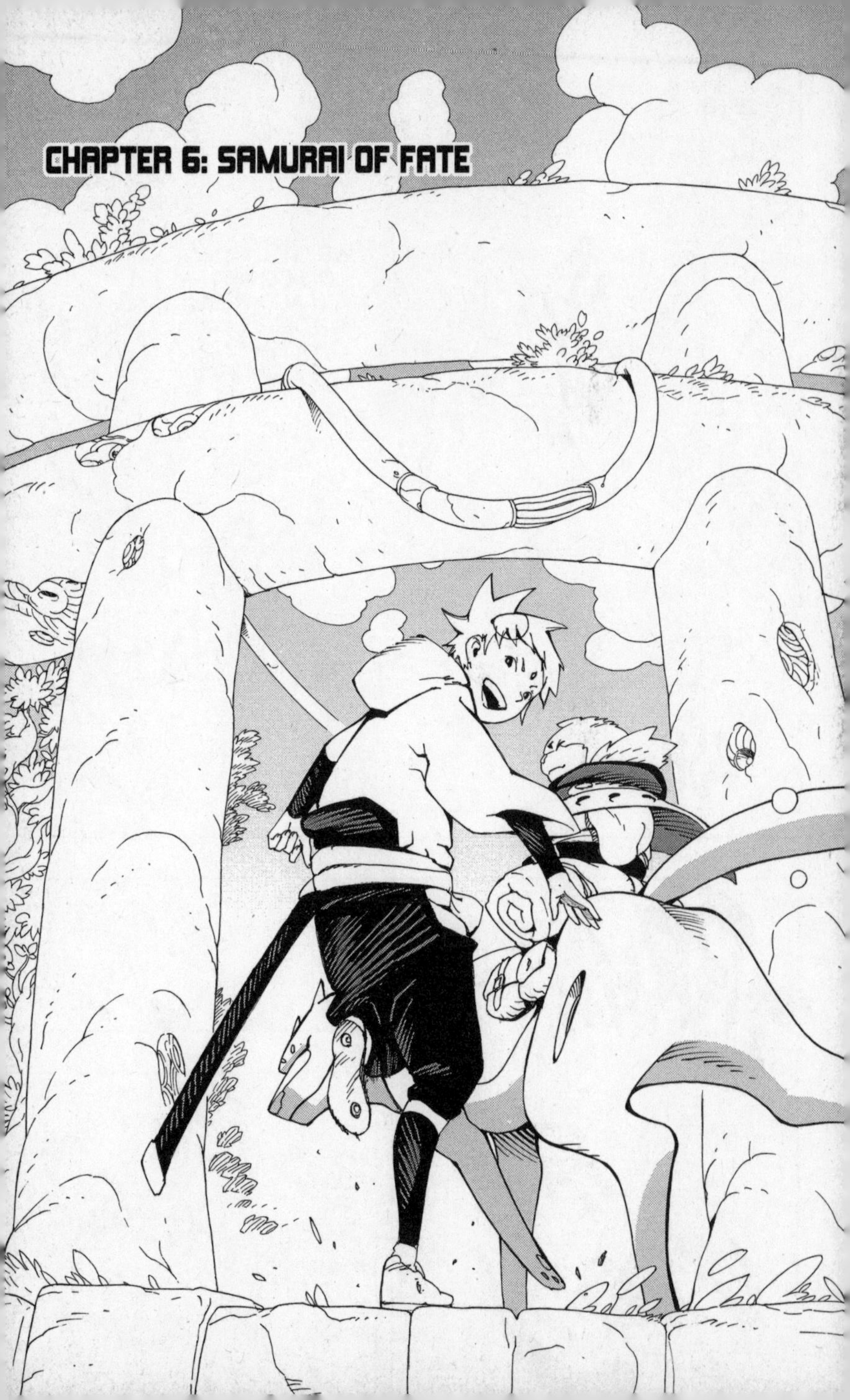
CHAPTER 6: SAMURAI OF FATE

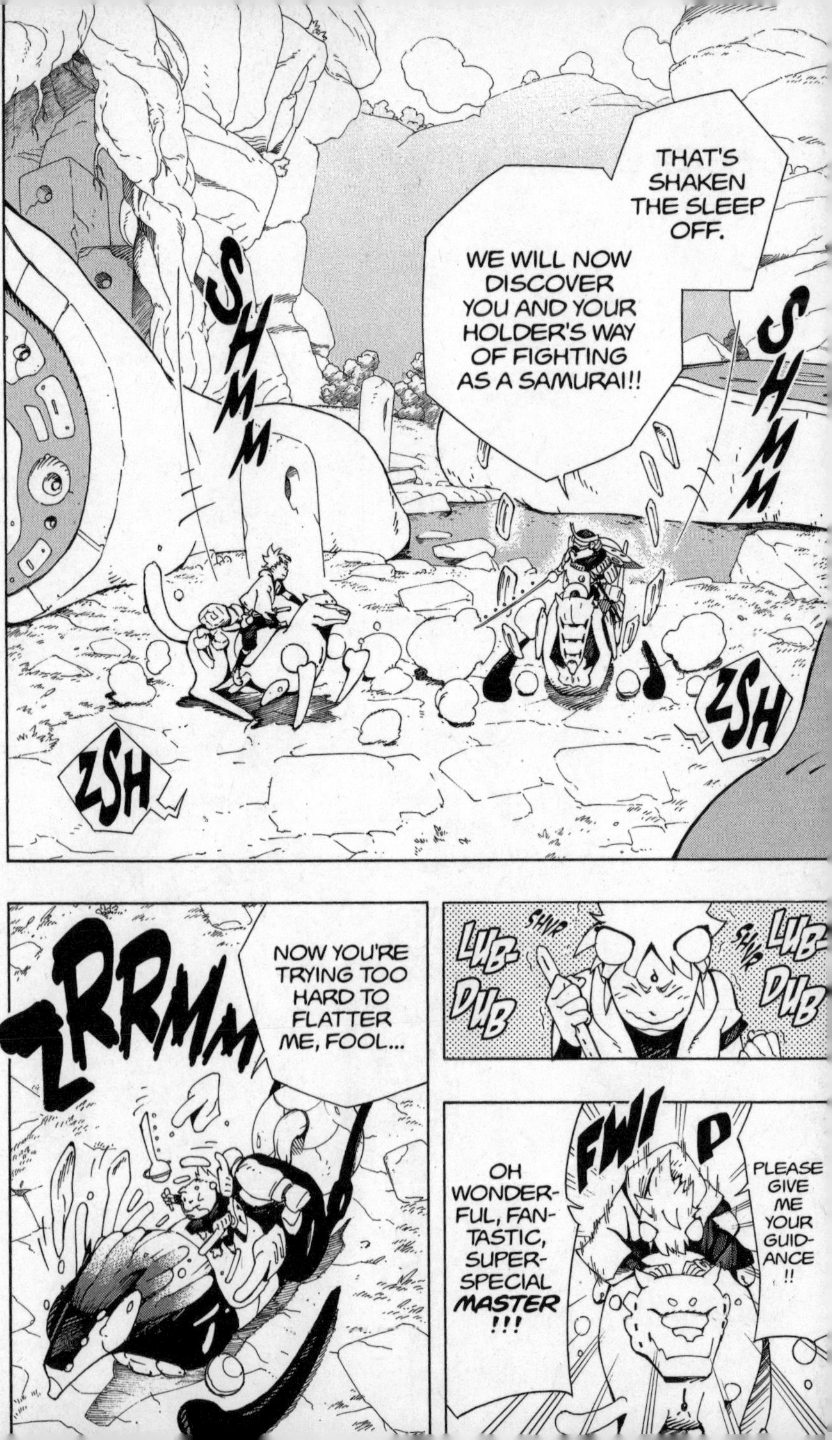
SHMM
THAT'S SHAKEN THE SLEEP OFF.
WE WILL NOW DISCOVER YOU AND YOUR HOLDER'S WAY OF FIGHTING AS A SAMURAI!!
SHMM
ZSH
ZSH
LUB-DUB
SHVR
SHVR
LUB-DUB
FWIP
PLEASE GIVE ME YOUR GUIDANCE!!
OH WONDERFUL, FANTASTIC, SUPER-SPECIAL **MASTER**!!!
ZRRMM
NOW YOU'RE TRYING TOO HARD TO FLATTER ME, FOOL...

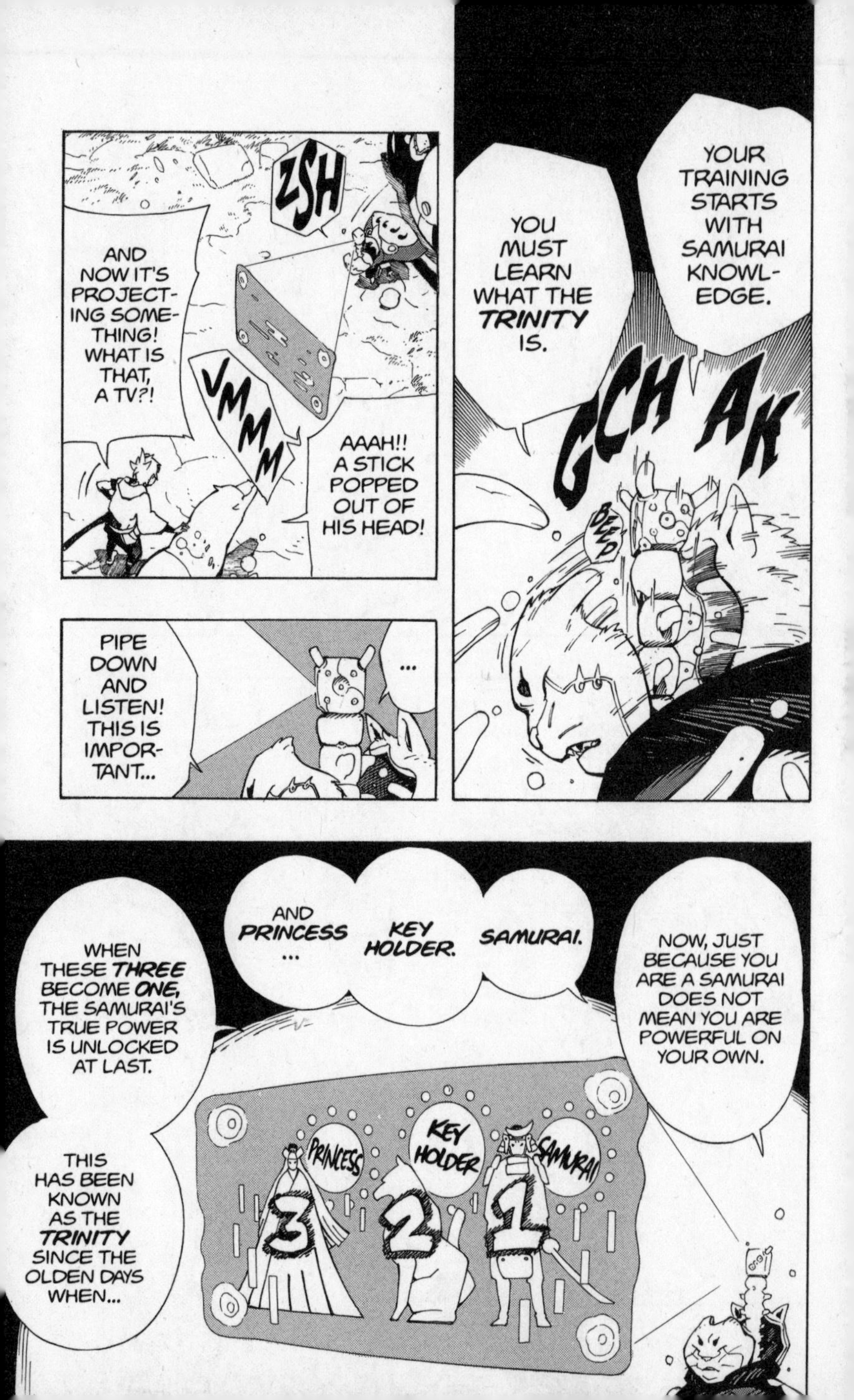
YOUR TRAINING STARTS WITH SAMURAI KNOWL-EDGE.
YOU MUST LEARN WHAT THE TRINITY IS.
GCCHAK
BEEP
ZSH
AND NOW IT'S PROJECT-ING SOME-THING! WHAT IS THAT, A TV?!
VMMM
AAAH!! A STICK POPPED OUT OF HIS HEAD!
...
PIPE DOWN AND LISTEN! THIS IS IMPOR-TANT...
NOW, JUST BECAUSE YOU ARE A SAMURAI DOES NOT MEAN YOU ARE POWERFUL ON YOUR OWN.
SAMURAI.
KEY HOLDER.
AND PRINCESS...
WHEN THESE THREE BECOME ONE, THE SAMURAI'S TRUE POWER IS UNLOCKED AT LAST.
SAMURAI
KEY HOLDER
PRINCESS
1
2
3
THIS HAS BEEN KNOWN AS THE TRINITY SINCE THE OLDEN DAYS WHEN...

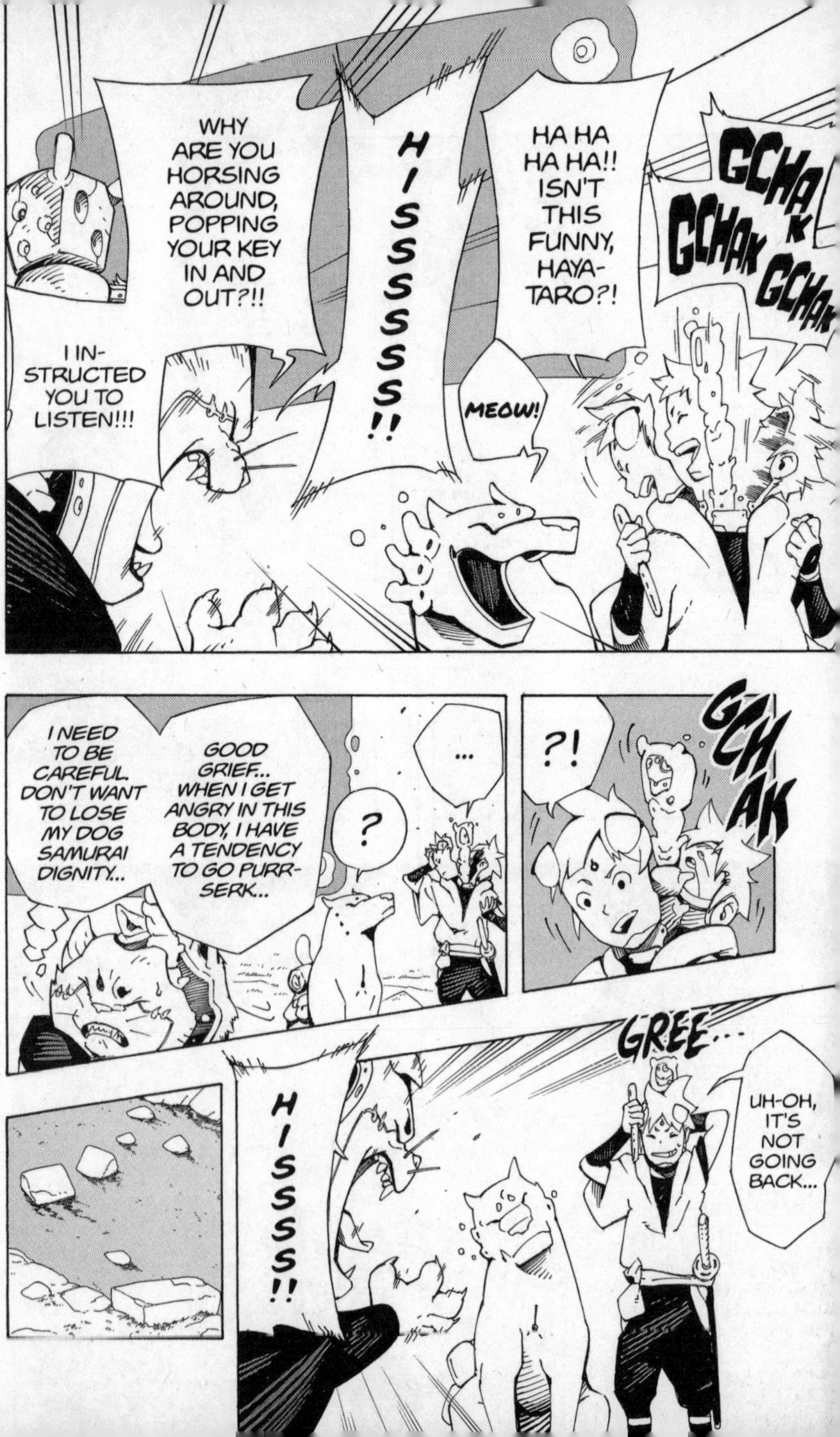

GCHAK GCHAK GCHAK
HA HA HA HA!! ISN'T THIS FUNNY, HAYA-TARO?!
HISSSSSSS!!
WHY ARE YOU HORSING AROUND, POPPING YOUR KEY IN AND OUT?!!
MEOW!
I IN-STRUCTED YOU TO LISTEN!!!
GCHAK
?!
...
?
GOOD GRIEF... WHEN I GET ANGRY IN THIS BODY, I HAVE A TENDENCY TO GO PURR-SERK...
I NEED TO BE CAREFUL. DON'T WANT TO LOSE MY DOG SAMURAI DIGNITY...
GREE...
UH-OH, IT'S NOT GOING BACK...
HISSSS!!

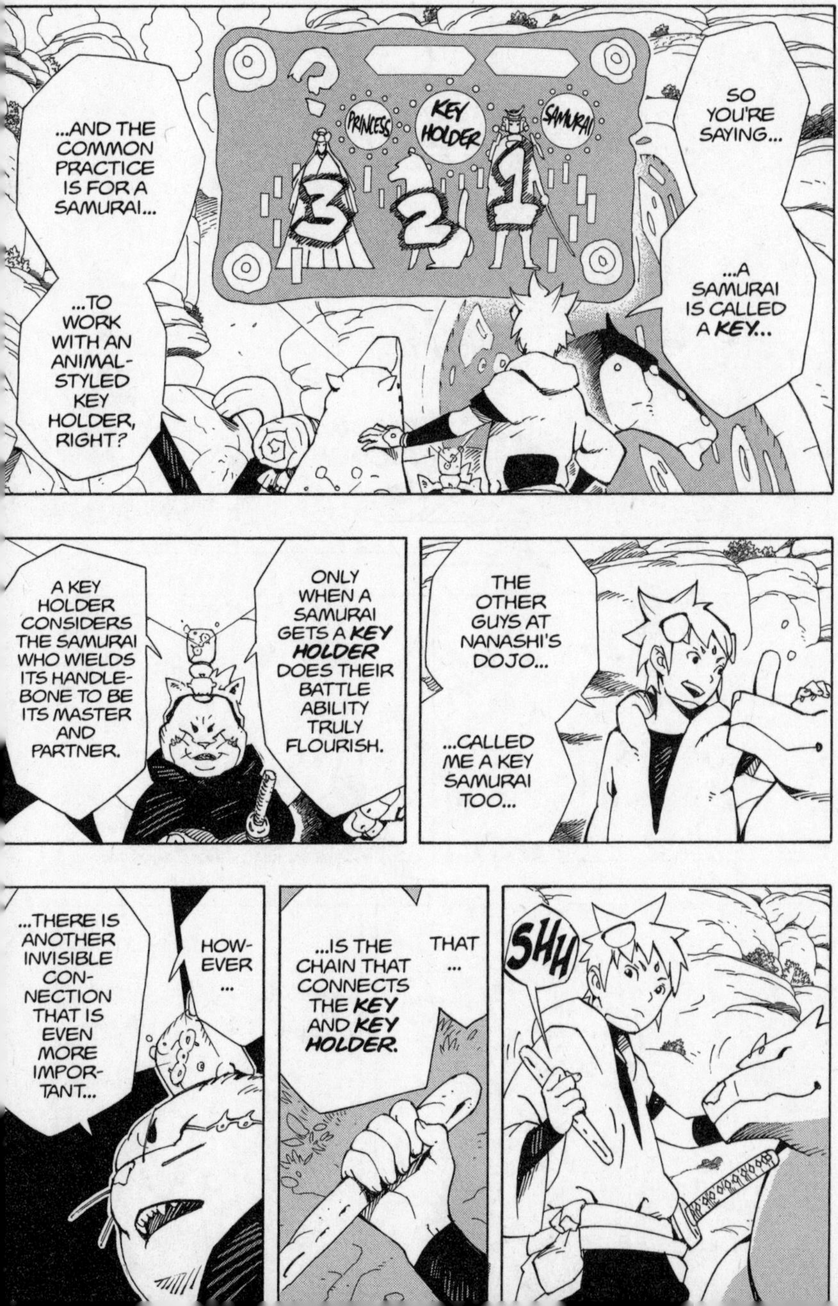
SO YOU'RE SAYING...
...A SAMURAI IS CALLED A **KEY**...
SAMURAI
1
KEY HOLDER
2
PRINCESS
3
...AND THE COMMON PRACTICE IS FOR A SAMURAI...
...TO WORK WITH AN ANIMAL-STYLED KEY HOLDER, RIGHT?
THE OTHER GUYS AT NANASHI'S DOJO...
...CALLED ME A KEY SAMURAI TOO...
ONLY WHEN A SAMURAI GETS A ***KEY HOLDER*** DOES THEIR BATTLE ABILITY TRULY FLOURISH.
A KEY HOLDER CONSIDERS THE SAMURAI WHO WIELDS ITS HANDLE-BONE TO BE ITS MASTER AND PARTNER.
SHH
THAT...
...IS THE CHAIN THAT CONNECTS THE ***KEY*** AND ***KEY HOLDER***.
HOW-EVER...
...THERE IS ANOTHER INVISIBLE CON-NECTION THAT IS EVEN MORE IMPOR-TANT...

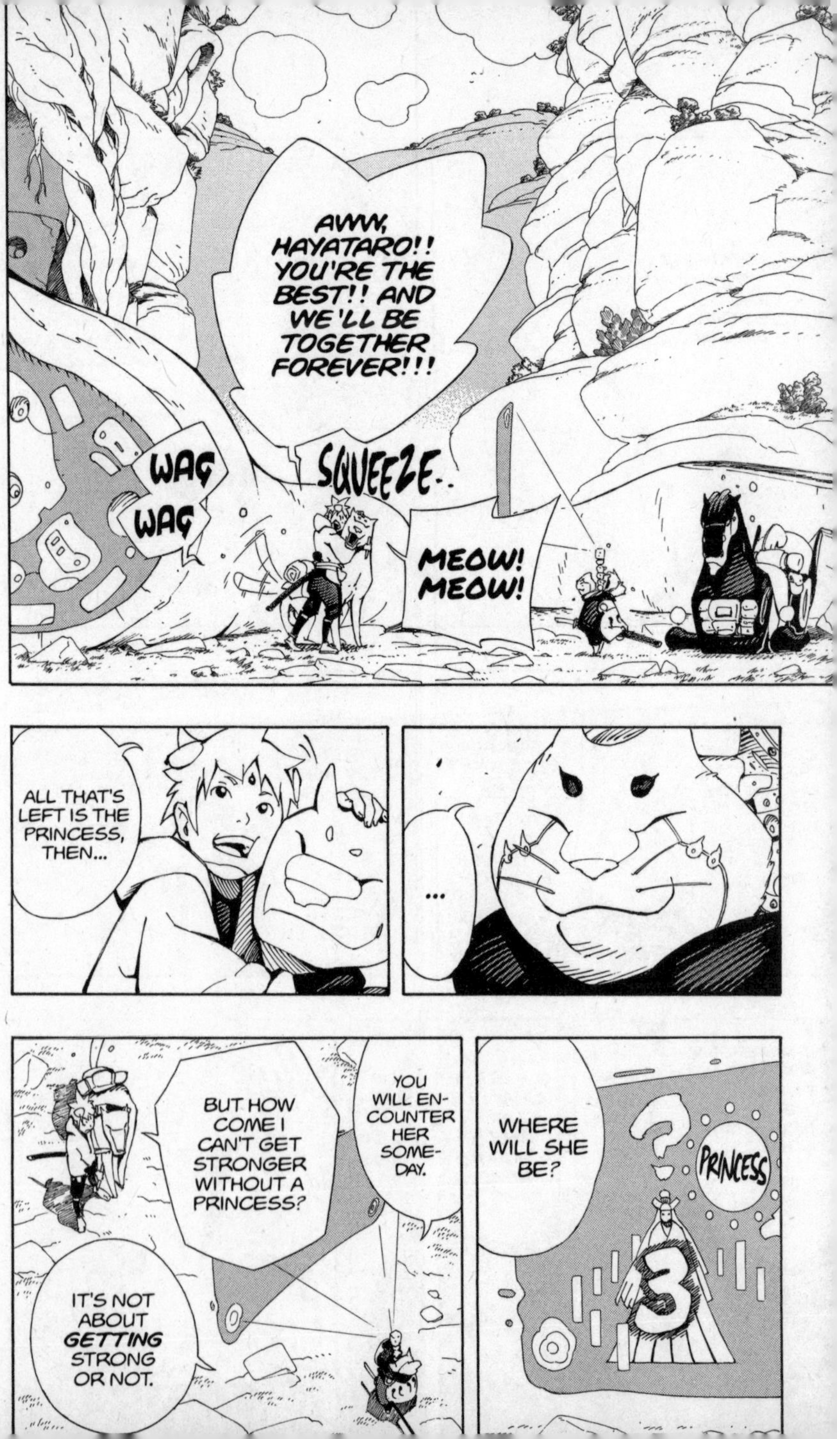
AWW, HAYATARO!! YOU'RE THE BEST!! AND WE'LL BE TOGETHER FOREVER!!!
SQUEEZE...
MEOW! MEOW!
WAG WAG
...
ALL THAT'S LEFT IS THE PRINCESS, THEN...
WHERE WILL SHE BE?
PRINCESS
3
YOU WILL EN-COUNTER HER SOME-DAY.
BUT HOW COME I CAN'T GET STRONGER WITHOUT A PRINCESS?
IT'S NOT ABOUT **GETTING** STRONG OR NOT.

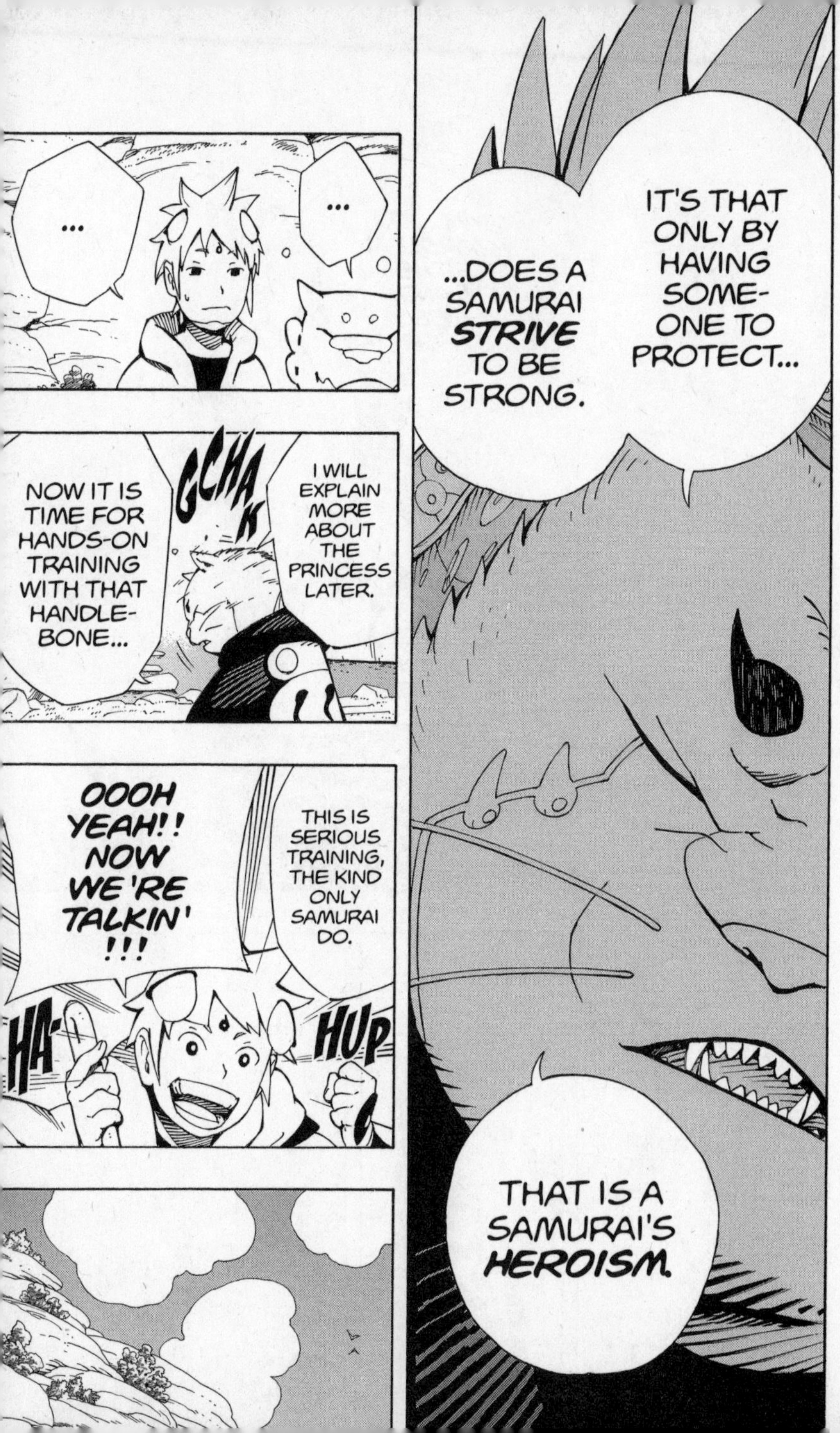

IT'S THAT ONLY BY HAVING SOME-ONE TO PROTECT...
...DOES A SAMURAI STRIVE TO BE STRONG.
THAT IS A SAMURAI'S HEROISM.
...
...
I WILL EXPLAIN MORE ABOUT THE PRINCESS LATER.
GCHAK
NOW IT IS TIME FOR HANDS-ON TRAINING WITH THAT HANDLE-BONE...
THIS IS SERIOUS TRAINING, THE KIND ONLY SAMURAI DO.
HUP
OOOH YEAH!! NOW WE'RE TALKIN'!!!
HA-

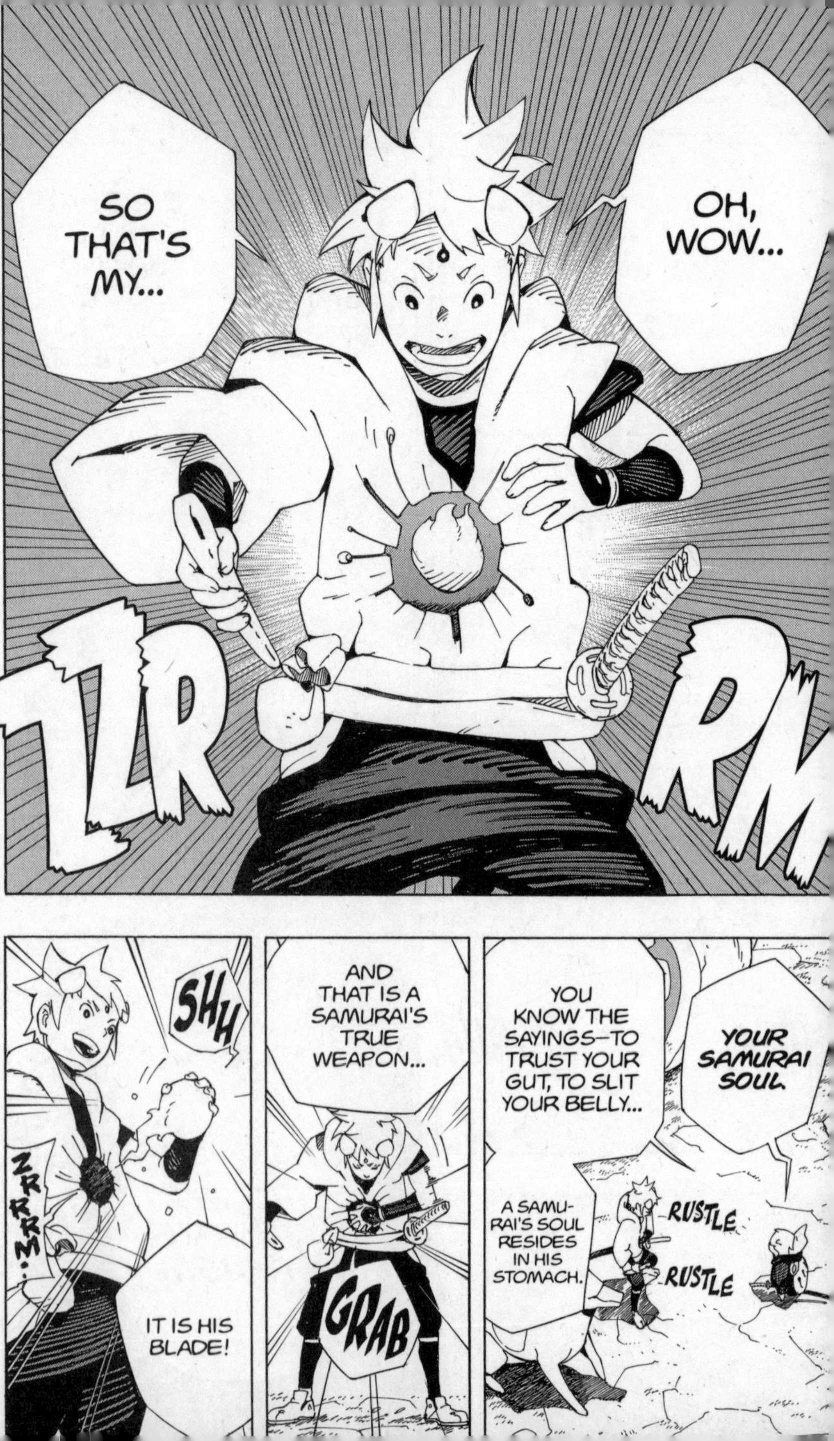
OH, WOW...
SO THAT'S MY...
ZZR
RM
YOUR SAMURAI SOUL.
YOU KNOW THE SAYINGS—TO TRUST YOUR GUT, TO SLIT YOUR BELLY...
A SAMURAI'S SOUL RESIDES IN HIS STOMACH.
RUSTLE
RUSTLE
AND THAT IS A SAMURAI'S TRUE WEAPON...
GRAB
SHH
ZRRRM...
IT IS HIS BLADE!

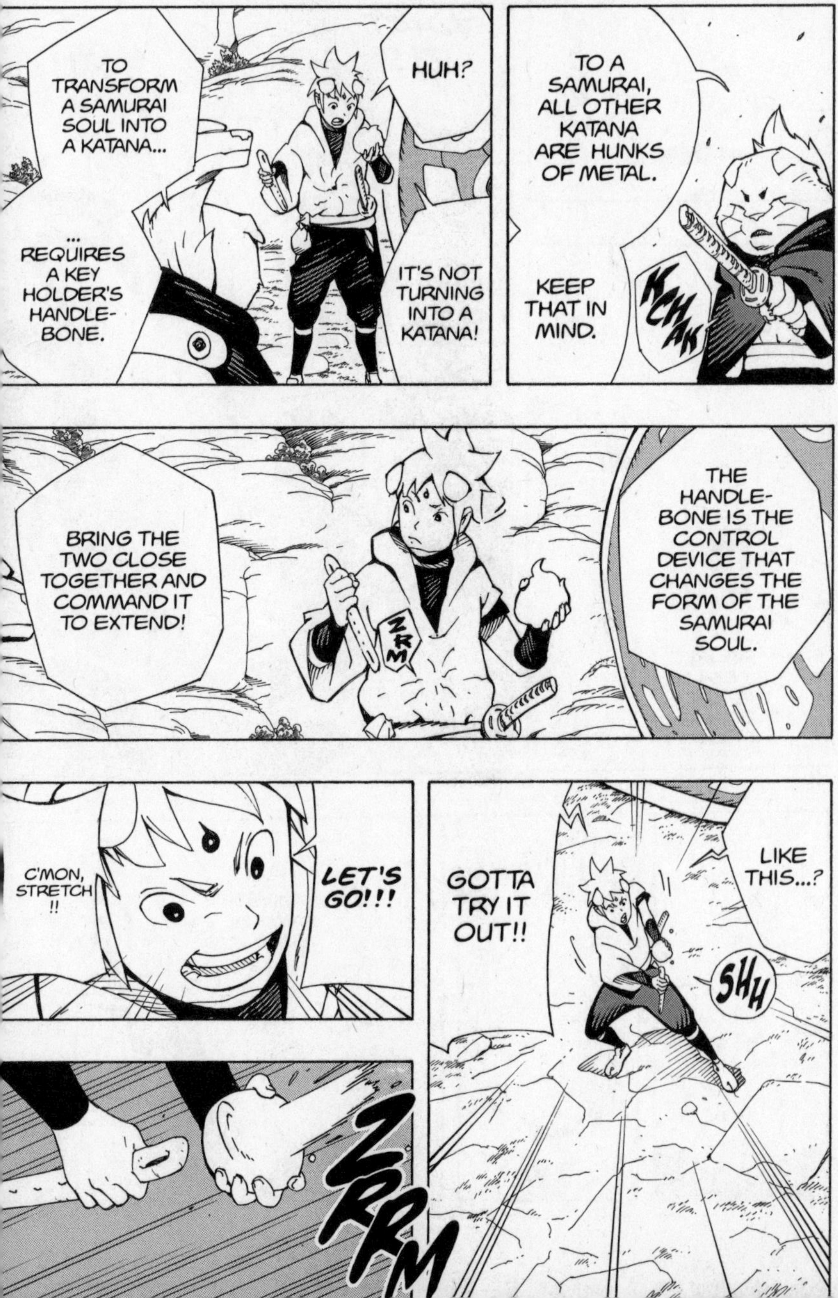
TO A SAMURAI, ALL OTHER KATANA ARE HUNKS OF METAL.
KEEP THAT IN MIND.
KCHAK
HUH?
IT'S NOT TURNING INTO A KATANA!
TO TRANSFORM A SAMURAI SOUL INTO A KATANA...
...REQUIRES A KEY HOLDER'S HANDLE-BONE.
THE HANDLE-BONE IS THE CONTROL DEVICE THAT CHANGES THE FORM OF THE SAMURAI SOUL.
ZRM
BRING THE TWO CLOSE TOGETHER AND COMMAND IT TO EXTEND!
LIKE THIS...?
GOTTA TRY IT OUT!!
SHH
LET'S GO!!!
C'MON, STRETCH!!
ZRRM

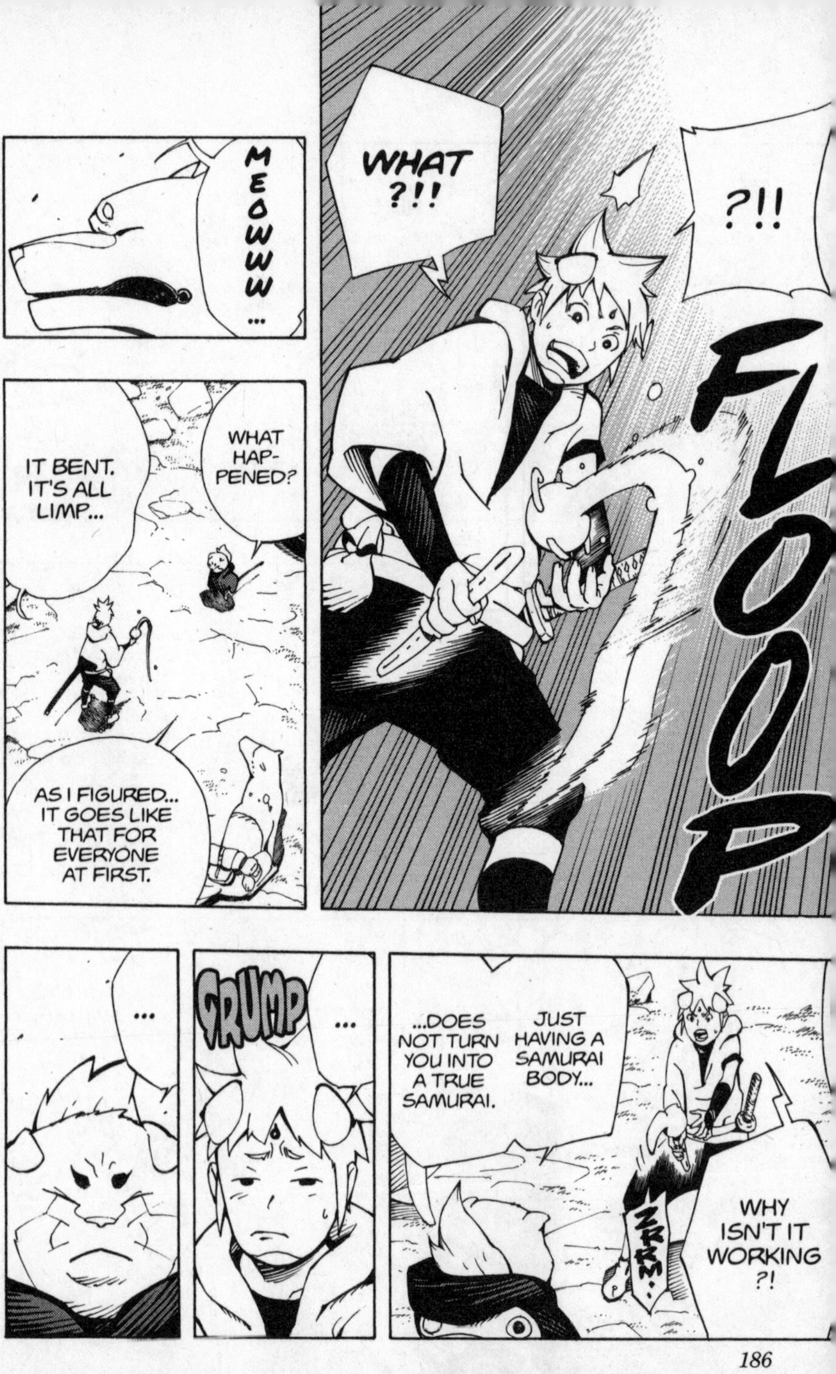
?!!
WHAT ?!!
FLOOP
MEOWWW...
WHAT HAP-PENED?
IT BENT. IT'S ALL LIMP...
AS I FIGURED... IT GOES LIKE THAT FOR EVERYONE AT FIRST.
JUST HAVING A SAMURAI BODY...
...DOES NOT TURN YOU INTO A TRUE SAMURAI.
ZRRM
WHY ISN'T IT WORKING ?!
...
GRUMP
...

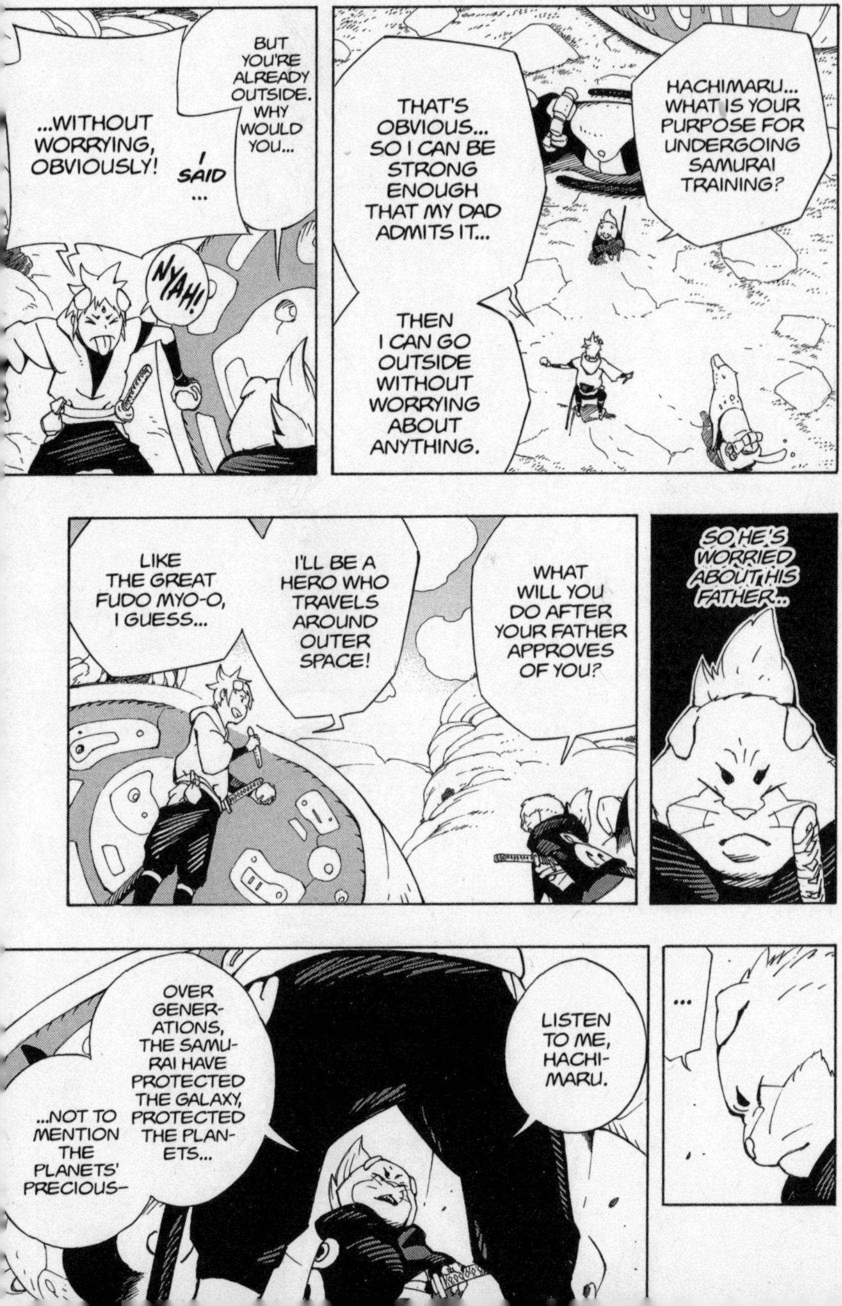
HACHIMARU... WHAT IS YOUR PURPOSE FOR UNDERGOING SAMURAI TRAINING?
THAT'S OBVIOUS... SO I CAN BE STRONG ENOUGH THAT MY DAD ADMITS IT...
THEN I CAN GO OUTSIDE WITHOUT WORRYING ABOUT ANYTHING.
BUT YOU'RE ALREADY OUTSIDE. WHY WOULD YOU...
I SAID...
...WITHOUT WORRYING, OBVIOUSLY!
NYAH!
SO HE'S WORRIED ABOUT HIS FATHER...
WHAT WILL YOU DO AFTER YOUR FATHER APPROVES OF YOU?
I'LL BE A HERO WHO TRAVELS AROUND OUTER SPACE!
LIKE THE GREAT FUDO MYO-O, I GUESS...
...
LISTEN TO ME, HACHIMARU.
OVER GENERATIONS, THE SAMURAI HAVE PROTECTED THE GALAXY, PROTECTED THE PLANETS...
...NOT TO MENTION THE PLANETS' PRECIOUS–

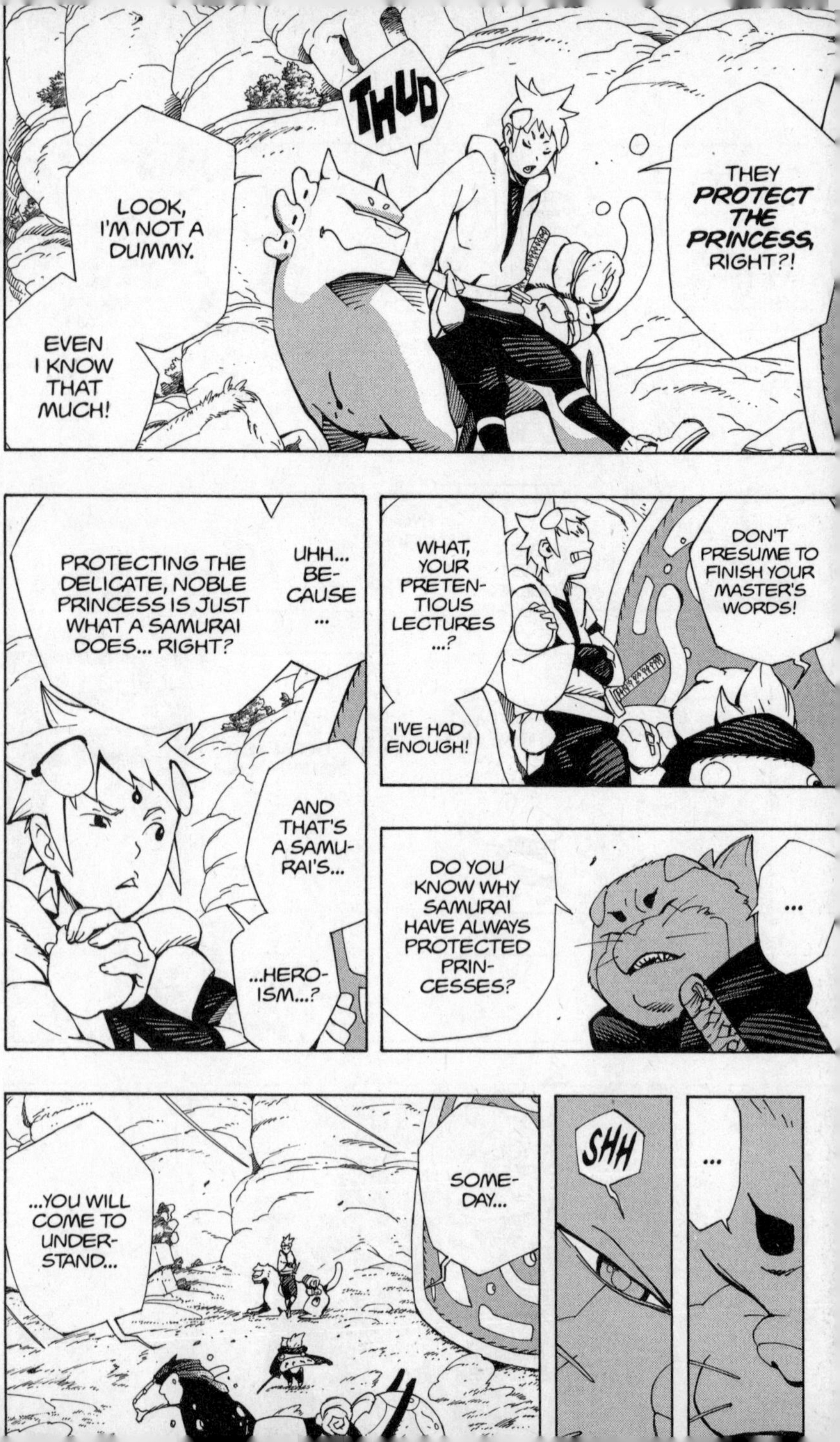
THEY PROTECT THE PRINCESS, RIGHT?!
THUD
LOOK, I'M NOT A DUMMY.
EVEN I KNOW THAT MUCH!
DON'T PRESUME TO FINISH YOUR MASTER'S WORDS!
WHAT, YOUR PRETEN-TIOUS LECTURES ...?
I'VE HAD ENOUGH!
...
DO YOU KNOW WHY SAMURAI HAVE ALWAYS PROTECTED PRIN-CESSES?
UHH... BE-CAUSE ...
PROTECTING THE DELICATE, NOBLE PRINCESS IS JUST WHAT A SAMURAI DOES... RIGHT?
AND THAT'S A SAMU-RAI'S...
...HERO-ISM...?
...
SHH
SOME-DAY...
...YOU WILL COME TO UNDER-STAND...

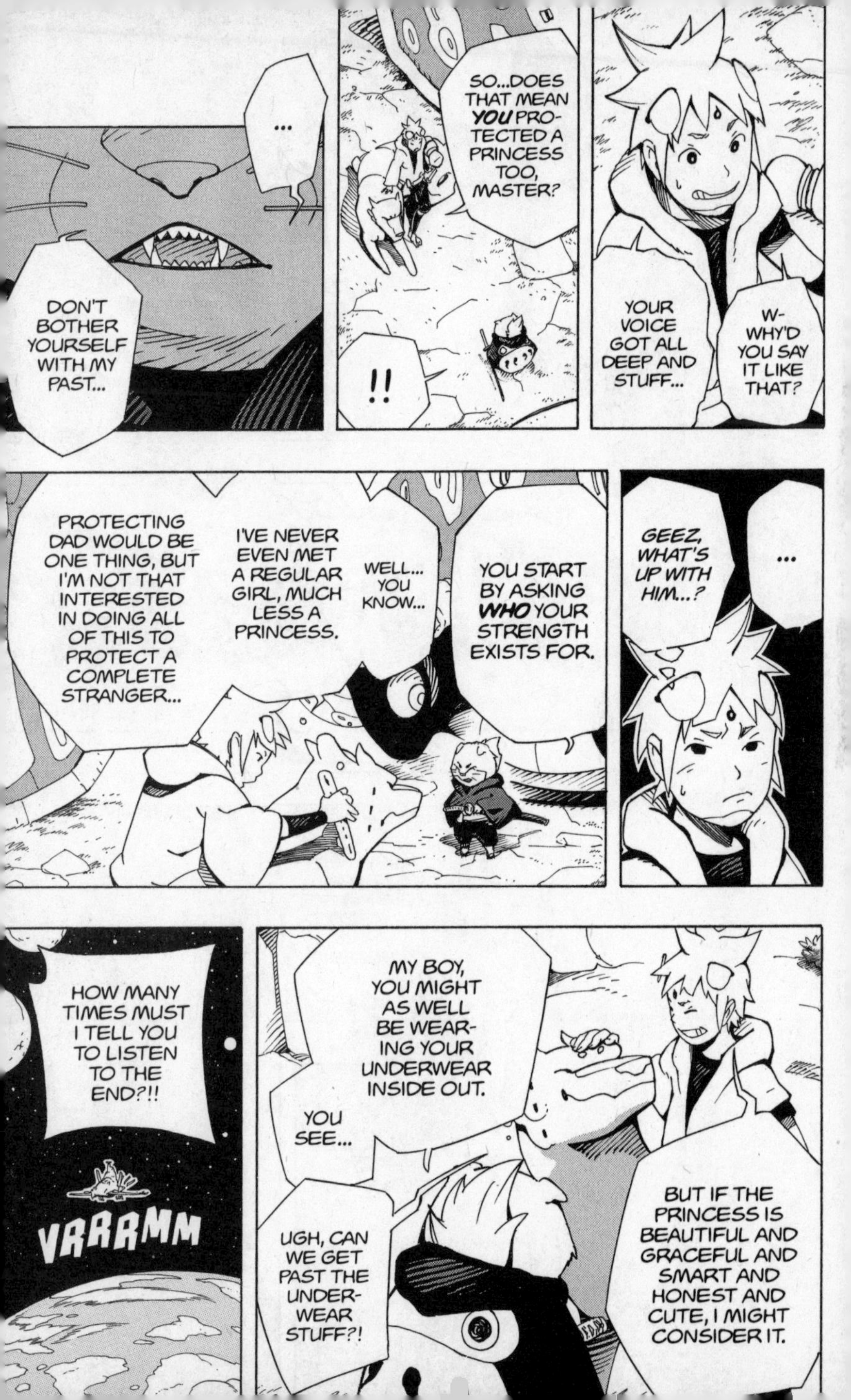
W-WHY'D YOU SAY IT LIKE THAT?
YOUR VOICE GOT ALL DEEP AND STUFF...
SO...DOES THAT MEAN YOU PROTECTED A PRINCESS TOO, MASTER?
!!
...
DON'T BOTHER YOURSELF WITH MY PAST...
...
GEEZ, WHAT'S UP WITH HIM...?
YOU START BY ASKING WHO YOUR STRENGTH EXISTS FOR.
WELL... YOU KNOW...
I'VE NEVER EVEN MET A REGULAR GIRL, MUCH LESS A PRINCESS.
PROTECTING DAD WOULD BE ONE THING, BUT I'M NOT THAT INTERESTED IN DOING ALL OF THIS TO PROTECT A COMPLETE STRANGER...
MY BOY, YOU MIGHT AS WELL BE WEARING YOUR UNDERWEAR INSIDE OUT.
YOU SEE...
BUT IF THE PRINCESS IS BEAUTIFUL AND GRACEFUL AND SMART AND HONEST AND CUTE, I MIGHT CONSIDER IT.
UGH, CAN WE GET PAST THE UNDERWEAR STUFF?!
HOW MANY TIMES MUST I TELL YOU TO LISTEN TO THE END?!!
VRRRMM

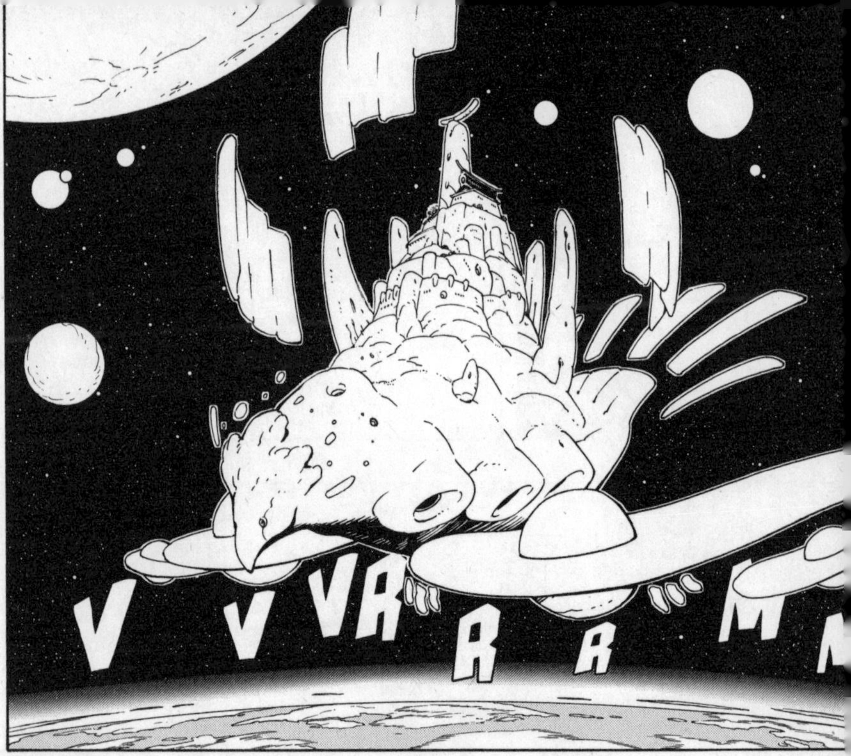
VVVRRRMM

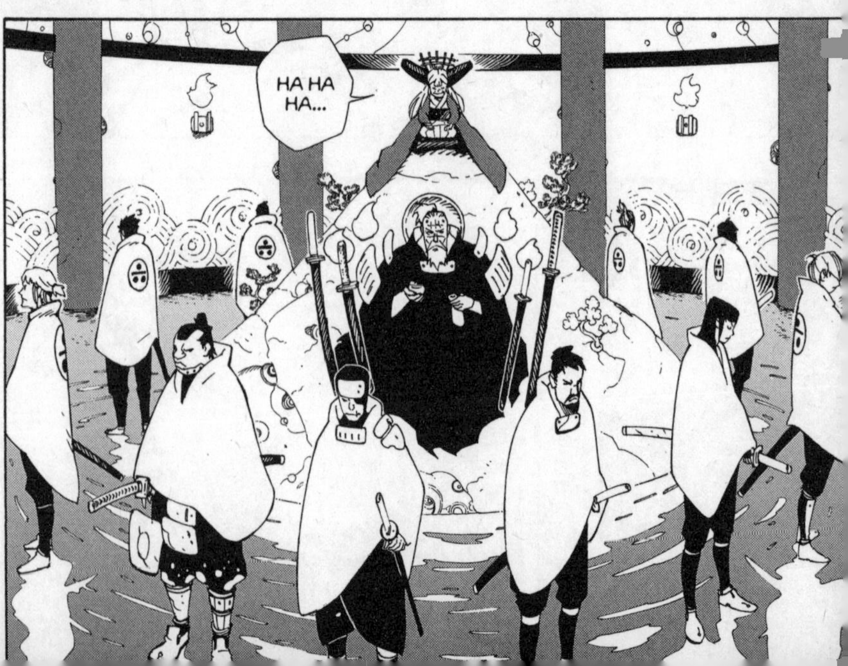
HA HA HA...

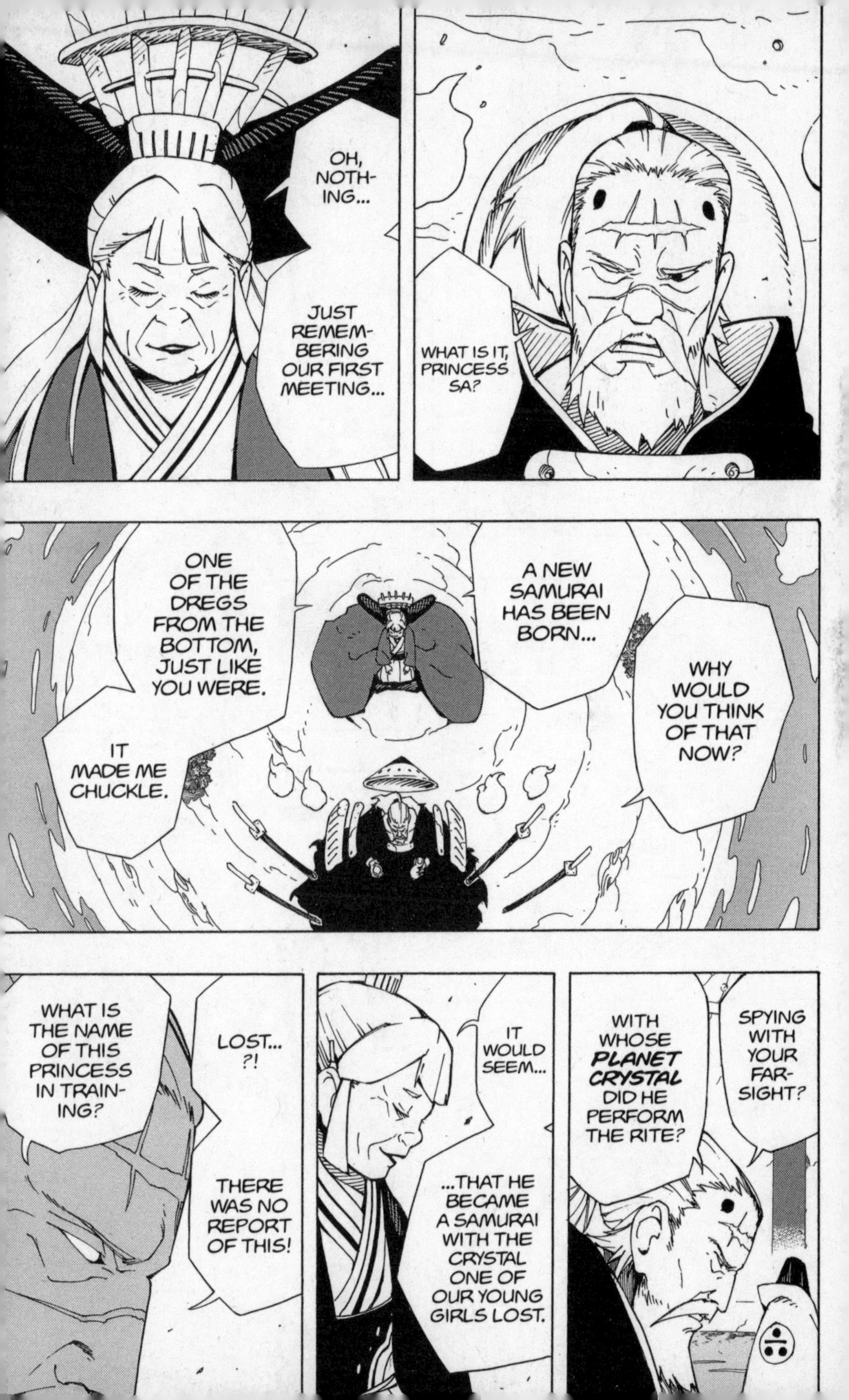
WHAT IS IT, PRINCESS SA?
OH, NOTHING...
JUST REMEMBERING OUR FIRST MEETING...
WHY WOULD YOU THINK OF THAT NOW?
A NEW SAMURAI HAS BEEN BORN...
ONE OF THE DREGS FROM THE BOTTOM, JUST LIKE YOU WERE.
IT MADE ME CHUCKLE.
SPYING WITH YOUR FAR-SIGHT?
WITH WHOSE **PLANET CRYSTAL** DID HE PERFORM THE RITE?
IT WOULD SEEM...
...THAT HE BECAME A SAMURAI WITH THE CRYSTAL ONE OF OUR YOUNG GIRLS LOST.
LOST...?!
THERE WAS NO REPORT OF THIS!
WHAT IS THE NAME OF THIS PRINCESS IN TRAINING?

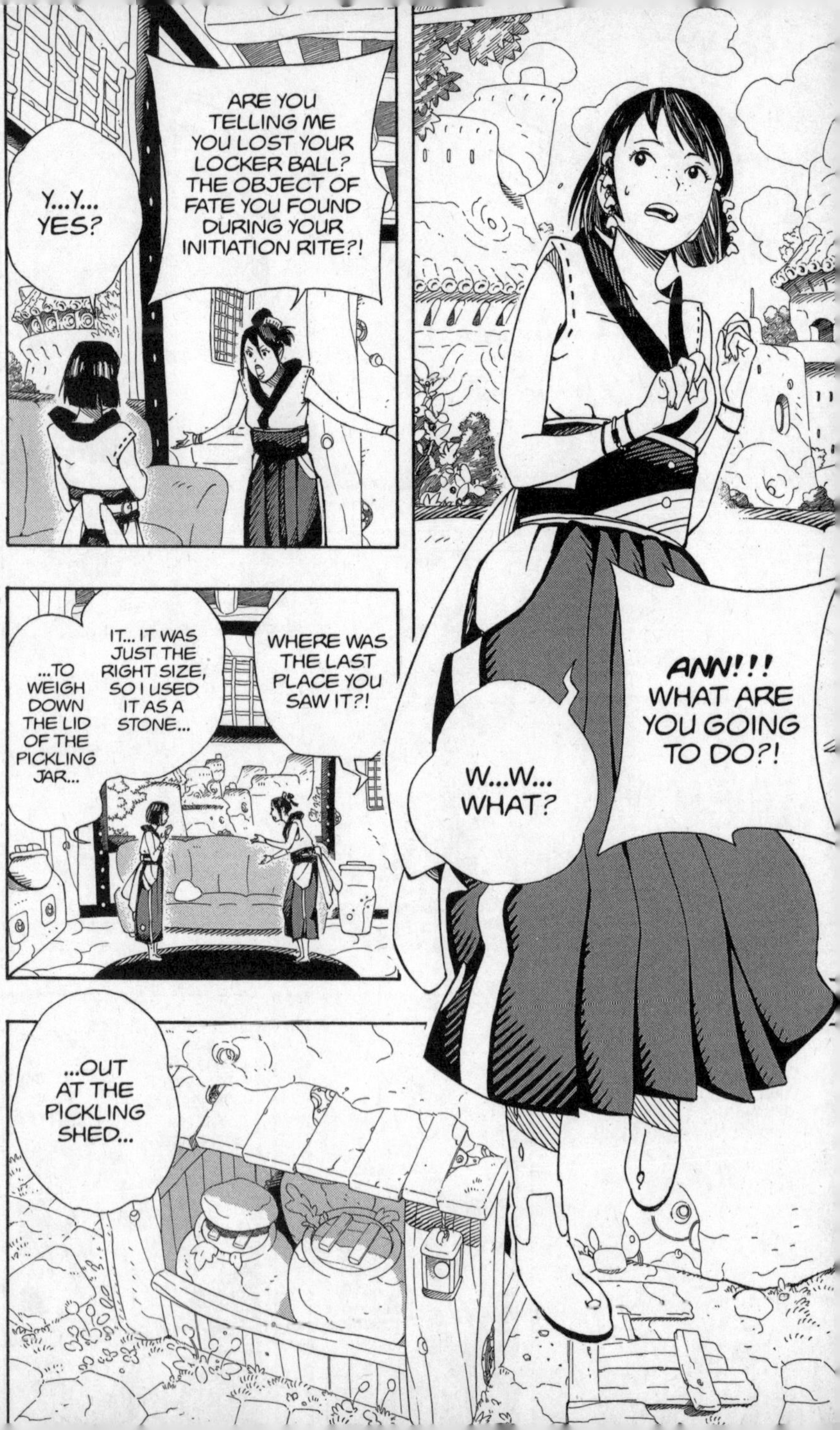
ANN!!! WHAT ARE YOU GOING TO DO?!
W...W... WHAT?
ARE YOU TELLING ME YOU LOST YOUR LOCKER BALL? THE OBJECT OF FATE YOU FOUND DURING YOUR INITIATION RITE?!
Y...Y... YES?
WHERE WAS THE LAST PLACE YOU SAW IT?!
IT... IT WAS JUST THE RIGHT SIZE, SO I USED IT AS A STONE...
...TO WEIGH DOWN THE LID OF THE PICKLING JAR...
...OUT AT THE PICKLING SHED...

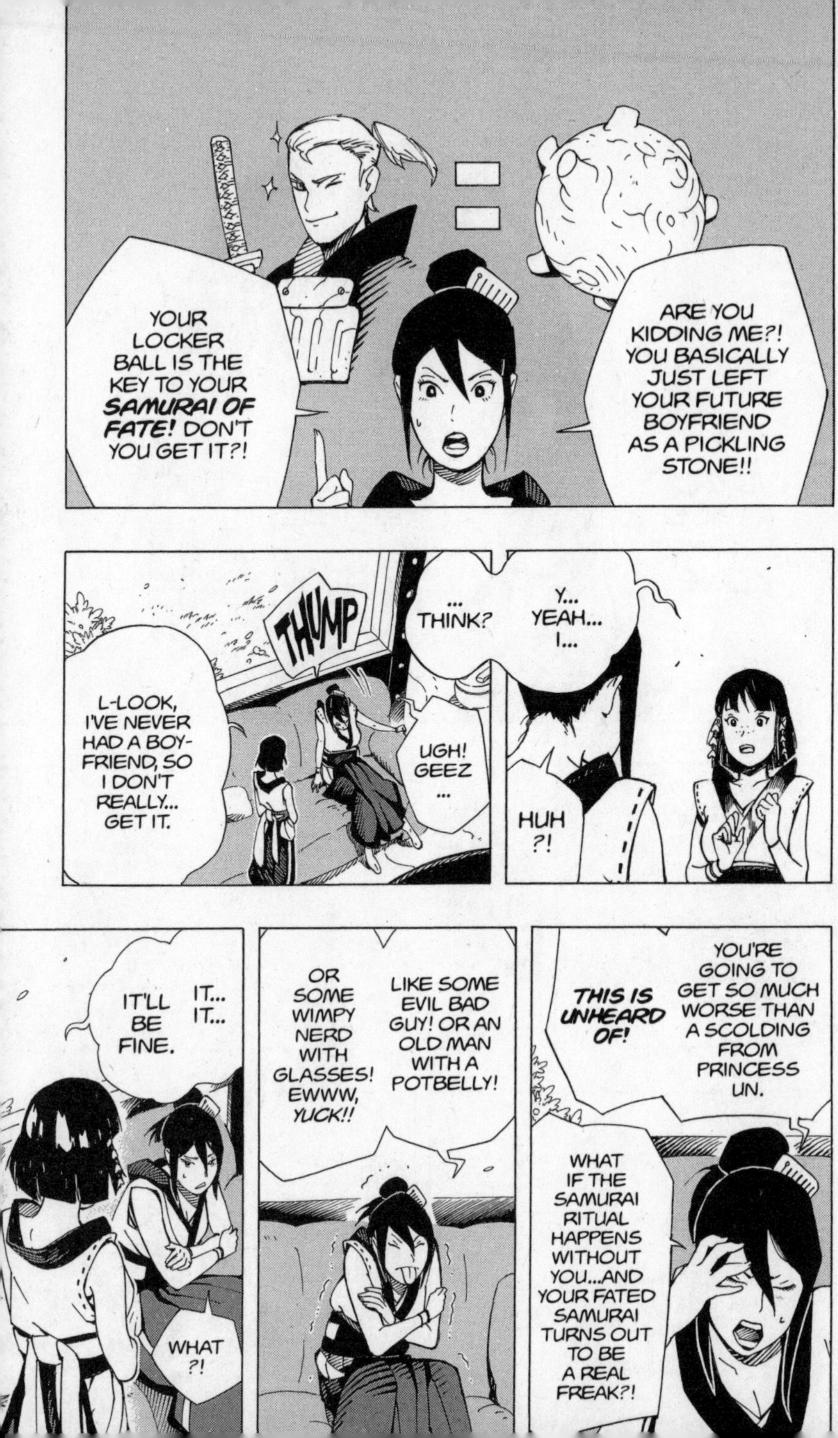

ARE YOU KIDDING ME?! YOU BASICALLY JUST LEFT YOUR FUTURE BOYFRIEND AS A PICKLING STONE!!
YOUR LOCKER BALL IS THE KEY TO YOUR ***SAMURAI OF FATE!*** DON'T YOU GET IT?!
Y... YEAH... I...
... THINK?
HUH ?!
THUMP
UGH! GEEZ ...
L-LOOK, I'VE NEVER HAD A BOY-FRIEND, SO I DON'T REALLY... GET IT.
YOU'RE GOING TO GET SO MUCH WORSE THAN A SCOLDING FROM PRINCESS UN.
THIS IS UNHEARD OF!
WHAT IF THE SAMURAI RITUAL HAPPENS WITHOUT YOU...AND YOUR FATED SAMURAI TURNS OUT TO BE A REAL FREAK?!
LIKE SOME EVIL BAD GUY! OR AN OLD MAN WITH A POTBELLY!
OR SOME WIMPY NERD WITH GLASSES! EWWW, ***YUCK!!***
IT... IT...
IT'LL BE FINE.
WHAT ?!

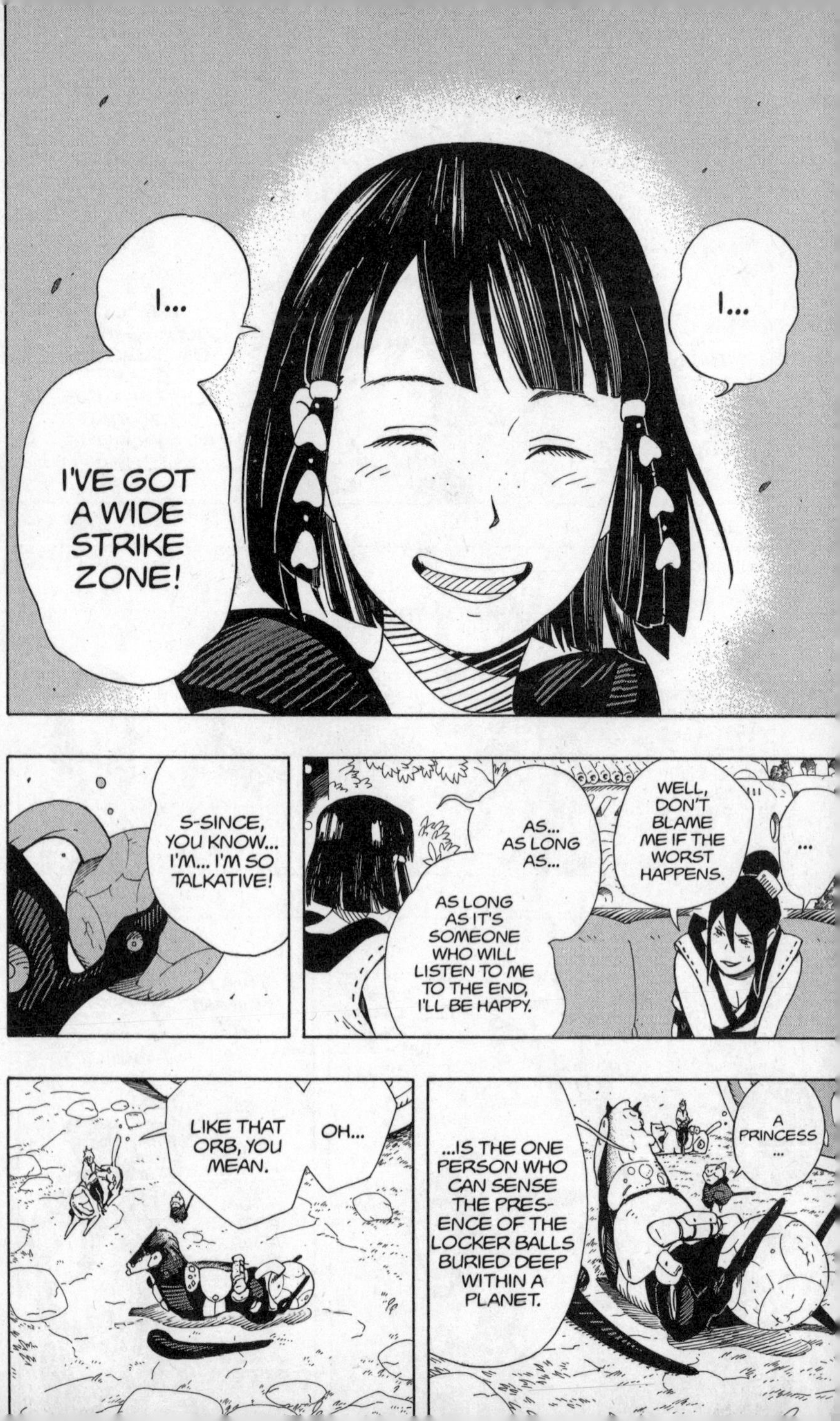
I...
I...
I'VE GOT A WIDE STRIKE ZONE!
...
WELL, DON'T BLAME ME IF THE WORST HAPPENS.
AS... AS LONG AS...
AS LONG AS IT'S SOMEONE WHO WILL LISTEN TO ME TO THE END, I'LL BE HAPPY.
S-SINCE, YOU KNOW... I'M... I'M SO TALKATIVE!
A PRINCESS ...
...IS THE ONE PERSON WHO CAN SENSE THE PRES-ENCE OF THE LOCKER BALLS BURIED DEEP WITHIN A PLANET.
OH...
LIKE THAT ORB, YOU MEAN.

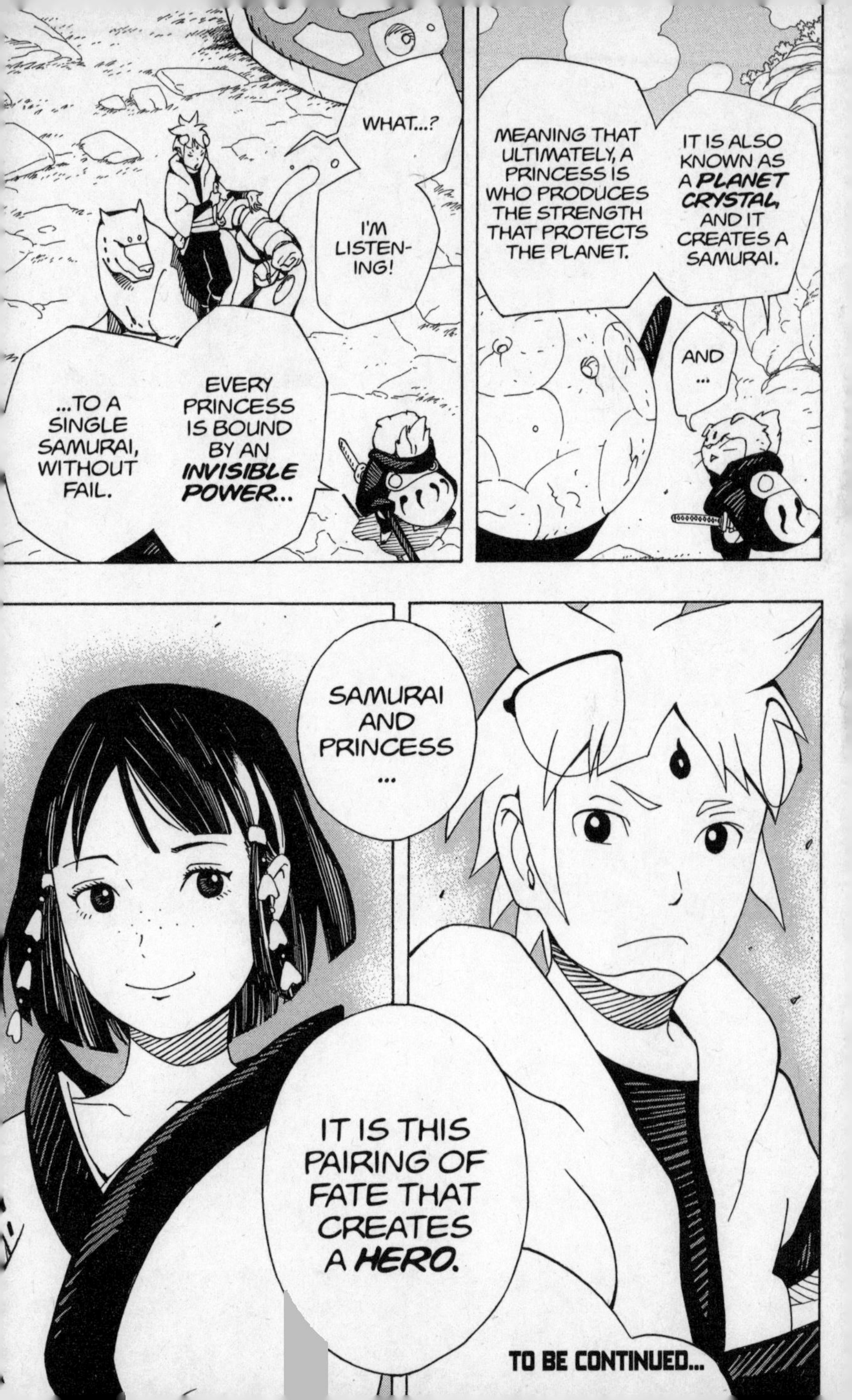
IT IS ALSO KNOWN AS A **PLANET CRYSTAL,** AND IT CREATES A SAMURAI.
MEANING THAT ULTIMATELY, A PRINCESS IS WHO PRODUCES THE STRENGTH THAT PROTECTS THE PLANET.
AND ...
WHAT...?
I'M LISTEN-ING!
EVERY PRINCESS IS BOUND BY AN ***INVISIBLE POWER...***
...TO A SINGLE SAMURAI, WITHOUT FAIL.
SAMURAI AND PRINCESS ...
IT IS THIS PAIRING OF FATE THAT CREATES A ***HERO.***
TO BE CONTINUED...

SAMURAI 8
THE TALE OF HACHIMARU

THE PROMISED NEVERLAND

STORY BY KAIU SHIRAI
ART BY POSUKA DEMIZU

Emma, Norman and Ray are the brightest kids at the Grace Field House orphanage. And under the care of the woman they refer to as "Mom," all the kids have enjoyed a comfortable life. Good food, clean clothes and the perfect environment to learn—what more could an orphan ask for? One day, though, Emma and Norman uncover the dark truth of the outside world they are forbidden from seeing.

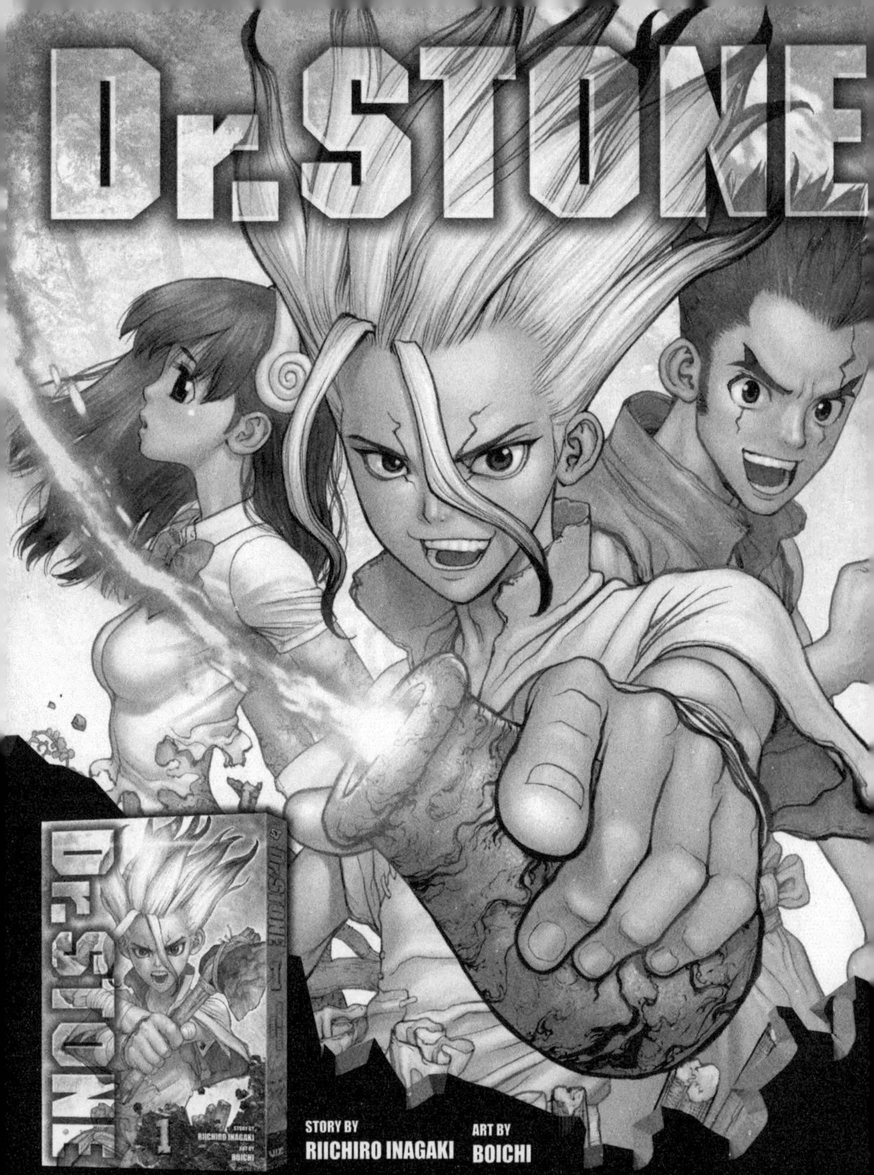

Dr. STONE

STORY BY
RIICHIRO INAGAKI

ART BY
BOICHI

One fateful day, all of humanity turned to stone. Many millennia later, Taiju frees himself from petrification and finds himself surrounded by statues. The situation looks grim—until he runs into his science-loving friend Senku! Together they plan to restart civilization with the power of science!

YOU'RE READING THE WRONG WAY!

SAMURAI 8
THE TALE OF HACHIMARU

reads from right to left, starting in the upper-right corner. Japanese is read from right to left, meaning that action, sound effects and word-balloon order are completely reversed from English order.

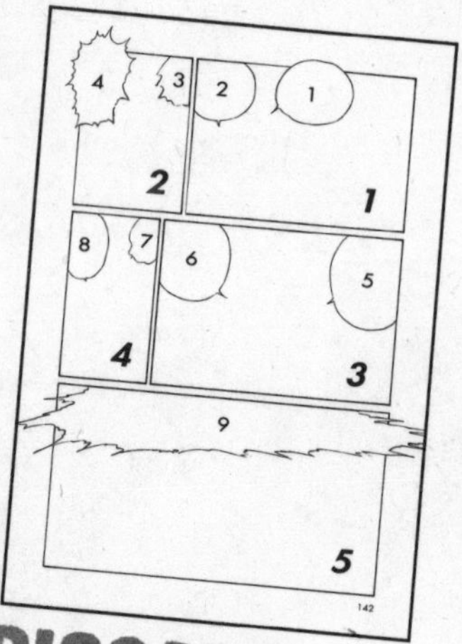
1
2
3
4
1
2
5
6
7
8
3
4
9
5
142

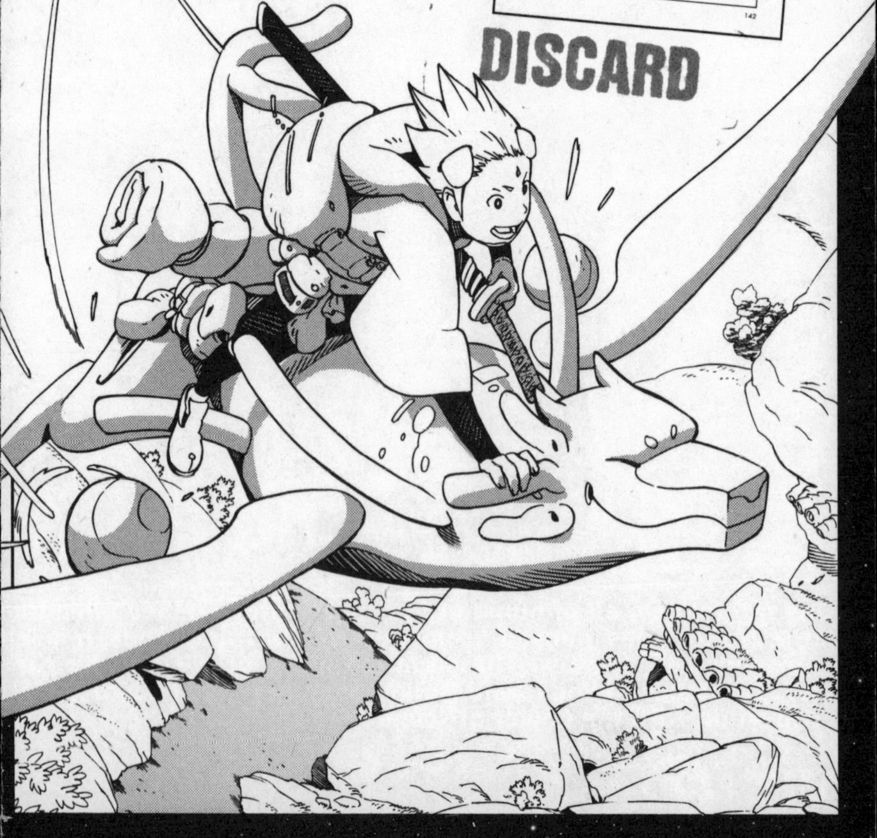